INDIAN WARS

Also by the Bill Yenne

On the Trail of Lewis and Clark, Yesterday and Today

The Story of the Boeing Company

Missions of California

A Damned Fine War (A Novel based on General George Patton)

Great Northern Empire Builder

The American Brewery

Operation Cobra & The Great Offensive: 60 Days that Changed World War II

Secret Weapons of World War II

Secret Weapons of the Cold War

Aces: True Stories of Victory & Valor in the Skies of World War II

San Francisco Then and Now

INDIAN WARS

The Campaign for the American West

BILL YENNE

WESTHOLME
Yardley

Published by Westholme Publishing, LLC
Eight Harvey Avenue, Yardley, Pennsylvania 19067.

www.westholmepublishing.com

ISBN 1-59416-016-3

0 9 8 7 6 5 4 3 2

Printed in the United States of America
on acid-free paper

Contents

Introduction

The Indian Wars in the West were the longest and most misunderstood campaigns ever waged by the U.S. Army. My purpose here is to present the military history of these conflicts—the where, when, what, and how of the Indian Wars—in as much detail as possible in a single volume. The place is the American West, the region of what is now the United States that is west of the Mississippi River. The time period is generally from the California Gold Rush of 1849 through 1890, when the United States Census Bureau deemed the western frontier closed (some exceptions are noted). The whats and hows are the stories of the many strategies and battles that took place during this era. The whys and whethers are questions that are beyond the scope of this book; they are, and will continue to be, subjects for debate. I hope that the facts contained herein will help to inform those discussions.

Americans' cultural misunderstanding of the Indian people themselves is longstanding and only slowly changing. Likewise, misunderstanding of the Indian Wars grows out of stereotypes that emerged in the absence of a solid factual background. This is especially true with regard to the Indian Wars in the West, many of which were fought in places that are still very remote from the population centers of the United States.

To start with, the popular stereotype of Indian culture in North America is of a monolithic society of individuals living in harmony with one another and with their environment. The popular view of the Indian Wars casts this society in opposition to the encroachments of European, and later American, settlement and exploitation. In fact, Indian culture was far from monolithic, and Indian conflicts long predated contact between the indigenous people and the Europeans.

In the days before contact, the indigenous people of North America were extremely tribal-centric. In most cases, the word for their tribal group in their language meant "the people." The North American peoples were as varied culturally and linguistically as the ethnicities of Europe. Separate language groups had little or nothing in common. Culturally, tribes also differed greatly. At the time of contact, the tribes of the Northwest Coast lived in plank houses, used ocean-going vessels, and created graphic arts that are still regarded as highly sophisticated. Meanwhile, many people in the Great Basin were still essentially hunter-gatherers, who possessed little in the way of complex tools or technology. In the Southwest, people lived for generations in large cities filled with multi-storied buildings.

On the Plains, a nomadic culture existed in which the people used their remarkably mobile tipis to easily and routinely move entire settlements as they followed the buffalo. Known to zoologists as the American Bison (*Bison bison*), these powerful bovids provided the people of the Plains with food, clothing, and shelter. During the nineteenth and most of the twentieth century, the American Bison was known universally to English-speaking people throughout the West as the "buffalo," the term I will use for the American Bison in this book.

Contrary to the popular stereotype, the Indian Wars, especially those that took place before 1848, were not always between the indigenous people of North America on one side opposing European settlers and their descendants on the other. Prior to contact with Europeans, warfare was a constant reality among the indigenous people throughout North America. In what is now the Northeastern United States, the Algonquian-speaking tribes of the Eastern Seaboard were often in a state of war with their traditional rivals, the Iroquoian-speaking tribes of the Iroquois Confederacy (the Mohawk, Oneida, Onondaga, Cayuga, Seneca, and later the Tuscarora). So great was this animosity that Indians would ally themselves with Europeans against opposing tribes. During the eighteenth century, the Iroquois sided with the English, when the Algonquians allied themselves with the French.

On the Northern Plains, the Sioux had become the acknowledged dominant political power, not by sensitive diplomacy, but through practiced military policy. Indeed, the U.S. Army exploited the rivalry between the Sioux and their neighbors by recruiting members of tribes such as the

Crow to serve as scouts in the Army's campaigns against the Sioux. In the Southwest, the Navajo were in conflict with the Pueblo, and the Apache were in conflict with the Navajo. Eventually, the Navajo aided the U.S. Army in its campaigns against the Apache. In fact, rival Apache bands participated in Army actions against one another.

Throughout North America, just as throughout Europe, inter-tribal rivalries went on for decades or even centuries, punctuated with frequent raids and occasional major battles. The raids routinely involved the taking of captives, including women and children who frequently were never repatriated, and who often became slaves. On the other hand, just as in Europe, alliances were formed, some of which lasted for several generations. When the Europeans arrived, the indigenous people treated them as they would another tribe. In some cases, there would be conflict and kidnapping, while in other cases there would be accommodation and even alliances.

The idea of traditional tribal homelands is another misleading stereotype. Though the Euro-Americans would displace indigenous people from the homelands that they occupied at the time of contact, this displacement was only a phase in a long series of displacements that had occurred through the years. The Blackfeet were encountered by Euro-Americans in north-central Montana, but this group had been displaced from an earlier homeland north of the Great Lakes by other Algonquian-speaking people. The Navajo were the largest tribe in the desert Southwest at the time of contact (as they are today), but they probably arrived in that region after the Norman conquest of England in the eleventh century. Indeed, their arrival occurred at about the same time as the disappearance of the ancient Anasazi people, whose complex culture vanished abruptly.

Indians throughout the continent had traditionally used bows and arrows, lances and other such weapons in both for warfare and for hunting. However, soon after their contact with Europeans, they obtained firearms through trading or other means. By the early nineteenth century, guns were available and widely used by Indians, although they continued to also use bows and arrows through most of the century. A good bowman was often as effective at long range as a rifleman was, and until the widespread use of repeating firearms late in the century, a bow was much faster to reload than a gun.

As with any war whose scope is continental, the Indian Wars of the West can be divided into theaters, some of which saw more major combat than others. The California and the Pacific Northwest theaters saw less action than others, although each was the site of significant battles. Texas was a theater that saw intense combat early in the nineteenth century, but less after the Civil War. The most active theaters of operation were the Southwest and the Plains, both of which would see major combat through the 1870s.

In the twenty-first century, more than one hundred years after the majority of the battlefields fell silent, a few military encounters, such as that at the Little Bighorn, are still household words. Others are well remembered locally, but more have fallen into obscurity. Several leaders of these fights, such as Sitting Bull and Custer, are well known. The names of many individuals who played a much greater role in these long-ago battles, however, have faded from collective memory. This book places the people and the battles in the context of the overall history of the nineteenth century and the Indian Wars in the West so that their place in American history will be better understood and their names not forgotten.

INDIAN WARS

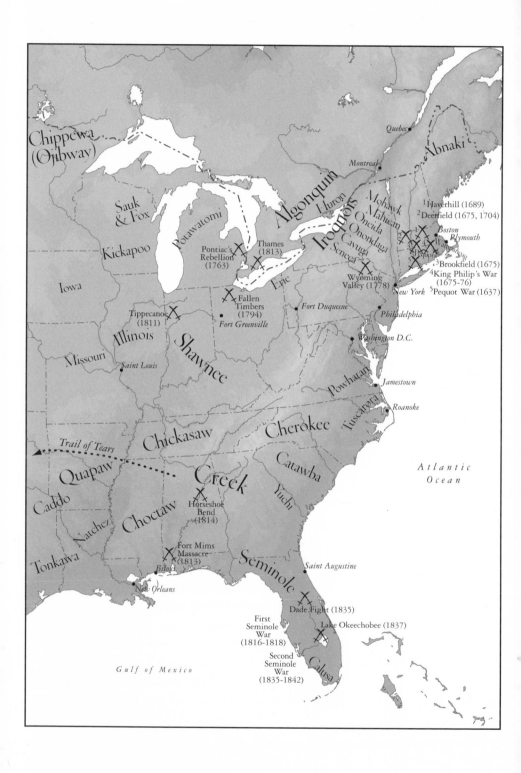

Chippewa
(Ojibway)

Quebec

Abnaki

Montreal

Algonquin

Huron

Iroquois

Mohawk
Mahican
Oneida
Onondaga
Cayuga
Seneca

[1]Haverhill (1689)
[2]Deerfield (1675, 1704)

Boston
Plymouth
Wampanoag

[3]Brookfield (1675)
[4]King Philip's War
    (1675-76)
[5]Pequot War (1637)

Sauk
& Fox

Potawatomi

Kickapoo

Iowa

Illinois

Missouri

Saint Louis

Pontiac's
Rebellion
(1763)

Thames
(1813)

Fallen
Timbers
(1794)

Fort Greenville

Tippecanoe
(1811)

Shawnee

Erie

Wyoming
Valley (1778)

New York

Fort Duquesne

Philadelphia

Washington D.C.

Powhatan

Jamestown

Roanoke

Tuscarora

Trail of Tears

Chickasaw

Cherokee

Catawba

Atlantic
Ocean

Quapaw

Creek

Yuchi

Caddo

Natchez

Choctaw

Horseshoe
Bend
(1814)

Fort Mims
Massacre
(1813)

Tonkawa

Biloxi

New Orleans

Seminole

Saint Augustine

Dade Fight (1835)

First
Seminole
War
(1816-1818)

Lake Okeechobee (1837)

Second
Seminole
War
(1835-1842)

Calusa

Gulf of Mexico

1

CLASH OF CULTURES

When Christopher Columbus made landfall at San Salvador on October 12, 1492, it was a milestone both for European culture and for the indigenous people of North America who greeted him on that sandy shore. Although Europeans and Native Americans had made contact before, this time the Europeans had come to stay.

Columbus didn't "discover" America. There were several million people—population estimates vary—living on the continent at the time. He wasn't even the first European to make landfall in the Western Hemisphere. What the voyages of Columbus did do was to initiate the permanent European presence in what romantic Europeans would refer to as the "New World." Prior to Columbus, the vast majority of Europeans were unaware of America, and the people living in America were unaware that Europe existed.

Within a few decades of the arrival of Columbus, Spain had substantial permanent colonies in the Caribbean and Mexico, and a century of ever-increasing European exploration on the North American continent led to the establishment of permanent French and English settlements in what are now the United States and Canada. Initially, the Europeans saw the Western Hemisphere as a place to exploit for its resources. The Spanish had come looking for spices, but they discovered that most dazzling of commodities—gold. The French found little gold, but they began exploiting the abundant supply of beaver for their luxurious fur.

The English saw value in the land as a place for colonization. By the beginning of the seventeenth century, a new generation of English entrepreneurs began to conceive of the New World as not so much a place to exploit, but as a place to put down roots and live. With this, serious attempts at settlement began. This territory was then already occupied by Algonquian-speaking indigenous people who were to be generally less than accommodating to the interlopers from across the Atlantic.

In 1585, encouraged by reports brought back by early explorers, Sir Walter Raleigh sent an expedition under Sir Richard Grenville and Sir Ralph Lane to establish a colony on Roanoke Island off the coast of what is now North Carolina. They failed, but the undaunted Raleigh sent a second band of settlers, under John White, in 1587. In turn, White made a supply run to England, but was delayed in his return until 1591. When he arrived back at Roanoke, the colony had vanished without a trace, initiating one of the most enduring mysteries of early American folklore.

James I came to the throne of England in 1603. High on his list of priorities was the project of colonizing his American "possessions." He issued patents to groups of colonists authorizing them to colonize sections of North America between 34 and 45 degrees north latitude, or the area from the Cape Fear River in present North Carolina to Passamaquoddy Bay between what are now Maine and New Brunswick. In 1607, Captain John Smith founded his settlement at Jamestown (named for the king) in the territory of Virginia. Though conditions were rough and hardships many, Jamestown escaped the fate of Roanoke and survived as the first permanent English settlement in America. In 1620, a second English colony was established by the Pilgrims at Plymouth in what is now Massachusetts, and in 1626, the Dutch colonists of New Amsterdam bought Manhattan from the Algonquian-speaking Lenape (Delaware) people.

At first, the Indians treated the interlopers more as a curiosity than as a serious threat. They were as likely to want to trade with their new neighbors as to attack them. During the early years of colonization, the settlers faced more adversity in the harsh climate than in the intentions of the natives.

The legend of the first Thanksgiving notwithstanding, relations between the colonists and the indigenous people gradually became more and more strained. The tension grew in proportion to the increase in the number of the colonists, who became bolder as they gradually adapted to the environment. This same pattern would be repeated again and again, from the Eastern seaboard to beyond the Mississippi River. In the early days, hostilities were characterized by occasional skirmishes and attacks on isolated settlements. Eventually, however, the situation boiled over in a full-scale warfare.

EARLY MAJOR COMBAT IN AMERICA

By the 1630s, the Dutch had a thriving colony in the lower Hudson River Valley, while the English had growing settlements in Massachusetts and Rhode Island, with a Connecticut colony in the works. In 1636 the Pequot people living in the Connecticut River Valley came into conflict with the settlers. Small skirmishes later escalated into larger battles. Their initial major attacks in April 1637 brought a counterstrike from Massachusetts, and the Pequot War was under way. This conflict provides an early illustration of how divergent the political and economic interests of the various tribes really were, as the Mohican (Mahican) people allied themselves with the colonists against the Pequot.

A generation later, New England experienced its bloodiest major conflict with the indigenous people of the region. This clash would be known as King Philip's War, after the English name for the Wampanoag chief, Metacomet. Born in 1639, he was the youngest son of the venerable sachem, or chief, Ousamequin (Yellow Feather). Better known as Massasoit, or "Great Chief," Ousamequin was one of the Wampanoag leaders who interacted with the Plymouth colony in the 1620s, and he figures prominently in the legend of the first Thanksgiving.

After Massasoit died in 1661, Metacomet and his brother Wamsutta ruled the Wampanoag. Initially, relations with the English settlers were good, and the two leaders were given the English names Philip and Alexander. When Alexander took sick and died in 1662, rumors spread that he had been poisoned. The ensuing cold war, which prevailed between the Wampanoag and the colonists for more than a decade, turned hot in January 1675, when a Harvard-educated, converted Christian Wampanoag man named John Sassamon was found dead. The rumor was that "King" Philip was planning to attack the colonists and that Sassamon was murdered en route to warning them. Three Wampanoag men were arrested, tried, and executed for the homicide. If King Philip had not been planning a war against the colonists, circumstances now pushed him in that direction.

In June 1675, a group of people returning from church in Swansea were fired upon by Wampanoags, who killed three settlers and burned barns and cabins. Several villages were then attacked, and soon all of Plymouth colony was involved. Members of the Nipmuck tribe joined the fray in August, and Brookfield became the scene of a conflict. The Naragansett people joined with the Wampanoag, although the Iroquoian-speaking Mohawk specifically refused King Philip's call to arms. The struggle continued for more than a year with great loss of life and property on both sides. Cities such as Deerfield and Haverhill became battlefields, and more than half of the settlements in New England suffered damage. More than 1,200 English homes were burned, and the death toll was over 600 for the colonists and as many as five times that number for the Indians. King Philip himself was killed in August 1676 near his old home in Rhode Island, and the war would grind to a close with both sides exhausted. The largest major Indian war to that time within the territory of today's United States had ended, but the seeds of conflict were still present.

THE FRENCH AND INDIAN WARS

The next round of Indian wars in North America were theaters within a series of four formally declared wars between England and its perpetual European rival, France. It is important to note that, in waging war in North America, the two European enemies exploited the existing bitter rivalry between the Algonquin and Iroquois people. In North America, these conflicts were to be known as the French and Indian Wars, a reference to the fact that the English colonists were at war simultaneously against the French and the Indians.

The French had obtained a footing in Nova Scotia and on the banks of the St. Lawrence River in an area populated by the indigenous Iroquoian-speaking people. Well into the eighteenth century, the tribes of the Iroquois Confederacy—the Mohawk, Oneida, Onondaga, Cayuga, and Seneca—were the dominant non-European political force on the southern side of the St. Lawrence. On the northern side, the dominant tribe was the Huron people, who were also Iroquoian-speakers. Although the French made a general claim of sovereignty over the lands of the interior, they did little to disturb the Iroquois, who benefited economically through the fur trade. French settlements were established at Quebec in 1608, and in 1623 French explorer Etienne Brulé became the first European to see Lake Superior, the largest of the Great Lakes and the largest body of fresh water on earth.

Initially, because of the vastness of North America, and because European population density was so small, the French and English had little contact with one another, but by the end of the seventeenth century, things began to change.

The first three of the French and Indian Wars were each named for the sitting English monarch, just as the Indian war preceding them had been named King Philip's War after the Wampanoag leader. King William's War began in 1689, the first year of the reign of William III. The war was characterized by a series of bloody raids carried out by European forces, or by Indians whose animosity toward a particular target was stirred up by one side or the other. Again, Haverhill, Massachusetts, was a target. A shaky truce in the form of the Treaty of Ryswick ended King William's War in 1697.

In 1703, one year after Queen Anne succeeded William III on the throne, her namesake war began as a theater of the European War of the League of Augsburg—also known as the War of English Succession because of the ongoing French effort to restore James II to the English throne. In North America, actions ranged as far south as Charleston, South Carolina, but were concentrated mainly in the north, where the English captured Acadia, now Nova Scotia. As with King William's War, Queen Anne's War saw numerous Indian raids against villages throughout New England. As in King Philip's War, Deerfield was sacked and burned. Many were killed and about one hundred English people, mainly women and children, were taken captive. One of the captives, Reverend John Williams, was ransomed, but his daughter would remain with her captors for most of her life. His book about the ordeal would remain in print, one of many such narratives that would galvanize public opinion against the alleged savagery of the continent's indigenous people for years to come.

The Treaty of Utrecht in 1713 ended both the war in Europe and Queen Anne's War in North America. Though major combat between the English and French in North America remained in abeyance for a generation, tensions between Indians and settlers continued. In 1715, warfare between the English and the Iroquoian-speaking Tuscarora people in the Carolinas was the catalyst for their joining the five tribes in the north as part of the Iroquois Confederacy.

The third of the French and Indian Wars, known as King George's War, began in 1744 as the North American Theater of the War of Austrian

Succession, which had begun in Europe four years earlier. Named for George II, whose thirty-three-year reign began in 1727, this conflict saw the British capture of the French citadel at Louisbourg on Cape Breton Island in 1745, which was the most significant action in North America. However, Louisbourg was returned to France under the terms of the 1748 Treaty of Aix-la-Chapelle (Aachen), which ended both the European conflict and the war in North America.

King George's War was merely a prequel to the final war in the series. Known simply as the French and Indian War, this was the decisive contest between Britain and France in North America. It lasted from 1754 to 1763 and was the American Theater of the Seven Years War in Europe, which began in 1756 and lasted for the duration suggested in its name.

The French and Indian War saw a major participation by the indigenous people of the Northeast. The Algonquian-speaking tribes generally allied themselves with the French against the British and their Iroquois allies. Major combat began badly for the British, notably in the defeat and death of General Edward Braddock during his 1755 campaign against Fort Duquesne. By 1758, the tide had turned when General John Forbes finally took Fort Duquesne and many Indian allies of the French changed sides. In 1759, troops under General James Wolfe executed a dramatic capture of Quebec, although the general himself was killed in action.

The war ended under terms of the Treaty of Paris, by which France lost most of its possessions in Canada to Britain, and their possessions east of the Mississippi to Spain. The treaty forever ended major direct combat between Britain and France in North America (excluding France's support of the colonies in the Revolutionary War), but it did not affect the underlying clash of cultures within the continent. The war saw the emergence of another important military and political leader.

Pontiac was the war chief of the Algonquian-speaking Ottawa people living in the vast area between the Ohio River and the Great Lakes, and forces under his command and control had been a serious thorn in the side of British operations in the interior. When the war ended, Pontiac moved to resist efforts by the British to extend their political dominance into areas under his control.

The extension of the French and Indian War known as Pontiac's Rebellion saw the Ottawa taking control of many of the former French

This woodcut dating from around the late seventeenth century shows a New England militia engaged in a firefight with an Indian raiding party. (*Author*)

forts and besieging Detroit. Pontiac's star shone brightly, albeit briefly. The withdrawal of French support after the Treaty of Paris led to desertions from his ranks, and in 1765 he signed a peace treaty with the British.

The American Revolution

As had been the case during the series of Anglo-French wars in North America, the native people of the continent played a role in the war between the English monarchy and its American subjects in the colonies. Unlike the situation in the previous conflict, where the two sides had actively sought Indian allies, neither side wanted to put its official imprimatur on Indian warriors involved in what was initially seen as a family feud. As a practical matter, however, both sides actively recruited Indian scouts and warriors.

One of the most notable was the great Mohawk chief, Thayendanega, who worked to unify the Iroquois Confederacy in support of the British. A committed Anglophile, Thayendanega had taken the name Joseph Brant, had traveled to England to meet George III, and had been commissioned as a colonel in His Majesty's Army. Indeed, Thayendanega was being wined and dined in London in July 1776 when the colonists met to declare their independence. Two years later, his cohort, Tory Colonel John Butler, led a British and Iroquois force against the Americans in the Wyoming

Valley of Pennsylvania that decimated a militia army and laid waste to the settlements, while Thayendanega and John Butler's son, Walter, led an attack on Cherry Valley, New York, which culminated in a notorious massacre of civilians.

Despite Thayendanega's effort to keep the Iroquois pro-British, the powerful Iroquois Confederacy was divided. While most of the tribes followed the Mohawk sachem's lead, the Oneida and Tuscarora supported the colonists, helping General Horatio Gates to stop General John Burgoyne's redcoats in the Hudson Valley, for instance. In 1779, George Washington ordered the largest action against indigenous people in the war, a three-prong strike into the Iroquois homeland. Following Washington's orders to "not merely overrun, but destroy," the seasoned Continental troops moved along the Mohawk River from the east, the Susquehanna River from the south, and the Allegheny River to the west, laying waste to the Iroquois food supplies and villages, and ending any further serious military threat from the Iroquois. This same strategy would be employed nearly a century later in the West, notably by Kit Carson in his campaign against the Navajo in 1864.

In the South, the dominant tribes were the Iroquoian-speaking Cherokee people, as well as the Choctaw, Chickasaw, and Creek, whose languages belong to the Muskogean linguistic group. The British attempted to recruit them for action against the Americans, but received only lukewarm support.

On the western frontier, the tribes saw the war between the English and the colonists as an opportunity to attack remote settlements. It was on this front of the war that men such as Daniel Boone and George Rogers Clark first made names for themselves.

When the Revolutionary War ended in 1783, the new United States became the dominant political force in North America. It was a fast-growing nation of energetic people, and it had a generally robust economy. In the West, the Spanish owned a vast tract that was larger than the United States, but it was lightly populated and likely to stay that way.

After the war, Thayendanega returned to England to lobby for support for his scheme of a vast uprising against the new United States, but the recently defeated British were not yet in the mood to resume hostilities. Iroquois attacks would continue, but for the moment, they would be without active British logistical support.

With the sovereignty of the United States came the need for a new government policy toward the indigenous people of the continent. The Articles of Confederation, approved in 1777 but not made effective until 1781, divided responsibility for Indian affairs between the central government and the states. At the same time, it was agreed in principle that the central government should regulate Indian affairs and manage Indian trade. The notion of giving the thirteen original states responsibility for Indians residing within their boundaries and investing in the central government responsibility for all other Indians outside their collective boundaries strengthened the concept of "Indian Country," but it perplexed many people. President James Madison, writing in The Federalist (1788), called it "absolutely incomprehensible" and likened it to subverting a mathematical axiom, "by taking away a part, and letting the whole remain."

The framers of the U.S. Constitution attempted to eliminate the problem by calling for specific constitutional authority for federal supervision of indigenous people in the Commerce Clause. Provisions for making treaties with indigenous people were established, and Congress was charged with the responsibility "to regulate commerce with foreign nations, and among the several States and with the Indian tribes."

In 1778, the newly formed United States government had signed its first treaty with an Indian tribe, the Lenape (Delaware). In signing this treaty, the United States was following the English and European tradition of dealing with tribes as political entities. Early U.S. policy remained consistent with the European practice of recognizing tribes as governments with full internal sovereignty. At one point it was even expected that certain tribes might be organized into states and one day be granted representation in Congress. In grouping Indian tribes with states and foreign nations in the Commerce Clause, the United States was recognizing the indigenous people as separate and distinct political entities to be dealt with on a government-to-government basis. This idea would not last long.

The United States at War

With the end of the American Revolution in 1783, the open warfare involving the indigenous people of North America was just a distant memory in most of the thirteen new states of the United States. Grandparents could still frighten the children with tales of Haverhill and Deerfield, but those days were gone forever, and the people of the new nation were entering another era. Indian attacks were no more likely in Boston or Philadelphia than they were in London or Paris.

On the western frontier, however, it was a different story. Actually, it was the same story that had unfolded in New England a century earlier. In the relative wilderness beyond the Cumberland Gap and in the Ohio Country of the Old Northwest, the nuances of America's recognition of tribes as governments with full internal sovereignty was far from anyone's mind. The tribes themselves did not care that their sovereignty was defined by a distant government. They did not believe that it was. The tribes treated the settlers the same way, regardless of whether they flew the Union Jack or the Stars and Stripes. The colonists were just rival tribes, and as such, they were subject to armed raids.

The settlers and farmers, meanwhile, did not care whether the people attacking them were distinct political entities or rival tribes. They were being attacked, and they wanted their government to come to their aid.

The principal theater of operations where military action was required was in the Northwest Territory, north of the Ohio River in what is now the states of Ohio and Indiana. The antagonist was a loose confederation of Algonquian people from the Chippewa (Ojibway or Anishinabe), Miami, Potowatomi, and Shawnee. These tribes were united militarily under the leadership of a Miami chief named Mishikinakwa (Little Turtle). A brilliant tactician, he would lead the warriors of the confederated tribes in one of the most successful campaigns ever waged by an Indian force.

As the United States would do after the Civil War, both world wars and the Cold War, the new nation had largely disbanded its regular army after having won its War of Independence. In order to underscore the doctrine of state's rights, the emphasis was on state militias, rather than a federal army. This gave President George Washington little flexibility in crafting a military response. He authorized Major General Arthur St. Clair, then governor of the Northwest Territory, to raise a militia to augment a small regular army contingent. With this, Brigadier General Josiah Harmer penetrated deep into the area controlled by the Indians in 1790, looking for a decisive battle. He found it, but not on his own terms. When Harmer's force became strung out along the trail, they were easy prey for an ambush by Mishikinakwa, and they were badly mauled.

In 1791, St. Clair led a follow-up expedition himself, taking 1,400 troops into the Old Northwest. Again, the Americans got their battle with Mishikinakwa's confederacy, and again it was a disaster. This time, Mishikinakwa inflicted the worst defeat that would be suffered by the U.S. Army during the Indian Wars. St. Clair suffered 65 percent casualties, including thirty-seven officers killed. He survived both the battle and a subsequent Congressional inquiry.

It would take three years before the U.S. government would try again to bring Mishikinakwa into submission. The 1794 offensive would take the Army's General "Mad Anthony" Wayne into the field with 3,000 troops. Far from being a madman, Wayne was a strict disciplinarian and a master tactician. Mishikinakwa had met his match. After some initial skirmishes with Wayne, he realized this and abdicated his leadership role to Shawnee Chief Blue Jacket. The decisive encounter, the Battle of Fallen Timbers, occurred on August 20, 1794, near today's city of Toledo, Ohio. General Wayne soundly defeated the Indian confederacy with minimal casualties.

Mishikinakwa reemerged in 1795 as a delegate to the treaty conference at Fort Greenville. The Greenville Treaty defined Indian land claims in the Old Northwest and brought temporary peace to the region. Mishikinakwa reinvented himself as an advocate for peace and accommodation with the Americans, and this led to his becoming unpopular with many members of his tribe and his former confederacy.

Gradually, the Old Northwest was becoming pacified, as New England had a generation earlier. Once the settlers had been outnumbered by the Indians living there, but by the turn of the nineteenth century, this was no longer true. The population density of the settlers was growing, and demographics were shifting. Kentucky had become a state in 1792, and neighboring Tennessee joined the Union in 1796, just a year after the Greenville Treaty. A virtual wilderness at the time that George Washington was president, Ohio became a state in 1803.

Also in 1803, President Thomas Jefferson doubled the size of United States territory on the continent by acquiring the Louisiana Purchase from a cash-strapped Napoleon.

By 1811, however, as the United States was embroiled in events on the international scene that would lead it into its second war with Great Britain, the indigenous people of the Northwest were also moving toward the revival of old hostilities. Indeed, from the Indians' perspective the War of 1812 would serve as an ideal backdrop for this unrest because the United States would have to divert resources to fight the militarily superior British.

TECUMSEH AND THE PROPHET

This time, the leadership would be that of a pair of Shawnee brothers. Actually, they were ethnically only part Shawnee because their mother was Creek, but they had been raised among the Shawnee and their father was a highly regarded Shawnee warrior. The two men were Tecumseh (Leaping Panther), the fifth of nine siblings, and Tenskwatawa (Open Door), one of a set of triplets, born last. They were an interesting duo. Tecumseh was a pragmatic military and political leader, while Tenskwatawa became what we would now call a shaman, and what was long referred to as a "medicine man." Most references call Tenskwatawa the "Shawnee Prophet," or simply "The Prophet." His birth name had been Lalawethika (Noisemaker).

Tecumseh participated in actions against American settlements as early as 1782, and had taken part in the Battle of Fallen Timbers in 1794. Tecumseh's ambition was political, while his brother's was more esoteric.

In contrast to his more athletic brother, the Prophet was a clumsy man, unskilled at hunting. His fortunes changed in 1805, when he is said to have had a vision from which he extracted a religious doctrine that was remarkably similar to the Ghost Dance religion of Plains Indians tribes that would be promulgated by Wovoka nearly a century later. An essential tenet of both religions was the belief that white men were inherently evil. Both Wovoka and the Prophet taught that the hard times that the Indians were experiencing could be reversed by rejecting Euro-American culture, rejecting its food, drink and tools, and by re-adopting traditional ways. When he successfully predicted a solar eclipse, the Prophet suddenly attracted an enormous following to his headquarters on the Tippecanoe River, near what is now Lafayette, Indiana.

Tecumseh saw the value in exploiting his brother's supporters for political purposes. Using the Prophet's teachings, Tecumseh gradually assembled an army of younger warriors who would be prepared to fight to the death to rid the Old Northwest of the Americans. Tecumseh proved himself to be a brilliant politician and respected leader who sought to unite the various tribes of the region into a single political and military force. William Henry Harrison, the governor of Indiana Territory, recognized what Tecumseh was attempting to do and acknowledged his skill as a leader and organizer.

Harrison attempted to outmaneuver Tecumseh and the Prophet politically by getting other Indian leaders to support the United States role in the Old Northwest. In the Treaty of Fort Wayne in 1809, Harrison succeeded somewhat in undercutting Tecumseh's influence by getting a faction of the tribes in the Old Northwest to accept American settlement in the region.

Nevertheless, skirmishes along the frontier continued, and in July 1811 some settlers were killed on a farm in Illinois. In November 1811, while Tecumseh was in the South attempting to enlist southern tribes to join his growing confederacy, Harrison went to meet with the Prophet at his headquarters on the Tippecanoe, known as Prophetstown, where it was rumored that the killers from the Illinois incident had taken refuge.

Harrison camped near the Prophet's stronghold and sent word that he wanted to talk about the fugitives. Not waiting for the conference, the Prophet sent warriors to attack Harrison's camp by night. The Americans were able to resist the initial assault, and after daybreak on November 7, Harrison led a counterattack. Harrison's command suffered sixty-eight men killed in action, and about 120 wounded. The Indian casualties were estimated to have been slightly fewer, although they abandoned Prophetstown as a result of the battle. Harrison burned the village after the battle and withdrew. The Battle of Tippecanoe was a costly draw militarily, but politically it was a huge defeat for Tecumseh and the Prophet. They had reached and passed the high point in their search for disciples to their cause.

When the War of 1812 began the following year, Tecumseh formed an unlikely alliance with the British, even going so far as to ride into battle in a red officer's jacket. This was almost directly counter to the teachings of the Prophet, who admonished his followers to eschew the accouterments of the Euro-Americans. In August 1812, Tecumseh and his followers rode alongside the British in the capture of Detroit. The following spring, Tecumseh and his Indian force joined with British Colonel Henry Proctor in a failed attempt to capture Fort Meigs. Located near what is now Toledo,

Ohio, the fort was successfully defended by none other than William Henry Harrison. The Prophet continued to accompany his brother, but he took no part in combat operations and his leadership role among the Indians was now subordinated to that of Tecumseh.

By September 1813, the Americans were on the offensive. Commodore Oliver Perry defeated the British fleet on Lake Erie, while Harrison chased the redcoats—as well as Tecumseh and his mainly Shawnee contingent—out of Detroit and into Canada. Tecumseh goaded the retreating Proctor into stopping to make a stand on the Thames River near the site of present-day Chatham, Ontario. In the Battle of the Thames on October 5, Harrison soundly defeated Proctor's force, although the Indians led by Tecumseh fought bravely. During the battle, Tecumseh was killed, although it is not known exactly what happened to his body. The Prophet, who again took no active role in the fighting, escaped the battlefield and remained in exile in Canada until 1825. He died near Kansas City in 1836.

William Henry Harrison went on to a political career, serving in the U.S. House of Representatives and the U.S. Senate. After running for president in 1836 and in 1840, he was elected on his second try. He took ill with pneumonia at his inauguration and died a month later.

A recurrent myth from American folklore holds that Harrison fell victim to a curse placed on him by Tecumseh or the Prophet after Harrison's victory at Tippecanoe. Essentially, the curse stated that Harrison would be elected president, but that he would die in office, and everyone elected president in twenty-year increments thereafter would also die in office. Harrison was elected in 1840 and he died in office. Two decades later in 1860, Abraham Lincoln was elected and he too died in office. Thereafter, the presidents elected in 1880, 1900, 1920, 1940, and 1960 all died in office, and through the end of the twentieth century, they were the only American presidents to pass away while in office. Because these years were the only presidential election years during that time frame that ended in zero, the curse became known as the "zero-year curse." Had only Harrison died in office, it would have been a coincidence. However, the fact that the pattern continued for 120 years kept the myth of the curse alive.

The United States concluded its "Second War of Independence" in 1815 with a renewed sense of confidence that would help it fulfill what it saw as its destiny, to become the dominant power in North America. Moreover, the War of 1812 ended with the British finally recognizing that

A nineteenth-century print depicting the death of Tecumseh at the Battle of the Thames in 1813. (*Library of Congress*)

the United States could not be bullied, and that the new nation was, indeed, the dominant power in North America. Though the term would not be coined for a quarter century, Americans now viewed dominance of the continent as their "manifest destiny."

TECUMSEH'S LASTING INFLUENCE AND THE CREEK WAR

Although the myth of the so-called zero-year curse took on a life of its own after the Prophet's death, Tecumseh's own influence also survived his demise. His vision had been of a new paradigm of Indian identity. He had imagined a virtual United Nations of tribes in which individual tribal identities were subsumed by their shared identity, and unified against the common enemy of American encroachment on Indian land. He was survived by many who shared that vision.

Though skirmishes would continue, Tecumseh's final defeat seemed to have marked the end of major combat in the Northwest Territory. In a recurring theme throughout the history of the relationship between the U.S. government and its indigenous people, the Indians living in the Old Northwest were told that they would be left alone if they would abandon the territory in question and move farther west. Wanting to be left in peace like anyone else, many did, albeit with resentment. With this, the Old Northwest became open to settlement, the demographics shifted and the United States expanded to further fulfill the notion of Manifest Destiny. Ohio had been a state since 1803, and with the War of 1812 over, two more states were carved from the Northwest Territory. Indiana was added to the Union in 1816, and Illinois achieved statehood in 1818.

It was in the latter state that residents would experience a major exception to the general rule of peace in the Old Northwest after the war. In 1831, eighteen years after the death of Tecumseh, that long-simmering antagonism would again flare into the serious warfare in the Old Northwest.

The guiding force behind the 1831 uprising would be a sixty-four-year-old member of the Sauk (Sac) tribe known as Makataimeshekiakiak (Black Hawk). He had been a follower of Tecumseh and had led a pro-British contingent of Sauk warriors against the Americans in the War of 1812. In 1814, he had even defeated a force under the command of future president Zachary Taylor. After the war, he and his more conciliatory rival, Keokuk, rose to positions of political prominence among the Sauk. Like many of their tribe, they had crossed the Mississippi to live.

By 1831, as had happened so often before, settlers were spreading west into the areas promised to the Indians. Against this backdrop, Black Hawk began leading raids into Illinois. He imagined that he might be able to put together the sort of broad coalition that Tecumseh had once assembled, but those days were gone. Aside from a few hundred Sauk, the only people that Black Hawk was able to attract to his multi-tribal coalition were a few members of the Mesquaki (Fox) tribe, traditional Sauk allies. Within the Sauk, his rival Keokuk did not support the renewed hostilities.

The United States responded with a show of force and attempted to negotiate an end to hostilities. When this failed, the local newspapers called for all-out war. The Black Hawk War consisted of running skirmishes as far afield as Wisconsin, and the climactic battles did not occur until the summer of 1832. Though defeated, Black Hawk himself escaped, but with a price on his head. He was captured by the Winnebago people and exchanged for the promised ransom. The Old Northwest was once again quiet.

Black Hawk aside, it had been in the South where Tecumseh had found the indigenous people most receptive to his ideas. Indeed, while the Prophet was battling Harrison at Tippecanoe in 1811, Tecumseh had been in the South making converts to the cause. Tecumseh had inspired a new generation of people in that region, especially among the Creek

(Muskogee), who would attempt to do there what Tecumseh and his brother had tried in the Old Northwest. A Muskogeon-speaking tribe whose traditional homeland had been in the present states of Georgia and Alabama, the Creek had been pro-British during the Revolutionary War, but had pledged loyalty to the United States after the war. When American promises to restrict settlement on Creek lands were broken, it created fertile ground for the seeds sewn by Tecumseh to take root.

However, Tecumseh's ideology served to divide rather than unite the Creeks. The two sides that evolved from this division were the Lower Creeks, or "White Sticks," who had become farmers and who remained loyal to the United States, and the Upper Creeks, the "Red Sticks," who advocated rebellion. The Creek War of 1813-1814 might have been essentially a civil war among the Creeks, but Red Sticks insisted on attacking settlers. The United States would ultimately be drawn in by these actions, and by the fact that the Red Sticks had the tacit support of the redcoats in the midst of the War of 1812.

The Creek War began in August 1813 with an attack by Red Sticks against Fort Mims, north of Mobile in what would become the state of Alabama six years later. More than 350 people who had taken refuge in the fort, many of them women and children, were killed by the Creeks. Something had to be done to avenge the massacre and put down the rebellion. Andrew Jackson was authorized to organize a Tennessee militia force to intervene and stop the Creek War. Known as "Old Hickory" for his tenacity, Jackson was a lawyer and politician who was on the threshold of a brilliant military career in which he would be seen as a determined and courageous leader.

In two decisive battles during November, Jackson's troops achieved two overwhelming victories over the Red Sticks. Jackson continued to pursue the Red Sticks through the winter, during which time his force was augmented by regular army troops as well as Cherokee and even White Stick volunteers.

In February and March 1814, Jackson aggressively pursued the Red Sticks, delivering a final defeat at Horseshoe Bend on the Tallapoosa River in eastern Alabama. Having soundly defeated the Creeks, Jackson was not magnanimous in drafting the cease-fire agreement. In the treaty that ended the war, Jackson demanded that the Creeks, and not just the Red

Sticks, relinquish a sizable portion of their lands in both Georgia and Alabama. This would not be the last time that he would err on the side of harshness in his dealings with America's indigenous people.

Jackson went on to greater glory in January 1815, soundly defeating the British under General Edward Pakenham in the Battle of New Orleans. Neither side had gotten the word that the treaty ending the War of 1812 had already been signed, but the fact that the battle was a postscript diminished neither the impact of Jackson's victory nor the British defeat. As the Battle of Tippecanoe would send William Henry Harrison to the White House in 1841, so too the Battle of New Orleans catapulted Old Hickory to the presidency in 1829.

For the Indians of the mid-South, Jackson's defeat of the Red Sticks at Horseshoe Bend, and of the redcoats at New Orleans, marked a turning point. As had been the case with the tribes of the Old Northwest, the increasing population density of American settlers in the mid-South was leading to a demographic reversal. At the same time, it was no longer possible to play the Americans against the British, as many tribes had been doing for the better part of three decades.

THE SEMINOLE WARS

It would be in Florida, which remained as Spanish territory until it was purchased by the United States in 1819, that the last major clash of cultures between Indians and American settlers east of the Mississippi River would take place. The dominant tribe in the area were the Seminole, who spoke a Muskogeon dialect related to the language of the Creek, and who shared many aspects of their custom and culture.

There would be two major Seminole Wars, also called Florida Wars. The first consisted of a series of border skirmishes while Florida was still Spanish. The second lasted from 1835 to 1842 and was one of the bloodiest in American history.

In the wake of the War of 1812, the Seminole had been joined by many Red Stick Creek warriors who had been inspired by the Tecumseh creed and who did not want to become farmers loyal to the U.S. government. Among these was a man named Osceola, who was born Billy Powell in Tallahassee in 1804. He was the son of a British trader named William Powell and a Creek woman who had taken the English name Polly

Copinger. He took the name Osceola, which roughly translates as one who enjoys "asi" or strong, dark tea. Osceola had fought in the Creek War, and he would play a central role in the Second Seminole War, as well as in the future folklore of the Southeast.

When the Seminole and Red Stick Creek undertook a campaign of cross-border raids into Georgia in 1818, the United States sent war hero Andrew Jackson to deal with the situation. Not one for defensive action, Jackson crossed the border himself to attack Seminole towns—as well as Spanish outposts—within Florida. Indeed, it was Jackson's aggressive response to the Seminole raids that hastened Spain's desire to sell Florida before Jackson simply took it.

Detail of a portrait of Osceola that was executed by George Catlin at Fort Moultrie. Catlin painted numerous portraits and documented Indian life both east and west of the Mississippi in the early nineteenth century. (National Archives)

By 1832, Andrew Jackson, now president, was winding up his first term in the White House, running for re-election and enforcing the Indian Removal Act, an 1830 federal law that called for the relocation of all Indians living east of the Mississippi River. For the Seminole in Florida, it was the year that they were being asked to agree to the Treaty of Payne's Landing. Under the terms of this treaty, the entire tribe was to leave Florida en masse for the newly created Indian Territory in what is now Oklahoma.

Past the midpoint of Jackson's second term as president, the Seminole people remained in Florida. Most, but not all, kept a low profile. By now, Osceola had risen to prominence as a leader of the armed resistance movement among the Seminole. When his growing band began raiding settlements, there was a call for action.

Major Francis Dade was sent in to put down the rebellion and to enforce the order for the Seminole to leave Florida. He led a contingent of regular army infantry and artillery into the interior, but they were ambushed north of Tampa Bay on December 28, 1835, by an estimated 180 Seminole warriors. A hundred soldiers, including Dade himself, were killed in the open-ing action of the Second Seminole War. A few days later, Osceola attacked a force of 250 regular infantry and 500 Florida militiamen on the south bank of the Withlacoochee River. Osceola won, but was wounded in the process.

During 1836 and 1837, the Second Seminole War played out like a haunting premonition of the Vietnam War. The enemy turned to guerril-la warfare, for which the jungle terrain was ideal. In the face of intense scrutiny from Washington, the U.S. Army and Marine Corps sent ever-increasing numbers of well-armed regular troops who consistently failed to lure the enemy into a decisive battle. In the Florida Theater, a series of commanders came and went, including Winfield Scott, who went on to command U.S. forces in the Mexican War of the 1840s.

Throughout the better part of two years, Osceola earned a well-deserved reputation as a guerrilla leader. In October 1837, however, Colonel Thomas Jessup succeeded in capturing the elusive warlord in October 1837, when he traveled under a white flag to Fort Peyton, Florida for peace talks. He was then incarcerated at Fort Moultrie, South Carolina. Osceola had been suffering from malaria for some time, and his condition deterio-rated in captivity. Despite receiving medical care from Dr. Frederick Weedon, the chief died on January 30, 1838 at the estimated age of 33.

When General Zachary Taylor took command of U.S. forces in 1837, he adopted tactics similar to those that would eventually be used in Vietnam. He mapped the state in a grid pattern and used continuous search and destroy missions to patrol each quadrant to keep the enemy on edge. He was eventually able to force the Seminole into a major battle—a defeat—in December 1837 at Lake Okeechobee.

The guerrilla war continued, but Taylor's victory and the loss of Osceola marked the turning point. The U.S. government sought to exploit this turn by attempting a negotiated settlement. As in Vietnam, this was inter-preted by the enemy as weakness, and the war devolved into a three-year stalemate. Mounting casualties—some 1,500 troops were killed—led to demands for decisive action. In 1841, General William Worth finally won the war through a policy of destroying the Seminoles' villages and torch-ing their crops. The same tactic would be used a quarter century later against the Navajo in the Southwest.

Seminole warriors attacking an American blockhouse during the Second Seminole War in 1837. (*Library of Congress*)

Most of the Seminole surrendered in 1842 and submitted to removal to Indian Territory. A few remained in the deepest corners of the Everglades, and they were involved in minor skirmishing as late as the 1850s, but essentially, the Seminole Wars were over.

In his thesis submitted to the faculty of the Marine Corps Command and Staff College in 1995, Major John C. White, Jr., wrote: "The most obvious flaw in the Army's campaigns in Florida concerned the strategy itself. . . . [which] was totally out of place with the Seminoles' methods of warfare." He goes on to say that several attacks, "point out the Indian's preference for using ambushes to terrorize their opponent. They would not stay and offer the Army a fixed engagement unless it held out a strong chance for success."

It was a lesson in which the United States military would be schooled in Vietnam and Southwest Asia, but before that, there would be the Indian Wars in the West.

THE INDIAN REMOVAL ACT OF 1830

The clash of cultures that began with the first English settlements on the Atlantic coastline in the early seventeenth century reached its climax with the Indian Removal Act. Passing by a close vote in the House of Representatives in May 1830, and signed by President Andrew Jackson, the new law called for the relocation of all Indians living east of the

Mississippi River. Today, the whole idea seems unimaginable, both in its moral dimensions and in the incredible scale of such an operation, but in the 1830s, it was national policy, and it was carried out.

President Jackson, who had long opposed treating tribes as independent entities and who favored removal, enthusiastically executed the measure, and with the exception of the Quakers, the act enjoyed widespread popular support in the United States.

The fact that the Indian Removal Act was passed, and that it was enforced, provides a vividly clear picture of how dramatic this clash of cultures had been. As the United States had grown, it had become apparent that the two civilizations could not coexist. At the same time, there was the idea that American civilization could be contained entirely within the states east of the Mississippi, and that there was more than enough room in the vast and relatively empty trans-Mississippi West to absorb all the Indian people living in the East, as well as those already in the West. Little consideration was given to the potential clash of cultures between the eastern tribes and western tribes if the former were suddenly transported across the Mississippi.

Throughout the eighteenth century, various tribes had been edged out, bought out, wiped out, and pushed out of various places, especially along the Atlantic coast. By the beginning of the nineteenth century, few remained in areas such as New England, which were densely populated with Euro-Americans. The idea of developing an overall plan to systematically remove all Indians began to take shape early in the nineteenth century. On the western edges of the United States rapidly growing populations were in conflict with the indigenous people, many of whom had already moved from farther east. For instance, between 1790 and 1830 the population of Georgia increased sixfold. Against the backdrop of events such as the Creek War and the ongoing unrest in the Old Northwest, settlers were not interested in coexistence and compromise. Rather, they called for a complete eviction of all indigenous people from within their borders.

In 1804, Congress authorized the president to exchange Indian lands east of the Mississippi River for land to the west, and under this authority some tribes were moved. However, it was not until the 1820s and the presidency of James Monroe that the policy of large-scale removal, and the establishment of separate government-designated Indian homeland, gained momentum.

The focus of the attention of the Indian removal advocates was on the indigenous people living in the South, particularly the Creek, Cherokee, Choctaw, Chickasaw, and Seminole. Ironically, these people—with the exception of the Seminoles living deep in the Florida Everglades—no longer fit the eighteenth-century stereotype of Stone Age savages. Indeed, they were referred to routinely in the 1830s as the Five Civilized Tribes. Most of these people had embraced Euro-American culture, and many had completely assimilated to the new way of life. They lived in wood-frame houses, practiced modern farming methods, dressed like Americans, and took American names. The Cherokee, for example, had developed a written language with a roman alphabet and published a newspaper. The Creek and the Cherokee had even begun setting up a form of representative government.

The impact of the Indian Removal Act on the Cherokee Nation was especially devastating. John Ross, a Cherokee leader, wanted to fight the act through the courts, but this only slowed the removal. In 1835, a working treaty was made between the Cherokee and the United States. The terms of the agreement included the forfeiture of current lands for new land in the West, plus a cash settlement. Ross petitioned against the treaty, but the appeal was ignored. Deportation was to start in October 1838.

What ensued is one of the most tragic episodes in American history. Although Georgia had been their home for generations, men, women, and children were taken from their land, herded into makeshift forts with minimal facilities and food, and then forced to march a thousand miles. Under the generally indifferent Army commanders, human losses for the first groups of Cherokee removed were extremely high.

John Ross made an urgent appeal to Washington to let him lead his tribe west, and the federal government agreed. Ross organized the Cherokee into smaller groups and let them move separately through the wilderness so they could forage for food. The parties under Ross left in early fall and arrived in Indian Territory during the brutal winter of 1838-1839. Ross was able to significantly reduce the loss of life among his people. However, approximately 4,000 Cherokee died as a result of the removal. The route they traversed and the journey itself became known as the Trail of Tears, or in the direct Cherokee translation, "the trail where they cried."

The withdrawal called for in the Indian Removal Act was all but complete by 1837, with the Five Civilized Tribes each assigned to a specific sector in the eastern part of what is now Oklahoma. The sectors were roughly equal except for that of the Seminole, which was substantially smaller. Each of these districts was separately organized and entitled to its own internal government. The U.S. government stipulated that according to law and treaty that the tribes were entitled to live in the "Permanent Indian Country" for "as long as grass shall grow and water run."

The notion that the two cultures would coexist on opposite sides of the Mississippi River in perpetuity was both unrealistic and short-lived. This naive concept was soon to be overtaken by events.

2

INTO THE WEST

In the early decades of the nineteenth century, the image of the West as the "Great American Desert" was the accepted understanding of the region. The popular conception held that it was a dangerous and even deadly terra incognita filled with ferocious wildlife and equally ferocious indigenous people, inhabiting a world of extremes in terms of both topography and climate.

The area of what is now the contiguous United States west of the Mississippi River comprises more than two million square miles. At the beginning of the nineteenth century, the region was sparsely populated with a native population estimated at only about a quarter of a million. Of these, the large majority lived in the mild climates along the Pacific coast in what is now California and the Pacific Northwest. In the interior, there were approximately 75,000 indigenous people, members of dozens of tribes and smaller bands, who spoke a wide variety of languages.

Most of the languages spoken in the West were loosely grouped into five major linguistic groups, including the Penutian of the Pacific Coast, the Uto-Aztecan of the Southwest and Great Basin, the Algonquian of the northern tier of what is now the United States, and the Dené or Athapaskan. The latter included tribes that were widely dispersed geographically, including those of far northern Canada, people such as the Haida and Tlingit of the Pacific Northwest, the Hupa in California, and the Navajo and Apache of the Desert Southwest. There are numerous smaller languages groups and subgroups, including the Hokan group who are indigenous to the interior of what is now northern California. Across the Great Plains, most indigenous languages were grouped into the Siouan linguistic group. The people who spoke languages in this group included not only the Sioux, but many of their traditional enemies, including the Crow, as well as lower Missouri River tribes such as the Omaha, Osage, and Oto.

The Sioux people were the most important political, military, and cultural force on the Plains. They were the most populous tribe in the interior of the West, estimated to number between 20,000 and 30,000 at the beginning of the nineteenth century. (For the sake of comparison, the three largest tribes in the United States today according to the 2000 Census are the Cherokee, with 281,069 people identifying themselves as purely Cherokee, followed by 269,202 Navajo and 108,272 Sioux.) The second most populous tribe in the interior were probably the Navajo, whose population is estimated at up to about 12,000.

On the Plains, the tribes were essentially nomadic because the base of their economy was the American bison, or buffalo, herds of which were constantly on the move. Rarely staying in one place for very long, the tribes were frequently in contact with one another. This contact probably was the catalyst for the contest for dominance in which one tribe would naturally emerge as a superpower. That superpower was the Sioux.

The Sioux dominated the Northern Plains from before the eighteenth century until the 1870s. At its apogee, the Sioux homeland spanned the area from the Rocky Mountains to the Mississippi River, including the southern parts of what are now Montana, the Dakotas and Minnesota, as well as much of Wyoming, Nebraska, and Iowa.

They were first called "Sioux" by the eighteenth-century French traders, a name that would be almost in universal use throughout the nineteenth century and most of the twentieth. The term Sioux is still widely used, although today the largest subgroup, the Teton Sioux, use their traditional name for themselves, Lakota. "Sioux" was a truncation of the Chippewa word Nadouessioux, which means "little snakes." The Chippewa applied this derogatory nomenclature to all the Plains tribes that shared the Hokan-Siouan language. The Sioux are the principal people of this linguistic group, which also includes tribes on the Plains such as the Iowa, Oto, Omaha, Ponca, Osage, Kansas, Quapaw, and Winnebago. On the Northern Plains, the Hidatsa and Mandan also spoke a Hokan-Siouan dialect.

The Sioux are, in turn, geographically subdivided into three distinct, but closely related, groups, each speaking a separate but similar Hokan-

Siouan dialect. Each group refers to itself by a name that means "all Sioux people." From east to west, these three groups refer to all members of the tribe as "Dakota," "Nakota," and "Lakota," respectively.

The people themselves never used the term "Sioux" until after the beginning of the reservation era in the late nineteenth century. I use the term Sioux in this work because it is the most widely used term in historical references, it is the official term used by the Indian Bureau and the Census Bureau, and it is widely used in the Dakotas and adjacent states today. Where an individual person was a member of a specific Sioux group or subgroup, I identify him or her as such. Living generally in what is now Minnesota, the eastern branch of the tribe, known as the Dakota or Santee, included such subgroups as the Mdewakanton, Sisiton (Sisseton), Wahpekute, and Wahpetonwan. The central branch or the Nakota, living in what are now the Dakotas, included the Yankton and Yanktonai (Little Yankton), subgroups.

Accounting for about three quarters of the Sioux population, the largest division of the Sioux was the western branch, the Lakota or Teton (Titonwan). Within this group were the Brulé (Burnt Thighs), the Hunkpapa or Uncpapa, the Itazipacola (Sans Arcs or No Bows), the Minneconjou, the Oglala, the Oohenonpa (Two-Kettle), and the Sihasapa. The latter group were also known as the Blackfoot Sioux—not to be confused with the Blackfeet tribe, who were culturally similar, but who speak an Algonquian language, and who were geographically separate.

The non-Indian population of the West was small at the beginning of the nineteenth century, and mainly concentrated along the Pacific Coast or the Mississippi River. It is thought that the highest concentration of native peoples in the West at the start of the eighteenth century was on the Pacific coast, especially in California. However, here and in the Pacific Northwest, there were generally no large dominant tribes because resources were more evenly distributed. With a few exceptions, the people living in the region were members of a myriad of smaller self-contained bands that were related linguistically rather than politically to adjacent bands.

Long before the American Revolution, the French and Spanish had surveyed the Mississippi River, and the Spanish had explored parts of the Southwest. Between 1540 and 1542, Francisco de Coronado led the first Spanish expedition, and Santa Fe, the oldest permanent European city in the West, was established in 1609.

Juan Cabrillo had explored the California coast for Spain in 1542, and British adventurer Sir Francis Drake had landed on Point Reyes north of San Francisco in 1579 to spend the winter and to name the area New Albion. The first permanent European settlements in Alta California—what is now the state of California—would not appear until after 1769, when military governor Gaspar de Portoló, and Franciscan Father Junípero Serra arrived in what is now San Diego to begin an organized effort to establish settlements and missions in the region. By the end of the eighteenth century, there were eighteen missions and four presidios or military posts, as well as a few other settlements between San Diego and San Francisco. However, all of these were close to the Pacific coastline.

English mariners such as Captain James Cook and Captain George Vancouver explored this coastline north into the Pacific Northwest during the late eighteenth century. However, it was not until 1792, that an American, Captain Robert Gray, discovered the mouth of the Columbia River, the waterway that is the defining geographic feature of the Pacific Northwest.

Meanwhile, the area between the Mississippi and the Pacific Coast, and north of Santa Fe, had remained largely uncharted by Europeans or Americans. A quarter century after the United States Declaration of Independence, Boston, Philadelphia, and New York had paved streets and regular mail delivery, but the interior of the American West was still a mysterious land, a vast void on the maps.

The interior was so remote that there was little impetus for going there. Distances were great, so travel time was measured in months, or often seasons—one had to wait for the spring thaw and return before the snows fell. The few who did go into the interior of North America were trappers. Beaver pelts were so highly valued in the "civilized" world that the fur business became big business. For most of the eighteenth century, the French had controlled the trade, and by the turn of the nineteenth century, two British firms, the North West Company and the Hudson's Bay Company, dominated the market in Canada. As with the French before them, the British were especially active around the Great Lakes and extended their reach into the interior and into the Pacific Northwest. The trappers at the bottom of the fur industry ladder were hearty souls who lived off the land and learned to coexist with the indigenous people. Many trappers, who were as likely to be ethnically French as British, had Indian wives and lived among the Indian people.

LEWIS AND CLARK

In 1803, even before the Louisiana Purchase, President Thomas Jefferson had commissioned U.S. Army Captain Meriwether Lewis to explore the interior, all the way to the Pacific Coast. After the Louisiana Purchase, the Lewis mission took on an even greater importance. With his co-captain, William Clark, Lewis and the U.S. Army Corps of Discovery would travel from the mouth of the Missouri River to its headwaters in Montana, then across the Continental Divide and down the Columbia to its mouth.

French, British, and American trappers had been in parts of the territory that Lewis and Clark surveyed, but none had gone all the way to the ocean. Lewis and Clark were the first people known to have traveled across the continent from the Atlantic to the Pacific within the territory of what is now the United States, although Scottish explorer Alexander MacKenzie, an employee of the North West Company, had crossed what is now Canada, from Montreal to the Pacific, in 1793. Lewis and Clark departed St. Louis in May 1804, reached the Pacific in November 1805, and returned to St. Louis in September 1806.

As would be the case with the Apollo lunar exploration missions of the twentieth century, Jefferson's motivation for launching the Lewis and Clark expedition had been primarily scientific—but with an important political dimension. In 1804, there was an urge to show the American flag to the British and the Spanish. In 1969-1972, the United States was showing the flag to the Soviet Union.

The response of the indigenous people to Lewis and Clark varied. As the explorers crossed the Plains on the lower Missouri River, they were in contact with people who had some, albeit limited, experience with Europeans and Americans. Among these, the Sioux, who dominated the Plains politically and militarily, treated the Corps of Discovery with a wariness that verged on hostility. The interaction between the two sides almost turned deadly. In contrast, the Mandan and Hidatsa welcomed the Corps with generosity. Indeed, the Americans spent their first winter on the trail camped across the Missouri from a combined Mandan and Hidatsa village that had a population larger than St. Louis.

An artist's conception of Captain Meriwether Lewis speaking with Indians during the expedition to explore the Louisiana Purchase (*Library of Congress*)

It was here that they were joined by Touissant Charbonneau, a French Canadian trapper, and his sixteen-year-old wife Sacagawea. She was a member of the Shoshone tribe, who had been taken captive at about age twelve by a Hidatsa raiding party. She was then taken six hundred miles from her home, where she was incorporated into life in the Hidatsa village. In turn, she was sold to Charbonneau and became one of his two wives. He and Sacagawea would then travel west with the Corps of Discovery, all the way to the Pacific.

As Lewis and Clark traveled west into what is now Montana and Idaho in 1805, they came upon indigenous people who had never encountered ethnically European people, or had very limited experience with them. Among the Shoshone—Sacagawea's people—as well as among the Nez Percé (Sahaptini) people, Lewis and Clark were received warmly. Both tribes shared food with them, even though provisions were scarce. The story of fellowship and sharing between Pilgrims and Wampanoag that forms the basis of the legend of the first Thanksgiving at Plymouth, Massachusetts, is now thought to have not actually occurred. The affable cooperation that we celebrate is a myth. However, among the Shoshone, and later with the Nez Percé, Lewis and Clark experienced it for real.

Both the Shoshone and the Nez Percé made it clear that they feared and disliked the Blackfeet people more than the strangers from the distant land to the east. Of course, having Sacagawea along as the expedition reached Shoshone country didn't hurt.

By contrast, the Chinook and Clatsop people with whom the Corps of Discovery spent their second winter at the mouth of the Columbia were more indifferent than hospitable. Here, Lewis and Clark traded with the indigenous people for food, and complained in their journals that the Indians charged high prices for goods.

On their return, the captains split up to cross Montana, and Lewis was involved in the only shootout that the Corps experienced with the Indians. This incident, which left at least one Blackfeet man dead, seems to have taken place when the Blackfeet misinterpreted Lewis's sign language when he spoke of having had a peaceful encounter with the Shoshone. The Blackfeet apparently thought that the strangers and the Shoshone were allied against the Blackfeet.

In the years that followed the Lewis and Clark expedition, an increasing number of people from the East traveled into the West, although most were adventurers and mountain men, who made their living with a bit of freelance trapping. One of these men was John Colter, a former member of the Corps of Discovery, who discovered what is now Yellowstone National Park during one of his adventures. His reports of the geysers and hot pools were regarded as laughable tall tales; it was only long after his death that his stories were finally confirmed by a subsequent expedition.

In the wake of the Corps of Discovery, Colter was one of only a handful of hearty American frontiersmen who went west from what was then the United States into the vast region west of the Mississippi. Immediately after the Lewis and Clark Expedition, Zebulon Pike surveyed the route from the Missouri southwest to Santa Fe. He discovered—but did not ascend—the Colorado peak that bears his name, and he surveyed the route that would later evolve into the Santa Fe Trail. Pike was neither as lucky nor as well organized as Lewis and Clark. His party got lost, nearly died, and were detained by the Spanish.

The major impetus for re-examining the places where Lewis and Clark had boldly gone before was the fur trade. John Jacob Astor established Astoria at the mouth of the Columbia River as a base for harvesting beaver pelts, and Manuel Lisa established a series of posts along the Missouri River also for that purpose. However, it would be nearly two decades before further major efforts were made to explore the interior of the West. A few small expeditions, such as that of Steven Long, crossed the continent from the Pacific to the Mississippi, but the next significant expedition was that of William Ashley in 1822. He went into the upper Missouri for the beaver, but would end up making a number of important geographic discoveries. Most notable about Ashley's expedition was two of the young men who signed on to accompany him. Jedediah Smith and Jim Bridger would go on to careers that would make their names synonymous with the term "mountain man."

Jedediah Smith is credited with surveying more of the West than anyone before him, including Lewis and Clark. He explored the central Rockies, as well as Arizona, thus becoming probably the first American to travel overland to California by way of the Southwest. In 1824, he confirmed the existence of South Pass in Wyoming, the easiest crossing point of the Rocky Mountains between northern Alberta and central New Mexico. This would pave the way for a new era of immigration that was to come.

Trails and Forts

Even before the end of the era of the trappers and the free-ranging mountain men, people were beginning to envision the notion of routine crossings of the immense and forbidding West. By 1821, William Becknell, a trader from Kansas City, took a mule trainload of manufactured goods overland to Santa Fe, the northern outpost of recently independent Mexico. Within a year, wagons were following what would come to be known as the Santa Fe Trail.

Gradually, settlements grew up at strategic points along the Santa Fe Trail. Perhaps the most famous was Bent's Fort or Fort William, established in 1833 by Ceran St. Vrain, along with William and Charles Bent, on the upper Arkansas River near what is now La Junta, Colorado. This fort was only one of many such privately financed fortified trading posts that would soon appear across the West.

Meanwhile, William Sublette, who had experience with the Santa Fe Trail, imagined an offshoot of that road that would go from Independence, Missouri, to the Pacific Northwest by way of South Pass in Wyoming. As early as 1827, he had surveyed the route, and by 1830, the first wagons were making use of what would be known as the Oregon Trail. While the Santa Fe Trail was primarily a trade route, the Oregon Trail was an emigrant trail used by settlers bound for the lush Willamette Valley south of what is now Portland, Oregon.

Unlike the trappers and traders, travelers on the Oregon Trail were coming to stay. In the years before the Civil War, it was the major thoroughfare of Western expansion. The Oregon Trail also carried the California traffic through South Pass, at which point, a separate California Trail branched off to cross the arid wasteland of what is now Nevada, and the almost impenetrable Sierra Nevada mountains. Crossing the Sierras, California immigrants then found themselves in the immense and fertile Central Valley of California. During the California Gold Rush that began in 1849, the California Trail would be used by an almost continuous flow of people, many of whom returned on the trail after they achieved whatever fortune—or misfortune—the gold fields provided them.

In the decades before the Civil War, the number of forts and outposts along the trails gradually increased, but for most part the object was to pass through, not to linger. Between the 1820s and the 1840s, the American West had gone from a terra incognita feared by Americans and ignored by Mexicans, to a highway to be endured for the sake of what lay across the horizon. Even after the United States took possession of the region from Mexico in 1848, it would remain a highway rather than a destination. After the Civil War, the popular image of the American West would continue to evolve—this time from mere highway to land of opportunity.

The pre–Civil War emigrant trails were not single lane highways, nor were they the only trails that crossed the American West in the 1840s and 1850s. Both the Santa Fe Trail and the Oregon Trail, like the California Trail and the Mormon Trail that led to the Great Salt Lake after 1846, were actually multiple parallel tracks, punctuated by numerous cut-offs. As these and short cuts and side tracks multiplied, they affected the lives of the indigenous people of the region to a greater and greater extent.

INITIAL SKIRMISHES IN THE WEST

Lewis and Clark managed to cross the continent without losing a single member of the Corps of Discovery to hostile action, and with only one such encounter that drew blood. Other early expeditions were not always so lucky, but generally the indigenous people of the West avoided the strangers rather than confronting them. Attacks on traders using the Santa Fe Trail were rare because the Indians benefited from the trade goods that the freighters were carrying—especially guns. They had an economic motivation not to interfere.

While the Sioux dominated the Northern Plains, West Texas and the Southern Plains were controlled by the Uto-Aztecan-speaking Comanche and Kiowa. The Santa Fe Trail ran through their sphere of influence, and its traffic moved at their pleasure, so there were demands for United States military support and protection on the section of the trail north of the Arkansas River.

The first hostile contact between the U.S. Army and the Comanche and Kiowa on the Santa Fe Trail came in June 1829. Major Bennet (also spelled Bennett) Riley was leading an escort detachment of the 6th Infantry Regiment when the wagon train they were escorting was surrounded and attacked near the site where Fort Riley, Kansas, would be established in 1853. The troopers managed to drive off the attackers with the loss of just one man, but were unable to give chase because, being infantry rather than cavalry, they were afoot. The infantry was soon replaced by regiments of mounted dragoons, which were redesignated in 1861 as cavalry regiments.

One of the first areas of the American West to see large-scale settlement by Anglo-Americans—Texas—was not actually part of the United States. As had been the case east of the Mississippi River, conflict between settlers and the indigenous population boiled over when the population density of the newcomers reached critical mass.

Having won its independence from Mexico, Texas declared itself as an independent republic in 1836 and flourished as such until it joined the United States as the twenty-eighth state in 1845. During this time, the Republic of Texas relied on an official paramilitary organization known as the Texas Rangers. The Rangers were organized into three companies, each commanded by a captain and two lieutenants, who in turn were under the command of a major, who answered to the commander-in-chief of the regular army of Texas. During the Texas War of Independence, they took part in neither the defense of the Alamo in February and March 1836 nor the climactic Battle of San Jacinto on April 21, 1836. Beginning in 1838, however, President Mirabeau Lamar began using the Texas Rangers to aggressively pursue the Comanche and Kiowa. After a series of successful skirmishes, the Rangers delivered a major blow to the power of the Comanche in March 1840 at the Battle of Plum Creek, near the site of present-day Lockhart, Texas.

Across the continent in the Pacific Northwest, Oregon had become de facto American territory with the arrival of large numbers of settlers via the Oregon Trail. The region would officially become American territory in 1846 by way of the agreement between the United States and Great Britain that ceded all the territory south of 49 degrees north latitude to the Americans, thus fixing the southern border of Canada. Thereafter, Oregon was settled by even larger numbers, much to the consternation of the indigenous population.

The event that set off Indian-American hostilities in the Pacific Northwest occurred on November 29, 1847, seven miles from the site of present-day Walla Walla, Washington. Dr. Marcus Whitman and his wife, Narcissa, were Presbyterian lay missionaries who originally came into the area in 1836. They had established a mission at Waiilatpu, an Oregon Trail way station on the Walla Walla River to minister to the Penutian-speaking people of the central Columbia River Valley, including the Cayuse, Palouse, and Walla Walla. In 1847, a rumor spread among the Cayuse that a measles outbreak was a deliberate effort by the Whitmans to kill them. Led by a man named Tilokaikt, the Cayuse attacked the Whitman mission. The Whitmans themselves, along with sixteen others, were murdered, and more than fifty people, mainly women and children, were captured and tortured.

The Whitman Massacre led to reprisals by the Oregon militia, raids, counter raids, and general bloodshed that gripped the region well into the following year. Tilokaikt and several other perpetrators of the Whitman Massacre were captured in 1850 and executed.

The Whitman incident and the ensuing warfare were the catalyst for organizing the Pacific Northwest region into Oregon Territory in 1848. In 1853, the part north of the Columbia River became Washington Territory. Oregon became a state in 1859, but Washington would not follow it into the Union for thirty years.

As had occurred previously in New England, in the Old Northwest and, indeed, in all of the United States territory east of the Mississippi River, the indigenous people of the Pacific Northwest were learning that the increasing population of light-skinned outsiders was a tide that could not be stemmed. Throughout the West, two dramatically dissimilar cultures were on a collision course.

3

THE WEST AT WAR

The year 1848 marked a major turning point in the history of the United States, and in the perception by Americans of the continent on which they lived. In the space of just nine days, two events transformed the United States. On January 24, a New Jersey immigrant named James Marshall was building a sawmill on the property of Swiss immigrant John Sutter near the present location of Coloma, California, when he saw something shiny in the water of Sutter Creek. It turned out to be gold, and not just a little. He soon discovered that the area was literally littered with gold nuggets. When news of his discovery reached the eastern United States and the world beyond, it touched off the California Gold Rush of 1849, which began one of the largest voluntary mass migrations in human history.

Nine days after Marshall found gold, representatives of the United States and Mexico met in the Mexico City suburb of Guadalupe Hidalgo to sign the treaty of the same name, thus ending the Mexican War. In this treaty, which concluded two years of major combat between the two powers, American claims in Texas were confirmed, and Mexico ceded to the United States all of the present states of California, Nevada, and Utah, as well as parts of Arizona, New Mexico, Colorado, and Wyoming in exchange for $15 million and the assumption by the United States of claims against Mexico by American citizens.

Since the Louisiana Purchase and the War of 1812, the United States had imagined itself as the dominant power in North America. Now, with the incorporation of Texas in 1845, the acquisition of Oregon in 1846, and the addition of the former Mexican territory in 1848, the United States spanned the continent and encompassed an area roughly equivalent in size to all of Europe. The subsequent Gadsden Purchase, ratified by the U.S.

Congress in 1854, added a strip of land across the southern tier of what are now the states of Arizona and New Mexico. This provided the United States with an advantageous route for a future transcontinental railroad line, while Mexico gained a buffer zone to keep Apache raiders—based in the mountains of Arizona and New Mexico—out of its territory.

In revisionist histories, the United States had stolen land from Mexico through the agreements of Guadalupe Hidalgo and Gadsden, but, in fact, Mexico was well compensated for territory in which it had shown little interest since it had been inherited from Spain a quarter century earlier. Indeed, General Stephen Watts Kearny—marching southwest on the Santa Fe Trail—occupied Santa Fe without a fight in 1846, and General John Charles Frémont met little resistance in California.

The majority of the people living in the territory that the United States gained from Mexico were members of Spanish families who had been living here since the Spanish period, Americans such as James Marshall, and Europeans such as John Sutter—or they were members of the tribes who had lived here for centuries and who swore no allegiance to any outside government. Because the Mexican army had never offered much in the way of protection from the Indians, the settlers in the new territories welcomed the promise of support from the U.S. Army.

Meanwhile, the Indians themselves were happier with the prospect of the Americans. For many years, Spain provided aid and supplies to the indigenous people in their territory, just as the U.S. Indian Bureau would in the latter half of the nineteenth century. After Mexico declared its independence from Spain in 1821 and took over the territory, the payments ceased along with any interest in interacting with the native people.

With the discovery of gold and the incorporation of the Far West into the United States, Americans looked west, and in greatly increasing numbers, they began to travel into the West to stay.

THE U.S. ARMY IN THE WEST

In the years after the Mexican War, the mission of the U.S. Army in the West would evolve from one of protecting the trails to one of enforcing the reservation system. As the balance of the population shifted between 1848 and 1890, the West changed from a few sinuous trails sketched against a vast Indian backdrop to small patches of Indian reservations dabbed onto a predominantly non-Indian canvas.

To fulfill its initial post-1848 mission of guarding the trails, the U.S. Army undertook the establishment of forts along these trails throughout the West. These forts would eventually anchor the reservations as well. The creation of the forts changed the operational nature of the Army. Prior to 1848, most army posts in the West were on navigable waterways, such as the Mississippi River, the Columbia River, or along the Pacific coast. After 1848, most new forts would be established well inland. There were eight such installations in 1848, but by 1854, the number had grown to fifty-two.

The inland forts posed new problems for both logistics and communication. A well-armed ship or barge could travel with impunity on any river in the West and it could carry substantial tonnage. Overland supply routes offered neither of these benefits. For this reason, conditions at the frontier forts developed a well-deserved reputation for being austere at best.

Organizationally, the U.S. Army organized the trans-Mississippi West into numbered divisions, or departments. Based at St. Louis, the 6th Department had responsibility for the Northern Plains, while the 7th Department, based at Fort Smith, Arkansas, oversaw military activity on the Southern Plains, excluding Texas. In 1853, the U.S. Army redesignated its departments with names, rather than numbers, and the 6th and 7th were merged as the Department of the West.

Indian Territory (what is now Oklahoma) and Texas were initially the 8th Department, headquartered at San Antonio, but were redesignated in 1853 as the Department of Texas. The 9th Department, which became the Department of New Mexico, included all of what is now part of that state as well as eastern Arizona and a slice of southern Colorado.

Prior to 1848, all of the Far West had been designated as the Pacific or 3rd Division, but it was subdivided into the 10th and 11th Departments. The 10th Department, redesignated in 1853 as the Department of California, included that state, as well as most of Arizona, some of Nevada, and the Oregon Coast as far as Coos Bay. The Pacific Northwest, including much of Idaho, was originally the 11th Department, but it became the Department of Oregon. In the center of the West, the Department of Utah encompassed what is now that state as well as parts of Nevada and Colorado. Here, the task of the U.S. Army was to impose American sovereignty as much onto the Mormons as onto the Indians.

Spokane Plain
(Coeur d'Alene War, 1858)
Seattle
Toppenish Creek   Tohotonimme Creek
(1855)   (Coeur d'Alene War, 1858)
Fort Vancouver   Yakima War (1855-56)
Fort Dalles
Portland   Fort Walla Walla
    Helena
Grande Ronde (1856)

Missouri River

Rogue River Wars
(1851-56)
Fort   Table Rock/Fort Lane
Humboldt
    Yellowstone River
Pit River Actions
(1857-61)   Black Hills
Pomo   Paiute War   Fort Laramie Fight (1853)
Campaign   (1860)   Grattan Fight (1854)
(1850)   Fort Laramie   Platte River
Coloma   Salt Lake City   Omaha
Sacramento   Council
San   Denver   Bluewater Creek   Bluffs
Francisco   Mariposa War   Gunnison Fight   (1855)
(1851)   (1853)   Solomon River (1857)   Kans
    City
    Fort Leavenworth
    Fort Riley   Independence
    Mountain Meadows   Cienquilla
    (1857)   (1854)   Bent's Old Fort   Crooked Creek (1859)
Los Angeles   Fort Union
    Canyon de Chelly   Santa Fe
    (1858)
    Fort Defiance   Fort Sill
Pacific   San Diego
Ocean   Oatman Incident
    (1851)   Red River
    Tucson   Fort Stanton   Pease River
    (1860)

    Rio Grande   Austin
    Del Rio   San Antonio
    Eagle Pass

    Rio Grande

Within these departments was a vast landmass, and relatively few troops to cover it. In 1853, the regular U.S. Army was comprised of 10,417 officers and men, of which 15 percent were assigned to the border with Mexico, and 51 percent were stationed elsewhere in the West. The post–Mexican War U.S. Army consisted of eight infantry regiments and four artillery regiments, but only three mounted regiments. The latter included the 1st and 2nd Dragoons, as well as one regiment of mounted riflemen. As was becoming apparent in the early battles being fought against the Comanche and Kiowa in Texas, only mounted troops were effective against the Indians except in a purely defensive role.

The Indian warriors of the West in the 1848-1890 period were almost all mounted, hence it was impossible for foot soldiers to pursue them after an engagement. Indeed, the warriors of the Plains were often described romantically as the best light cavalry in the world. Certainly, like the mounted warriors of Central Asia, their mobility and their inherent understanding of the terrain made them a cavalry force to be reckoned with, and a force with which infantry could not reckon.

Prior to the arrival of the Europeans, horses were unknown to the indigenous people of North America. Ancestors of modern horses had once existed in the Western Hemisphere, but had been extinct since around the end of the Pleistocene epoch. The vast horse herds that would become such an integral part of the life, culture and image of the Western tribes, especially those on the Plains, were descendants of the horses that were brought over in large numbers by the Spanish.

Beginning early in the sixteenth century, many Spanish horses were either lost or stolen. When the Indians had first encountered Spanish cavalry on horseback, they were frightened, thinking that horse and rider were a single animal. Very soon, however, the Indians came to realize the value and utility of horses. Meanwhile, the horses themselves adapted quickly to the environment, and wild herds soon became common.

Throughout the American West, people such as the Blackfeet, Apache, Cheyenne, Comanche, Nez Percé, and Sioux soon became expert horsemen. Just as quickly, the use of horses revolutionized the way that the buffalo were hunted, and horses changed the nature of warfare throughout the West. The tribes who had the most horses had a clear advantage in military operations.

To address this imbalance between the mounted Indians and the infantry on foot, the regular U.S. Army added the 1st and 2nd Cavalry Regiments in 1855. In 1861, all three types of mounted regiments—dragoons, riflemen, cavalry—were redesignated as cavalry. The 1st and 2nd Dragoons became the 1st and 2nd Cavalry, while the original 1st and 2nd Cavalry were redesignated as 4th and 5th Cavalry, and the Mounted Rifles became the 3rd Cavalry Regiment. The 6th Cavalry Regiment was added to the regular U.S. Army in 1861.

Despite the US Army's apparent emphasis on the horse in the western campaigns, the infantry would comprise the largest number of troops posted to the West, although most infantry regiments were not sent west until after the Civil War. Infantry regiments were seen as being less expensive to equip and maintain, and under the leadership of officers such as Nelson Miles, they would prove effective in combat operations. By 1876, there were 25 infantry regiments assigned to the West, or which had seen service there. This compared to ten cavalry regiments and five artillery regiments. While the cavalry regiments saw a great deal of service in the West, the artillery regiments saw very little service at regimental strength. When artillery was deployed, it usually involved component companies of the regiments being attached temporarily to infantry or cavalry units for a specific campaign.

The regiments of regulars, both infantry and cavalry, were distinct from the state regiments that accounted for the vast majority of U.S. Army personnel during the Civil War. State militias were, however, involved in many of the Indian Wars in the West through 1865. This was especially true of the Texas Rangers.

Each of the mounted and infantry regiments was comprised of ten companies. Those companies assigned to cavalry regiments were alternatively known as "troops," but I use the term "company" in this book for the sake of consistency.

Because the U.S. Army was spread so thin in the West, and because most regiments were substantially understrength, the company tended to be the basic operational unit. Operations involving full regiments would be extremely rare. In the West, the strength of both mounted and infantry companies was authorized for seventy-four privates, but the actual number was almost invariably less, with an average of half that number. A captain, aided by two lieutenants and a sergeant, commanded the company, which theoretically included four squads led by a sergeant and a corporal. In turn, the regiment was commanded by a colonel and/or a lieutenant colonel, two majors, and various quartermaster and other personnel, who might be officers or sergeants. In the early days, most of the officers assigned to the U.S. Army in the West had been trained and commissioned at the U.S. Military Academy at West Point. Advancement beyond the rank of lieutenant was slow.

Overall strategic policy theoretically flowed from the War Department in Washington, but the generals commanding the departments had a great deal of flexibility in determining tactical direction. More often than not, however, actions would be determined by events on the ground as they unfolded.

Military life in the West was difficult, owing more to boredom and environmental conditions than hostile fire. The extremes of heat and cold affected both daily life and the ability of the troopers to do their work. More often than not, this work consisted of non-combat duty, such as caring for the horses and mules and maintaining the physical structure of the fort. Military personnel also conducted some of the earliest geographic survey work done in the West, including surveying rights of way for future roads.

Monotony was more common than combat, and the U.S. Army lost more men to disease and desertion than to enemy action. Eventually, civilian settlements grew up around the forts, and these included saloons and bawdy houses that provided the troopers with the various diversions that made life more bearable.

The U.S. Army in the West became a refuge for recent immigrants eager for a regular paycheck. As many Irish immigrants as American-born men volunteered, and together they comprised two-thirds of the force. Most of the remaining troops were recent immigrants from Bavaria, Prussia, and other German-speaking principalities of central Europe.

Just as the U.S. Army was being called upon to play an ever-increasing role in the West, Congress deemed that it should share its authority to do so. The four decades from 1848 to 1890 would be marked by armed conflict between the U.S. Army and the Indians, just as they would be marked by a bureaucratic conflict between governmental departments. Beginning in

1789, the Department of War, the cabinet-level office overseeing the U.S. Army, had the responsibility for Indian affairs. The post of commissioner of Indian Affairs was created within the War Department in July 1832, and the Office of Indian Affairs (later Bureau of Indian Affairs) was organized two years later. On March 3, 1849, a year after the end of the Mexican War, Congress created the Department of Interior and transferred the Indian Bureau to this new cabinet-level department.

The new bureau would be responsible for establishing formal relations with the Indian "nations," and for administering the evolving and shifting U.S. governmental Indian policy. One aspect of this policy that was adopted early in the life of the bureau was the payment of an annual annuity to Indians who remained peaceful. The annuity was paid by the Indian Bureau agents in the form of supplies, such as food and tools.

The U.S. Army, meanwhile, would be responsible for security and enforcement. The division of responsibility sounded good on paper, but in the field, the two missions were not always parallel and complementary. This was especially true when the supplies distributed by Indian agents included firearms. These were theoretically intended to be used for hunting, but they could easily be turned against the soldiers, and occasionally they were.

Beginning with the treaties of Fort Laramie in 1851 and Fort Atkinson in 1853, the United States government began moving toward the policy of setting aside sections of the West as "Indian reservations." Formalized in 1868 after the next Fort Laramie Treaty, this policy would include assigning civilian Indian agents to manage the reservations on behalf of the government until or unless relations between the Indians and the government got out of hand. Then the Army was called in.

The Texas Theater in the 1850s

In the Lone Star State, the troubles with the Comanche and Kiowa that had preceded the Mexican War continued, even as the Northern Plains remained relatively quiet in the wake of the treaties of Fort Laramie and Fort Atkinson. The terms of the treaties prescribed specific territory that was to be set aside for the use of the respective parties, Indians and settlers. There was relative peace, because both sides knew where they stood—at least for a while.

Many of the actions continued to involve detachments of Texas Rangers, including those commanded by men such as Captain William "Bigfoot" Wallace and the legendary Captain John Salmon "Rip" Ford, who later went on to a career in state politics. Parenthetically, Ford had been involved in the last battle of the Mexican War, at Sequaltipan, and he commanded Confederate forces in the Battle of Palmito Ranch, the last battle of the Civil War. For the purpose of the military history of the region, the Texas Theater also includes western Oklahoma, wherein the Texas Rangers would fight some of their biggest battles.

By the 1850s, the Texas Rangers had developed tactics that were usually effective in fighting the Indians. Part of this involved their ability to successfully track the Indian raiding parties to their own camps after a raid on a town or settlement, in order to launch a counterstrike. Usually, the skirmishes were just that, with casualties less than a half dozen.

While most of the battles cast the Rangers opposite the Kiowa and Comanche, there were other combatants involved in Texas actions. Mescalero and Lipan Apache based in northern Mexico often forded the Rio Grande to conduct cross-border raids on settlements and roads in West Texas. On October 3, 1854, and July 22, 1855, companies of U.S. Army Mounted Rifles tracked and engaged large Apache raiding parties near Eagle Pass and Eagle Springs, but they were able to escape with light casualties, crossing the Rio Grande into the sanctuary of Mexican territory where the U.S. Army could not pursue them.

The Apache did not always operate close to the border. In 1856, units of the 2nd Cavalry Regiment were involved in a number of skirmishes with both the Lipan Apache and the Comanche deep in Texas and far from the Rio Grande. These actions included battles on March 8 north of San Antonio, on April 13 on the Nueces River, and another on July 1 on the Brazos River. Between November 26 and December 22, the 2nd Cavalry fought a series of four battles with both Apache and Comanche in West Texas in which the regiment lost its first two troopers killed in action. The fight continued into 1857, with the 2nd Cavalry involved in skirmishes with the Comanche during February in the Concho River drainage near the center of the state, and on July 20 after trailing a large group of Comanche south toward the Rio Grande crossing at Del Rio.

After 1857, the number of pitched battles between the Indians and the military declined. Patrols by the Texas Rangers and the United States Cavalry generally kept the Indians at bay within the radius that could easily be reached from the forts, although the Indians continued their raids on more remote settlements. The attacks on towns and settlements were a continuation of a long-standing Indian reaction to rival tribes or bands camping in disputed territory. As it had been long before the arrival of Euro-American settlers, the raiding policy was partly in retaliation against trespassers, and partly an opportunity to plunder and pilfer desirable property. Just as the Apache enjoyed a sanctuary within Mexico, the Comanche raiders rode north to regroup in the remote Llano Estacado, or Staked Plains, the vast tall grass prairie encompassing parts of northeastern New Mexico and northwestern Texas south of the Canadian River.

In the spring of 1858, incoming Texas governor Hardin Runnels decided that more aggressive action was required, and he ordered Captain Rip Ford to cross the Red River and go after the Comanche. Planning for a major—and hopefully decisive—battle, Ford assembled a large force that included a number of Indian scouts from rival, smaller tribes, including the Anadarko and Shawnee, who were living at the Brazos Reservation in Texas. The Comanche raiders had also been harassing these people, and allying themselves with the Rangers offered a good possibility of getting back at their enemies. The force numbering 215, including 102 Rangers, would face about 300 Comanche warriors under Chief Iron Jacket, who took his name from the old Spanish chain mail that he liked to wear into battle.

On May 11, near the Canadian River at Antelope Hills, some of Ford's Indian scouts attacked a small Comanche encampment about three miles from the main Comanche camp. The Rangers reached the scene just as the main Comanche force from the village arrived. In the ensuing seven-hour battle, the Comanche suffered 76 dead—including Iron Jacket himself—while the opposing side lost just two.

The success of Rip Ford's bold Texas Ranger campaign demonstrated that the U.S. Army's policy of mounting reactive operations within a short radius of their forts was probably too cautious a strategy. Indeed, it inspired the U.S. Army to undertake a similar mission. Veteran cavalry commander Captain Earl Van Dorn led a 225-man detachment across the Red River into present-day Oklahoma in September 1858. His command consisted of four companies of 2nd Cavalry and a small infantry detachment, plus 135 Indian scouts from the Brazos Reservation that were coordinated by Lawrence Sullivan "Sul" Ross, the son of Indian agent Shapely Ross.

Without being detected, the troopers located a large Cheyenne encampment on Rush Creek, a tributary of the Washita River. Present in the camp were an estimated 500 Cheyenne, including women and children, under the leadership of Buffalo Hump.

Van Dorn ordered a dawn attack on October 1 that caught the Comanche by surprise. The Battle of Rush Springs was the second major defeat for the Comanche during 1858. They lost fifty-six men on the battlefield, plus another twenty-five who died of their wounds soon after. Van Dorn's command lost four killed, and eleven wounded. Among the wounded were Sul Ross and Van Dorn himself, who was seriously injured. Both, however, survived to rise to the rank of general in the Confederate Army.

Two Comanche women were also killed, but most of the Comanche, including Buffalo Hump, managed to escape. They split up, with some scattering to Mexico and others remaining in the Oklahoma. Shortly after the first of the year, they resumed raiding settlements, and on February 24, 1859, a Comanche raiding party ambushed a detachment from the 1st Cavalry Regiment, based at Fort Arbuckle on the Washita River. The 1st Cavalry dispatched a force to run down the raiders, and this unit caught up with them three days later. In the ensuing fight, seven Comanche were killed.

In May, Earl Van Dorn resumed the pursuit with five hundred troopers from six companies of 2nd Cavalry plus fifty-eight Indian scouts. By this time, the Comanche were moving north, and Van Dorn followed them across present-day Oklahoma and into Kansas Territory. On May 13, 1859, the 2nd Cavalry caught up with the Comanche near the Cimarron River at Crooked Creek. The Comanche attempted to escape, but were cut off. The rough terrain consisting of steep-sided gulleys meant that the battle would be characterized by fierce close-in action. As with Rush Springs, the Battle of Crooked Creek was a Van Dorn victory. His troops killed forty-nine Comanche fighters, while capturing five men and thirty-two women. The 2nd Cavalry lost two, and four Indian scouts died as a result of the battle.

Lesser engagements aside, the next major battle between the U.S. Army and the Comanche in the Texas Theater came the following summer, although it was a mere skirmish compared to Rush Springs and Crooked

Creek. Major George Thomas departed Camp Cooper, Texas, in late July, leading elements of two companies of the 2nd Cavalry on what amounted to an extended search and destroy mission against Comanche insurgents. On August 26, they crossed paths with a Comanche raiding party on the Clear Fork of the Brazos River. In the ensuing firefight, each side lost one killed in action.

Despite the losses, the Indians continued their raids, both from a desire to plunder supplies, and a general sense that continued pressure would eventually compel the settlers to withdraw from Indian land.

The last major battle in Texas before the state succeeded from the Union on the eve of the Civil War came on December 19, 1860, on the Pease River, just south of its confluence with the Red River. In this case, it was a joint operation involving a detachment of 2nd Cavalry and a company of Texas Rangers. The latter were under the command of Sul Ross, who was now a Ranger captain. The combined force of approximately 150 men caught up with a smaller group of Comanche, led by a man named Nocona, on the Pease River. In the battle, the soldiers and rangers overwhelmed the Comanche, killing fourteen, including Nocona, while losing none of their own.

Among the Comanche people captured was Nocona's blue-eyed wife. She turned out to be thirty-five-year-old Cynthia Ann Parker, who had been captured by the Comanche as a child in 1836, and who had lived with them ever since. She had several children by Nocona, including Quanah Parker. The teen-aged Quanah escaped capture at Pease River, and would go on to become an important chief of the Quahadi Comanche and lead his people into battle.

Cynthia Ann Parker was repatriated to white society reluctantly, because she had lost her Comanche family and was taken away from the culture that she knew. Although she never returned to live with the Comanche, neither did she ever fully assimilate to her new life. She died in 1870, having suffered the pain of being torn from her family twice.

THE ROGUE RIVER WAR

The Pacific Northwest saw more major combat before the Civil War than after. A parallel with Texas was that much of the early military action between the tribes and the new arrivals pitted the indigenous warriors against a militia, in this case the Oregon volunteers, rather than regular U.S. Army troops. The latter were under the command of the Department of Oregon, based at Fort Vancouver, located on the site of the present city of the same name in Washington State. Most of the forts in the department were located on the Columbia River or around Puget Sound.

Southwestern Oregon, where a great deal of the major combat would take place, was under the command of the Department of California, based at the Presidio of San Francisco.

The Whitman Massacre of November 29, 1847, had essentially begun the open hostility between the indigenous people of the region and the newcomers who imagined they would find paradise at the end of the Oregon Trail.

As had happened in other regions of the United States, as non-Indian population density reached a critical mass, armed conflict tailed off as indigenous people moved out of the region or assimilated. Hence, the Willamette Valley would experience no major combat after 1850, and the Columbia River area would experience very little.

The major center of conflict during the 1850s was in the Rogue River region of southwestern Oregon. The Rogue River War is today recalled as the signature military campaign in the Pacific Northwest during this period, although it was by no means the only important conflict.

Settlers had been passing through the region since 1846, when Jesse Applegate pioneered the trail that bore his name. The Applegate Trail, actually a southern spur of the Oregon Trail, led into the Willamette Valley from the south. With the 1849 California Gold Rush, the traffic became two-way, as treasure seekers headed south across the Siskiyou range into California. In the meantime, a discovery of gold on the Rogue River in 1851 led to a minor gold rush that brought a surge of prospectors into southwestern Oregon.

The Rogue River War was a running conflict that began in 1851 and reached its climax in 1856. The protagonists were settlers, militia, and the U.S. Army on one side, and a group of indigenous people referred to by historians as the "Rogue River Indians" on the other. The Rogue River Indians were not a tribe, but a confederacy of small bands in the region who were simultaneously at war. According to the Oregon State Museum of Anthropology at the University of Oregon, they encompass the Penutian-speaking Takelma—including the Umpqua, Tutuni, and Klamath—and the Athapaskan-speaking Dakubetede—which include the Coquille. While the bands spoke differing Penutian and Athapaskan languages, they shared many cultural features, and they had a common enemy. The Hokan-speaking Shasta, who lived to the south in the interior of what is now northern California, also allied themselves with the Rogue River people.

The first battles in the Rogue River War occurred during June 1851. On Bear Creek, near present-day Ashland, a group of ambushed miners fought a four-hour pitched battle on June 2 in which seven Indians and a miner were killed. Eight days later, an estimated one hundred Rogue River Indians attacked a group of settlers on the Oregon coast at present-day Port Orford. The settlers withdrew to a large outcropping of rock just offshore and managed to hold out for two weeks.

The first contact between the U.S. Army and the Rogue River Indians came on June 17, 1851, in the form of a skirmish at Table Rock, a prominent bluff just north of present-day Medford. The Indians ambushed a detachment of the 1st Regiment of Mounted Rifles under the command of Major Philip Kearny, the nephew of Stephen Watts Kearny, who would have an illustrious Civil War career before being killed in action in 1862. The attackers lost eleven men at Table Rock, while Kearny lost one officer.

Having briefly withdrawn to the safety of another settlement at Coos Bay, the Port Orford settlers sent an expedition back into the area three months later. On September 14, this group came into conflict with members of the Athapaskan-speaking Coquille band at the mouth of the river of the same name near present-day Bandon. Five settlers were killed in what is known as the Coquille Massacre.

In November, the U.S. Army sent three companies of the 1st Dragoons into the region on a retaliatory mission. They located a Coquille encampment, against which they launched a surprise attack on November 22 in which two soldiers and fifteen Coquille were killed.

The following summer, as incidents continued, Indian agent Alonzo Skinner arranged for a meeting which he envisioned as a peace conference. Indians, settlers, and militia volunteers met near Table Rock on July 17, but the discussion turned into an argument, which became violent when a Shasta man was shot. After the dust settled, about twenty people, including most of the Indian conferees, were dead.

Meanwhile, a parallel conflict to the Rogue River War saw even greater casualties along the Applegate Trail immediately south of the Rogue River area. During September, a group of Penutian-speaking Modoc warriors ambushed a wagon trail near Tule Lake just south of the Oregon border, killing sixty-two immigrants and capturing two young girls. Ben Wright, a settler from Yreka, west of Tule Lake, organized a militia to track down the Modoc, and their encampment was located near present-day Merrill, Oregon. As at Table Rock four months earlier, a discussion turned violent. In a shootout on November 15, 1852, the well-armed volunteers killed an estimated fifty-two Modoc. It would be two decades before there would be further major combat between the Modoc and the settlers.

Throughout 1853, the fighting in the Rogue River continued to escalate, with raids and counter-raids. In August, the volunteers joined forces with the U.S. Army 4th Infantry Regiment in two pitched battles near Table Rock, during which they lost ten men and killed fifteen Indians. In the aftermath, the Rogue River people agreed to a cease-fire under the terms of the Table Rock Treaty of September 10.

Despite the treaty, which established a reservation near Table Rock, the violence continued. A cattle rustling incident in October led to another battle near what is now Cave Junction that cost the lives of two soldiers and fifteen Indians. Further skirmishes, in which settlers raided Indian villages, continued through the winter and into 1854, resulting in several dozen Indian deaths throughout southwestern Oregon and northern California. The U.S. Army concentrated elements of both the 1st Dragoons and 4th Infantry at Fort Lane, newly established near Table Rock.

The region saw little major combat for about a year, although the Indians continued their occasional raids against outlying settlements. In response to these raids, a Yreka, California, man named James Lupton organized a group of volunteers for the purpose of conducting search and destroy operations in the rugged Siskiyou Mountains. In a predawn raid on October 8, 1855, they attacked a sleeping village on Little Butte Creek near Table Rock, where they massacred about two dozen Indians—including women and children.

The following day, Indians living on the reservation at Table Rock retaliated, attacking and killing about twenty nearby settlers who had not been involved in the previous attack. The Indian raiders continued their attacks, striking a mining camp at Skull Bar on October 17 and a field encampment of 4th Infantry Regiment men at Grave Creek on October 25. In the two engagements four miners, two soldiers, and several Indians were killed. The settlers and the Army were now clearly on the defensive.

By the end of October, a group of Indian leaders, notably Tecumtum, also known as Old John, had assembled a small army of about five hundred to support their continued raids. This was about double the size of the combined force that the Army and the volunteers had available. Battles fought at Hungry Hill on October 31 and Little Meadows on November 26 resulted in a total of about twenty deaths on each side, but with neither side achieving a clear victory.

As winter set in and the snow fell, warfare typically slackened, but not so in the winter of 1855-1856. On Christmas Eve, a contingent of volunteers attacked and burned two Indian camps on Little Butte Creek, killing nineteen men and leaving women and children without food or shelter. A week later, the volunteers entered into a running battle with another group of Indians on the Applegate River that lasted several days, but cost only a few lives on either side. The pursuit continued, with a series of small but bloody skirmishes through January.

On February 23, 1856, the Tutuni band of Rogue River Indians launched several major surprise attacks in and around the settlement of Gold Beach at the mouth of the Rogue River. The Tutumi achieved a complete rout, managing to kill forty volunteers or settlers, including militia leader Ben Wright, before breaking off their attack.

The fighting around the mouth of the Rogue River would continue with separate and uncoordinated campaigns launched by the volunteers and the U.S. Army. On March 18, a volunteer contingent was surrounded on the Pacific shoreline about ten miles south of Gold Beach, but the Indians broke off the attack when the battle lasted into the night. Over the next week, near Gold Beach itself, units attached to the 4th Infantry Regiment engaged the Indians in two indecisive firefights with the Indians led by Old John. Raids and small skirmishes involving both volunteers and troops would continue for two months.

Minimal headway was made toward a negotiated cease-fire, because Old John was still holding out for a decisive victory. It would come, but not the way he had convinced the other Indian leaders that it would. A cease-fire meeting had been arranged for a place on the Big Bend of the Rogue River about twenty miles upstream from Gold Beach, but Old John had other ideas.

One company each from the 1st Dragoons and the 4th Infantry Regiment were present on the morning of May 27, when Old John led his attack aimed at enveloping the troops. The soldiers responded with a howitzer. They kept the attackers at bay, but remained surrounded and running out of water. The following morning, Captain Christopher Augur arrived on the scene with a sizable 4th Infantry Regiment force. He struck the Indian rear, breaking the siege. Each side lost

Tecumtum, Elk Killer, also known as Old John (178?–1864), around 1863 following his release from prison. (*Oregon Historical Society*)

about a dozen men, but the Indians surrendered. The Rogue River War was over, and Old John was imprisoned at Alcatraz in San Francisco Bay. With the Rogue River people pacified, Oregon could contemplate statehood.

THE YAKIMA AND COEUR D'ALENE WARS

In Washington Territory, the young governor, Isaac Stevens, had managed to broker peace treaties with most of the tribes living within his jurisdiction. The exception that caused things to unravel—even as the Rogue River War was reaching a crescendo in Oregon—was an internal power struggle among the Penutian-speaking Yakima people. Their principal chief, Kamiakin, is said to have favored peace, but younger men, including his nephew Qualchin, favored random attacks on miners and settlers. When Qualchin murdered a number of people in unprovoked attacks, including Indian agent Andrew Bolon in September 1855, Kamiakin found his people at war.

Captain Granville Haller led a 4th Infantry Regiment contingent out of Fort Dalles on the Columbia River to strike the large Yakima force that Kamiakin was assembling on Toppenish Creek not far from the present city of Yakima. On October 6, Haller was overwhelmed by 1,500 Yakima and Palouse warriors and forced into a retreat. Over the next three days, he fought his way back to Fort Dalles, losing five men killed in action.

Kamiakin's victory in the first battle of the Yakima War served to inspire other tribes to join the war. When a combined force of 4th Infantry Regiment and volunteer troops moved south from the Puget Sound area in early November to attack the Yakima, other tribes, such as the Nisqually and Puyallup, moved in to attack settlements left unguarded. Other western Washington tribes, such as the Chinook and Klickitat, joined the Yakima in battle.

In December, the focal point of the Yakima War moved east to the Walla Walla River area and the vicinity of the old Whitman Mission, when six companies of Oregon volunteers under Lieutenant Colonel James Kelly rode into the area. An attempt at a cease-fire conference failed on December 4, and Walla Walla Chief Peopeomoxmox, a leading pre-war peace advocate, was taken into custody.

On December 7, Kelly attacked the Walla Walla and Cayuse, who were prepared for battle. For four days, a see-saw battle raged within about two miles of the old mission site. Finally, the exhausted Indians withdrew and the volunteers claimed victory. Peopeomoxmox himself was killed during the battle when he allegedly tried to escape.

During the spring of 1856, the volunteers pursued the Palouse and Walla Walla warriors to the east and north. More often than not, they attacked unguarded villages and non-combatants, but they succeeded in keeping the warriors on the run and on the defensive. On March 27, however, a U.S. Army contingent under Major Edward Steptoe met a sizable Indian force in battle on the north side of the Columbia River only twenty miles east of Fort Vancouver and the mouth of the Willamette. Steptoe defeated the Indians and captured a few, but most escaped.

The end of Washington Territory's Yakima War came in an unlikely place—Oregon. In July 1856, Governor Stevens sent his Washington militia under Lieutenant Colonel Benjamin Shaw across the Columbia in pursuit of the Yakima. He caught up with and defeated them in the Grande Ronde Valley. Shaw's victory here on July 18 led to a formal surrender two months later in eastern Washington.

A relative peace reigned in Washington for two years until the Palouse began attacking mining settlements near Colville in northeast Washington in the spring of 1858. By now, the Yakima and Palouse were allied with the Spokane and Coeur d'Alene tribes living in this area. It was the Coeur d'Alene who would become the namesake for this new war, although the Yakima and Palouse were still involved.

Again, it was Edward Steptoe, now a lieutenant colonel, whom the U.S. Army sent to deal with the situation. Leading a force that contained three companies of the 1st Dragoons, Steptoe moved north from Fort Walla Walla. On May 16, he detected a contingent of Palouse and allied tribes following his troops and attempting to intimidate them. Outnumbering the troopers five to one, the Indians attacked the following morning at Tohotonimme Creek. Steptoe managed to hold them off all day, but he expected the worst, so he led a nocturnal escape that was amazingly successful, and they reached Fort Walla Walla on May 22.

After Steptoe's defeat in the first major battle of the new Coeur d'Alene War, the U.S. Army moved to react swiftly and decisively. On August 15, three companies of 9th Infantry under Major Robert Garnett and one company of the 4th Infantry Regiment under future Indian Wars legend Lieutenant George Crook managed to surround and capture seventy Palouse on the Yakima River in central Washington.

The decisive battle of the Coeur d'Alene War would come two weeks later, on September 1, 1858, on the flat plains west of Spokane. Colonel George Wright led six hundred men drawn from five companies of the 1st Dragoons, five companies of the 3rd Artillery Regiment, and two companies of the 9th Infantry Regiment. Opposing him were a combined force of Yakima, Palouse, Spokane, and Coeur d'Alene, who were confident and ready for battle. Both Kamiakin and his nephew Qualchin, who had been the catalyst for the Yakima War three years earlier, were present.

The Indians attempted to break up the Army force by allowing them to capture a hill, and then drawing them into a series of ravines and woods on the far side, but Wright turned the tables. Wright integrated his various elements masterfully. He managed to draw the Indian line out onto the open hillside, where his cavalry enveloped them, and the artillery blasted the covered positions in the ravines and woods. Since 1856, the standard guns used by the U.S. Army's light field artillery units in the West were the three-inch Rodman Ordnance rifle, and the smooth-bore Napoleon twelve-pounder field gun. The rounds fired included canister or case shot that was particularly effective against massed formations such as those encountered on the Spokane Plain. The infantry were now equipped with the Model 1855 rifles, whose long-range accuracy accounted for a significant number of Indian losses. In the Battle of Four Lakes, fifty Indians were killed in action, while the U.S. Army suffered no losses.

Wright kept up the pressure, catching the Indians four days later in another fierce battle. Again, he used his artillery to its full effect, and his cavalry to attack the Indians once they had been knocked off balance by the artillery barrage. The U.S. Army's success in the Battle of the Spokane Plain rounded out the earlier victory at Four Lakes. The Indian force that had been so confident a week earlier was in disarray, and within a few days the Army had rounded up a sizable number of prisoners.

Though there would be a few minor skirmishes in eastern Oregon after the Civil War, Wright's victory at Spokane essentially marked the end of the Indian Wars in the Pacific Northwest north of the Great Basin. Qualchin was captured and executed for his part in the killings in 1855. Kamiakin had been injured by a falling tree branch at Four Lakes, but he was rescued by his wife Colestah. They escaped to Montana, and later Canada. They returned to eastern Washington in 1860, where they lived peacefully. Colestah died four years later, and Kamiakin remained in the area until his death in 1877.

THE CALIFORNIA THEATER IN THE 1850s

Before contact with Europeans, the native culture of California was similar in many respects to that of the Pacific Northwest. There were many small tribes, but few large tribes dominating large geographic areas as was the case on the Plains. Most people lived in small, self-contained enclaves and there were sufficient resources for the people to hunt and gather in order to survive. They hunted wild game, including quail, deer and rabbits, and they gathered the acorns which are abundant throughout California. Most native peoples throughout California were adept at making intricate baskets that were woven so well as to be watertight.

An important difference between the hunters in California when compared to hunters in other regions, especially on the Plains, was in terms of scale. In California, and along the coastal valleys of the Pacific Northwest, a hunting trip might take hunters out of a fixed village for several days or weeks, whereas on the Plains, the annual buffalo hunt consumed an entire season, and the entire village folded up its portable tipis and traveled with the hunters.

In such a vast area, there were numerous ethnic and linguistic groups. In the south, the people spoke dialects of the Uto-Aztecan linguistic group called Yuman that were related to the languages spoken in what are now the Desert Southwest of the United States and northern Mexico. In the deserts and the west of what is now California, people spoke Uto-Aztecan languages related to those of the Great Basin tribes such as the Paiute.

In central California, most people spoke languages associated with the Penutian linguistic group. Among these were the people living along the Pacific coast between Monterey Bay and San Francisco Bay that the Spanish referred to as Los Costanos, or "the Coastal People." Anthropologists now refer to this family as Costanoan. Other Penutian people included the Yokuts (Tulare), who lived in the vast San Joaquin Valley; as well as the Maidu, Wintun, and Miwok, who lived in enclaves north of San Francisco Bay from the Pacific to the western foothills of the Sierra Nevada, and in the Sacramento Valley as far north as the Trinity River. Another Penutian group were the Modoc, who lived in the deserts of the distant northeastern part of California as well as in adjacent areas of Nevada and Oregon.

Also living along the coast, especially along the shores of the Santa Barbara Channel, were the linguistically distinct Chumash people, who were noted for operating fishing fleets of ocean-going canoes.

Hokan-speaking tribes lived throughout California. In the valleys of the coastal ranges south of Monterey Bay, a number of tribes spoke the Salinan dialects of Hokan. In the areas north of San Francisco Bay, both along the coast and in the interior were the Hokan-speaking Pomo, Shasta, Karuk (Karok), and Achomawi (Pit River) people. In northern California, there were also tribes associated with the Athapaskan linguistic group, such as the Hupa, and with the Algonquian linguistic group, such as the Yurok. Indeed, California was, as it still is, an ethnically diverse region.

To the Spanish, there were two Californias, Lower, or Baja California, and Upper, or Alta California. It would be Alta California that became the American state. The Spanish made several attempts to establish a presence in Baja California during the seventeenth century, and finally succeeded in 1697 with a permanent mission at Loreto. It would nearly a century before they did the same in Alta California. In 1769, the expeditions that would establish Alta California's first permanent settlements arrived in San Diego in a coordinated effort by the Spanish government and the Catholic Franciscan missionary order. Arriving together were future military governor Gaspar de Portolá, and Franciscan Father Junípero Serra. Within the first decade, Father Serra and his Franciscans had established eight missions, and Portolá's military personnel had established presidios, or military posts, at San Diego, Monterey, and San Francisco, overlooking the Golden Gate. By the end of the century, there were eighteen missions and another presidio at Santa Barbara, and cities such as Los Angeles were growing commercial hubs.

The relations between the Spanish and the native Californians were generally good. The only major incidents involving Indian attacks on missions during the Spanish period were in November 1775 at Mission San Diego de Alcalá, and one year later at Mission San Luis Obispo de Tolosa. In 1824, after Mexico took over Alta California, another incident occurred after a Mexican military guard at Mission Santa Inés beat a Chumash neophyte from Mission La Purísima Concepción. Only in the first instance did the attackers deliberately kill a Franciscan missionary.

In 1832, a Zacatecan priest named Father José Maria Mercado led an ambush of a group of Pomo people that he mistakenly thought were going to attack the mission. The ensuing firefight resulted in the deaths of more than twenty unarmed Pomo. Both the native and Spanish population in the San Francisco Bay area were outraged at this incident, and Father Mercado was relieved of his pastorship and disciplined.

In revisionist histories, the Franciscan missionaries are faulted for bringing disease and enslavement to the indigenous people of California. In fact, they were much more benevolent and cooperative than fundamentalist Protestants such as Cotton Mather in New England or Marcus Whitman in Oregon Territory. The Franciscans resided with the local people for years at a time, often outnumbered several dozen to one within the mission complexes themselves. They made an effort to understand the native people. At Mission San Antonio de Padua, Father Buenaventura Sitjar mastered the local Teleme dialect of the Salinan language to the extent that he was able to produce a written dictionary. Father Felipe del Arroyo de la Cuesta did similar work at Mission San Juan Bautista.

The Mexican government inherited, but never supported, the California mission system established under the Spanish. A succession of Mexican government officials sent in to serve as Alta California governors seized mission lands and eventually sold off even the mission churches. These were not finally restored to the Church until after California became a state.

Populated mostly by Spanish families, American immigrants, and Indians—rather than by Mexicans—California declared itself an independent republic in July 1846. Unlike the Republic of Texas, which had remained independent for a decade before joining the United States in 1845, the Republic of California would last just a few weeks. It ceased to exist before the news that it had been a republic had reached many corners of the state. The U.S. Navy under Commodore John Sloat captured the Mexican provincial capital at Monterey on July 7, and two days later, the United States flag went up in the village of Yerba Buena, which would soon become the city of San Francisco.

Gold was discovered in January 1848, and California became the thirty-first state in September 1850. The U.S. Army took over the Presidio of San Francisco, which became the headquarters of the Department of the Pacific, later the Department of California. The Department of California would encompass not only California, but also southwestern Oregon and most of Arizona. After the Civil War, when the entire West was organized into two divisions, the Missouri and the Pacific, split at the continental divide, the Presidio would be the headquarters of the Division of the Pacific as well as the constituent Department of California. Arizona would become a separate department within the Pacific Division in 1870.

One of the legacies that the United States inherited from the Spanish in the state of California was generally good relations with the native population. After 1850, there were only a handful of major incidents south of San Francisco Bay and none within a day's ride of the coast.

In May 1850, the U.S. Army was involved in a brief campaign against the Pomo which would be the largest action to involve the Army in the southern three-quarters of the state. After several miners had been killed during the winter near Clear Lake, north of San Francisco Bay, Captain Nathaniel Lyon led a contingent including three companies of the 2nd Infantry Regiment and a company of the 1st Dragoons on a search and destroy mission. In a series of engagements between May 14 and May 19, more than one hundred Pomo were killed. No soldiers were lost in the Pomo campaign, but one trooper was killed in action on July 25 in a skirmish with the Achomawi in the far northern part of the state.

During 1851, the action in California followed a pattern familiar from contemporary actions in Texas and the Pacific Northwest. Aggressive civilian volunteers went on the offensive in reaction to Indian attacks. In this case, what would be known as the Mariposa War began with raids on settlers organized by Chief Tenaya, who led a mixed force of about 350 Miwok, Chowchilla, and Yokuts warriors. In the process, they attacked a trading post owned by Mariposa county businessman James Savage, killing several of his employees. In January and February, Savage led a well-armed force into the Sierra Nevada foothills to attack known Yokuts strongholds. A series of firefights left an estimated thirty-seven Indians and two militiamen dead.

Similar civilian volunteer actions on the South Fork of the Trinity River in April 1852, and near Oroville in March 1853, resulted in 140 and thirteen Indian dead, respectively.

Excluding the operations in the far north that were associated with the Rogue River War in Oregon, the U.S. Army saw little major combat in California during the 1850s after the Pomo campaign. An exception was in the Pit River country of northeastern California. Here the opposition included the Achomawi, known as the "Pit River Indians," as well as the Shasta. Among the officers leading the soldiers was young Lieutenant George Crook of the 4th Infantry Regiment, who would later, as General George Crook, serve as one of the Army's most famous Indian War commanders. He would earn his stellar reputation as a field commander during the Paiute campaign of the late 1860s and his series of campaigns in the Southwest during the 1870s.

In June 1857, with Crook heading Company D, the 4th Infantry Regiment went into the Pit River country in response to a series of fatal attacks against settlers that had occurred through the winter. In a skirmish on June 10, Crook was hit in his hip by an arrow, the head of which would remain in him for the rest of his life. In a series of engagements lasting though July, Crook and his men killed about two dozen Indians, lost none of their own, and managed to recover some stolen cattle.

A portent to his long career, Crook was in the center of the action in California during 1857. Toward the end of the year, he and his company were assigned to a post near the mouth of the Klamath River, where they put down a Klamath uprising on November 17. Again, the casualty figures were lopsided, with ten Indians killed in action, and no losses among Crook's force.

This lopsidedness prevailed in actions involving civilian volunteers. Indeed, there would be several incidents that can clearly be called massacres. On January 13, 1860, volunteers killed an estimated thirty Indians at Round Valley in Mendocino County, and nearly two hundred Indians were murdered near the mouth of the Eel River in neighboring Humboldt County in late February 1860.

By the 1850s, the Indians throughout most of California were clearly no match in terms of either mobility or firepower for the well-armed irregular militias, or for the U.S. Army.

THE GRATTAN FIGHT AND THE PLAINS THEATER IN THE 1850s

No theater of the Indian Wars could have been more different from California than the Plains. By the 1850s, California cities, especially San Francisco, rivaled any city in the East for their cosmopolitan sophistication. The idea of an Indian uprising was just as distant in the mists of the past throughout most of California as it was in New England. The U.S. Army headquarters for the region, designated as the Department of the West, would be at St. Louis, a city that was about as far, at least psychologically, from the Indian Wars as the cities of the Eastern seaboard.

Yet on the Plains, the Sioux, especially the western Lakota branch, remained dominant. They were being challenged by the U.S. Army for military supremacy, but they, not the Army, still controlled most of the Plains north of Texas and Oklahoma. There were no major Indian War actions in either Montana or Dakota Territory during the 1850s because the local tribes, including the Sioux, Cheyenne, and Blackfeet, essentially remained unchallenged.

This status quo seemed to have been formalized by the 1851 conference arranged by Superintendent of Indian Affairs David Mitchell and Indian Agent Thomas Fitzpatrick held at Fort Laramie, located on the Oregon Trail in eastern Wyoming (which was part of Idaho Territory until 1868). There were an estimated 10,000 Indians representing most of the Northern Plains tribes, including the Arapaho, Arikira, Assiniboine, Crow, Gros Ventre, and Hidatsa, as well as the Sioux and Cheyenne. The result was the Treaty of Fort Laramie, which recognized Indian hunting grounds and provided annuities in the form of food and other supplies in exchange for the right to build roads. A similar treaty signed at Fort Atkinson, Kansas, in 1853 essentially added the Comanche and Kiowa as signatories to the same agreement.

The initial phases of the conflict between the interlopers and the indigenous people in the interior of the West involved actions along the emigrant trails and roads, as discussed in Chapter 2. Subsequently, it moved to include forts and settlements.

Events such as the one on June 15, 1853, at Fort Laramie, in which three Lakota were killed during an argument, could have precipitated an enormous conflict. The fact that the Fort Laramie incident did not devolve into massive bloodshed indicates the state of relations on the Plains at the time. The fact was that the Indians did not yet consider the outsiders as a threat and accommodated them for their value as a source of guns and other supplies, through either trade or the generous grants being made through the Indian Bureau.

A year later, however, the era of coexistence came to an end and thirty-six years of major combat between the U.S. Army and the Plains Indians began.

The Grattan Fight, or Grattan Massacre, was a battle that should not have happened. The incident began on August 18, 1854, just east of Fort Laramie at a time when the Brulé Lakota were camped there waiting for their government annuities. High Forehead, a Minneconjou man camping with the Brulé, shot a lame cow belonging to a group of emigrants passing through on the Oregon Trail. A complaint was filed with Lieutenant Hugh Fleming, the post commander at Fort Laramie. He was inclined to let the matter slide in order to maintain peaceful relations with the Indians. However, a capricious young recent West Point graduate, Lieutenant John Grattan, insisted that he lead a detachment to arrest the man who had shot the cow. Fleming agreed, apparently with reluctance.

On August 18, Grattan took thirty men from Company G of the 6th Infantry Regiment to the camp of Brulé leader Conquering Bear at nearby Ash Hollow. Grattan proceeded to parley with Conquering Bear through an interpreter who is variously described as drunk, malicious, or both. The Brule offered to exchange horses for the sick cow—a deal that Grattan should have accepted—but Conquering Bear would not surrender High Forehead.

The discussion turned to an argument and a shot was fired, possibly by accident. Conquering Bear was shot down even as he tried to stop the ensuing firefight. Greatly outnumbered, Grattan attempted to retreat to Fort Laramie, but his command was surrounded and decimated. Only one survivor made it to safety, and he soon died of his wounds.

Rather than retaliating, the U.S. Army declared that Grattan had exceeded his authority. An explosive situation was not allowed to escalate, but the seeds of distrust and future violence had been sewn.

The distrust ran both ways. In Washington, U.S. Secretary of War—and future Confederate President—Jefferson Davis eventually decided that allowing the Grattan Massacre to go unpunished sent the wrong message to the Sioux. In August 1855, a year after Grattan's death, the U.S. Army launched a show of force on the Oregon Trail that was designed to send the correct message. Seminole War veteran Colonel William Selby Harney led six hundred troops out of Fort Leavenworth, Kansas, bound for Fort Laramie. His command included five companies of the 6th Infantry Regiment, two companies of the 2nd Dragoons, and a company each of the 4th Artillery and 10th Infantry Regiment.

With the best interests of his charges in mind, Fort Laramie Indian Agent Thomas Twiss cautioned the tribes camped near the fort not to cross paths with Harney's task force. Most heeded the warning, but a group of Brulé led by Little Thunder, the successor to the late Conquering Bear, did not. They remained camped at Bluewater Creek, not far from Ash Hollow. On September 3, 1855, Harney told Little Thunder to surrender those Brulé involved in the Grattan Massacre. Naturally, he refused, and, as might have been expected, Harney attacked immediately.

Harney had prepositioned his troops for a pincer action, with the dragoons on the north side of the Brulé encampment, and the infantry on the south. The Bluewater Creek fight, often misnamed as the Battle of Ash Hollow, was a resounding defeat for the Brulé. Though Little Thunder himself escaped, most of his people were killed or captured. Harney lost seven troopers, but there were between eighty-six Brulé warriors killed in action, along with a number of women and children. In addition, about seventy Brulé women and children were taken captive.

Harney would continue to patrol the West through the winter but failed to lure any other bands into a major battle. Bluewater would be his last major battle. During the Civil War, General Harney remained in the U.S. Army, but his Confederate sympathies would result in his being relieved of command. He retired in 1863, but never served openly with the Confederate Army.

As noted previously, much of the ongoing conflict in the West had been, and continued to be, between tribes. In the summer of 1856, for example, a round of fighting in Nebraska between the Cheyenne and their traditional enemies, the Pawnee, spilled over into attacks on settlers and wagon trains that led to retaliation and counter-retaliation that involved elements of the 1st Cavalry Regiment based at Fort Kearny.

The following spring, continued Cheyenne attacks on travelers on the westbound trails was the catalyst for a show of force involving six companies of the 1st Cavalry and three companies of the 6th Infantry Regiment under the command of Colonel Edwin Sumner.

As would be the pattern throughout the coming decades of warfare on the Plains, the Indians assiduously avoided contact with the large task force, knowing that while Sumner could control the roads, they owned the countryside. On July 29, 1857, however, the Cheyenne paused on the South Fork of the Solomon River in western Kansas to do battle, having been convinced by their shamans that it was a propitious time and place to do so.

Sumner's three hundred cavalrymen attacked a like number of Cheyenne in what is recalled as having been the only major cavalry charge of the Indian Wars to involve drawn sabers as the primary offensive weapon. In the ensuing battle, Sumner lost only two soldiers, with Cheyenne losses numbering less than ten. The low casualties in fights such as this throughout the Indian Wars were attributable to the nature of the combat. It was difficult to aim a gun accurately while riding a fast-moving horse in rugged terrain, and the nature of the action was mainly hit and run. The Indians would lead the troops on high speed chases, that were often broken off by the soldiers for fear of being sucked into an ambush. Though most of the Cheyenne escaped, the battle would be seen by them as a significant psychological defeat. One of the men taking part in the historic charge was young Lieutenant J.E.B. "Jeb" Stuart, later a legendary Confederate cavalry commander.

Though Sumner had managed to achieve something of a victory over the Cheyenne, their raids against wagon trains on the emigrant trails would continue both during and after the Civil War.

THE GREAT BASIN THEATER IN THE 1850s

As remote as the Northern Plains were in the 1850s, they were surpassed in their isolation by the Great Basin. Still the most geographically remote and desolate part of the United States, the Great Basin is a vast desert encompassing much of Utah, Nevada, Idaho, and Oregon—as well as the Lava Beds of California east of the Siskiyous. Even to this day, there are virtually no significant settlements in the area—more than twice the size of New England—that is bounded by Interstate 84 on the north, Interstate 15 and the Great Salt Lake on the east, Nevada's Clark County on the south, and the Sierra Nevada and Cascade ranges on the west.

After 1846, the Mormons had begun to colonize Utah Territory, but their settlements were mainly in the Wasatch Range of the Rockies on the eastern side of the Great Salt Lake. To the west were six hundred miles of waterless desert and virtually impassable mountains that the emigrant trails had to cross in order to reach the fertile valleys of California. It was at Camp Floyd, near the Mormon capital of Salt Lake City, that the U.S. Army situated the headquarters for its Department of Utah, an area that stretched from the Continental Divide (now in the state of Colorado) to the middle of the Nevada desert.

The indigenous people of this region belonged primarily to the Shoshone branch of the Uto-Aztecan linguistic group. The tribes included the Shoshone, Paiute, and Ute, who were ethnically related to the Comanche and Kiowa of the southern Plains and to the people living at the Rio Grande pueblos in New Mexico.

As had been the case with Lewis and Clark and their Corps of Discovery in 1804-1806, the government, by way of the U.S. Army, sponsored numerous geographical expeditions into the West. Most notable were a series of such surveys conducted by Colonel John Charles Frémont across the Great Basin between 1838 and 1846. He mapped much of the area west of the Great Salt Lake and charted routes through the difficult Sierra Nevada—which he described as a "White Saw" because of their snow-capped ruggedness.

The horror of attempting to cross the Sierra Nevada is perhaps best illustrated by the story of the party led by George Donner that were marooned in the mountains through the winter of 1846-1847. Only forty-six of the eighty-seven people survived the ordeal, half of whom resorting to cannibalism. The Donner Party story became an instant legend and a clear warning to those who would attempt to cross the mountains too late in the season.

Major incidents involving conflict between Indians and outsiders in the Great Basin were few and far between during the 1850s, and usually involved isolated parties caught in the wrong place at the wrong time. One such event involved one of Frémont's successors, Captain John Gunnison of the U.S. Army Corps of Topographical Engineers. On October 26, 1853, he and a ten-man detachment were camped on the Sevier River in central Utah when they were attacked by a band of either Ute or Paiute raiders. Gunnison, along with six others, was killed.

Another such wrong place, wrong time story involved the Holloway Party, which attempted to cross the Great Basin with just ten people. Most wagon trains banded together because of there being safety in numbers. Just as the Donner Party tale taught a lesson, so too did the Holloway Party story. They were ambushed by the Paiute at Humboldt Wells in northern Nevada on August 13, 1857. Six of the people were killed, three escaped, and a fourth, Mrs. Holloway, was wounded as she tried in vain to save her baby. She was then scalped, although she survived. The story of her fashioning a wig from her own recovered scalp, and her subsequent insanity and death are another enduring legend of the Old West.

Less than a month after the Holloway incident, an incident occurred that also helped to define the folklore of the Old West. The undercurrent was the growing animosity of certain Mormon settlers in Utah toward non-Mormon emigrants passing through the region. On September 7, 1857, at Mountain Meadows in southeastern Utah, the Fancher Party wagon train was attacked by Paiute who had been encouraged to do so by a Mormon group led by John D. Lee. The wagons were circled into a defensive position and the situation became a stalemate. The following day, two men slipped out to go for help. They met a group of Mormons who, instead of helping them, shot them. One survived and returned to the circled wagons.

John D. Lee approached the wagons on September 11 and offered aid if the emigrants surrendered their weapons to the Mormons. The emigrants agreed, but as soon as they did so, they were attacked and murdered by Mormons aided by Paiute warriors. Of the 140 people in the party, seven were killed in the September 7 attack, and 121 four days later. The Mormons spared just seventeen young children. John D. Lee was the only person ever charged in the Mountain Meadows Massacre and he was not arrested and tried until 1877. He implicated numerous others who were never charged.

Though the Mormon involvement at Mountain Meadows made it an isolated incident, attacks by the Basin tribes against unguarded wagon trains continued, reaching a crescendo in the Paiute War of 1860, the last major conflict in the West prior to the Civil War. The catalyst was an attack by renegade Paiute and Bannock warriors on the western Nevada trading post known as Williams Station. Though Paiute leader Winnemucca counseled peace, the deaths of five people at Williams Station had already given the impending war a momentum of its own. A volunteer militia under Major William Ormsby had already set out from Virginia City bent on revenge.

Things did not go as planned for Ormsby's 105-man detachment. Though they outnumbered the Paiute four to one, they were outmaneuvered and beaten in the Battle of Pyramid Lake on May 29, 1860. The Paiute lost about ten warriors killed in action, but they managed to kill seventy-six of the volunteers and send the rest running.

The settlers around Virginia City and Carson City organized a response that would be led by the legendary former Texas Ranger John Coffee Hays. Leading a force of nearly seven hundred, Hays rode north. A U.S. Army detachment from San Francisco including elements of the 1st Dragoons, the 6th Infantry Regiment, and the 3rd Artillery Regiment reached Carson City, but halted to wait orders and did not accompany the volunteer strike force. Hays found the Paiute force entrenched at Williams Station, but they withdrew after a fierce firefight on May 29.

Now backed by the U.S. Army contingent, Hays continued the pursuit toward Pyramid Lake, catching the Paiute in an indecisive battle on June 3. Again, the Paiute withdrew, and again the volunteers and soldiers gave chase. After a hit and run ambush the following day, the Paiute escaped, this time not to return. The Paiute had killed three of their pursuers and lost twenty-five of their own to hostile gunfire, but the majority simply melted into the vast Great Basin desert. The Paiute War was over.

THE SOUTHWEST THEATER IN THE 1850s

The Southwest can be called the last frontier of the American West. Indeed, the two states which comprise it, Arizona and New Mexico, the last of the contiguous forty-eight to be admitted to the Union, did not achieve statehood until 1912. Though the area of the two states would be among the last to be settled, the route of the first scheduled transcontinental mail and transit line in the United States ran through here. Beginning in 1857, the Butterfield Overland Stage ran from St. Louis to California, crossing the southern tier of what would become the two states.

In the mid-nineteenth century, this area was divided by the U.S. Army between its Departments of California and New Mexico, with the latter also containing about a third of present-day Arizona. The California headquarters was at the distant Presidio of San Francisco, while the headquarters of the Department of New Mexico was in the heart of the Southwest at Fort Marcy in Santa Fe. Aside from Santa Fe and the Rio Grande Valley, the region was among the last to be widely settled by Anglo-Americans, and the last in which the indigenous people continued to maintain their sovereignty. Even today, the Navajo Nation exercises a level of sovereignty in its everyday affairs that is enjoyed by few other tribes.

In the Southwest, the largest tribes were the Navajo and the numerous subgroups that made up the Apache. Both tribes spoke a language associated with the Dené, or Athapaskan, people of far northern Canada, suggesting that the Southwestern tribes may have originated in the north and migrated south. This migration is thought to have occurred after the fourteenth century, with the Apache taking up residence on the Southern Plains, as well as in the Southwest.

The Navajo, who call themselves Dinéh, occupied the lands centering on northeastern Arizona that are known to have once been populated by the Anasazi. The latter were a very advanced culture who built elaborate cites with multi-storied buildings and flourished in the Southwest until they mysteriously disappeared around the fourteenth century. Archaeologists are still tying to figure out what happened.

Canyon de Chelly in northeastern Arizona, which contains a series of important Anasazi ruins, became—and continues to be—very important to the Navajo. A sacred stronghold for them in the nineteenth century, it would figure prominently in the Indian Wars in the Southwest. Today, the canyon is managed by the National Park Service, but access is granted only by permission of the Navajo Nation.

Originally hunter-gatherers, the Navajo eventually developed farming techniques, which were enhanced by way of contact with the Spanish in the seventeenth and eighteenth century. Also from the Spanish, they acquired sheep and horses, and learned metalworking, especially silver-smithing. From this, the tribe produced silver goods, and from the sheep, they produced woolen textiles. Both of these gave the Navajo the trade goods they used to become the wealthiest, as well as the most populous tribe in the region.

The Apache also acquired horses from the Spanish, but they remained mainly hunter-gatherers, with an emphasis on hunting, at which they were especially adept. Their intuitive understanding of the nuances of the terrain and meteorology of the Southwestern desert would make them both extraordinary hunters, but also formidable foes for any adversary. As the U.S. Army was to discover, their ability to vanish—as though into thin air—after a battle, was uncanny.

Prior to the eighteenth century, the Apache lived in a swath of territory across what is now the southern United States from Arizona through Texas and as far north as the Platte River, as well as south into Mexico. From east to west, the principal Apache subgroups were the Kiowa Apache, the Lipan and Jicarilla Apache of present West Texas, the Mescalero Apache of present New Mexico, and the Chiricahua Apache. The latter, who traditionally lived mainly in what is now Arizona, are now further subdivided into five major subtribes, the White Mountain, the Cibicue, the San Carlos, and the Northern and Southern Tonto. The western Apache groups are sometimes referred to collectively as Coyotero Apache.

The eastern Apache living on the Southern Plains were long involved in ongoing warfare with their traditional enemies, the Comanche and Pawnee, and by the early eighteenth century, they had been driven south and west. As the eighteenth century gave way to the nineteenth century, they continued to raid other tribes, as well as Mexican, Texan, and American settlers. Gradually, they continued to be pushed westward into New Mexico.

During the Mexican War, the Apache did not discriminate, striking targets of opportunity wherever they arose. Though the Mescalero and Jicarilla Apache entered into a treaty agreement with the United States government in 1851, the raids continued.

Another significant tribal grouping in the desert Southwest were the so-called Pueblo, or city-dwelling, people. Whereas the highly mobile Apache were considered nomadic, and the Navajo were only semi-sedentary, the Pueblo people lived in highly developed permanent cities, located near the present border between Arizona and New Mexico and in the Rio Grande Valley of New Mexico.

These cities were long established when the Spanish first visited the area in 1540, and these cities still exist in the twenty-first century. They are considered the oldest permanently occupied cites in the United States. Traditionally, the Pueblo people were farmers, growing corn, beans, and squash, with a highly developed cosmology that was closely associated with seasonal cycles and crop development.

Linguistically, the Pueblo people belong to two distinct groups, those who speak the Uto-Aztecan dialect known as Tanoan, and those who speak Keresan dialects, a language vaguely related to Hokan. The latter is spoken at the Rio Grande Pueblos of Cochiti, Santo Domingo, San Felipe, Santa Ana, and Zia, as well as at Acoma and Laguna, which are west of the river. The Tanoan-speaking Pueblos include Isleta, Jemez, Nambe, Picuris, Pojoaque, San Ildefonso, San Juan, Sandia, Santa Clara, Taos, and Tesuque. A Tanoan dialect is spoken by the Hopi people whose traditional home is on three mesa-tops in northeastern Arizona. The Zuni Pueblo of New Mexico has an entirely unique language called Zunian that has some similarity to the Penutian of California.

When the Spanish began to settle the Rio Grande Valley in the seventeenth century, the impact on the lives and traditions of the Pueblo people was more than that on other indigenous people. They eventually moved to evict the Spanish from their midst. The first major war in the Southwest to involve a European power was the Pueblo Revolt, which began in August 1680. For decades, the Spanish who settled in the upper Rio Grande Valley adjacent to the Pueblos had exploited the people living in these cities for cheap labor, and they had appropriated much of their farm produce. In 1680, an Indian priest known as Popé led a successful rebellion that drove the Spanish from the region for a dozen years. When they returned, the Spanish adopted a policy toward the Pueblo people that was much more equitable and conciliatory. After 1692, the two sides coexisted in relative peace.

Early in the eighteenth century, Father Eusebio Francisco Kino, a Jesuit missionary, established a chain of missions in the Southwest that was roughly analogous to the mission system that the Franciscans would establish in Alta California.

By the 1850s, the Americans and the Pueblo people coexisted, but there was friction in relations with other tribes. Smaller tribes that played minor roles in the history of the Southwest Indian Wars included the Uto-Aztecan-speaking Hopi, Papago, and Pima, as well as the Chemehuevi, Cocopah, Havasupai, Hualapai, Maricopa, Mojave, Quechan, Yavapai, and Yuma who spoke the Yuman dialect.

It was the Yavapai who would figure in one of the most notorious raids of the early 1850s. In March 1851, a small wagon train consisting of three Missouri families was crossing present-day Arizona en route to California. When the train split up, Royse Oatman, his wife, and their seven children carried on alone. On the Gila River, west of Yuma, they were approached by an estimated nineteen Yavapai who murdered the adults and four of the children. They left one wounded boy for dead and captured seven-year-old Mary Ann and fourteen-year-old Olive Ann, who were in turn, sold to the Mojave. Mary Ann died in captivity, but Olive Ann was rescued in 1856, having had her face heavily tattooed with markings identifying her as a slave. Despite the disfigurement, she attended college in California, married in 1865 and lived until 1903. However, she rarely appeared in public without her face being covered.

In the early years after the Mexican War, as it would be for another four decades, the Apache, mainly the Jicarilla and Mescalero, presented the U.S. Army with its greatest challenge in the Southwest. Leaders such as Chacon and Lobo Blanco assembled semi-permanent raiding parties that carried out fearsome raids against settlements and wagon trains that incited terror in among emigrants and residents alike. Nevertheless, during the 1850s, this conflict was characterized more by low-intensity combat than by anything resembling open warfare.

Once in a while, the Apache would also strike U.S. Army patrols and installations. In January 1852, three companies of the 2nd Dragoons were ambushed in the Jornada del Muerto area of central New Mexico, and two soldiers were killed. Two months later, Camp Yuma, near the Arizona border town of the same name, was attacked and five solders were killed in action. The Jornada del Muerto, meaning "the Route of the Dead," was so named by the early Spanish because of its utter desolation and its being more than a day's ride from any source of water. In 1945, the U.S. Army would explode the first nuclear weapon here.

North of Santa Fe, in the spring of 1854, the conflict intensified into a series of the largest battles of the decade in which the U.S. Army would face the Apache. When Lobo Blanco's Jicarilla rustled some cattle from near Fort Union, east of Santa Fe, Lieutenant Colonel Philip St. George Cooke sent Lieutenant David Bell and a company of 2nd Dragoons in pursuit.

On March 5, the two evenly matched opponents met on Congillon Creek. Typical of many such encounters in the West, heated words were exchanged, then a shot was fired. When the dust had settled, Bell's casualties numbered six, and those of the Jicarilla were sixteen. Among those killed in action was Lobo Blanco. Most of the Apache escaped to fight another day, and that day would come soon.

As the month progressed, the Jicarilla continued their raids, attacking traffic on the road leading north from Santa Fe to Taos. Major George Blake of the 1st Dragoons, based near Taos, sent out a detachment of sixty men under Lieutenant John Davidson to deal with them, expecting an engagement along the lines of what Lieutenant Bell had encountered three weeks earlier. In fact, Davidson took delivery of the worst thrashing that the U.S. Army would suffer in the Southwest during the decade.

On March 30, Davidson was ambushed at Cieneguilla in the Embudo Mountains by two hundred Jicarilla led by Chacon. After an intense three-hour firefight, the dragoons managed to break out of the canyon where they had been pinned down. Davidson left twenty-two men dead on the battlefield, and only two of the remaining thirty-eight escaped without being wounded.

After Davidson's resounding defeat, Lieutenant Colonel Cooke at Fort Union ordered all the troops that he could muster to fight the Jicarilla. This included elements from both the 1st and 2nd Dragoons, as well as from the 2nd Artillery and the 3rd Infantry Regiment. As the troops pursued Chacon into the Sangre de Christo Mountains, a spring storm dumped a great deal of snow on the landscape. This made the going more difficult, but it also aided in tracking the elusive Jicarilla.

On April 8, Chacon repeated his ambush tactic against the troopers in the rugged terrain on the Rio Caliente, but Cooke had sufficient forces to stand and to counterattack. Employing Lieutenant Bell's dragoons to effect a flanking maneuver, Cooke used his main force against Chacon's primary defensive position. The Jicarilla broke off the attack and attempted their usual tactic of trying to melt away into the jagged countryside. Cooke was able to keep up the pursuit for three days before the Apache finally escaped. The death toll for the action was a small fraction of that experienced at Cieneguilla. Five Jicarilla were killed, and just one soldier was lost, the sort of casualties that might have been expected in an engagement of a much smaller scale. This is indicative of the difficulty of effectively fighting large battles in the desert terrain of the Southwest.

While the Apache campaign of 1854 had cast the U.S. Army opposite the Jicarilla, the following year found the Mescalero as the troopers' main foe. In early January, General John Garland had sent a 160-man force in pursuit of a Mescalero band that had been raiding settlements on the Pecos River since December. Commanding the two-pronged offensive were Captains Henry Stanton and Richard Ewell. The undaunted Apache responded to the pursuit by ambushing their pursuers. They then made a tactical withdrawal, forcing the troops to follow them into the rough terrain of the Sacramento Mountains where the army's numeric advantage was reduced.

On January 19, Stanton led a small patrol of a dozen men up a canyon to try to find the Mescalero, but they were ambushed and Stanton was killed. Ewell's column, meanwhile, managed to kill fifteen of the enemy, including their leader, Santa Anna. The Mescalero disappeared into the Guadalupe Mountains and the troops lost their trail. Stanton became the namesake of New Mexico's Fort Stanton, and Ewell went on to a career as a Confederate general.

Meanwhile, on January 16, 1855, a small detachment of the 1st Dragoons managed to get on the trail of a Mescalero raiding party shortly after they had struck a ranch near Santa Fe. An intense firefight in the Manzano Mountains left the Mescalero and a soldier dead.

During the latter part of the decade, there would be numerous smaller skirmishes as the U.S. Army pursued western Apache groups into the isolated Mogollon Mountains that straddle the border between Arizona and New Mexico. In one such action on June 27, 1857, near the headwaters of the Gila River, Richard Ewell's 1st Dragoons managed to inflict an estimated forty casualties in a campaign that cost the lives of two soldiers. In December 1859, Ewell led two companies of the 1st Dragoons as part of a larger, comprehensive military sweep of Apache strongholds in the Pinal Mountains of central Arizona. His dragoons managed to kill eight Apache, with only one of their own, Ewell himself, slightly wounded.

Major conflicts between the U.S. Army and the Navajo began later in the decade. These mainly centered on the U.S. military base at Fort Defiance, located in northeastern Arizona near the present site of the town of Window Rock, which is the capital of today's Navajo Nation. Established by Colonel Edwin Sumner in 1851, Fort Defiance was tolerated by the Navajo for several years because there was little else in the way of outside settlement in the area during its early years. However, it eventually came to symbolize Navajo displeasure with having outsiders establishing themselves on their traditional land. Relations turned especially foul in September 1858, when Lieutenant Colonel Dixon Miles led four companies of the Mounted Rifles Regiment and two companies of the 3rd into Canyon de Chelly to arrest a Navajo man wanted for killing the African American "servant" of Captain William Brooks at Fort Defiance. In a series of firefights, the Navajo lost an estimated ten warriors, and two solders were killed.

The friction between the two sides over Fort Defiance turned violent again in the spring of 1860, as the Navajo, especially the followers of a leader named Huero, began a series of large overt actions against the fort itself. In January and February, Huero launched two attacks on the fort's satellite operations, including supply trains and its cattle herds, which were grazed some distance from the fort itself. The first series of attacks on January 17, involving a force of about 250 Navajo, cost the lives of four soldiers, but Huero was unable to steal the cattle. On February 8, Huero struck again with twice as many men, and again he was unsuccessful. This time, the troops were ready and were able to kill a number of Navajo.

On April 30, 1860, Huero mustered a force estimated at between 1,000 and 2,000 warriors for one of a few large-scale direct assaults on a U.S. Army fort during the Indian Wars in the West. In a scene reminiscent of the Vietcong assault on the United States Embassy in Saigon during the Tet Offensive 108 years later, the enemy actually penetrated Fort Defiance. As in Saigon, the troops eventually managed to repel the attack and drive the Navajo out, but their confidence was badly shaken.

Casualties were surprisingly light, about a dozen on the Navajo side, and one soldier was killed in action. Nevertheless, like Tet, it demonstrated that the U.S. Army was clearly not in control of the region beyond its fortified enclaves, and that the Navajo were still masters of their corner of the Southwest.

It was not until September 1860 that the U.S. Army finally organized a major campaign in response to the Fort Defiance debacle, and it was not until October that contact was actually made with Navajo warriors. Major Edward Richard Sprigg Canby commanded a six-hundred-man task force that included elements of the 2nd Dragoons and the 5th and 7th Infantry Regiments. The campaign was characterized by small skirmishes, as the cumbersome force of mainly infantry struggled through the rough terrain. Like the Apache—and like many guerrilla opponents that the U.S. Army would face over the coming 150 years—the Navajo warriors were able to avoid being forced into a major fixed battle. One firefight at Black Pinnacle on October 13 cost the life of an Army officer, and an estimated three dozen Navajo were killed in a campaign that dragged on into November.

The autumn offensive of 1860 was effective for the U.S. Army only in that it demonstrated that one of the Navajo strengths was also a major weakness. The Navajo had become economically successful through agriculture, and the Army was able to impact their livelihood by burning fields and taking livestock. In the coming decade, it would be a scorched-earth assault on the Navajo economy, like George Washington's campaign against the Iroquois nearly one hundred years before, not major combat, that would bring them into submission.

The Navajo of the 1850s were like the Anasazi people at that mysterious moment in the fourteenth century. They were the dominant tribe in the desert Southwest, both in cultural and in political terms. However, it had now been demonstrated that these days were numbered. The Anglo-American interlopers from the East had come to stay, and their numbers were reaching critical mass in the areas that were important to the Navajo.

The Apache, in contrast, still eluded domination. With their innate oneness with the land, they continued to outmaneuver the U.S. Army at every turn. In California and the Pacific Northwest—and even on the Plains—the army had the ability to track the ingenious people and launch decisive surprise attacks. The Apache's tracks, however, simply disappeared. With a skill that was unsurpassed by any other tribe on the continent, they could evade detection, frustrate attempts to force them into decisive battles that favored the army, and then strike out of nowhere. They proved this in the 1850s, and they would continue to do so for another generation.

4

AGAINST THE BACKDROP OF THE CIVIL WAR

No event affected and defined the United States in the nineteenth century more than the War Between the States. East of the Mississippi River, the Civil War seemed to touch nearly everyone and every place. If a town was not visited by the horrors of battle between 1861 and 1865, its cemetery was. In the interior of the Far West, however, across an area a half dozen times larger than all the states to see major combat, the Civil War was an abstract idea, a drama playing out on a distant stage. To the indigenous people, it hardly registered at all.

One of the most visible changes in the texture of the Indian Wars in the West would be in the order of battle. Just as the Civil War would pit brother against brother, within the U.S. Army officer corps, fellow officers and West Point classmates were suddenly on opposing sides. Many Southern-born officers in the regular U.S. Army resigned their commissions in order to don Confederate gray and be commissioned in the Confederate Army, although most regular army enlisted men remained in blue uniforms.

To meet the challenges of what was at the time the largest land war fought in the Western Hemisphere, the U.S. Army withdrew many of its regiments from the West, turning over responsibility for executing much of the Indian Wars mission to state militias. On the battlefields of the Civil War, the bulk of the fighting would be undertaken by state militia regiments that were placed under federal command. In the West, however, they fought on their home turf, led by local officers pursuing a strategy that was determined more by local concerns than by the distant and preoccupied War Department.

On the Western battlefield, the shift from regular troops to local volunteers would greatly change the complexion of the Indian Wars. The volunteers were local residents, who had come to make the region their home. Unlike troops from outside the area who were posted to the West temporarily, they had a stake in making the West safe for emigration and for settlement. Those who had lived in the West all or most of their lives had developed a more intuitive understanding of the region, of both its terrain and its indigenous people. Like westerners today, they viewed the West in practical terms, and they developed a direct, no-nonsense approach to the Indian Wars.

THE WEST AS A THEATER OF THE CIVIL WAR

Among the eleven states to secede from the United States in 1861 to form the Confederate States of America, Texas was the only state within whose borders there had been ongoing major combat between the U.S. Army and the Indian tribes. When Texas joined the Confederacy, it demanded that the U.S. Army surrender its facilities and withdraw its troops. This was a tall order, because one in five of the personnel of the prewar regular U.S. Army were stationed in Texas. The 1st and 2nd Cavalry and the 3rd Infantry Regiment evacuated Texas, but the 8th Infantry Regiment men were taken into custody as prisoners of war. Texas would also soon become a theater in the Civil War, as it was used as a base of operations to launch an 1862 invasion of New Mexico and Colorado with an eye toward occupying United States territory.

The Confederates had claimed the southern part of what is now Arizona and New Mexico in 1861, and sought in 1862 to capture the rest. Major Edward Canby was compelled to turn his attention from the Navajo to the Confederates under his former colleague General Henry Sibley.

Sibley's troops beat Canby's force at the Battle of Valverde, south of Albuquerque, in February and continued to march north through the Rio Grande Valley toward Santa Fe. In March, Sibley sent a force under the command of Major Charles Pyron to seize Glorieta Pass, a strategic location on the Santa Fe Trail southeast of Santa Fe itself. Control of the pass would allow the Confederate Army to advance north toward Colorado and the Plains. Standing in Pyron's way were Colorado militia units, including the 1st Colorado Volunteers under the command of Major John

Chivington. The following day, both sides pulled back to await the arrival of reinforcements under Confederate Lieutenant Colonel William Scurry and Union Colonel John Slough. The Battle of Glorieta Pass was resumed on March 28, and again it was a ferocious back and forth fight that resulted in a Confederate rout.

With this defeat, Sibley withdrew his forces into Texas, and the Southwest was never again seriously threatened by the Confederate Army. Conversely, New Mexico was never used—as it might have been—to launch a Union invasion of Texas. Later in 1862, the U.S. government moved to consolidate its political position by formally carving off parts of California and New Mexico Territory to create Arizona Territory.

COCHISE, BASCOM, AND IRWIN

In February 1861—even as Confederate General P. G. T. Beauregard was assuming command of Charleston, South Carolina, in advance of the bombardment, two months later, of Fort Sumter—the decades-long guerrilla war in the Southwest was moving into a new phase. This phase began with the emergence of a Chiricahua Apache leader whose name, Cochise, is synonymous with Apache resistance to the U.S. Army. Nearly fifty years old, an occasional employee of the Butterfield Overland Stage Company, and long a friend to the Anglo-Americans in Arizona, Cochise was an unlikely Apache war chief, yet circumstances thrust him into that role.

On February 4, Cochise and several members of his family were accused of an October 1860 kidnapping that had actually been conducted by a rival Apache band. As capricious Lieutenant George Bascom of the 7th Infantry Regiment tried to arrest them all at Apache Pass in what is now southeastern Arizona, Cochise escaped. The following day, Cochise attempted to negotiate the release of his family by offering to help locate the boy who had been kidnapped. Bascom argued, Cochise's men took Butterfield agent James Wallace prisoner, and the situation escalated. As the Apache took the situation as a cue to begin a series of raids, Bascom called for reinforcements.

The ensuing events not only heralded the ascendancy of Cochise as an important figure in the Indian Wars; they also marked the first instance of a member of the U.S. armed forces to warrant the Congressional Medal of Honor.

Seattle

Portland

Willamette Valley

Fort Humboldt

Feel River Campaigns (1861-64)

San Francisco

Sacramento

Los Angeles

San Diego

Pacific Ocean

Helena

Missouri River

Yellowstone River

Cache Valley (1862)

Salt Lake City

Spanish Fork Canyon (1863)

Canyon de Chelly (1864)

Gila River Campaign (1864)

Doubtful Canyon (1864)

Tucson

Fort Bowie

Apache Pass (1861, 1862)

Killdeer Mountain (1864)

Big Mound/Stony Lake (1863)

Fort Rice

Fort Abercrombie

Minnes Siou Uprisi (186.

Fort Ridgely

New Ulm

Black Hills

Fort Laramie

Platte River

Omaha

Counci Bluffs

Denver

Sound Creek (1864)

Fort Leavenworth

Fort Riley

Independence

Ka Cit

Fort Wise

Fort Lyon

Fort Larned

Glorietta Pass (1862)

Santa Fe

Fort Sumner

Wallen Fight (1863)

Basque Redondo (1864)

Adobe Walls (1864)

Fort Sill

Llano Estacado

Fort Stanton

Red River

Rio Grande

Austin

Del Rio

San Antonio

Eagle Pass

Rio Grande

The Congressional Medal of Honor was, and is to this day, America's highest military decoration for bravery under fire. The President on behalf of Congress presents the Medal of Honor, and as such it is often referred to as the Congressional Medal of Honor. The Medal of Honor was first authorized by joint resolution of Congress on July 12, 1862 to be awarded to U.S. Army personnel. The U.S. Navy Medal of Honor was created soon after, although the Navy had authorized a similar "Medal of Valor" in 1861. The original authorizing ordinance states that "The President may award, and present in the name of Congress, a Medal of Honor of appropriate design, with ribbons and appurtenances, to a person who while a member of the Army, distinguished himself conspicuously by gallantry and intrepidity at the risk of his life above and beyond the call of duty."

From 1862 through 2005, a total of 3,460 medals have been awarded to 3,409 different people. There were nineteen men who received a second award, including fourteen who received two separate Medals of Honor for two separate actions and five who received both the Navy and the Army Medals of Honor for the same action. In many cases, the award of the medal occurred a year or more, or even decades, after the action for which it was awarded. This was especially true for many Indian Wars awards.

During the Civil War and the Indian Wars, there was no award of slightly lesser stature, such as the Silver Star or Distinguished Service Cross (both of which have been awarded since 1918), so many Medals of Honor were awarded for actions that might have warranted the lesser awards instead.

There were 1,522 Medals of Honor awarded for actions during the Civil War and 426 for Indian Wars actions. This compares to 124 in World War I, 464 in World War II, 131 in the Korean War, and 245 in the Vietnam War. In 1916, every Army Medal of Honor award was reviewed and it was recommended that the Army rescind 911 medals. These included 864 medals awarded to members of the 27th Regiment, Maine Infantry (who received their medals from Secretary of War Edwin M. Stanton for extending their Civil War enlistment) as well as six awarded to civilians. The latter included Dr. Mary Edwards Walker, the only woman to ever be awarded the medal, and several Indian Wars scouts including William F. "Buffalo Bill" Cody. Dr. Walker's medal, as well as those of the scouts were ultimately reinstated, but not for half a century.

It was first awarded to nineteen participants in the April 1862 mission deep behind Confederate lines at Kennesaw, Georgia, which was led by James Andrews. This raid, best known as the "Great Locomotive Chase" involved capturing a locomotive traveling north toward Chattanooga destroying Confederate railroad bridges on the way. Though these men were the first to receive the medals, theirs was not the first action to warrant such an award.

The distinction of the first Medal of Honor action in American military history belongs to the Indian Wars, and to Dr. Bernard John Dowling Irwin, a thirty-one-year-old Army surgeon. Irwin did not receive his medal until 1894, after a long and distinguished career in the U.S. Army Medical Corps.

When it was learned that Bascom was surrounded at Apache Pass in the southeastern corner of Arizona, Irwin led a rescue party of fourteen from Fort Breckenridge on mules. They made a hundred-mile journey through a blizzard, while constantly on the lookout for a possible Apache ambush. On February 13, 1861, Irwin reached the place where Bascom's command was holding off the enemy. By careful placement of his minuscule detachment, Irwin was able to persuade Cochise that he had come with a substantially greater force. Cochise then ordered a tactical withdrawal, and Bascom and Irwin were able to go on the offensive. They chased the Apache into the mountains, and were able to rescue the young hostage whose capture had precipitated the incident.

In the two weeks centering on the Bascom engagement, nearly continuous fighting throughout the area cost the lives of eight Mexican civilians killed by the Apache, nine Apache killed or hung by soldiers, and two Butterfield employees, including Wallace.

A month later, Cochise struck again, ambushing a Butterfield stage and killing all five occupants. In angering Cochise, Bascom had turned the Chiricahua into an enemy with whom the U.S. Army would be at war for the better part of three decades.

Cochise then joined forces with his Mimbres Apache father-in-law, Mangas Coloradas (also known as Colorado), and assembled a band of warriors numbering close to two hundred. The purpose of this band was to conduct a continuing campaign of raids in retaliation for Bascom's impudence and for the hanging of Chiricahua prisoners. On July 21, they attacked a party en route to California at Cooke's Spring in what is now southwestern New Mexico. The travelers managed to hold out for the better part of two days before the last one was killed.

CARLETON, CARSON AND THE SOUTHWEST THEATER

In the wake of the Bascom incident, the U.S. Army in the Southwest faced three separate principal enemies—the Apache and the Navajo, as well as the Confederacy. With the Navajo and the Confederates, the action could be defined as conventional warfare, and it would be resolved before Appomattox. With Cochise and the Apache, the fighting was characterized by guerrilla actions, and there would be no resolution until well after the Civil War had ended.

With the ongoing Apache War, it is important to point out that, just as the indigenous people of the West had no interest in, or recognition of, the political nuances involved in the Civil War, the Apache did not recognize the border between the United States and Mexico. They readily and routinely crossed and recrossed it, raiding settlements and setting up their own semi-permanent camps wherever it suited them. However, the Apache saw that the two nations valued the artificial line in the sand, and they used this fact to their own advantage.

Confederate actions in the Southwest centered on their attempts to invade New Mexico as an entree to Colorado and California (see above). This threat was decisively removed as a result of the victory at Glorieta Pass in March 1862, but the U.S. Army continued to keep a watchful eye toward Texas, lest the Confederates decide to launch another invasion attempt.

So far as the Indian Wars are concerned, the Confederate invasion had the net effect of bringing Colonel James Carleton's 1,800-man California Volunteer Brigade into the Southwest. Their initial function was to protect the region from the next Confederate invasion. It never materialized, so the Californians would spend the Civil War fighting an Apache War.

Ironically, Carleton's first action would occur at Apache Pass, the site of the Bascom-Cochise fight in 1861. In this two-day battle in July 1862, Carleton's advance guard lost two men, while killing nine Apache and wounding several, including Mangas Coloradas.

It was also during this month that the second Congressional Medal of Honor action of the Indian Wars occurred. First Sergeant Charles Taylor of

Company D, 3rd Cavalry, earned his for his heroism at Big Dry Wash in Arizona Territory on July 17, although his medal would not actually be awarded until 1882.

One of the early actions undertaken by the Californians in New Mexico was in the Pinos Altos Mountains in the southern part of the territory, where the Apache were raiding the mining settlements.

In January 1863, after several months of usually fruitless search and destroy patrols, a group of Californians under the command of Captain Edmund Shirland captured Mangas Coloradas. He was lured into a trap under a truce flag and killed on January 18. The official version was that he was shot while trying to escape, but some witnesses said that he had been tortured and was shot while still bound. In the aftermath of his death, the military, notably the 1st California Cavalry under Captain William McCleave, would gain the upper hand in the Pinos Altos in fighting that continued into the summer of 1863.

James Carleton ended up being promoted to brigadier general in the U.S. Army and given command of the Department of New Mexico. At the time, it was administratively a subordinate command to the headquarters in San Francisco, but it was later transferred to the Division of the Missouri.

Carleton's command would consist of six full regiments, the U.S. Army 5th Infantry Regiment, as well as the 1st California Cavalry, the 1st and 5th California Infantry Regiments, the 1st New Mexico Cavalry and 1st New Mexico Infantry Regiment. To lead the latter outfit, Carleton called upon perhaps the best respected man for the job then available in the territory, Kit Carson.

Christopher Houston "Kit" Carson is a true legend of the Old West, and a man whose name figures prominently in the history of the Indian Wars in the Southwest. One of that unique breed of mountain men whose career coincided with the early nineteenth-century West, Carson was born in Missouri in 1809. He traveled from Missouri to New Mexico to seek his fortune when he was only about nineteen, and spent his early years as a trapper and guide throughout the Southwest and as far west as California. He accompanied John Charles Frémont on his expeditions during the 1840s, during which he earned a national reputation for his skill as a woodsman and mountaineer. He later guided Stephen Watts Kearny in his bloodless capture of Santa Fe in 1846.

James Carleton (1814–1873), left, during the Civil War. Christopher Houston "Kit" Carson (1809–1868), right, in the late 1860s. (*National Archives*)

By the 1850s, Carson was the most sought-after guide and scout in New Mexico, so he was frequently employed in that role by the U.S. Army. In September 1862, commissioned as a colonel, he led five companies of the 1st New Mexico Cavalry against the Mescalero Apache. The mandate from Carleton was to force the Mescalero onto the desolate Bosque Redondo Reservation, located on the Pecos River near Fort Sumner in east central New Mexico. Carson initially reactivated the previously closed Fort Stanton, southeast of Santa Fe, as a base of operations, and by the summer of 1863, he had made considerable progress in defeating the Mescalero raiders.

Carson's success with the Mescalero encouraged Carleton to assign him the same task with the Navajo. Forcing the dominant tribe in the Southwest onto a reservation that was three hundred miles from their revered homeland presented a monumental challenge, even for Kit Carson. In August 1863, Carson undertook a month-long expedition into the Navajo country in northeastern Arizona with six companies of 1st New Mexico Cavalry.

As had been the case in with Canby's similar mission in 1860, a large cavalry patrol was an unlikely way to achieve a decisive battle with Navajo warriors, but it was a useful means of conducting economic warfare against the Navajo infrastructure. The August 1863 campaign saw no major battles. Most of the Navajo encountered and captured were women or children, as were two of the four Navajo who were killed in the fighting. One U.S. Army officer, meanwhile, was killed by a sniper.

Carson launched a repeat campaign during the last half of November with similar results. Only women and children were taken prisoner, and there were only a few brief skirmishes. Though there was little contact with the Navajo through most of 1863, a sizable number of their sheep and other livestock were rounded up, and over two hundred acres of crops had been destroyed during August.

In December and January, it was the turn of the Navajo to go on the offensive, with raids against the Mescalero Apache on the Bosque Redondo Reservation. The aim was to capture livestock to make up for their previous losses. In response, elements of the 2nd California Cavalry, along with the 5th and 7th Infantry Regiments and a contingent of Mescalero scouts, tracked the Navajo and overtook them.

The major battle that had eluded Kit Carson in Arizona came for Major Henry Wallen's 7th Infantry Regiment on December 16, 1863. A dozen Navajo and a Mescalero were killed in the ensuing firefight. The Navajo escaped, albeit without the livestock they had stolen.

On January 4, 1864, the Navajo raided the Bosque Redondo reservation once more, and again the raid led to a major brawl. In this battle, Indian Agent Lorenzo Labadie and a group of Mescalero gave chase, with Lieutenant Charles Newbold's 5th Infantry Regiment detachment and elements of the 2nd California Cavalry arriving after the battle had been joined. In an all-day battle in freezing cold, an estimated forty Navajo were killed, with no losses reported on the other side. The surviving Navajo escaped, but again without their stolen livestock.

In the aftermath of the Bosque Redondo raids, Carleton ordered Carson to undertake another sweep of Navajo territory. This time, it would be a winter offensive into the sanctum sanctorum of the Navajo world, Canyon de Chelly, the 80,000-acre labyrinth of canyons surrounded by vertical cliffs into which few non-Navajo had ventured in the several centuries since the Anasazi had disappeared.

On January 12, two columns of 1st New Mexico Cavalry under Carson's command entered the maze. Though the Navajo held the high ground on the cliff walls, the troopers could cut them off from their supplies. In a series of firefights over two days, twenty-three Navajo were killed, and the number who came in shivering from the cold January weather to surrender mounted quickly. Nearly six hundred surrendered in January, and by the end of February the number had more than doubled. The last to give up was the band led by Manuelito, who held out long after most had gone to Bosque Redondo.

The Canyon de Chelly campaign marked the end of the organized resistance from the Navajo. The tribe formally agreed to cease hostilities and to live in peace with the Anglo-Americans. By the summer of 1864, in forced marches reminiscent of the Trail of Tears three decades earlier, an estimated eight thousand members of what had been the Southwest's dominant tribe had been relocated to the Bosque Redondo Reservation. The evacuation is still remembered as the "Long Walk."

Unlike the situation with the Cherokee and the other four civilized tribes, the Navajo exile was short—although internal conflict with the Mescalero sharing the reservation made it unpleasant. In 1868, the U.S. government uprooted the Navajo at Bosque Redondo and returned them to northeast Arizona, where they abided by their word not to conduct warfare against the settlers streaming into the Southwest. Today, the Navajo Reservation here is the largest Indian reservation in the nation, and it still encompasses Canyon de Chelly.

Even as the Navajo War had reached its climax and conclusion in northern Arizona, the Apache War continued in the Pinos Altos Mountains of the south. Captain James Whitlock's 5th California Infantry Regiment was in the center of the action against Cochise and the Chiricahua and Mimbres Apache who were raiding mines and settlements on the Arizona-New Mexico border.

In February 1864, the soldiers were able to ambush nineteen Apache who had brazenly ridden into the mining town of Pinos Altos. In a rare surprise on an Apache band, Whitlock's troopers killed thirteen, including Luis, reported to have been the successor to Mangas Coloradas.

In April, Whitlock successfully tracked an Apache raiding party into the Sierra Bonita after they had stolen some livestock. On April 7, Whitlock was again able to surprise his enemy, this time killing twenty-one of an estimated thirty in the band. The tables were turned on the 5th California a month later, when a small detachment was ambushed by

Apache on May 4 in Arizona's Doubtful Canyon. This time the soldiers lost two, while killing ten Apache.

Having finished the Navajo War, General James Carleton had drafted plans for a major spring offensive against the Apache that was designed along similar lines to Kit Carson's winter campaign. Elements of several regiments—including the 1st New Mexico Infantry, the 1st New Mexico Cavalry, the 1st California Cavalry, and the 1st and 5th California Infantry—would be involved. Because the Apache raiders were difficult to track and almost impossible to catch, the command would conduct the same sort of scorched earth warfare against the Apache infrastructure that had apparently succeeded against the Navajo. Marching north from Fort Bowie in southeastern Arizona, the object was to sweep the Gila River drainage area, destroying Apache encampments as they could be located.

Conducted during late May, the Gila River sweep skirmished with occasional war parties of Apache, but encountered no major resistance. On May 29, Captain Thomas Tidball attacked two large Apache settlements in Mescal Creek Canyon with an eighty-six-man strike force. In the course of destroying Apache homes and supplies, they killed fifty-one Apache and captured sixteen, mainly women and children.

Meanwhile, the 1st New Mexico Cavalry under Captain Julius Shaw was on patrol on the San Carlos River. His troops destroyed a small encampment early on June 7, and late in the day, he encountered a group of Apache who thought the cavalry were traders that they had been waiting for. The two sides camped for the night, with the Apache still thinking that the troopers were traders. The following day, Shaw revealed that he was with the U.S. Army and the Apache claimed that they had never raided settlements in the United States, only in Mexico. They further promised that they would release some of the hostages—who were usually an unwilling encumberment to Apache raiding parties. They rode off, telling Shaw that they would be right back. Of course they were not. The troopers caught up to them, and in the battle, an estimated thirty of seventy-six Apache were killed in action.

Carleton continued his large unit campaign against the Apache through the summer of 1864, with a large force under the 1st California Cavalry's Major Thomas Blakeney conducting a weeklong sweep through the Sierra Pinal beginning on July 28. In this case, Blakeney actually undertook negotiations aimed at inducing the Apache to surrender. However, the talks broke down, the shooting started, and Blakeney went on the offensive. Ten Apache were killed, two were taken into custody, and Apache property was destroyed. Blakeney also left a small detachment behind to wait for Apache that might return after the troops pulled out. This group killed a further five Apache.

Though raiding and skirmishing would continue, Carleton's campaigns during the first half of 1864 marked the last major combat involving the Apache to take place during the Civil War. When that conflict ended, the Apache War continued, albeit without Carleton, who went back to California with his volunteer regiments as the U.S. Army regulars returned to the Southwest.

THE GREAT BASIN THEATER DURING THE CIVIL WAR

As in the Southwest, major combat in the Great Basin during the Civil War years involved volunteer units from California. Indeed, the army units active in the Basin as well as the Southwest were administratively under the command of the Army of the Pacific.

Between late November and early December 1862, the 2nd California Cavalry under Major Edward McGarry were involved in a series of actions. These were against the Shoshone and their Bannock allies who had been raiding wagon trains on the Oregon Trail in the southern part of what would become Idaho Territory in 1863, as well as settlements in northeastern Utah for years.

The first major combat in this campaign followed an unusual pattern for engagements in the West. All too often, parleys turned to arguments which turned to firefights. In this case, McGarry attacked a force of about thirty Shoshone led by Bear Hunter in Utah's Cache Valley on November 23. After hours of gunfire and three Shoshone fatalities, Bear Hunter and McGarry agreed to a truce and a parley during which the troops recovered a boy thought to have been captured from a wagon train two years before. December 1862 found McGarry chasing Shoshone horse thieves southwest of Cache Valley. In this case, he took four Shoshone prisoner and offered to trade them for the purloined livestock. When the animals were not returned, he shot his captives as promised.

The following year, a 2nd California Cavalry contingent under Colonel George Evans undertook a campaign against the Ute south of the Great Salt Lake. The Ute responded by ambushing the troopers on April 12, then withdrawing into the protection of Spanish Fork Canyon. The two sides were fairly evenly matched, with the troops number about 170 and the Ute perhaps 200. The cavalry had the advantage of firepower in the form of a howitzer, the Ute had the advantage of a prepared defensive position and familiar terrain. On April 15, Evans used the howitzer against defensive concentrations, while outflanking the enemy with cavalry.

With their victory over the Ute at Spanish Fork and through continuing operations against the Shoshone, the military had essentially ended any further threat to emigrants and settlers from either tribe by the end of 1863.

THE TEXAS THEATER DURING THE CIVIL WAR

When Texas seceded from the Union, and the Civil War began, there were those who indulged the fantasy that the Comanche and Kiowa would ally themselves with the Texans against the common enemy, the U.S. Army. This did not come to pass. Operating from the Llano Estacado, or Staked Plains, the two tribes continued their raiding, compelling an abandonment of settlements in West Texas. Neither the Texas Rangers nor the Confederate Frontier Battalions were as effective at deterring Indian attacks as had been the much larger concentration of U.S. Army forces prior to 1861. The Mescalero also continued their raids against the Texans. On August 11, 1861, a detachment of the 2nd Texas Mounted Rifles under Lieutenant Reuben Mays was ambushed while on patrol in southern Texas by eighty Mescalero. His entire command, save for his Mexican guide, was killed.

Ironically, the major Indian battle within Texas during the Civil War involved a Union force. Kit Carson's success in militarily resolving the Navajo conflict led to his being tasked with leading a campaign against Comanche and Kiowa raiders on the Santa Fe Trail in November 1864. He took a strike force of more than three hundred men from the 1st New Mexico Cavalry and two California regiments into the Texas panhandle. On November 25, he attacked Chief Little Mountain's Kiowa encampment at a place called Adobe Walls, near the ruins of Bent's Fort on the Canadian River. Carson soon discovered that he was pinched between the Kiowa and Chief Stumbling Bear's even larger Comanche camp, and his troops were outnumbered three to one.

Firepower turned out to be the decisive factor that allowed Carson to turn the tide in the Battle of Adobe Walls. His two howitzers shattered the

Indian counterattack, and they broke off the fight after several hours, leaving sixty killed in action. As he had done against the Navajo in Arizona, Carson burned food stores and other property in the two villages. With winter coming on, these losses could not be replenished any time soon, and hardship would ensue. Under Carson's economic warfare doctrine, making life difficult for the Indians was seen as hastening the day that they would submit to living under the terms and conditions of the federal government's reservation policy. At this time, the reservation policy was still taking shape. Finally formalized in 1868, it is discussed in the following chapter.

THE CALIFORNIA THEATER DURING THE CIVIL WAR

While General James Carleton's California volunteers were the centerpiece of the major combat in the Southwest, the Indian Wars continued in the Golden State itself. During the early 1860s, the action was centered in the Eel River country of Humboldt and Trinity counties in northwestern California, an area that remains fairly remote from the rest of the state even today. As noted previously, the indigenous people of this region lived as small, generally autonomous bands, and were members of several tribes including the Pomo, Shasta, Karuk (Karok), Hupa, and the Yurok. As was the case with the Apache in the Southwest, some elements of these tribes conducted raids against settlements and other targets of opportunity, after which they escaped into the wilderness of redwood forests.

The principal U.S. Army base in the region was Fort Humboldt, overlooking Humboldt Bay on the Pacific Ocean at a site that is now within the city limits of Eureka. Since its establishment in 1853, the fort had been home to the 4th Infantry Regiment, commanded during the Civil War by Colonel Francis Lippit. During the 1850s, both George Crook and Ulysses S. Grant had served at the post. The 4th Infantry was augmented by other units, both regular army and California volunteers, especially the 2nd California Infantry Regiment.

The operational military strategy during the Civil War, as before, was to conduct search and destroy campaigns against the isolated Indian bands with the purpose of keeping them off-balance and unable to organize systematic raids against settlements in the area. In general, this strategy was far more effective in northern California than it was during the same period in the Southwest. The steep and heavily wooded terrain allowed for much less freedom of maneuver than did the mountains and canyons of the deserts, so it was easy for the offensive side—usually the army—to locate its quarry because there were fewer possible routes that could be taken. Usually, these paralleled the Eel River and its adjacent streams and tributaries. The effectiveness of these operations is evident in the casualty figures, in which the Indians lost a disproportionately larger number of people, including women, in battle.

The first major campaign of this type to take place during the Civil War was conducted between April 14 and June 17, 1861. In one phase of this operation, Lieutenant Joseph Collins's 4th Infantry Regiment detachment attacked nine separate villages or encampments, reporting ninety-three warriors killed in action with no losses. Simultaneously, Lieutenant James Martin led a combined force of 6th Infantry Regiment and California volunteers in attacks on five encampments along the South Fork of the Eel River. Martin's men reported thirty-nine Indians killed, although this number included at least three women killed accidentally and four men who were shot as "spies" after being captured. Martin resumed operations in the same area six weeks later, killing twelve of the forty people found at one encampment, including another woman who was shot by "mistake."

Limited offensive operations in northwestern California resumed in the spring of 1862, but on a smaller scale than in 1861. During May and June, elements of the 2nd and 3rd California Infantry Regiments killed thirteen Indians in three separate engagements.

During 1862, there were also a series of major raids by large numbers of Indians, something of a rarity in California. On June 6, an estimated fifty Indians attempted to rob Daley's Ferry, near Arcata. They killed a man and a woman, captured a child, and set fire to buildings at the settlement. Two soldiers of the 2nd California Infantry Regiment who were present returned fire, though one was wounded, and eventually the attackers withdrew. On July 28, a raiding party struck a ranch in the area, killing two men. The survivors held off the raiders until a detachment of the 2nd California arrived on the scene. On September 8, a 2nd California pack train was ambushed, but the attackers withdrew with no one killed on either side.

In 1863, the 2nd California Infantry began its search and destroy operations in the Eel River drainage on March 10. Their first action came eleven days later, with a surprise attack in which one soldier and eleven

Indians—including a woman—were killed. The next day, they struck another camp, killing ten men. On March 24, the infantrymen were involved in two separate firefights during which they lost another of their own, while killing two dozen Indian men and two women.

Later in the spring, the 2nd California took to the field in search of two groups of Indians who had murder several settlers in the Williams Valley and near Shelter Cove. In the first instance, the main body of Indians managed to escape into the mountains, but the troopers caught up to and killed a half dozen stragglers on April 9. One month later, infantrymen led by Captain William Hull succeeded in catching their quarry in the Shelter Cove incident. Though about twenty Indians escaped, one of the four who was killed was identified as the man who had committed the murder at Shelter Cove.

In 1864, Captain Hull was at the head of the 2nd California spring offensive, which went into the Eel River drainage in mid-March. In four separate engagements between March 19 and March 28, the infantrymen killed twenty-five Indians and captured fifteen, with the latter being mainly women and children. In another sweep a month later, Hull's men killed another eight Indians in a firefight on April 28.

On May 1, a 6th California Infantry Regiment pack train was ambushed, and one soldier killed. The following day, elements of this unit plus members of the 1st California Mountaineers located the ambushers and attacked their camp in a classic pincer operation. Among the seven Indians killed were three women. The 1st California Mountaineers continued their patrol, tracking and killing five Indians, including a woman, in two separate engagements on May 27 and 28.

By the time that the Civil War came to a close at distant Appomattox in the spring of 1865, the Indian campaigns conducted by the military in northwestern California had come to a close as well. Such fighting was just a distant memory in most of the state, but there would be one final chapter to be played out during the coming decades in the lava beds of the northeast.

The Minnesota Uprising of 1862

Before the Teton Sioux, or Lakota, became the central focus of America's Indian Wars, their cousins in the East, the Santee Sioux, or Dakota, would stun Minnesota with major combat in a region where the Indian Wars were thought to be a thing of the past. The fact that the Minnesota Uprising occurred in an area closely linked to the population centers of the East through roads, rails, and telegraph lines made it easy grist for the major media and particularly frightening—especially as the Civil War entered its second uncertain year.

It was axiomatic to Minnesotans that the Santee had been pacified. The last major deadly incident involving the Santee had occurred in March 1857 in the far south of the state in the vicinity of Spirit Lake, Iowa. A small Santee band led by a man named Inkpaduta had terrorized farm families and had killed forty-two people, but these renegades had long since left the area.

If the Santee had not been pacified in Minnesota, although there was every reason to suspect they had, they had certainly been marginalized. The Santee youth were angry, and they had a sense that there was nothing to lose.

On August 17, 1862, for no better reason than a whim, some young Santee men murdered five settlers near Acton, Minnesota. The action quickly escalated into widespread violence that had a fierce momentum of its own. On August 18, a large party of Santee attacked the Redwood Agency near Morton, Minnesota with shocking savagery. They raped, pillaged, tortured, and murdered people throughout Renville County and beyond. Settlers were burned alive and children were hacked to pieces while their mothers watched.

The survivors attempted to reach the safety of Fort Ridgely, and many made it. At the fort, Captain John Marsh led a contingent of the 5th Minnesota Infantry Regiment to confront White Dog, a Santee leader whom he knew. As the two leaders met, the Santee ambushed the soldiers. Badly outnumbered, and rapidly losing men to Santee musket fire, Marsh attempted a tactical withdrawal to the fort. Only fourteen of the forty-eight soldiers made it, and Marsh himself died while trying to swim across the Minnesota River to escape. By the end of August 18, at least 250 settlers and soldiers, and perhaps as many as four hundred, were dead.

On August 19, the Santee were divided, with the group led by Little Crow wanting to attack Fort Ridgely, and the another faction wanting to strike the town of New Ulm, a much softer target. The two groups went their separate ways, with the latter group reaching New Ulm by mid-afternoon. The townspeople had quickly organized a defense, and they were able to repulse the attackers. About a half dozen people were killed on each side.

Little Crow did not attack Fort Ridgely until August 20, by which time reinforcements had brought the fort's contingent to nearly two hundred, which was about half the Santee strength. The attackers managed to penetrate the fort's outer defenses, but they were turned back by artillery. Little Crow assembled an estimated eight hundred warriors for another attack on August 22, but the defend-

Little Crow (c. 1810–1863) photographed in Washington, DC in the late 1850s. (*National Archives*)

ers were better prepared. Despite a penetrating attack in which some Santee managed to start fires within the fort, the defenses held. When the dust had settled that day, Little Crow had given up. His losses numbered about one hundred, and only five soldiers had died in the siege.

The Minnesota Uprising changed direction on August 23, when Little Crow and his followers abandoned their assault on Fort Ridgely to join in the final attack on New Ulm. In the meantime, a group of about 125 men from nearby St. Peter who were led by Judge Charles Flandrau had ridden to New Ulm to join the townspeople in their defense. Together, they resisted repeated attacks by about 350 Santee. When the day ended, the attackers gave up, having lost about one hundred of their men. In New Ulm, the dead numbered thirty-two.

The successful defense of New Ulm did more than save the town. By preventing another Santee victory, it convinced other factions to stay out of the fight. A number of bands, including the Sisiton at the Yellow Medicine Agency and some Yankton as far west as the recently organized Dakota Territory, had been ready to join the uprising and probably would have if Little Crow had swept New Ulm. The battle may have been won, however, but the war was not over.

As the civilian volunteers were riding to the aid of New Ulm, the state government of Minnesota was sluggishly organizing its own response.

Former governor Henry Hastings Sibley—not to be confused with Henry Sibley, the Confederate officer—was commissioned as a colonel in the state militia and given the task of organizing a relief column. He managed to put together a force of about 1,500 that included the new 6th Minnesota Infantry Regiment, but they did not reach Fort Ridgely until August 28.

On September 1, he sent a 160-man detachment under Major Joseph Brown and Captain Hiram Grant to Redwood Agency to bury the dead. Early the next morning, a Santee force led by Big Eagle, Gray Bird, and Mankato attacked the detachment's camp at nearby Birch Coulee. The soldiers and volunteers managed to hold off the initial assault, but they were surrounded and short of water. Sibley sent a relief column of 240 on September 2, but they were turned back by the Santee.

On September 3, a thousand troopers rode to relieve the siege at Birch Coulee. This time, the Santee scattered in the face of a superior force. The relief column found that the detachment at Birch Coulee had lost twenty-four men, and were on the verge of running out of ammunition—and what they did have was the wrong caliber. The men had been forced to whittle down the lead in order to get it to fit their muskets.

Even as the Santee were within a few musket balls of overwhelming the men at Birch Coulee, another band was preparing for an attack on the towns of Hutchinson and Forest City, Minnesota. Though the townspeople managed a successful defense at both locations, the Santee badly mauled a contingent of the 10th Minnesota Infantry Regiment that was en route to Forest City. About half of the inexperienced troops were killed or wounded.

Much to the outrage of the people and media in Minnesota, Sibley waited for two weeks before he moved his sizable main force against the Santee. Finally, on September 19, he led 1,619 up the Minnesota River toward Wood Lake. It included elements of the 3rd, 6th, and 7th Minnesota Infantry, as well as numerous paramilitary volunteers. Four days later, Little Crow ambushed the column near Wood Lake, sending its advance guard into disarray. Though the Santee were outnumbered by more that two to one, Little Crow's flanking attacks were remarkably successful in the opening actions of the battle. At last, thanks to the tenacity of the troops and the timely action by a 6th Minnesota detachment commanded by Colonel William Marshall, the troops rallied and defeated the enemy. The losses were twenty-five Santee and seven from Sibley's force killed.

Hanging of the forty Indians convicted of conspiring against the United States in Minnesota in 1862. (*Library of Congress*)

Although Little Crow made a brief and unsuccessful attack on Fort Abercrombie on September 26, the Battle of Wood Lake on September 23 marked the end of major combat in the 1862 Minnesota Uprising. Over the course of the coming weeks, Sibley obtained the release of hostages that had been captured by the Santee, and took approximately two thousand Santee into custody. In November, 303 Santee were convicted by a military tribunal for crimes against civilians, but President Abraham Lincoln personally reviewed the case and commuted the sentences of all but forty. These were hanged in December.

Sibley's force was kept on alert for further action, while Little Crow's followers crossed into Canada to regroup. The following year, the Santee leader crossed back into Minnesota with a small band. On June 29, 1863, they murdered four members of a farm family near Howard Lake. This might have been the harbinger of a new offensive, but Little Crow's once powerful military force had dwindled to just a handful of bandits. On July 3, he was killed by a hunter while he was picking berries in the woods near Hutchinson, Minnesota. The Sioux would never again threaten Minnesota or points east, but on the Plains, it would be another matter entirely.

The Northern Plains Theater During the Civil War

Prior to the Civil War, the Plains had been just one of many theaters in the Indian Wars, but the region was moving to the forefront. Through the 1860s, the actions by the no-nonsense volunteer militias were gradually eliminating the threat to commerce and settlement in all of the other theaters except the Plains and Southwest. At the same time, the 1860s were seeing the gradual awakening of what can be described as the fury of the powerful Sioux war machine.

The sovereigns of the Plains since long before an Anglo-American had set foot in their territory, the Sioux, especially the Teton Sioux, or Lakota, had been slow to take the threat from the newcomers seriously because so few had previously lingered long in their territory. The Minnesota Uprising of 1862, however, alerted both sides to the potential consequences of the clash between two powerful adversaries. It would not take long. During 1863, a series of running battles in Dakota Territory that involved numbers of combatants on each side would dwarf any engagements yet seen anywhere in the Indian Wars in the West.

After the Minnesota debacle, there was a groundswell of support for a strategy of pushing the Sioux out of Minnesota and placing them on reservations in the vast open range that had been designated as Dakota Territory in 1861. By this time, the federal government was developing the policy, formalized in 1868 and discussed in the following chapter, of establishing prescribed reservations throughout the West. Conveniently, a military contingent was available to enforce such a strategy. Henry Sibley, now a brigadier general, had not disbanded his brigade after the 1862 campaign. Indeed, by the summer of 1863, he had doubled the size of his Minnesota Brigade to more than 3,300 men. They included the three infantry regiments that had taken part in the earlier battles, as well as nine companies of the 1st Minnesota Mounted Rangers, an artillery battalion and other units.

Meanwhile, the U.S. Army had created a new military Department of the Northwest under the command of Major General John Pope, who had recently been relived of command of the Army of Virginia after his defeat in the Second Battle of Bull Run in August 1862. Under him, Sibley would command the District of Minnesota troops, and there would be a District of Iowa brigade under Brigadier General Alfred Sully. This force would consist of elements of the 6th and 7th Iowa Cavalry, the 2nd Nebraska Cavalry, and the 45th Iowa Infantry Regiment, as well as artillery and other units.

Sibley's brigade marched west, establishing a base near Devil's Lake in northeastern Dakota Territory, while Sully's men marched north into Dakota Territory along the Missouri River. Sibley made contact with the

Santee in the area and arranged for a conference with Santee leaders Standing Buffalo and Sweet Corn on July 24 at Big Mound, south of Devil's Lake.

An aura of tension and suspicion hung over the meeting, so when a nervous Santee shot and killed a militiaman he thought was threatening him, violence erupted. Given that there were 2,000 troopers and 1,500 Santee at Big Mound that day, the casualty figures were minuscule. The Santee, who were outgunned by the troops with their artillery, lost forty, but Sibley lost just four, the man shot in the beginning, two in the battle and a fourth who was killed by a lightning strike.

Most of the Santee escaped, and Sibley gave chase. He would not catch them, but on July 26, he crossed paths with another mixed Sioux gathering of about 1,650 Santee and Lakota near Dead Buffalo Lake, who promptly attacked the advance guard of Sibley's column with aggressive flanking maneuvers. As had happened at Big Mound, the Sioux broke off the attack after a fierce firefight. Also as at Big Mound, the casualties were tiny compared to the number of combatants on the field. Only one soldier and fifteen Sioux were killed in action.

Two days later, as Sibley's command camped near Stony Lake, they were ambushed by an estimated 2,500 Sioux. It was a determined attack that might have succeeded had not artillery been brought into play. Again, as at the two major battles earlier in the week, casualties were surprisingly light, with none among the Minnesotans, and an estimated eleven among the Sioux.

Through August, as Sibley was engaged in some of the largest engagements ever fought west of the Mississippi, General Sully's column was making its way northward with little contact with any of the indigenous people of the region. This would soon change however, as August gave way to September.

On September 3, a 6th Iowa Cavalry patrol under Major A. E. House came across a large Sioux encampment at Whitestone Hill, about one hundred miles east of the Missouri River. This group included the band led by Inkpaduta, the perpetrator of the Spirit Lake area massacre five years earlier. Sending a courier to alert Sully, House approached the camp to parley. The Sioux, however, recognized that they had a four to one numeric advantage over the three-hundred-man patrol and prepared to attack. Fortunately for House, Sully arrived just as the battle was joined.

The initial move by the Iowa brigade was to put the 2nd Nebraska Cavalry into the fight opposite the 6th Iowa Cavalry to squeeze the Sioux in a pincer. The Sioux offered determined resistance, and the offensive initiative shifted back and forth. The ferocious battle lasted until the Sioux made a tactical withdrawal at dusk. While Sibley's battles in August were marked by very light casualties, the Battle of Whitestone Hill was just the opposite. Sully had twenty troopers killed in action and thirty-eight wounded, while the Sioux may have lost between one hundred and three hundred. The Sioux also abandoned three hundred tipis, as well as food and other supplies, which the troopers burned. Lopsided casualty figures are often seen in actions such as Whitestone Hill and elsewhere, where the U.S. Army was able to launch a mounted attack against encamped Indians. As such, they had the initiative, as well as the advantage of speed and mobility. The Indian warriors, because they were dismounted, and defending their women and children, were at a tactical disadvantage. The casualty figures for the Indian side also often include noncombatants.

The U.S. Army had achieved a substantial victory over the Sioux at Whitestone Hill, but to place it in strategic context, it was small—both in terms of the enormous scale of the Plains and the number of Sioux warriors of various groups and subgroups that remained undefeated. Indeed, most of the warriors from Whitestone Hill and Sibley's engagements were able to get away and regroup to fight another day.

Meanwhile, the U.S. Army was simultaneously fighting the Civil War, and the Sioux Wars were tying down an enormous number of troops. The costly Battle of Gettysburg had taken place in July, just as Sibley and Sully were going into the field, and the army was in desperate need of personnel. There was a great deal of pressure on the troops in the West to eliminate the Sioux as a threat expeditiously.

Though there was light skirmishing through the winter, the grand strategy for the Plains Theater focused on another summer offensive in 1864. Moving his supplies and heavy equipment by Missouri River steamboat, General Sully went into the field in the late summer. He would have gone sooner, but there was not enough runoff in the rivers until July. His order of battle consisted of 2,200 men organized into two brigades. The first comprised the 6th and 7th Iowa Cavalry and another units for a total of twenty companies, while the second included the 2nd Minnesota

A panorama of the Whitestone Hill battlefield taken fifty years after the fact. This photograph gives an idea of the vastness of the landscape over which the U.S. Army and Indians fought in the upper Plains. (*National Archives*)

Cavalry and the 8th Minnesota Infantry Regiment, totaling fourteen companies. The four howitzers assigned to each brigade would prove vital.

On July 28, after a nine-day patrol, the troops made contact with an enormous Santee and Lakota encampment at Killdeer Mountain in northwestern Dakota Territory. Estimates placed the number of Sioux at eight thousand, at least a third of them warriors. Inkpaduta's band was among them, as were a sizable number of Hunkpapa Lakota led by two men who would figure prominently in the Indian Wars on the Plains in the coming decades—Gall and Sitting Bull.

Sully organized his force into a rectangular block, which he marched methodically across the field toward the Indian village, all the while pounding the enemy defensive positions with his howitzers. It was not the glorious cavalry charge of fictionalized accounts, but it was an efficient—and unstoppable—way to advance. Sully reached the encampment without the Sioux being able to penetrate his lines, and captured their supplies before they could be moved.

The Sioux withdrew having lost as few as thirty-one or as many as 150 warriors, while Sully lost just five. Sully's main objective in the Battle of Killdeer Mountain, as it had been at Whitestone Hill the year before, was to destroy the captured food and other supplies. To inflict such hardship on the Sioux with winter approaching was calculated to compel them to submit to the largesse of the U.S. government. It was a carrot-and-stick situation. In order to control the Indians, the government used the Army as the stick and the Indian Bureau to supply carrots. By destroying their supplies, the Army forced them to depend on the Indian Bureau. As an element of the developing reservation policy, the Indian Bureau provided supplies to the Indians under the condition that they camp peacefully in a designated area near an Army post. This way, the Army could more easily control hostile outbreaks. During the winter, especially when food was scarce, the Indians often acquiesced to this policy. In the summer, it was usually a different matter, and certain tribes, especially the Sioux, would remain fiercely independent for the better part of another generation.

After Killdeer Mountain, Sully energetically continued his patrol upriver on the Missouri to the mouth of the Yellowstone River, but if there were Sioux in these hills, they eluded his slow-moving task force. As successful as the Battle of Killdeer Mountain had been, it did little to terminate the perceived strategic threat of the Sioux.

SAND CREEK AND THE CHEYENNE CAMPAIGN OF 1864

If the Sioux were perceived by emigrants and settlers on the Northern Plains as the archetypical villain, that dubious distinction belonged to the Cheyenne and the Arapaho farther to the south. Signatories to the Fort Laramie Treaty of 1851, these tribes were guaranteed land in the West that was demanded by settlers only a decade later.

Under the Treaty of Fort Wise in 1861, their chiefs, including Black Kettle and White Antelope of the Cheyenne and Little Raven of the Arapaho, agreed to move the people onto smaller reservations on the Arkansas River and transform their way of life from hunting to farming. Many of the tribal members rejected this change and continued to follow the buffalo where they always had. This would put them in direct conflict with the emigrants following the Overland Trail to California, to the Colorado gold fields, and to Nevada's Comstock.

Military operations in the region were under the District of Colorado, which was a subsidiary command of the Department of the Missouri until January 1864 and of the newly formed Department of Kansas thereafter. With the two departments preoccupied by the Civil War, considerable autonomy of action was granted to the commander of the District of Colorado, Colonel John Chivington, the hero of the Confederate defeat at Glorieta Pass in New Mexico in March 1862.

By the summer of 1864, there was a virtual epidemic of raids on settlements and wagon trains through western Nebraska and eastern Colorado. During the first week of August alone, there were fifty-one people killed

A Cheyenne camp. One similar to this was attacked and destroyed at Sand Creek. (*Bureau of American Ethnology*)

and seven abducted by mainly Cheyenne raiders on the Little Blue River and in the Plum Creek area of Nebraska. Both the 7th Iowa Cavalry, part of Brigadier General Samuel Curtis's Kansas command, and Colonel Chivington's 1st and 3rd Colorado Cavalry undertook patrols aimed at apprehending the perpetrators. For the most part, the pickings were slim, as the Cheyenne meticulously avoided the troops.

In the meantime, diplomatic efforts were being made. The raiders by no means were representative of all of the Cheyenne in the theater, and Colorado Governor John Evans had gone so far as to issue a proclamation stating that Indians wishing to pursue peace should camp near military posts to disassociate themselves from the raiders and be safe from reprisals. Many Arapaho and some Cheyenne would take him up on this offer. However, Chivington and Curtis shared an antagonism and distrust for the Indians that would stack the deck against diplomacy.

On August 11, a Colorado detachment made contact with a band of Arapaho near Sand Creek, near the border between Colorado and Kansas. The Arapaho were uninvolved in the earlier assaults, and were actually en route to Fort Lyon (formerly Fort Wise) on the Arkansas River southeast of Denver in accordance with the Evans proclamation. Not knowing this, the troops gave chase. As the cavalry horses tired, the Arapaho might have overwhelmed the troops, but they chose not to attack.

On August 16, two 7th Iowa Cavalry detachments, one in Nebraska and one in Kansas, were ambushed by large Cheyenne war parties, which probably included participants from the earlier attacks. In one case, four out of six solders were killed, while in the other, a 125-man detachment under Captain Edward Murphy patrolling the Little Blue River lost two men before making a tactical withdrawal.

On September 20, about sixty Cheyenne ambushed a 7th Iowa Cavalry ambulance wagon on Cottonwood Creek in western Nebraska. Only two of the eleven soldiers present were armed. They returned fire, but were overwhelmed. Some of the soldiers managed to slip away, but four were killed or captured and tortured to death. Five days later, the advance guard of a 2nd Colorado Cavalry patrol out of Fort Larned, Kansas, ran into a Cheyenne encampment on the Pawnee Fork of the Arkansas River. They were surrounded and almost overwhelmed, but were relived by the main body of the force after a siege of about an hour.

On October 10, after weeks of raids by the Cheyenne against settlements throughout the region, a 3rd Colorado Cavalry patrol turned the tables in a target of opportunity raid against a Cheyenne encampment on White Butte Creek in eastern Colorado. Eleven Cheyenne were killed, including four women and children. The scalp and personal property of an emigrant woman were recovered at the scene.

As the skirmishes with the raiders went on, the diplomatic process was continuing. By October, Little Raven of the Arapaho had come in to camp near Fort Lyon, and the Black Kettle and Little Antelope Cheyenne bands arrived during the first week of November. Meanwhile, Major Scott Anthony had replaced Wynkoop at Fort Lyon, and he ordered the Indians to a new location on Sand Creek, forty miles from the fort until Anthony received specific orders from General Curtis authorizing him to officially take them into custody.

About this time, General Patrick Conner, commander of the District of Utah, passed through Denver on his way from Washington with orders directing him to aid Colonel Chivington in protecting the emigrant trails. Chivington took this as a War Department sanction for a general offensive against the Indians in the area, a project on which he enthusiastically set out. The core of Chivington's task force would be the 3rd Colorado Cavalry, who were just then winding up a hundred-day enlistment without having been involved in combat. They were anxious to rectify this situation, and Chivington was delighted with their eagerness.

Chivington marched to Fort Lyon, where he ascertained the location on Sand Creek of Black Kettle's village, and added a contingent of 1st

Colorado Cavalry to his task force. Because these Cheyenne had not been formally interned by the military, Chivington considered them fair game and acted accordingly. At dawn on November 29, about 575 troopers stared down at more than one hundred Cheyenne tipis, and another eight belonging to Left Hand's Arapaho, on the north side of Sand Creek.

As they approached the village, Black Kettle hoisted a white flag and an American flag to indicate that the Indians were not hostile. However, a stray shot was fired and the scene exploded. White Antelope ran out to try to stop the fight and was gunned down. The troops galloped into the village as howitzers dropped shells on a hastily assembled Cheyenne defensive line.

The Cheyenne managed to kill fifteen troopers, but Indian deaths numbered around 130. As the troops gained the upper hand, the battle turned into a slaughter, with women and children deliberately killed at close range and mutilated. Military discipline collapsed. From Chivington on down, an angry bloodthirstiness prevailed. Sand Creek is today recalled as an instance of hatred and reprisal at its worst.

A Congressional investigation condemned Chivington for "a foul and dastardly massacre." He escaped the arm of military justice by leaving the service, but a political career that he had hoped for was precluded by his Sand Creek misadventure. Black Kettle survived and escaped, but he was destined to face another, similar battle four years later. This time the forces would engage on the Washita River, and his foe would be George Armstrong Custer.

5

INDIAN WARS OF THE POSTWAR DECADE

With the end of the Civil War, the U.S. Army prepared to demobilize a force of more than 2 million. The reorientation to "peacetime" troop levels consciously ignored the fact that the United States was still at war in the Trans-Mississippi West.

Though there were those who wanted to embrace the peace that ended the horrible war between the states and ignore the distant conflict on the Plains and deserts, others suggested that the enormous Union Army should be sent into the West to subdue the Indians once and for all. These calls were never taken seriously in Washington. As would be the case after both world wars, there was a cry to get the boys home and out of uniform as soon as possible. In 1865, unlike in the world wars, the boys were mostly part of federalized state regiments, which reverted to state control as soon as the war was over, and local sentiment demanded that the troops be mustered out expeditiously. Only a handful of eastern regiments would see service in the West.

It would be interesting to speculate what course the Indian Wars would have taken if a million-man U.S. Army had been sent into the west in 1865. The Union Army had defeated the Confederate Army in four years, but it would take another quarter century to see the end of the Indian Wars. How long would it have taken with a million-man force? We'll never know. Certainly it would have been possible to conduct major offensives rather than small patrols, but the sheer scale of the western landscape and the elusiveness of people such as the Apache and the Sioux might have made the exercise just as frustrating as it actually was with a smaller overall force strength. As the U.S. Army had already discovered, their foe in the West had an uncanny ability to direct the battle to take place on their terms, and that large, slow-moving columns would almost never compel them into a decisive engagement.

As the war ended, General Ulysses S. Grant, the commanding general of the U.S. Army, recommended that the force level be set at 80,000, but Congress decided in 1866 to set the limit at 54,000. This was, of course, dramatically greater than the prewar 18,000. Much of this troop strength, however, would be earmarked for occupation duty in the former Confederate states. After the U.S. Army would reach a postwar peak of 56,815 in September 1867, Congress reduced the authorized force level. In 1869, it was lowered to 37,313, and in 1874 to 25,000.

The reductions in force levels were driven by a variety of factors. Chief among these was the omnipresent insistence within Congress to decrease the size of the military during "peacetime." One might recall the discussions of the "peace dividend" that filled the halls of Congress in the early 1990s after the end of the Cold War. So, too, did Congressmen seek to dramatically reduce military spending after the Civil War.

Another factor in reducing both force levels and military spending in the 1860s would be familiar to modern observers—the peace movement. In the 1860s, most Americans lived on or near the eastern seaboard, where no one had experienced an Indian war for generations. Their view had softened considerably from that of their eighteenth-century forebears. News of atrocities such as the Chivington massacre at Sand Creek inspired the altruistic factions to unite in support of conciliatory treatment of the indigenous people of the West. Such a spirit filled the editorial pages even as the regular U.S. Army was mobilizing to do battle in the West, and it would temper the mood of the majority of the nation until 1876. During the postwar decade, official government policy would vacillate between the hard line of the War Department and the more diplomatic and accommodating position taken by the Indian Bureau, where important policy-making posts were occupied by religious leaders, mainly from the Society of Friends or Quakers. Among these men were Lawrie Tatum, whom President Grant would appoint as the agent for the Kiowa and Comanche, and Brinton Darlington, who was given the Arapaho Agency.

Organizationally, the U.S. Army in the Trans-Mississippi West was now sectioned at the continental divide into two divisions generally comparable to the prewar arrangement. The Division of the Pacific contained two departments: the Department of California, containing the state of the same name, as well as the territories of Arizona and New Mexico; and the Department of the Columbia, which contained the state of Oregon and the territories of Washington and Idaho. The division was headquartered at the Presidio of San Francisco under the command of Major General Henry Halleck.

The Division of the Missouri contained four departments. The Department of the Missouri encompassed Colorado, Kansas, Missouri, and New Mexico. The Department of Arkansas included that state as well as Indian Territory. The Department of Dakota contained Minnesota, as well as parts of Montana Territory and Dakota Territory. Gerrymandered between the Dakota and the Missouri was the Department of the Platte, which contained the balance of Montana and Dakota Territory, as well as Nebraska and Utah. The postwar commander was Civil War legend William Tecumseh Sherman, the Army's only three-star lieutenant general.

Ulysses S. Grant, the Army's commanding general, had been given a fourth star, making him the first officer elevated to the rank of general since George Washington. When Grant was inaugurated as president in 1869, Sherman would succeed him as commanding general and hold that post for fourteen years, the climactic period of the Indian Wars.

Grant's fourth star was in contrast with what happened with most of the line officers in the postwar regular Army. Most found themselves being reduced in rank. During the war, many officers were given "brevet" or temporary rank a grade or two ahead of their actual rank. Captains became majors, and majors became colonels and sometimes generals. The reason was often patronage, but in theory it was because the men were in command of a force whose size justified the higher rank. After the war, as the force levels shriveled, the officers were returned to their nearly forgotten "actual" rank.

Postwar Strategic Doctrine

As the U.S. Army turned its gaze westward from the blood-soaked ground of the mid-South, there was also the question of strategy in dealing with the task at hand. The situation in California and the Pacific Northwest had been essentially stabilized. The population density in the Great Basin remained sufficiently thin to render it as a sideshow. The principal theaters of operations from 1866 forward would be the Southwest and the Plains, which were confusingly divided between several geographic military departments.

Prewar strategic policy in these two theaters had been geared to the notion of protecting the trails. During the war, the local militias had begun the effort to pacify large sections of the West. In short, the postwar strategic doctrine of the U.S. Army would be geared toward the Herculean task of forcing the West's entire indigenous population onto reservations.

While the theories of Indian policy were being debated in Congress and in the editorial pages of the eastern media, those on the ground in the West operated pragmatically. As for the Division of the Missouri, one had only to look at its commander. The Civil War record of General William Tecumseh Sherman, whose signature action was his brutal "March to the Sea" that cut the Confederacy in half, clearly illustrated his point of view with regard to strategic doctrine.

In theory, tactics were moving away from operating out of chains of fixed forts lining the trails. The Army would also move away from the idea of conducting summer campaigns with huge, slow-moving columns supported by wagons. Such columns carried formidable firepower, but they were restricted to terrain that the wagons could negotiate, and they were easy for a mobile, mounted enemy to avoid. The postwar Army would eventually trade supply wagons for pack trains, consisting of mules and/or packhorses, which were much more suited to operations in the western topography.

In addition, the U.S. Army would also begin to embrace the idea of winter, as well as summer, offensives. Heavy snow dramatically reduced the mobility of the nomadic Plains tribes, making them easier prey for the cavalry.

The Civil War had also helped to advance the technology of the weapons available to the U.S. Army. Muzzle-loading muskets were being replaced by breech-loaders, and other innovations such as metal cartridges revolutionized the weapons that individual soldiers carried. The metal cartridge dramatically reduced reloading time because the powder and projectile were prepackaged together rather than having to be loaded separately. The Springfield Arsenal modified a staggering 50,000 muskets as breechloaders by 1867. Troops were also receiving more advanced weapons, such as the Spencer repeating rifle and the Colt .45 caliber six-shooter. Beginning in the late 1860s, report after report credited the Spencer for allowing the troops to achieve extremely lopsided kill ratios in firefights against the Indians. Lever-action repeating rifles such as the Winchester and the Henry were not initially favored by the U.S. Army, although they found their way into the hands of the Western tribes by way of the Indian Bureau, which supplied them to the Indians for use as hunting rifles. They would prove to be an excellent weapon for close-in skirmishing.

In the decade after the Civil War, most of the artillery that was used by the U.S. Army was Civil War surplus equipment. By the early 1870s, the most common artillery piece of the half-dozen types in service with the U.S. Army in the West was the twelve-pounder mountain howitzer. In 1872, these guns accounted for half of the sixty-five artillery pieces assigned to the Department of the Missouri, half of the fifty artillery pieces assigned to the Department of the Platte, and 28 percent of the sixty-nine artillery pieces assigned to the Department of Dakota. Later in the Indian Wars, the Army would introduce the 1.65-inch, two-pounder Hotchkiss gun, which was much more versatile and more easily transported than the heavier Civil War-era artillery.

The ten-barrel Gatling gun, the precursor to the twentieth century machine gun, fired 350 rounds per minute and was theoretically a decisive weapon against any cavalry charge. However, many commanders in the West shunned the Gatling gun for a variety of reasons. It was considered too heavy and too awkward for a fast-moving cavalry patrol. It also had a reputation for inaccuracy at long distances, and for jamming too often. The latter criticisms are said to have been problems that could be overcome through proper training and maintenance.

In terms of communications and logistics, improvements in technology were also on the side of the soldier. The rapid growth of the railroad network in the West made the job of providing distant posts with large volumes of supplies dramatically easier that it had been with wagons and oxcarts before the war. In 1869, the completion of the transcontinental rail line by the Central Pacific and the Union Pacific revolutionized transportation on the continent. A trip that took several months in 1868 could be accomplished in less than a week in 1869.

Meanwhile, telegraph lines, although they could easily be cut, provided western outposts with virtually instant communications. In the sunny desert Southwest, heliographs were used to transmit Morse Code messages in the 1880s.

Despite their technology and their numbers, the postwar regular Army would face a skilled and determined foe who would not be subdued in the decade that followed the Civil War.

THE RESERVATIONS

The federal government formally adopted the policy of setting aside reservations, or prescribed blocks of land as permanent homelands for members of specific tribes, in 1868. However, this concept had been in development in the years prior to the Civil War. Pre-war treaties, such as those signed at Fort Laramie in 1851 and at Fort Atkinson in 1853, guaranteed the rights of Indians in certain areas, but the boundaries of these areas were generally ambiguous. The exception, of course, were the strictly prescribed boundaries within Indian Territory.

The need for strict reservation boundaries in the remainder of the vast and largely trackless West was not apparent until the wave of mass migration and settlement that followed the Civil War and the Homestead Act of 1862, which gave 160 acres of undeveloped land in the West to any family head provided he lived on it for five years. With this, it was necessary to strictly define the reservations as places not open to homesteaders.

According to the current definition of the United States Bureau of Indian Affairs, "An Indian reservation is a specific area of land which has been reserved, set aside or acquired for the occupancy and use of an Indian tribe." In essence, a reservation is land a tribe reserved for itself when it relinquished its other land areas to the United States through treaties.

The reservations that were established in the years after 1868 were managed by the Indian Bureau through the system of Indian agencies, some of which had been long established near military posts before the Civil War. The Indian Bureau's Indian Agent was based here, and the agency was also the disbursement point for aid, including food and material goods, that were given to the Indians by the government under the terms of the treaties.

As noted previously, under the presidency of Ulysses S. Grant, between 1873 and 1877, the United States government officially adopted a "Peace Policy" toward the Indians, and agents were appointed by either a missionary society or a church board. Part of Grant's rationale in bringing religious leaders into the governing of the Indians was to root out the corruption that had previously existed at many of the agencies.

According to the Secretary of the Interior's summary of the plan in 1873:

The so-called Peace Policy sought, first, to place the Indians upon reservations as rapidly as possible, where they could be provided for in such manner as the dictates of humanity and Christian civilization require. Being thus placed upon reservations, they will be removed from such contiguity to our frontier settlements as otherwise will lead, necessarily, to frequent outrages, wrongs and disturbances of the public peace. On these reservations they can be taught, as fast as possible, the arts of agriculture, and such pursuits as are incident to civilization. . . . Their intellectual, moral, and religious culture can be prosecuted, and thus it is hoped that humanity and kindness may take the place of barbarity and cruelty.

Military control was less of an issue on the reservations than off them. The Army's role was to coerce Indians outside the reservations to return to, or take up residence on, the reservations assigned to them.

RED CLOUD'S WAR AND THE PLAINS THEATER

After the campaigns in Dakota Territory conducted by General Henry Sibley and General Alfred Sully in 1863-1864, the locus of the Army's interaction with the Sioux shifted westward into what became Wyoming Territory in 1868. The focal point would be the Bozeman Trail, a spur road that split off from the Platte Road, a section of the old Oregon Trail that followed the Platte River. It departed from the Platte just north of Fort Laramie and traveled northwesterly into Montana Territory through the Powder River drainage, intersecting the Yellowstone River east of Bozeman.

Geographically important as the Indian Wars continued, this area of southeastern Montana and northeastern Wyoming is punctuated by a series of rivers flowing generally south to north into the Yellowstone, which flows generally west to east across Montana. From west to east, these rivers are the Bighorn River, the latter's Little Bighorn tributary, Rosebud Creek, the Tongue River, and the Powder River. The entire area, about the size of the state of Indiana, is often referred to as the "Powder River country." Parallel to the Powder River on the east is the Little Missouri, which flows into the Missouri just downstream from its confluence with the

Yellowstone. The Teton Sioux, or Lakota, and their Northern Cheyenne allies ruled this land and saw no reason to permit any outsiders to use a road such as the Bozeman Trail.

The first major campaign into the Powder River country came in early August 1865, shortly after the end of the Civil War. It was a three-column sweep, with the left column out of Fort Laramie led by Brigadier General Patrick Conner, and including elements of several cavalry regiments, including the 2nd California, the 6th Michigan, the 7th Iowa, the 11th Ohio, as well as nearly two hundred Pawnee and Omaha scouts. Operating farther east, the other two columns, also consisting of cavalry units, were led by Colonel Samuel Walker from Fort Laramie, and by Colonel Nelson Cole from Omaha.

After a few small skirmishes, the left column had its first major encounter when they came across an Indian encampment on the Tongue River in the early morning of August 29. Conner personally led the cavalry charge into the midst of the camp, while his howitzers blasted the tipis. The battle quickly devolved into vicious hand-to-hand combat, from which many Indians managed to escape. The general gave pursuit with a small contingent, but after ten miles, he turned back for fear of becoming too far separated from his main force. He lost two soldiers and three scouts in the fight. Reports of Arapaho dead, which included women and children, ranged from thirty-five to sixty-three.

The other two columns, meanwhile, had merged northwest of the Black Hills, and had moved into the Powder River country by the end of August. By now, they had been in the field for a month and they were both running short of supplies and having trouble finding adequate forage for their horses. On about September 1, a large combined force of Lakota and Cheyenne began shadowing the column, conducting several raids against the horse herds. On September 5 and 8, the Indians launched major direct attacks on the column of soldiers, and a dozen troopers were killed. A heavy early-winter snow fell on the night of September 8-9, and several hundred horses died. By September 13, the hungry troops of the right and center column had made contact with Conner's men, and the ordeal was soon over.

One Congressional Medal of Honor was awarded for heroism during the Powder River campaign. Sergeant Charles Thomas of Company E, 11th

Ohio Cavalry, earned it for carrying a message through an area occupied by hostile Lakota, and saving the life of a comrade en route.

The net benefit of the first of many Powder River campaigns was essentially nil. The U.S. Army had shown the flag in the Powder River country, and Conner had destroyed a great stockpile of Indian supplies on the Tongue, but the other columns lost an estimated seven hundred head of stock.

In June 1866, Indian Agent E. B. Taylor and Colonel Henry Carrington met with the Lakota leaders, including the great Oglala Lakota Chief Red Cloud (Makhpyia-luta), at Fort Laramie to discuss a treaty. The idea

Makhpyia-luta, Red Cloud, (c. 1821–1909) was a principal chief of the Oglala Lakota during the critical years following the Civil War. (*Author*)

was that substantial annuity payments would be made to the Lakota in exchange for freedom of passage on the Bozeman Trail. The chiefs whose people lived in the vicinity of the trail refused the offer, but the chiefs whose bands were unaffected agreed. Taylor either misunderstood or ignored what had happened, because he wired the Indian Bureau that a deal had been made.

In July, the Lakota struck. Red Cloud ordered attacks on every wagon train, military or civilian, that used the Bozeman Trail. Four civilians were killed in an attack on July 17, and two soldiers died three days later. Thus began the series of battles on the Northern Plains that would last until late in 1868 and be known collectively as Red Cloud's War.

To secure the Bozeman Trail, and to make it safe for civilian traffic, the U.S. Army undertook to build a series of forts north of Fort Laramie that were about seventy to ninety miles apart. These included Fort Reno, Fort Phil Kearny, and Fort C. F. Smith. This would institute an armed presence at various locations along the trail, and the troops based at each fort could provide a military escort when necessary, or serve as a rapid reaction force.

THE FETTERMAN DISASTER

As autumn faded into winter in 1866, Colonel Carrington's detachment at Fort Phil Kearny was working to finish construction on the fort. Carrington is commonly portrayed as defensively oriented in his approach to Indian fighting. His methods put the post commander at odds with more aggressive younger officers, like the brash, young, newly arrived West Pointer, Lieutenant William Fetterman. Carrington was also at odds with his boss, Department of the Platte commander General Philip St. George Cooke, who was actively pushing Carrington to undertake offensive winter patrols against the Lakota—despite most of the Powder River country being buried by impassible snowdrifts.

Captain William J. Fetterman (1833–1866) during the Civil War. (*National Archives*)

On December 6, when a group of Lakota attacked a woodcutting crew on Lodge Trail Ridge north of the fort, Carrington finally acted. He sent Fetterman and a thirty-man 2nd Cavalry detachment up to the west side of the ridge to relieve the siege and drive the Lakota across the ridge. Carrington, meanwhile, led a twenty-five-man detail of mounted 18th Infantry Regiment troopers on the Bozeman Trail to the east of the ridge to cut off the enemy. The plan fell apart when the advance guard of the two columns got too far ahead of the others, and inexperienced troops panicked. Two soldiers and an unknown number of Lakota were killed in a series of disorganized gunfights spread across the winter landscape.

Two weeks later, on December 21, the Lakota again attacked woodcutters working north of the fort. Carrington sent Fetterman out to respond to the attack with an eighty-man mixed detachment of 2nd Cavalry and 18th Infantry troops. His orders to Fetterman were to relieve the woodcutters, but not to cross Lodge Trail Ridge. As Fetterman reached the scene, the raiders withdrew up the slopes of the ridge. Among them was Crazy Horse (Tasunke Witko), the Oglala Lakota whose name would soon become synonymous with the ideal of the heroic warrior.

Whether he was deliberately disobeying Carrington, or just caught up in the spirit of the chase, Fetterman followed Crazy Horse up the hill, across the ridge, and out of sight of the fort. On the other side, Crazy Horse led Fetterman into a trap sprung by High Back Bone of the Minneconjou Lakota. Possibly as many as a thousand warriors pounced on Fetterman's men as they desperately sought defensive cover. It was for naught. Fetterman's entire command was wiped out to the last man in about thirty minutes. It was the worst defeat yet suffered by the U.S. Army in the West, and a source of reassurance for Red Cloud and the Lakota.

In the aftermath of the Fetterman Fight, General Cooke relieved Carrington of his command, and General Grant relieved Cooke. The impetuous Fetterman nonetheless became the namesake of a new fort constructed at the intersection of the Platte Road and Bozeman Trail.

The Hayfield and Wagon Box Fights

Encouraged by their defeat of the U.S. Army in December 1866, Red Cloud and the Lakota kept up the pressure on the Bozeman Trail through 1867, even boldly resuming their attacks on the troops. During this campaign, one 18th Infantry Regiment trooper performed acts of heroism that earned him the Congressional Medal of Honor. During the blizzards of February 1867, Sergeant George Grant volunteered to carry dispatches from Fort Phil Kearny, northwest to Fort C. F. Smith and back. The award citation credited him with "Bravery, energy, and perseverance, involving much suffering and privation through attacks by hostile Indians, deep snows, etc."

George Grant had braved the attacks on the two posts and the Bozeman Trail between, and these assaults continued through the spring and summer. On August 1, about eight hundred warriors attacked hay-cutters near Fort C. F. Smith. Lieutenant Sigismund Sternberg, heading a twenty-man 27th Infantry Regiment guard detail organized a defense and returned fire with their new breech-loading Springfields. The Lakota started a grassfire, but it blew back away from the troopers' defensive position. Private Charles Bradley was sent for help, and he managed to get through to the fort and return with a howitzer-equipped relief column. The Lakota withdrew, and the Hayfield Fight ended with Lieutenant Sternberg and one other soldier killed in action.

As dawn the following day, the Red Cloud personally led a major assault on the beleaguered Fort Phil Kearny, in which the Lakota warriors Crazy Horse and American Horse took part. As with the December attacks, the target was a woodcutting crew. Working northwest of the fort, they were escorted by a fifty-one-man detachment of 27th Infantry Regiment troopers led by Captain James Powell. The troops took cover behind a group of wagon boxes located at the woodcutting camp, and returned fire. Powell organized a defense that managed to turn back eight separate assaults over a period of more than six hours.

Some men who were outside the camp managed to slip back to the fort, and they returned with a relief column armed with a mountain gun. The siege was lifted and Red Cloud withdrew having been unable to execute a repeat of the Fetterman Fight. The Army lost seven men, although only three of these were among those within the wagon box defensive enclosure. Estimates of Lakota dead ranged from six to sixty.

The consequences of the Hayfield and Wagon Box Fights were a far cry from those of the Fetterman Fight, but the two battles demonstrated the Indian ability to strike at will on the Bozeman Trail despite the presence of the forts.

In the wake of the Fetterman Fight, General William Tecumseh Sherman, commanding the Division of the Missouri, came to believe that a brutal offensive like that he waged on the South during the Civil War was the strategy to use against the Plains tribes. To accomplish this mission he brought in two like-minded subordinates. General Christopher Auger would command the Department of the Platte in the north, and General Winfield Scott Hancock—one of the heroic figures from the Battle of Gettysburg—would execute operations in the Department of the Missouri. They shared the same strategic vision, agreeing that offensive action, rather than the maintenance of defensive forts, was the strategy most likely to make the area secure for emigration and settlement.

HANCOCK AND CUSTER

During the Civil War years, the Plains Theater had generally evolved into two theaters of operations. There was the Northern Plains region, encompassing Montana Territory, Dakota Territory, and what became Wyoming Territory in 1868. To the south, in Colorado, Kansas, and Missouri was the lion's share of General Winfield Scott Hancock's Department of the Missouri. Generally, the Lakota held sway in the north, and the Cheyenne in the south, but elements of both tribes traveled with one another, so members of both tribes were present in both areas. It was in the south where was where skirmishes and major combat with the Cheyenne had increased dramatically during the Civil War.

It was in the Department of the Missouri in 1867 that officers with reputations forged in the Civil War would emerge as the central figures in the strategy and tactics of the Indian Wars. Hancock had led the first division at Antietam and Chancellorsville. As II Corps commander at Gettysburg, he had held the center of the Union line against Pickett's charge and he later distinguished himself at Spotsylvania and Petersburg. Among his subordinates was a colorful Civil War hero who would go on to become the most recognized name in the history of the Indian Wars—George Armstrong Custer.

Custer graduated last in his class at West Point in 1861. Actually, he was last in the Class of 1862, which was graduated nearly a year early because of the war. He fought at Bull Run, commanded the Michigan Brigade at Gettysburg, and developed a reputation for bravery to the point of recklessness. Promoted to brevet major general as a division commander, the twenty-six-year-old "Boy General" went on to receive Robert E. Lee's truce flag at Appomattox.

In 1867, under his permanent rank of lieutenant colonel, the flamboyant Custer was in operational command of the recently formed 7th Cavalry Regiment in the Department of the Missouri. Technically, Colonel Andrew Smith was the 7th Cavalry commander, but he was also in charge of the U.S. Army's Upper Arkansas District, so Custer led the regiment in the field.

As he began his spring offensive into Kansas in April 1867, Hancock could not have picked a more like-minded right-hand man. Custer shared with Hancock both a fondness for flashy uniforms and a zealous desire to energetically take the battle to the enemy.

Large offensives against the Plains Indians were generally ineffective, and such was the case as Hancock got under way. On April 14, Hancock approached a large, mainly Cheyenne encampment on the Pawnee Fork of the Arkansas River and announced that he wanted to parley, but the Indians managed to break camp and move out under cover of darkness. They broke up into hard to track smaller bands, attacked an isolated settlement, and evaporated into the prairie even as Custer's troopers tried to follow.

A series of smaller skirmishes continued into the summer, and in late June, the Cheyenne under Roman Nose (Wookaynay) and the Lakota managed to besiege Fort Wallace in far western Kansas for two days, killing five defenders. On June 24, an Oglala Lakota party even managed to ambush Custer's camp as his column was escorting a wagon train bound toward Fort Wallace, escaping before anyone was killed on either side.

Two days later, the Indians struck twice, including a strike by the Oglala led by the warrior known as Pawnee Killer, against the wagon train, which was then being escorted by a fifty-man 7th Cavalry detachment. This three-hour firefight failed to halt the wagons, but it slowed their progress considerably. Meanwhile, another fifty-man 7th Cavalry detachment gave chase to a group of Cheyenne who had stolen some horses from near Fort Wallace. Instead of breaking up and fading away, the Cheyenne turned to attack. A half dozen were killed on each side in the ferocious, close-in gun battle.

The events of June 24-26 aside, 7th Cavalry operations in Kansas during the summer were characterized mainly as light skirmishes and patrols that reached the scene of a raid on an isolated station after the perpetrators had departed.

One of Custer's most pressing issues during the summer was dealing with a group of troopers who deserted in July in the wake of an excruciating forced march commanded by the Boy General. He ordered the deserters shot and three were, one fatally. Having dealt harshly with the deserters, Custer "deserted" himself later in the month. In a still controversial incident, he left Fort Wallace to visit his wife at Fort Riley. As a result, he was taken into custody, court-martialed in October, and relieved of rank and duties for a year.

Custer had been deprived of—some would say he had avoided—the major combat which he claimed to have craved. This greatly disappointed Hancock, who had expected more of the aggressive young officer, and who urged harsh treatment at the court-martial. Custer would have to wait until December 1868 for the major combat that would define his legacy as an Indian fighter. By this time, Hancock would be gone from the Plains.

GIVING DIPLOMACY A CHANCE TO END RED CLOUD'S WAR

In contrast to Hancock's offensive posture in 1867, his counterparts to the north remained on the defensive in the wake of the Fetterman debacle of

December 1866. Both General Augur, of the Department of the Platte, and General Alfred Terry, commanding the Department of Dakota, devoted their resources to bolstering defenses along the roads and trails, and to protecting the progress of the Union Pacific Railroad, which was building west from Omaha.

There were discussions of sending Colonel John Gibbon into the Powder River country with a two-thousand-man task force from western Montana, but this was postponed. Nathaniel Taylor, who became Commissioner of Indian Affairs in March 1867, convinced Congress to authorize a Peace Commission, which went into the field in September.

Taylor's objective was to hold large multi-tribe summit conferences in both Kansas and at Fort Laramie and to broker permanent peace agreements with all the Plains tribes. The Indian Bureau was ready with generous inducements in the form of annuities, which Congress had decided were worth the price if the warfare could be ended. General Sherman agreed to go along with the plan, commenting, "It makes little difference whether they be coaxed out by Indian commissioners or killed."

In the north, the Sioux and Cheyenne factions dealt from a position of strength. In the south, the tribes were more willing to go along with a negotiated treaty. In October 1867, an estimated five thousand Indians arrived to attend the southern conference, held on Medicine Lodge Creek, about seventy miles south of Fort Larned, Kansas. The Arapaho, Comanche, Kiowa, and Kiowa-Apache all attended, but initially the meeting was boycotted by the Cheyenne, who were still up in arms over the summer skirmishes with Hancock and Custer.

On October 28, however, the Cheyenne came in to sign the historic Medicine Lodge Treaty. By its terms, two large reservations in western Indian Territory, in which settlers were banned, were set aside for the signatories. The United States government would provide supplies and large quantities of farm equipment. The well-intentioned commissioners failed to recognize that the Plains tribes had been hunters for generations and that farming was profoundly alien to their way of life.

Buoyed by their success at Medicine Lodge, the commissioners traveled north to Fort Laramie. Here they found only a message from the powerful Red Cloud. He would not even speak to them unless the U.S. Army abandoned the Bozeman Trail forts. With chagrin Peace Commission returned to Washington to ponder a possible reply through the winter.

In April 1868, the Peace Commission left Washington as the capital lay beneath the dark cloud of the impeachment of President Andrew Johnson. They arrived at Fort Laramie with a treaty that essentially offered Red Cloud everything that he demanded. The Lakota would be granted sovereignty over a vast swath of territory across eastern Montana Territory and Dakota Territory, and the Bozeman Trail would be abandoned. The U.S. Army's senior leadership was livid at the idea of walking away from the forts over which so much blood had been spilled, but the Peace Commission was adamant. There could be no meaningful comprehensive agreement without the Lakota signing on.

As the commission presented the treaty, the Sioux bands came in one by one to sign. Spotted Tail (Sinte Gleska) signed for the Brulé, as did Sitting Bull (Tatanka Iyotake) of the Hunkpapa, and nearly two hundred other Sioux leaders. However, in May, Red Cloud sent a message that he would not come in until the forts were actually abandoned. By August, the troops had packed up and moved south on the Bozeman Trail toward Fort Laramie. Red Cloud set fire to Fort C. F. Smith, and then Fort Phil Kearny, scene of so much fighting nearly two years before.

It was not until November 6 that Red Cloud finally affixed his mark to the Treaty of Fort Laramie. The United States Senate approved the treaty on February 24, 1869, formally ending the two years of bloodshed that had been called Red Cloud's War.

SHERIDAN'S OFFENSIVE

History recalls that when he gave his word in the Treaty of Fort Laramie, the hard-nosed Red Cloud kept it. Not so for many the Cheyenne who had signed off on the Medicine Lodge Treaty of 1867. Of course, from the Indian perspective, the dilatory nature of government bureaucracy, and intra-agency corruption on the field level, made the Indian Bureau often appear to be going back on its word as well.

Meanwhile, the U.S. Army was making some important administrative changes on the Southern Plains. Two departments were in need of shaking up, so Sherman and Grant agreed to exchange the two departmental commanders. Winfield Scott Hancock, after a summer of inconclusive campaigning in the Department of the Missouri, was transferred to the Fifth Military District—comprising Texas and Louisiana—where Major General

This 1868 peace conference resulted in the Treaty of Fort Laramie, which effectively ended Red Cloud's War. The US Army's commanding general, General William Tecumseh Sherman, is third from right among the commissioners seated within the tent. (*National Archives*)

Philip Henry "Little Phil" Sheridan was in hot water with the local white population over his strict enforcement of Reconstruction laws. After 1868, the Fifth Military District would comprise Texas alone, and in 1870, it would be redesignated as the Department of Texas.

As General Grant's cavalry chief during the last year of the Civil War, Sheridan, who would now command in the Department of the Missouri, had distinguished himself in a series of battles culminating in his cutting off Robert E. Lee's final retreat and thus forcing the surrender at Appomattox. His prewar Indian Wars credentials included action with the 1st Infantry Regiment in Texas and with the 4th Infantry Regiment in Oregon. He would remain in command in the Department of the Missouri until 1869, when he succeeded Sherman as head of the Division of the same name, as Sherman took over command of the U.S. Army upon Grant's election as president. Sheridan, even more than Hancock, was on the same page as Sherman with regard to using a firm hand against the Indians who broke the treaty. The actions of the autumn of 1868 would demonstrate this.

As raids by mainly Cheyenne bands continued through the summer of 1868, Sherman ordered offensive action. Sheridan's mandate was to eliminate the threat of hostile Indians in the corridor from the Platte River in the north to the Arkansas River in the south, essentially across all of Nebraska and Kansas. This was to be accomplished by pushing the Cheyenne, Comanche, and Kiowa into what is now western Oklahoma, the area that had been guaranteed to them under the Medicine Lodge Treaty that many bands had chosen to ignore—as would the U.S. government in later years.

The core of the resistance was among a select group of Cheyenne warriors who were called "Dog Soldiers" (Hotamitaneo), who got their name from the leather dog tethers that they carried. The tethers symbolized the Dog Soldier's willingness to remain tethered to his position and not retreat in the face of an enemy if his comrades were still being threatened.

Like a cross between the medieval Knights Templar and the modern Delta Force, the Dog Soldiers were an extremely brave and unusually well disciplined organization. They were responsible for spearheading Cheyenne resistance through the late 1860s and beyond. After the massacre at Sand Creek, the Dog Soldiers became especially militant, and received a great deal of popular support from among the Cheyenne.

The constant but small-scale skirmishing that had gone on in the region between 1864 and 1868 had resulted in one action that earned a soldier the Congressional Medal of Honor. On May 12, 1865, a Lakota raiding party attacked a ranch on the North Platte River in central Nebraska which was being guarded by four 1st Nebraska Veteran Cavalry troopers. Another group of soldiers from the same unit came upon the scene and chased the Lakota across the river. Wounded while covering some of the other troops, Private Francis Lohnes was awarded the medal for his gallantry.

Sheridan had been delayed politically by the Peace Commission, but the timing did not upset his plan for an aggressive campaign. For 1868, Little Phil embraced the controversial strategy of a winter offensive, an idea that most planners had generally avoided. The conventional thinking steered away from winter actions because of the logistical problems involved in fighting in the snow. However, Sheridan was taking a page from Kit Carson's playbook from the Navajo campaign of 1864, which recognized that the logistical difficulties of a winter war presented far greater problems for the Indians than for the U.S. Army. The nomadic Plains warriors carried their entire infrastructure and their civilian population with them into winter quarters. The Army had only its soldiers to care for.

To support his own logistical requirements, Sheridan pre-positioned a huge supply depot, appropriately dubbed Camp Supply (later renamed as Fort Supply), deep in the interior on the North Fork of the Canadian River, near what is today the neck of the Oklahoma panhandle.

Sheridan's strategy was to push and prod through the autumn, then deliver a decisive blow as the snows grew too deep for the tribes to move their villages. The action would be played out across a broad landscape from the Republican River on the Kansas-Nebraska border, south into the Texas panhandle and what is now western Oklahoma, and as far west as eastern Colorado.

In September 1868, Sheridan ordered Brevet Brigadier General Alfred Sully, veteran commander of the Dakota Territory actions of several years prior, into the field with a five hundred-man strike force that included elements of Sully's own 3rd Infantry Regiment, as well as men from the 5th Cavalry, 7th Cavalry, and the African-American 10th Cavalry "Buffalo Soldiers." As an adjunct, Sheridan authorized Major George "Sandy" Forsyth to enlist a fifty-man contingent of experienced plainsmen, who would operate as essentially a special operations detachment. Lightly armed for high mobility, they were seen as the perfect force for fighting the Indian bands.

Sheridan and Sully also petitioned for Custer's court-martial to be overturned in order to place him back at the head of the 7th Cavalry. This would be done, but Custer would not be in a position to redeem his tarnished reputation for several months. When the opportunity presented itself, Custer would seize it zealously.

Sully's force fought a series of hit and run battles against the Kiowa, Comanche, and Cheyenne in the sand hill country along the North Fork of the Canadian River during the second week of September. The U.S. Army lost three men to an estimated twenty-two of the opposing forces. On September 15, a thirty-six-man 10th Cavalry detachment was ambushed by a Cheyenne raiding party on Big Sandy Creek in eastern Colorado. Though they were outnumbered three to one, the Buffalo Soldiers successfully beat off the attack, with seven men wounded and none killed.

Meanwhile, Forsyth's small command had been moving north out of Fort Wallace, Kansas, and into the Republican River drainage, following the trail of Cheyenne Dog Soldiers. On the morning of September 17, what was interpreted as a small band of Cheyenne struck Forsyth's camp to steal horses. As Forsyth ordered the men to mount up to give chase, they discovered that they were under attack by an estimated five hundred Lakota and Cheyenne Dog Soldiers. Forsyth quickly ordered the men to take up a defensive position on a small island in the Arikara Fork of the Republican River.

The siege continued until September 21, although the Indians made no major attempt to assault the island after the second morning. By the end, the men faced more of a threat from lack of food than from Indian bullets. The ordeal ended when four men who managed to get away at night returned with a 10th Cavalry relief column, commanded by Captain Louis Carpenter. The Battle of Beecher's Island, named for Lieutenant Frederick Beecher, became a staple of Western folklore. A good defensive position and Spencer repeating rifles kept the Army casualties lower than might have been expected. Six of the troopers, including Beecher, were killed, as opposed to an estimated thirty on the other side. Among the Cheyenne killed in action was the noted chief, Roman Nose.

Having gone into action as a wholly inexperienced unit in September, Carpenter's 10th Cavalry had found themselves very much in the thick of the action. In October, they would be involved in the biggest battle to take place in the theater since Beecher's Island.

The chain of events leading up to this point began on October 12, 1868, when a large patrol out of Fort Harker in central Kansas was reported as overdue. On the first of the month, Major William Royall had gone out with elements of seven companies of the 5th Cavalry, and had not been heard from—so the 10th Cavalry, together with additional 5th Cavalry elements under Major Eugene Carr, was sent out to search for them. Before the two units would run into one another, they would each find themselves in hostile action.

On October 14, Royall's camp on Prairie Dog Creek was attacked by a Cheyenne group under Tall Bull, and Royall's detachment lost one man in a brief firefight. Carr and Carpenter reached the same stream at a different point, saw no evidence of the battle, but picked up the trail of the Cheyenne and some Lakota. At midday on October 18, the Indians attacked, so the troopers established a defensive perimeter on a hilltop. The Indians launched repeated assaults until evening, when they broke off the attack. Carr's men suffered a few wounded but no losses, and the Indians lost a reported ten killed in action. One Indian was captured, and he betrayed the location of a large encampment of Cheyenne and Lakota who were off the reservation and in violation of the treaty.

Carr and Carpenter reached Fort Wallace on October 22, where they learned that Royall's command had safely reached Buffalo Tank Station on the Kansas Pacific Railroad. Carr then prepared for a mission against the Indian village about which he had learned from the prisoner captured on October 18. Carr's 480-man force made contact with a group of Indians on October 25, so their arrival at their village the following day was not a surprise.*

The troops caught the Cheyenne and Lakota in the process of breaking camp and attacked. This engagement, like the one the previous week, cost the Indians an estimated ten lives, with the only cavalry casualties being a few wounded. As the battle wound down, Carr's men destroyed captured supplies and gave chase, but the Indians split into small groups and got away.

CUSTER ON THE WASHITA

On November 12, George Custer led the 7th Cavalry south from Fort Dodge, Kansas to play his role in Phil Sheridan's 1868 winter offensive. His regiment was part of Alfred Sully's task force in what is now western Oklahoma. At Camp Supply, the task force rendezvoused with General Sheridan himself, who had come out to observe operations personally. In the meantime, the trail of an especially large Indian force had been detected, and it was interpreted to be heading north into Kansas, presumably to attack settlements there. The 7th Cavalry was to intercept and destroy this column.

Custer left Camp Supply on November 23 with more than eight hundred men, including his cavalry and Indian scouts. Though a heavy snow obscured the trail, Custer located a sizable Cheyenne encampment on the Washita River and prepared for a dawn attack on November 27. This was the camp of Black Kettle, the same Cheyenne chief whose village had been the target of Chivington's brutal onslaught four years earlier.

*For actions during September and October, Captain Carpenter was awarded the Congressional Medal of Honor. His citation mentions gallant and meritorious service throughout the campaign, especially in the relief of Forsyth's embattled team at Beecher's Island.

Custer's battle plan followed the model that he would employ eight years later at the Little Bighorn, that is, a multi-pronged attack from opposite directions. While Custer himself rode from the west with four companies, Major Joel Elliot came from the northeast with three. A pair of two-company incursions under Lieutenant John Johnson and Captain William Thompson from the southwest and south rounded out the encirclement.

The troops charged into the village with guns blazing. As the intense firefight turned to hand-to-hand combat, many of the Indians fled. Major Elliot led an eighteen-man contingent after one group that was escaping. Some distance from the scene of the battle, the troopers were ambushed and all were killed.

As the battle at the Washita fight scene ended, Custer learned from prisoner interrogation that there was another, possibly larger encampment a short distance downstream with Arapaho, Kiowa, and Comanche, as well as Cheyenne present.

In a scene tailor-made for the future Hollywood depictions of the battle, mounted riders from these villages suddenly appeared on the hills surrounding the river valley. Custer could have mounted a follow-up attack against the second village, but he did not. He feinted such a move, mounting his troops and ordering his buglers into action, but instead, he departed the Washita and returned to Camp Supply. The remains of Major Elliot's men were found en route.

A great deal of speculation has always swirled around Custer's decision not to attack the other Indian encampment. Had he done so, he would probably have prevailed, but that is by no means certain. In any case, General Sheridan congratulated Custer on his victory over Black Kettle, and concurred with his decision to stop with just one decimated village.

In terms of losses, the Battle of Washita River is recalled as having been the major conflict in the Plains Theater during 1868. Estimates of the Cheyenne dead range from fifty to more than one hundred, including a number of women and children. Among the dead were both Black Kettle and another chief, Little Rock. The 7th Cavalry lost twenty-one men killed in action, most of them in Elliot's group.

The overall losses to the Cheyenne also included the destruction of the supplies that the 7th Cavalry burned at the scene, and more than eight

A sketch of Custer's troops moving a column of prisoners through heavy snow after the attack on Black Kettle's encampment along the Washita River. Theodore R. Davis' illustration originally appeared in the December 26, 1868 edition of *Harper's Weekly*.

hundred head of Indian horses that they killed. This was an important element of the strategy of Sheridan's winter campaign, like Kit Carson's against the Navajo, to put pressure on the Indians logistically. It was not, however, nearly as decisive a victory as Carson's Navajo campaign in 1864.

The 7th Cavalry troops also captured fifty-three women and children, including Black Kettle's sister, whom Custer would use as an intermediary in future efforts to persuade other Cheyenne bands and Dog Soldiers into surrender. According to a popular folklore, among the other Washita prisoners there was also the stunningly beautiful, seventeen-year-old Cheyenne daughter of Little Rock, named Monaseetah.

Monaseetah and two other women ended up being taken under the wing of the 7th Cavalry after the battle, and they traveled with the unit through the winter of 1868-1869. Although technically prisoners, they were accorded the privileges of honored guests and they traveled in the regiment's weatherproof ambulance wagon. Custer wrote often of Monaseetah in a series of articles that were published in Galaxy magazine beginning in 1872, and which later were published in book form as My Life on the Plains. His captivation with the young woman is evident in his describing her "handsome appearance, both in form and feature," her "bight, laughing eyes," "pearly teeth" and "silken tresses . . . which she allowed to fall loosely over her shoulders, to below her waist." That the enchantment may have been mutual is evident in his comment that she possessed "a bright, cheery face, a countenance beaming with intelligence, and a disposition more inclined to be merry than one usually finds among Indians."

Apparently Monaseetah proved herself quite valuable to the 7th Cavalry as a scout and tracker during the campaign that winter. For example, she was able to correctly tell Custer how many people had camped in a particular place, and how much time had elapsed. Though such a task was not beyond the ability of male scouts, Custer expressed particular fascination with Monaseetah's powers of deduction, writing that "No detective could have set about the proposed examination with greater thoroughness than did this Indian girl."

Custer notes that Monaseetah "exhibited marked feelings of regret" when she departed his company to return to her own people. Although it was never substantiated, legend has it that she became Custer's mistress, and bore him a son. Her later life remains shrouded in myth and mystery.

Greatly overshadowed by Custer at Washita was the last major battle of 1868, which took place on Christmas Day at Soldier Spring on the North Fork of the Red River in what is now western Oklahoma. Major Andrew Evans had been in the field with six companies of the 3rd Cavalry and two of the 37th Infantry Regiment for five bone-numbing weeks. They had picked up the trail of some of the Indians who had been involved at the Washita, and on Christmas, they stumbled into a Comanche camp.

Evans began blasting the village with artillery, then sent in his cavalry. The ensuing battle matched two adversaries who were tired, cold, and hungry. The troops managed to capture the village, but their horses were too spent to give chase when the Indians rode away. Evans destroyed the village, along with stockpiles of food, and eventually most of the Comanche would surrender to U.S. Army authorities in order to eat.

Custer took to the field again in January 1869, using hard-handed diplomacy to wheedle the cold and hungry bands into surrendering to the largesse of the Army and the Indian Bureau. He met with Little Raven's Arapaho, and the Cheyenne led by Little Robe and Medicine Arrow. Aside from dissident factions of Cheyenne, who traveled north of the Platte to join the Lakota, most of the tribes grudgingly acquiesced.

It was Washita that solidified Custer as a star. His dashing persona, his fringed buckskin jacket, and his golden hair—which he always wore long—made him the ideal grist for the tabloid press in the East. Even the Indians bought into the Custer image, dubbing him "Yellow Hair." Over the coming years, the heavily embellished Custer myth would continue to grow and evolve. There would be a great deal to be written before the opera that was Custer's career came to its tragic climax at the Little Bighorn.

CARR, CODY, AND OPERATIONS ON THE PLAINS

As the winter campaign officially wound to a close in April 1869, General Sheridan transferred the 5th Cavalry under Major Eugene Carr north to the Department of the Platte to aid General Augur in a summer offensive against the Cheyenne Dog Soldiers, particularly those under the leadership of Tall Bull, who were conducting a campaign of raids against settlements in the Republican River drainage of western Nebraska. Carr's regiment had participated in the winter campaign, but had not seen action. Carr, who considered himself a rival to Custer, was anxious to get into the fight.

As a guide for his column, Carr was now utilizing the services of a colorful character whose flair rivaled even that of Custer—William Frederick "Buffalo Bill" Cody. Having earned his distinctive nickname for his work as a hunter supplying meat for workers on the Kansas Pacific Railroad, Cody was a skilled marksman who styled himself as a frontiersman in the mold of Kit Carson. Unlike the quiet-mannered Carson, however, Buffalo Bill was flamboyant and extroverted, and would ultimately find his niche in show business.

Having left Fort Wallace for Fort MacPherson, Nebraska, on May 10, Carr's command discovered an Indian trail on Beaver Creek on May 13, near a stone outcropping known as Elephant Rock. Carr sent a scouting party, including Cody and Lieutenant Edward Ward, to investigate, and they discovered a sizable Lakota encampment. They were attacked as they raced back toward the main force of 5th Cavalry, but Cody got through. Leaving part of his force to guard his wagons, Carr moved to attack the village. Fighting his way through a series of gun battles spread across a dozen miles, Carr reached the Lakota camp too late in the day for an attack, so he withdrew, harassed by further Lakota attacks. The Lakota broke camp overnight, so there was little left for Carr to attack in the morning. The fight had cost Carr four men killed in action, while an estimated twenty-five Lakota were killed.

Undaunted, Carr decided to follow the Lakota north toward the Republican River in Nebraska. On May 16, near Spring Creek, the troops sighted their quarry. Carr sent Cody out with a small reconnaissance team, then decided to send a company, led by Lieutenant John Babcock, as backup. They were pounced upon by a group of about two hundred Lakota. Babcock ordered the small force into a defensive position on a hill. For his leadership in the ensuing firefight, the lieutenant would be awarded the Congressional Medal of Honor. As his citation points out, Babcock ordered his men to dismount and take cover, but he remained mounted himself, in an effort to "encourage them, and there fought the Indians until relieved, his horse being wounded." Carr had sent a second relief party, which succeeded in scattering the Lakota.

Babcock had lost three men killed in action, with no reported losses on the other side. Carr attempted to continue to follow the Lakota, but their trail dissipated, and his column was too exhausted for a pursuit action.

On June 9, Carr's regiment departed Fort MacPherson, headed back into the Republican River country in search of Tall Bull and the Cheyenne. This time, his column was augmented by three companies of Pawnee Scouts under Frank North. While the U.S. Army employed Indian scouts throughout the West during the Indian Wars, the latter group was one of a handful of instances wherein the Army had organized Indians into disciplined military units. Despite North's experiment having been deemed a success, it was not widely copied.

On June 15, Carr's 450-man task force made contact with the Cheyenne, or rather vice versa, when a raiding party hit their horse herd. The Cheyenne were chased off, with two of the raiders killed. The column continued on, with Carr sending patrols out from the main force to look for Cheyenne. Three weeks later, one such patrol under Major William Royall—who had campaigned with Carr the previous year—was involved in a brief skirmish in which three Cheyenne were killed.

Despite advice from Royall that the parched landscape of eastern Colorado could not support the forage needs of a large cavalry formation, Carr continued to march westward. By the first week of July, they were operating on the Colorado border north of the Republican River.

On July 8, Carr sent Corporal John Kyle with two men to round up some cavalry horses that they had left in the vicinity of Dog Creek, a tributary of the Arikara River, which is the northern fork of the Republican River. They were spotted by eight Cheyenne Dog Soldiers, who gave chase. Kyle and his men took cover and returned fire, killing three warriors. When the Indians broke off their attack, Kyle's men joined the main column. That night, the Cheyenne struck the bivouac area of the Pawnee scouts in an attempt to steal horses.

William Frederic "Buffalo Bill" Cody (1846–1917) in 1911. (*National Archives*)

Two Medals of Honor were awarded for actions on July 8. Corporal Kyle received one for his leadership and bravery in the incident with the Dog Soldiers, and Mad Bear (Coruxtechodish), a sergeant in the Pawnee Scouts, earned one that evening for running out from the command in pursuit of a dismounted attacker. Mad Bear, also called Angry Bear by some sources, was shot down and badly wounded by a bullet from his own unit.

The next day, Carr ordered the column to move north, still following the trail of Tall Bull's Cheyenne. As they worked their way upstream on Frenchman Creek (now Frenchman River), they discovered several abandoned campsites, indicating that they were on the right track. By July 11, they were near Summit Springs, moving northward toward the South Platte River, when the scouts spotted Tall Bull's village. The Cheyenne were camped, waiting for low water in the river so they could cross and go north into Wyoming.

Carr organized his tired troops for a three-pronged afternoon assault and launched a surprise attack. The 5th Cavalry and the Pawnee killed more than fifty of the Cheyenne, while losing none of their own. Among the dead was Tall Bull himself, shot down either by Buffalo Bill Cody or by Frank North, depending upon which of the Old West legends one believes.

There were also two hostages, previously seized by the Cheyenne in Kansas, present at the camp and they were shot by their captors as the troops attacked. Susanna Alderdice was killed, but Maria Weichell was wounded and recovered.

Though a number of Cheyenne had managed to escape, the Summit Springs battle had dealt a decisive blow against the Cheyenne raiders operating in western Kansas and Nebraska. Historically, it would prove to be a decisive blow against the military cohesiveness of the Dog Soldiers. Their victory would give Carr and his 5th Cavalry the military equivalent to what Custer and the 7th Cavalry had achieved at the Washita, although it never inspired nearly the newspaper attention that Custer was getting.

In mid-September 1869, the 5th Cavalry deployed from Fort MacPherson into the Republican River country once again, this time under the command of Lieutenant Colonel Thomas Duncan, and accompanied by three companies of the 2nd Cavalry. As before, they were joined by the Pawnee Scouts and guided by Buffalo Bill. Their only major confrontation with the Indians came on September 26, on Prairie Dog Creek. A small Lakota raiding party ambushed Cody and several others as they were hunting. When other troops arrived on the scene, the Lakota fled. The troops chased them but killed only one. One of a myriad of tributaries flowing north into the Republican from Kansas, Prairie Dog Creek had been where Tall Bull's Cheyenne had ambushed Major Royall's detachment in October 1868.

There would be no winter campaign in 1869. President Grant, much to the surprise of the field officers who expected a tough Indian policy from the former general, decided to give peace a chance. Further offensives would be put on hold while he gave the Indian Bureau wide latitude in drafting an Indian policy for the West.

Despite the peace initiative, fighting in Nebraska continued into 1870, with a notable small-unit action on May 17. Five men of Company C of the 2nd Cavalry under Sergeant Patrick Leonard held off the attackers for two hours, killing at least one. For the action, the Congressional Medal of Honor was awarded to the sergeant, as well as to privates Heth Canfield, Michael Himmelsback, George Thompson, and Thomas Hubbard, who was wounded.

The next major battle in Nebraska to warrant the Congressional Medal of Honor occurred on the South Loup Fork of the Platte River (also known as the South Loup River) on April 26, 1872. When a band of Minneconjou rustled some horses belonging to the Union Pacific Railroad, Captain Charles Meinhold took a detachment of 3rd Cavalry troopers out to recover them. Buffalo Bill Cody, then working as a scout with the regiment, joined the patrol. Cody took eleven men to scout the south bank of the river, while Meinhold and the balance of the command rode across to reconnoiter the opposite shore. It was Cody's contingent who found the Minneconjou. They attacked, killing three, one of whom was claimed by Cody. The Congressional Medal of Honor was awarded to Sergeant John Foley, Private William Strayer, and Sergeant Leroy Vokes, as well as to Cody. Buffalo Bill's medal was rescinded in 1916, along with many others that had been awarded to civilians in the nineteenth century because it was felt that only military personnel should have them. But in June 1989, the U.S. Army Board of Correction of Records restored the medal to Buffalo Bill.

The early 1870s would not see a repeat of 1869's intense campaigning on the central Plains. The region was no longer a major theater operations in the Indian Wars, but action on the Northern Plains had barely begun.

The Southwest Theater and the Hualapai War

In the early postwar years, media attention was focused on the Plains. The Fetterman Fight, the Fort Laramie Treaty, and Custer on the Washita symbolized the Wild West to readers of the eastern newspapers, but in the desert Southwest, the U.S. Army would be waging the continuing war against the Hualapai (also spelled Hualpai) in Arizona, and the Apache in both Arizona and New Mexico.

The Southwest was a distant and divided theater. It was split between the Division of the Missouri, commanded out of Chicago, and the Division of the Pacific, with headquarters in San Francisco—and it was distant from both.

As General James Carleton's California brigade had departed at the end of the Civil War, the Territory of Arizona organized its own volunteer militia to deal with the Apache raiders. The latter were analogous to the Cheyenne Dog Soldiers, insofar as they were a militant contingent of a larger tribe. However, because the Apache were a tribe that consisted of a myriad of smaller, self-contained groups and bands, the raiders did not have the overall cohesiveness of the Dog Soldiers. Each group of raiders was defined by the leader of that group, invariably a man who inspired respect and loyalty, and who could get his group to follow him into battle.

Not all of the Arizona Territory volunteers were Anglo-Americans. As with Frank North's companies of Pawnee Scouts on the Plains, members of tribes such as the Maricopa and Pima, who were traditional enemies—and victims—of the Apache were organized as companies of Arizona Territorial militia. These individuals were especially adept at tracking the elusive raiders in the rugged Southwest terrain, but showed little mercy when they had their enemy in their crosshairs. In one such incident in March 1866, a group of Pima under Lieutenant John Walker, a part-Wyandot officer, tracked about two dozen Apache into the Sierra Pinal, ambushed them and wiped them out to the last man.

For its part, the U.S. Army sent the 14th Infantry Regiment and the recently formed 8th Cavalry Regiment into Arizona Territory. The first major offensive campaign for the 8th Cavalry came in 1867, against the Yavapai in northwestern Arizona. Operating out of Fort Whipple, near Prescott, two 8th Cavalry companies under Captain James Williams were involved in four separate fights in the Black Mountains and Verde River country between April 10 and 18, in which an estimated fifty-three Yavapai and one trooper were killed.

Shortly after this sweep, the 8th Cavalry conducted operations in western Arizona in response to an attack by two hundred Hualapai on Beale's Spring Station that left one civilian dead. In two battles on May 30 and June 14, the troops killed an estimated thirty-five Hualapai with no Army losses. In a further incident on July 9, the Hualapai managed to seriously wound two troopers while losing three of their own.

The Hualapai War continued into the winter, with search and destroy sweeps into the mountains of western Arizona. Major combat occurred on November 7, 1867, and on January 14, 1868. In the former incident, elements of the 8th Cavalry and the 14th Infantry Regiment attacked a Hualapai village, killing nineteen and capturing seventeen women and children. In the latter, an 8th Cavalry patrol out of Fort Mojave stumbled across a Hualapai encampment in Difficult Canyon. In the ensuing firefight, twenty-one Hualapai were killed. In another fight on March 21, the casualty figures were more evenly balanced. A 14th Infantry Regiment contingent escorting a mail train was ambushed by an estimated seventy-five Hualapai, and the battle left two dead on each side.

The 8th Cavalry in Arizona

As the Hualapai War seemed to be winding down during the middle of 1868, the postwar phase of the Apache War in Arizona was heating up. It was a true guerrilla campaign, characterized by numerous small unit skirmishes rather than battles with dozens of combatants on either side.

Despite the sideshow aspect of the Southwest Theater in 1868 and 1869, the 8th Cavalry actions in Arizona during this period resulted in an unusually high number Congressional Medals of Honor, although in one action, they shared the harvest of medals with the 1st Cavalry. These incidents provide an insight into the campaign that was ongoing in Arizona at the time.

The first such 8th Cavalry action came on April 29, 1868. Private James Reed received his Medal of Honor for "defending his position against a party of 17 hostiles under heavy fire at close quarters." He was the only trooper not wounded in the battle. A month later, on May 30, two men from Company L, Privates Edgar Aston and William Cubberly, volunteered to search for a wagon passage out of a four-thousand-foot valley in which an infantry column was bogged down. They scouted through six miles of rugged territory, in which Apache warriors were known to be present, and located a usable wagon route. On their way back, they were ambushed, but successfully beat off the attack. For this, each man received the Medal of Honor. On October 21, Private John Kay, another Company L man, received his medal for retrieving a severely wounded comrade who was under fire from a sizable Apache force.

These three 8th Cavalry Medals of Honor were awarded for specific actions. On July 24, 1869, thirty-seven additional Medals of Honor were awarded to enlisted men from companies B, E, K, and L of the 8th Cavalry for "Bravery in scouts and actions against Indians" from August to October 1868, or simply in 1868, with no further details mentioned in their citations.*

*The men included Heinrich Bertram, James Brophy, Patrick Burke, Thomas Carroll, George Carter, Charles Crandall, Charles Daily, William Dougherty, James Dowling, Henry Falcott, Daniel Farren, William Folly, Nicholas Foran, Charles Gardner, Thomas Gay, Patrick Golden, John Hall, Clamor Heise, Thomas Higgins, John Keenan, Albert Knaak, James Lawrence, Thomas Little, Bernard McBride, James McDonald, Daniel McKinley, Charles McVeagh, George Miller, John O'Callaghan, Michael O'Regan, Lewis Phife, William Shaffer, Benoni Strivson, John Sutherland, Andrew Weaher, Joseph Witcome, and George Wortman.

Eight Medals of Honor were awarded on September 6, 1869, to 8th Cavalry sergeants and enlisted men for bravery in actions against Indians in Arizona. The dates of the action were noted in the citations as "1868 and 1869," again with no further elaboration.* Meanwhile, Julius Stickoffer, a Swiss-born saddler with Company L of the 8th Cavalry, earned a Medal of Honor far to the north at Cienaga Springs, Utah, on November 11, 1868.

During 1869, the string of Congressional Medal of Honor actions would continue for the troopers of the 8th Cavalry in Arizona Territory. On June 4, Private Joseph Watson and Bugler George Gates of Company F each "killed an Indian warrior and captured his arms," thus earning the medal. On June 29, Private Albert Sale, also of Company F, earned his on the Santa Maria River for "killing an Indian warrior and capturing his pony and effects." On July 3, the Medal of Honor was awarded for "Conspicuous gallantry in action," in the Battle of Hell Canyon to three men from Company L: Sergeant Sanford Bradbury, Corporal Paul Haupt, and Corporal John Mitchell.

On August 25-26, the 8th Cavalry's Company E was in action on the Agua Fria River north of present-day Phoenix, while Company F was fighting at Seneca Mountain. Three men from the former company earned the Medal of Honor in their engagement: Sergeant Cornelius Donovan, Corporal Michael Corcoran, and Private Frank Hamilton.[†]

A month later, as Company D was fighting at Red Creek on September 23, three men earned the Medal of Honor, Corporal George Ferrari, Sergeant Charles Harris, and Private John Walker, not to be confused with Lieutenant John Walker of the Arizona Pima militia. Three Company L privates, David Goodman, John Raerick, and John Rowalt, would be awarded the Medal of Honor for gallantry in action near a stream then known as Lyry Creek on October 14.

October 1869 found Cochise and his Chiricahua Apache band terrorizing the southeast corner of Arizona Territory in the Pedregosa and Chiricahua Mountains north of the border with the Mexican State of Sonora. On October 5, his Chiricahua attacked a stage near Dragoon

---

*These men included Jacob Gunther, David Matthews, Sergeant James McNally, Sergeant John Moriarity, Samuel Richman, Otto Smith, and Wilbur Taylor.

[†]Among those fighting at Seneca Mountain, five were awarded the medal for their gallantry in action: Private Herbert Mahers, Private John Moran, Corporal Philip Murphy, Corporal Thomas Murphy, and Corporal Edward Stanley.

Springs and killed six people aboard. When word reached nearby Fort Bowie, Company G of the 1st Cavalry responded. After an exhausting forced march, they caught up with Cochise and his men in the Pedregosa foothills on October 8. A fierce firefight ensued in which the Chiricahua lost a dozen warriors, but Cochise and most of the band escaped.

Captain Reuben Bernard of the 1st Cavalry promptly set out from Fort Bowie with a larger force—consisting of men drawn from Company G of the 1st Cavalry and Company G of the 8th Cavalry—bent on tracking Cochise and his Chiricahua, and forcing the elusive decisive battle. He picked up Cochise's trail on October 18, but the next day, the Chiricahua sprang an ambush. The battle raged, but Cochise held the high ground and Bernard knew his force was too light to overcome the Apache advantage, so he made a tactical withdrawal. Bernard lost two men, and claimed having killed a dozen Chiricahua.

This battle in the Chiricahua Mountains was one of the most studded by Medal of Honor actions of any in the Indian Wars. There were eighteen such medals awarded to the men of the 1st Cavalry, while the 8th Cavalry added twelve to their tally for the year.* Another 8th Cavalry trooper, Private John Carr, was awarded a Congressional Medal of Honor for actions in the Chiricahua Mountains on October 29, and Sergeant John Crist of the 8th Cavalry earned the medal for actions on November 26.

It is illustrative of the composition of the U.S. Army in the West during this era that about half of these men, especially in the actions during the summer, were foreign born, most of them natives of Ireland or Germany.

George Crook, Desert Warrior

If George Custer's name is the most recognized by the general public among the U.S. Army officers of the Indian Wars, that of George Crook

*The men of the 1st Cavalry included Sergeant Frederick Jarvis, Trumpeter Bartholomew Keenan, Private Charles Kelley, Corporal Nicholas Meaher, Private Edward Murphy, Sergeant Francis Oliver, Corporal Thomas Powers, Private James Russell, Private Theodore F. Smith, Private Thomas Smith, Private Thomas J. Smith, Private William H. Smith, Private George Springer, Private Thomas Sullivan, Private James Sumner, Sergeant John Thompson, Private Charles Ward, and Private Enoch Weiss. From the 8th Cavalry, there were Corporal Charles Dickens, Private John Donahue, Private Edwin Elwood, Private John Georgian, Blacksmith Mosher Harding, Private Edward Pengally, Private Charles Schroeter, Private Robert Scott, Sergeant Andrew Smith, Private William Smith, Private Orizaba Spence, Saddler Christian Steiner, and Private John Tracy.

has become synonymous with the wars' most successful type of operational doctrine.

An 1852 graduate of the U.S. Military Academy at West Point, Crook had served with the 4th Infantry Regiment in the Indian Wars on the California-Oregon border before the Civil War, and had distinguished himself during both conflicts. He led the Ohio Brigade at Antietam, and was a division commander at Chickamauga and in the Shenandoah Valley campaign.

Having risen to the brevet rank of major general, Crook reverted to his regular rank of lieutenant colonel after the war, and again he was posted to the West. Here, in the years immediately after the Civil War, he would develop the tactics that would be his trademark in the Southwest. Crook's methods, considered revolutionary for the U.S. Army of the late 1860s, were a harbinger of the special forces doctrine of the late twentieth century. He modeled them after the techniques of the frontiersmen and the Indians, who lived off the land.

His basic tactical element was a small, highly mobile, and well-armed unit composed of skilled marksmen, rather than a large, slow-moving column. He did away with supply wagons, using a pack-string of mules instead. He hired experienced guides who knew the lay of the land intimately, and he actively enlisted members of the same tribe that he pursued.

Rather than integrating Indian scouts into each military unit, he drilled his regular troops to think and operate as Indians would. Crook himself became a voracious student of the flora, fauna, and terrain of the environment where he would operate, and he studied his opponents so that he came to understand them as well as they understood one another. This astute preparation would serve him well in the Paiute War.

THE PAIUTE WAR

George Crook was sent to Fort Boise in 1866 as commander of the 23rd Infantry Regiment and tasked with a mission similar to what he would later face in the Southwest. Under terms of a treaty negotiated in 1864, the tribes of the upper Great Basin, including Klamath, Modoc, and Paiute bands, had agreed to settle on the Klamath Lake Reservation in southern Oregon. However, not all of the bands within these tribes subscribed to the treaty, and raids against travelers and settlements occurred throughout eastern Oregon and southern Idaho Territory. Crook's first job after the Civil War was to bring the outlaw bands into compliance.

On December 18, 1866, he went into the field with forty-five men of the 1st Cavalry in pursuit of a band of Paiute raiders in southern Oregon. Eight days later, he successfully ambushed them on the Owyhee River, killing 30 and capturing seven. A month later, on January 29, 1867, Crook's 1st Cavalry troopers ambushed another renegade Paiute band at Steen's Mountain, killing sixty and capturing twenty-seven. His aggressive campaign continued into summer. In July, he led one hundred 1st

General George Crook (1828–1890), West Point Class of 1852, was perhaps the best U.S. Army field commander to serve in the Indian Wars of the West. (*National Archives*)

Cavalry troopers and about the same number of Indian scouts on a sweep through the region that netted forty-six Paiute killed or captured.

In September 1867, Crook led his command into the desolate lava beds of northeastern California, which were recognized as some of the most difficult terrain in which any of the Indian Wars would be fought. On September 26, Crook led a 280-man mixed force of 1st Cavalry and 23rd Infantry Regiment troops against a hundred-man force of mainly Paiute warriors who had taken up a defensive position in a section of the lava beds known appropriately as Infernal Caverns. In two days of fighting, Crook had killed twenty Indians and had captured or wounded another fourteen, but he had lost eight of his own men.

Crook's relentless campaigning eventually achieved the desired objective. On July 1, 1868, Weawea, the last of the outlaw Paiute leaders, came into Fort Harney in central Oregon to sign a treaty agreeing to live on a reservation. He credited Crook with eventually wearing him down. The U.S. Army also recognized Crook for his accomplishment. General Halleck, the divisional commander, made him the acting head of the

Department of the Columbia, a post he would hold until his reassignment to the Southwest—despite Crook not having a permanent general's rank.

CROOK IN THE SOUTHWEST, AND THE TONTO BASIN WAR

The increasing intensity of the Apache guerrilla war in Arizona Territory in 1868-1869 was the catalyst for the War Department decision to separate the territory from the Military Department of California on April 15, 1870, and designate it as the independent Department of Arizona under the Division of the Pacific. The headquarters would be located at Whipple Barracks near Prescott. Initially, the department would be commanded by General George Stoneman, but he would soon be replaced by George Crook.

Under the new government peace process promulgated by President Grant, the Indian Bureau established a network of supply depots and temporary reservations across Arizona where the Apache who had disowned the raiders and the guerrilla war could receive rations and other annuities. One such depot was at the U.S. Army's Camp Grant, near Tucson.

Despite the largesse and the annuities of the of the federal government, not all of the many autonomous Apache bands subscribed to the peace process, and the leaders of the bands who did often had little or no influence over young hotheads within their communities who looked upon raiding as a right of passage.

On April 27, 1871, Lieutenant Howard Cushing led a nineteen-man contingent of Company E, 3rd Cavalry troops into the Whetstone Mountains of southern Arizona Territory on a scouting mission reminiscent of those of two and three years previously. The objective was to locate any Chiricahua, and among them, hopefully, Cochise himself.

On May 5, the men were ambushed by an estimated 280 Apache. There ensued a ferocious firefight, during which Cushing was killed and eight men would earn the Congressional Medal of Honor for gallantry in action.*

While the president's peace policy may have pleased the eastern humanitarian movement, the settlers living in Arizona and the other ter-

---

*They were Private Hermann Fichter, Private John Kilmartin, Private Daniel Miller, Sergeant Henry Newman, Private John Nihill, Sergeant Rudolph Stauffer, Private John Yount, and Sergeant John Mott. Mott pulled a wounded Lieutenant Cushing out of the line of fire, but Cushing was later killed. Another Medal of Honor action occurred in the Whetstone Mountains on July 13, 1872. Irish-born Private Michael Glynn of the 5th Cavalry singlehandedly beat off an attack by eight Apache, killing or wounding five.

ritories in the West were still living in fear of the periodic raids. On April 30, they took the law into their own hands. Three days after Cushing had gone into the Whetstone Mountains, a group of 148 vigilantes, mainly residents of Tucson, launched a midnight attack upon the Apache encampment at Camp Grant, which was under the supervision of the Indian Bureau. In an orgy of rape, torture, and killing, between 86 and 150 Apache, primarily women and children, lost their lives.

Another victim of the Camp Grant Massacre was President Grant's peace process. The eastern media denounced the bloodbath, while the Apache lost what little trust they had for the U.S. government.

Indian Bureau Commissioner Vincent Colyer went to Arizona as a peace emissary, where he was joined by Brigadier General Oliver Otis Howard. A deeply religious military officer who had lost his right arm during the Civil War, Howard nevertheless went on to command XI Corps at Gettysburg. After the war he headed the Freedman's Bureau and founded the all-black Howard University. Now he was being tapped by Grant as peace emissary for Arizona. However, the Arizona citizens wanted firmness, even in the wake of the Camp Grant pogrom. Arizona Territorial Governor Anson Safford lobbied the U.S. Army to replace General Stoneman with Crook, and he got his wish.

Crook arrived in June 1871, even as the peacemakers were coaxing Apache onto reservations, and immediately set out to get a sense for the lay of the land. Crook's plans for a campaign remained on hold, as the official plan was to give peace a chance. In the face of these noble efforts, the Wickenburg Massacre, near the town of that name on November 5, started tipping the scales the other way. In this incident, a group of Apache attacked a stage, killing six men and leaving a wounded man and woman for dead. The peace thereupon unraveled, with forty-four people killed in various raids through September 1872.

In one incident on August 27, 1872, two 5th Cavalry mail couriers were ambushed in Davidson Canyon, near the U.S. Army's Camp Crittenden. One man was killed, and Corporal Joseph Black was in the process of being tortured when Sergeant James Brown intervened with four others. He was awarded the Congressional Medal of Honor for saving Black, defeating a superior force, and delivering the mail to Tucson.

Less than two weeks later, Crook was on a peace mission of his own. Acting on a tip that the perpetrators of the Wickenburg incident were there, he rode into the Date Creek Reservation with a small 5th Cavalry contingent on September 8. He was planning to discuss the surrender of the Wickenburg perpetrators. As he was meeting with Chief Ochocama, one Apache tried to shoot Crook. In the firefight that followed, seven Apache were killed, and four of Crook's party wounded. During the action, Sergeant Frank Hill earned the Congressional Medal of Honor. As the citation states, Hill had "Secured the person of a hostile Apache Chief, although while holding the chief he was severely wounded in the back by another Indian."

By now, it was clear that the peace process was not working. The raids continued, settlers died, and Cochise remained at large as a rallying point.

On November 16, Crook began the long-awaited offensive. As has been demonstrated by Carson in Arizona, and by Hancock on the Plains, a winter offensive could be effective owing to its logistical impact on the enemy. If captured or destroyed, stockpiles of food and other supplies could not easily be replenished during the cold winter months.

Crook moved into the Tonto Basin at heart of central Arizona Territory, using elements of the 1st and 5th Cavalry and the 23rd Infantry Regiment. He configured them as five light and mobile units, just as he had done with his men in Oregon. Each of the columns would be accompanied by Indian scouts, including Paiute and Hualapai, as well as Apache.

The first major combat of the winter offensive came on November 25, when eleven Apache warriors were killed in a firefight at Hell Canyon. Another action on December 7 in the picturesque red rocks area near present-day Sedona, Arizona, resulted in thirteen Apache and one 5th Cavalry member killed. During the following week, a 23rd Infantry Regiment detachment under Captain George Randall chased the Apache led by Chief Delshay into the Sierra Mazatzal. Here they fought two significant battles that resulted in a total of twenty-five Apache killed in action.

On December 28, the companies of the 5th Cavalry cornered what they thought was Delshay's band, in a cave in the Four Peaks area of the Tonto Basin. Obviously trapped, the Indians refused to surrender, perhaps thinking that their position was defensible. After trading insults for a while, the troopers sprayed the cave with rifle fire. When the dust settled, it was discovered that the people within were not Apache, but their Yavapai allies. Of the seventy-seven occupants of the cave, fifty-seven had

Apaches photographed in Arizona by C. S. Fly in 1871. (*National Archives*)

been killed. The survivors were mainly women and children, and most of them were wounded.

As the campaign progressed into January, three actions warranted the Congressional Medal of Honor, all of them to the 5th Cavalry. Irish-born Private James Lenihan earned his medal at Clear Creek on January 2, 1873, and Sergeant William Day was awarded his for a series of actions on the Agua Fria and East Verde rivers between December 30 and January 19. On the former date, Day was leading a patrol that surprised and killed six Apache warriors. On the latter date, he led his patrol to attack and kill a group of Apache that were sending smoke signals warning of the approach of the troops. The third Medal of Honor of the month was awarded posthumously to Private George Hooker, who led a charge against an Apache stronghold on Tonto Creek. He was the only trooper killed in a firefight that claimed seventeen Apache.

The next Medals of Honor in the Tonto War were awarded for actions in the Battle of Turret Mountain, which took place between March 25 and 27. As Captain George Randall's 5th Cavalry and 23rd Infantry Regiment troops worked their way up from the Verde River and into the mountains, they knew that the Apache knew they were coming. The Apache, however, did not know exactly where they were. A group of soldiers snuck to the top of the ridge, located the Apache and launched a surprise attack. An estimated twenty-three Apache were killed, to no losses among Randall's men. For their actions during this encounter the Medal of Honor was awarded to Sergeant Daniel Bishop, Sergeant James Hill, and Private Eban Stanley, all of the 5th Cavalry, and to Sergeant William Allen of the 23rd

Infantry Regiment. An additional nine Medals of Honor were awarded to members of the 1st and 5th Cavalry for the 1872-1873 winter campaign in which no specific date or place is noted in the citation.*

Ten of Crook's Indian scouts—Alchesay, Blanquet, Chiquito, Jim, Elsatsoosu, Kelsay, Kosoha, Machol, Nannasaddie, and Nantaje—were also awarded the Medal of Honor for actions during the 1872-1873 winter campaign. They were among only a handful of Indian scouts to receive the award. Both Alchesay and Jim were given the rank of sergeant, and Elsatsoosu was made a corporal.

The Battle of Turret Mountain essentially ended the winter campaign. In the weeks that followed, many Apache surrendered at reservations, or scattered so deeply into the mountains of the Southwest that the cavalry patrols saw no sign of them. The war was not, however, finished.

A series of skirmishes that would occur through the summer of 1873 included several actions for which troopers would receive the Congressional Medal of Honor. Samuel Hoover, a bugler with Company A of the 1st Cavalry, earned his in the Santa Maria Mountains on May 6, 1873. Sergeant Richard Barrett of the same company would earn his for leading a charge against the Apache at Sycamore Canyon on May 23. Sergeant Patrick Martin of Company G, 5th Cavalry, was awarded the Medal of Honor for a series of actions in June and July at Castle Dome and in the Santa Maria Mountains.

Early in July, the warfare spilled across the divisional demarcation line into New Mexico. When the Apache raided at settlement near Las Cruces, Captain George Chilson responded with a small detachment of 8th Cavalry troops out of Fort Selden near the present-day U.S. Army White Sands Missile Range. Chilson's men trailed the Apache through rough terrain into the Canada Alamosa, finally forcing them into a shootout, in which three Apache and one trooper, Corporal Frank Bratling, were killed in action.[†]

---

*These were awarded to Sergeant James Blair, Sergeant Lehmann Hinemann, Private James Huff, Sergeant Henry Hyde, Private Moses Orr, and Sergeant William Osborne, all of the 1st Cavalry. Those awarded to 5th Cavalrymen went to Sergeant James Bailey, Sergeant Clay Beauford, and Sergeant James Turpin.

[†]Bratling was posthumously awarded the Congressional Medal of Honor. For service in both the battle and pursuit, four of the other men, Sergeant Leonidas Little, Sergeant James Morris, blacksmith John Sheerin, and Private Henry Wills, also received Medals of Honor.

Schuyler and Randall Against the Apache

George Crook's 1872-1873 campaign effectively curtailed the surge of Apache raids that had reached epidemic proportions in the year before he was brought in to take over the Department of Arizona. When he was finished, the majority of the Apache who had once been raiders now chose a more reliable, if less exciting, life on the reservations.

Crook's winter offensive is recalled as one of the most successful campaigns of the Indian Wars in the West, and it earned Crook a well-deserved promotion to the permanent rank of brigadier general. This having been said, the operation did not totally stop the Apache from raiding in Arizona. To address this problem, Crook would continue the offensive pressure in the winter of 1873-1874. In this campaign, one of the key leaders would be Lieutenant Walter Scribner Schuyler of Company K, an 1870 West Point graduate and now with the 5th Cavalry Regiment, based at Camp Verde.

Beginning in mid-September, the determined Schuyler led a series of search and destroy sweeps through central Arizona in the Verde River and Cave Creek country. Like Crook had on a large scale, Schuyler used Indian—especially Yavapai—scouts as a key element in his operations. Indeed, he often had more Indians riding with him than cavalrymen, and they were even more anxious to kill the Apache than were the troopers. On September 23, a detachment of Yavapai scouts attacked an Apache encampment on Hardscrabble Creek, killing fourteen Apache before Schuyler had even arrived on the scene.

Like Crook, the relentless Schuyler kept up his offensive even in weather when Indians would not expect to find the U.S. Army on the prowl. On December 4, Schuyler tenaciously attacked two Apache encampments during a heavy snowstorm. He killed fifteen in a dawn surprise attack. In another dawn attack near Cave Creek on December 23, Schuyler used part of his column as a decoy to get the Apache to betray their positions. This attack cost the Apache nine killed in action, with no Army losses.

Schuyler continued his operations into 1874, conducting a series of offensive sweeps into the Verde River country in January, into the Superstition Mountains east of Phoenix in March, in the Aravaipa Mountains east of Tucson in April and Four Peaks country in the Tonto

Basin through May 25. In five battles, his Company K troops killed seventy-seven Apache, including Chief Natotel, and took more than two dozen prisoners.*

Among the other officers who led operations through the winter of Schuyler's string of successful campaigns was Major George Randall, who had—as a captain—figured prominently in the campaigns of the previous winter. Randall went into the Sierra Pinal in March 1874 with a 5th Cavalry Regiment force, guided by Apache scouts. In two major attacks on Apache encampments on March 8 and April 2, his troops killed sixty Apache and captured about seventy-five, mainly women and children.

A detailed comparison of the Schuyler and Randall campaigns illustrate two contrasting tactical doctrines. Schuyler followed the pattern that Crook had used so effectively against the Paiute in 1866-1867, while Randall used the large formation approach such as Sibley, Sully, and Hancock had employed on the Plains. Schuyler went out with a relatively small command, fewer than the fifty-eight men that were average for a cavalry company in the postwar U.S. Army. Randall took elements of six companies. Schuyler moved fast, traveling light and lean. With a small force, roughly equivalent to the size of a band of Apache raiders, he was able to maintain stealth and employ the element of surprise.

Randall, on the other hand, was able to launch a surprise attack in neither of his major battles. Furthermore, lack of adequate communication and coordination between separate elements of his large, cumbersome force led to confusion and mistakes.

Both commanders made extensive use of Indian guides. As Crook had found in Oregon, and the previous year in Arizona Territory, the use of Indian auxiliaries had a profoundly demoralizing effect on the Apache. This effect was far deeper than even Crook might have expected.

Of course, both cavalry forces were able to inflict high casualties on the Apache, while capturing and destroying hard-to-replace stockpiles of food and other supplies. The aggregate effect was that the Apache were beaten—at least for a while.

---

*Congressional Medals of Honor awarded to men of the 5th Cavalry for actions in Arizona during this period went to Sergeants George Deary, Bernard Taylor, and Rudolph von Medem. Taylor was cited for rescuing the 5th Cavalry's Lieutenant King from the Apache on November 1, 1874.

The Modoc War

Back in the Great Basin, the postscript to George Crook's Paiute War was the last major campaign to be fought by the U.S. Army in California. It took place among the desolate Lava Beds in the remote northeastern part of the state where Crook had battled the Paiute in September 1867. The Lava Beds here consist of a vast jumble of jagged rocks strewn across a landscape that consists a withering maze of narrow canyons and semi-subterranean tunnels, each composed of the same razor-sharp rocks.

The Lava Beds were the traditional homeland to the Modoc people, a tribe whose population stood at just a few hundred. The area is scarcely more populated in the twenty-first century than it was in the middle of the nineteenth century. Of all the tribes living in the barren Great Basin, they had the environmental booby prize of the bleakest corner. For the Modoc, the only good thing that could be said of the Lava Beds was that they were the best naturally occurring defensive terrain that the U.S. Army had thus far had occasion to fight in.

By the treaty negotiated in 1864, the Modoc had been relocated to the Klamath Lake Reservation in southern Oregon. Here, however, they found themselves bullied by the more numerous Klamath and Paiute. They numbered just a few hundred, and they found themselves at the bottom of the pecking order in any social situation.

As was the case with many isolated tribes, they had names that were unpronounceable to outsiders, so they were given English nicknames which sound almost like practical jokes. There were Boston Charley, Scarfaced Charley, Bogus Charley, Steamboat Frank, and Hooker Jim. Intriguing stories probably precipitated the nicknaming of Ellen's Man George and Shacknasty Jim. The shaman most closely associated with the command and control of the Modoc resistance was known as Curley Headed Doctor. The most influential leader was Kientpoos (or Kintpuash), known by the English name of Captain Jack.

The Modoc, who longed for the sharp black rocks of home, jumped the reservation in 1865 and went back to the Lava Beds. They were coaxed back to the reservation at the end of 1869, but Captain Jack's band remained for only a few months before returning to the Lost River section of the Lava Beds.

In July 1872, after discussions between the Indian Bureau and the War Department, Superintendent of Indian Affairs Thomas Odeneal finally decided that Captain Jack's Modoc group should be forced back to the reservation. The task fell to the U.S. Army, specifically to forces under the command of Brigadier General Edward Richard Sprigg Canby, a highly regarded officer who had previously served as commander of the Department of the Columbia. The chain of command ran down through Lieutenant Colonel Frank Wheaton of the 21st Infantry Regiment at Camp Warner and German-born Major Johnny Green of the 1st Cavalry at Fort Klamath, to Captain James Jackson, who would lead a forty-three-man contingent of Company B into the Lava Beds.

Captain Jack and his followers, which included about sixty warriors, were camped on the Lost River near Tule Lake when Jackson's cavalry approached on November 29. Jackson demanded that they return to the reservation, and an argument ensued. Either Jackson or Scarfaced Charley discharged a weapon, and a gun battle ensued. The Modoc escaped with one of their number having been killed, although Jackson would claim that he killed sixteen. Two soldiers were killed in action. As the Modoc retired to the other side of the lake, they killed between thirteen and eighteen settlers, further aggravating tensions.

The Modoc withdrew into the labyrinth of the Lava Beds, knowing that it was a virtually impregnable fortress that greatly favored the defender. The U.S. Army would soon become painfully aware of this fact. After the Battle of Lost River, Lieutenant Colonel Wheaton took command of the operation, leading three companies of his own regiment, plus three of the 1st Cavalry under Major Green, and about one hundred state militiamen. They moved into the Lava Beds, taking up positions surrounding the natural fortress that would come to be known as Captain Jack's Stronghold, or simply the Stronghold.

At dawn on January 17, 1873, the U.S. Army went in with a three-pronged assault, supported by artillery fire, that was expected to make quick work of the Modoc defenders. It was not to be. The troops found themselves in impassible topography, taking fire from an unseen enemy. Wheaton tried to maneuver and reposition his forces, but the terrain and the Modoc rifle fire made this impossible.

At the end of the day, the U.S. Army withdrew, having suffered thirty-seven casualties, including eleven killed in action. There were no

General Edward R. S. Canby (1817–1873), left, seen in his Civil War uniform. Captain Jack, far right, and Schonchin in prison shackles. Both were hung in October 1873. Captain Jack's body was preserved and taken on tour back east where it could be seen for a ten-cent admission charge. (*National Archives*)

Modoc lost in the Battle of the Stronghold. This defeat of the U.S. Army—that had recently defeated the Confederacy—by a people who were perceived as unsophisticated, played as a scandal of immense proportions in the newspapers.*

With military action having failed, the Indian Bureau insisted on using diplomacy, and former Superintendent Alfred Meacham himself was sent west to negotiate with the Modoc. For two months, Captain Jack and Curley Headed Doctor toyed with the venerable Washington bureaucrat, and finally, the Indian Bureau asked for Army backup. William Tecumseh Sherman ordered Canby himself to assume direct command of operations at the Stronghold, and Wheaton was replaced by Colonel Alvin Gillem.

In March, Canby established a tight perimeter around the Stronghold, as Meacham continued to try to negotiate. Meanwhile, Toby Riddle, the

*For actions on January 17, both Major Green and Army contract surgeon Dr. John Skinner were awarded the Congressional Medal of Honor. Green's citation recalls that "In order to reassure his command, this officer, in the most fearless manner and exposed to very great danger, walked in front of the line; the command, thus encouraged, advanced over the lava upon the Indians who were concealed among the rocks." Dr. Skinner, meanwhile, "Rescued a wounded soldier who lay under a close and heavy fire . . . after two soldiers had unsuccessfully attempted to make the rescue and both had been wounded in doing so."

wife of Frank Riddle, an interpreter employed by Canby and Meacham, whispered that she had heard talk of a plot to kill the negotiators, a warning that they did not take seriously.

On April 11, Good Friday, the two sides met at the Panmunjom of the Lava Beds, a tent erected in the desolate no-man's-land between the Army's perimeter and the Stronghold. Meacham was accompanied by Reverend Eleasar Thomas, a Methodist minister and member of the negotiating team, and by General Canby, who went unarmed and in full dress uniform. The Modoc demanded that the Lava Beds be made their reservation, and Canby gave no quarter, insisting that they would have to do as they were told.

At this, Captain Jack pulled a gun and shot Canby in the face, as Ellen's Man George cut his throat. Several Modoc, including Shacknasty Jim, opened fire on Meacham, and Boston Charley shot Reverend Thomas. Only Meacham would survive, although he was seriously wounded. As the Modoc prepared to scalp their victims, Toby Riddle warned them that soldiers were coming. The Modoc escaped back into the Stronghold as news of Canby's death was telegraphed to the nation. He was to be the highest ranking officer, and the only man with the permanent rank of general to be killed in action in the Indian Wars.

If Wheaton's failure to win the Battle of the Stronghold was bad for the Army's image, the murder of an unarmed general in the midst of negotiating was an outrage. Sherman ordered General John Schofield, commanding the Division of the Pacific, to go on the offensive and he passed the order down through the chain of command by way of Brigadier General Jefferson Davis (no relation to the Confederate president).

In the field, Gillem needed no urging. He moved into the Stronghold in a campaign not unlike that undertaken by Wheaton in January. Five companies of the 1st Cavalry, six of the 4th Artillery, two of the 12th Infantry Regiment, and three of the 21st Infantry, assisted by Indians hostile to the Modoc, methodically swept the Stronghold beds by day, as howitzers rained shells on the oceans of black rock by night. On April 17, after three days of operations, the troops discovered that the Modoc had abandoned the Stronghold, leaving behind just eleven bodies, eight of them women.

Nine days after wrapping up the actions in the Stronghold, Gillem ordered Captain Evan Thomas of the 4th Artillery to lead a sixty-five-man search and destroy force across the Lava Beds in search of the escaped

Modoc. Evans's command consisted of men from his own regiment as well as from the 12th Infantry Regiment. Having seen no sign of the enemy during the morning, Evans ordered a lunch stop near Hardin Butte. As the soldiers ate, a twelve-man patrol went out to reconnoiter, but they were promptly ambushed.

At the sound of gunfire, another patrol went to investigate, and they too were clobbered. The Modoc then attacked the main force with withering rifle fire from high ground as the troops scampered about in confusion. When the battle was over,

A U.S. Army picket station in the lava beds. Because of the siege-like conditions, the Modoc War produced some of the few photographs from the Indian War period showing actual combat. (*National Archives*)

the two dozen Modoc slipped away, having lost nobody killed in action. Among the troopers, eighteen enlisted men were killed, seventeen were wounded, and five out of six officers were dead, including Evans.

The Hardin Butte Fight on April 26 was one of the most lopsided losses that the U.S. Army would suffer anywhere in the West. Morale had sunk to new depths, but it would continue to slump.

On May 7 and May 10, Captain Jack's men conducted two further ambushes of troops in the field. In the first attack, they captured horses from a wagon train while forcing the soldiers, three of them having been wounded, to flee. In the second fight, Captain Jack attacked a bivouac of three companies under the command of Captain Henry Hasbrouck of the 4th Artillery, killing two men. In this action, Ellen's Man George was the first Modoc to die since the last sweep through the Stronghold in April.

Hasbrouck pursued the Modoc, catching Hooker Jim's band on Willow Creek Ridge on May 19. Having put the Modoc on the run, Hasbrouck, along with 1st Cavalry detachments under Captain James Jackson and Captain David Perry, were able to capture the band piecemeal as they grew tired and slowed down. On May 22, Hooker Jim surrendered with the last of his group—and then he promptly offered to help the Army capture Captain Jack.

Armed by the soldiers, the turncoat Modoc caught up with Captain Jack six days later and urged him to surrender. Jack refused, but the following day the Perry's cavalrymen picked up his trail. Again the Modoc were on the run, split into small groups that were easy pickings for the troopers. On June 3, Perry cornered Captain Jack in a cave and persuaded him to give up.

Though there was a great deal of popular sympathy for prompt executions of the Modoc leaders, they were put on trial before a military tribunal at Fort Klamath. Captain Jack, Boston Charley, and two others were found guilty of the murder of General Canby and were hanged. Hooker Jim and Shacknasty Jim were both pardoned for having turned sides, but all of the surviving Modoc captured in the Lava Beds were exiled to Indian Territory.

The net result of the publicity surrounding the Modoc War was the turning of national public opinion away from the peace process that President Grant had pursued during his first term in office. The peace process would be tested in other theaters as well.

TEXAS AFTER THE CIVIL WAR

Throughout the Civil War, as the Confederate Army was fighting for national survival east of the Mississippi River, Indian raids on the towns and settlements of West Texas had been on the increase. The Confederate Frontier Battalions, which had taken over the role of the much larger prewar U.S. Army force, fought a number of skirmishes, but for the most part Texans went on the defensive, withdrawing into settlements.

When the war ended, there was a great deal of political pressure for the regular U.S. Army to resume its prewar role in Texas, because the alternative would be state militias that would essentially be reconstituted Confederate regiments, with former Confederate troops led by former Confederate officers. While such a thing was not such a bad idea tactically, it was unpalatable to the politicians in Washington.

The period between the collapse of Confederate military effectiveness and a return of the U.S. Army was marked by increased Indian activity in the Lone Star State. The Comanche and Kiowa were active in the north, and in the south, the Mescalero Apache routinely crossed the Rio Grande from their sanctuary in northern Mexico.

The Kickapoo, who had migrated south from Indian Territory to northern Mexico to avoid the Civil War actions that spilled over from adjacent states, were also a factor. This was especially true after an incident in January 1865 in which a Kickapoo party was mistaken for Comanche raiders and attacked. Captain Henry Fossett's Confederate battalion, and a larger contingent of Texas militia under S. S. Totten, trailed the Kickapoo to their camp on Dove Creek, a tributary of the Concho River near San Angelo. A dawn attack was met with stiff resistance, and the Kickapoo forced the Texans to retreat.

Though the Kickapoo had won the battle and had killed twenty-six Texans, they had lost nearly that many of their own. They had done nothing to provoke the attack, but the Kickapoo were sufficiently angered that they went on the offensive, conducting a growing number of raids throughout Texas in the early years after the Civil War.

Prior to the Civil War, the U.S. Army had a very comprehensive system of forts across Texas, but most were abandoned and not occupied once the war started. Four or more years of deferred maintenance meant that a great deal of rehabilitation had to be done to bring the military to its 1860 level of readiness. During the latter part of the decade, the U.S. Army gradually reestablished itself in West Texas, making cavalry patrols a regular part of operations, with units such as the 6th and 9th Cavalry Regiments involved in occasional skirmishing.

On September 14, 1868, the 9th Cavalry fought a major battle against a band of Lipan and Mescalero Apache who had attacked a wagon train south of Fort Stockton in West Texas. In the Battle of Horsehead Hill, the troops killed more than two dozen raiders, effectively crippling that particular band for the time being.

THE KIOWA-COMANCHE WAR

By the late 1860s, all of West Texas was essentially a war zone in the ongoing conflict between the U.S. Army and the Kiowa and Comanche, who, as often as not, combined forces. In 1869, two 9th Cavalry encounters with the Kiowa and Comanche on the tributaries of the Brazos resulted in significant battles. On September 16, 1869, four companies under Captain

Henry Carroll and Captain Edward Heyl had been on patrol for two weeks when they discovered an encampment of about two hundred lodges on the Salt Fork of the Brazos near the Llano Estacado. Carroll ordered an immediate assault that resulted in an estimated twenty Indian casualties, and three troopers were wounded.

A month later, another five-company 9th Cavalry patrol under Captain John Bacon was one element of a large sweep conducted by the regiment. As they prepared to break camp on the Freshwater Fork of the Brazos on the morning of October 28, the troops were attacked by an estimated five hundred Kiowa and Comanche warriors. Though the two hundred troopers were surprised, they fought back bravely. In fact, it was a rare instance of troops suffering a surprise attack by an overwhelming enemy in which they carried the day.

Bacon and his command not only beat the attackers and forced them to flee; they also chased them into the following day, inflicting further casualties. The 9th Cavalry suffered eight men wounded, while killing an estimated forty of the enemy. Both Bacon and Lieutenant Byron Dawson were commended for their service.

In a separate action on the Brazos the same day, Lieutenant George Albee received the Congressional Medal of Honor for attacking eleven Indians while leading a three-man reconnaissance mission. Albee and the others "drove them from the hills, and reconnoitered the country beyond."

Another small unit action in Texas resulting in the award of the Medal of Honor occurred on May 20, 1870. Sergeant Emanuel Stance of the 9th Cavalry was leading a patrol near Kickapoo Springs, when his men intervened to save a wagon train that was under attack from a band of Comanche. Stance received the medal for leading the initial charge, as well as a counterattack when the Comanche reappeared.

Kiowa and Comanche raiding parties continued to confront the U.S. Army wherever possible. On July 20, Captain Curwen McClellan was leading a fifty-six-man 6th Cavalry detail in pursuit of raiders that had hit a stagecoach, when he ran into 250 Kiowa warriors from Kicking Bird's band on the North Fork of the Wichita River. McClellan was immediately surrounded, but the troops broke out and the two sides led a running gun battle across the Plains until the troops finally reached the South Fork of the Wichita, and Kicking Bird broke off his pursuit. Two soldiers and an estimated fifteen Kiowa were killed in action. For gallantry in action during the July 20 fight, thirteen Medals of Honor were awarded.*

On October 5, Captain William Rafferty's Company M of the 6th Cavalry caught up with a Wichita raiding party at Spy Knob near the Wichita River.†

Meanwhile, the U.S. Army was crippled from an unlikely source, President Grant's peace process. Rules of engagement were promulgated under which the Comanche and Kiowa were provided with a sanctuary in the heart of the Plains. In the south, the Apache could slip

Tene-Angopte, Kicking Bird, (c. 1835-1875), photographed by W. S. Soule. (*National Archives*)

back across the Rio Grande into Mexico, while the northern tribes could raid Texas, then cross the Red River into Indian Territory, with the U.S. Army troops based in Texas prohibited from following.

Operations within Indian Territory had to be cleared with the Indian Bureau agents at the Fort Sill Reservation, and these agents were members of the nonviolent Society of Friends, the Quakers. They operated under the theory that all of the Indians in Indian Territory were to remain safe from the U.S. Army, regardless of whether they had been living there peacefully all their lives, or they had just returned from ambushing a wagon train in Texas the night before.

It was a situation similar to that which would frustrate U.S. Air Force pilots during the Korean War, when they were forbidden from chasing

---

*The recipients were Corporal John Conner, Sergeant George Eldridge, Sergeant Thomas Kerrigan, Sergeant John Kirk, Sergeant John May, Private Solon Neal, farrier Samuel Porter, Corporal Charles Smith, Sergeant Alonzo Stokes, Corporal James Watson, bugler Claron Windus, Sergeant William Winterbottom, and Corporal John Given, one of those killed in action.

†Actions during the ensuing battle resulted in the Congressional Medal of Honor being awarded to Private James Anderson, Corporal Samuel Bowden, post guide James Doshier, Corporal Daniel Keating, Sergeant Michael Welch, and Private Benjamin Wilson.

Chinese MiGs north of the Yalu River, and in the Vietnam War, when much of North Vietnam was declared by the United States government as a sanctuary for enemy aircraft. The rules of engagement would change for the U.S. Air Force in Vietnam in May 1972 with Operation Linebacker I, just as they had for the U.S. Army in Texas 101 years earlier.

In May 1871, General William Tecumseh Sherman was conducting a fact-finding excursion into Texas, when he found himself nearly at the center of the action. On May 18, as he and his party crossed the Salt Creek Prairie south of the Red River near Fort Richardson, they were under the eye of a large Kiowa raiding party, which included the noted leaders Satanta (White Bear), Satank, and Big Tree. Their shaman, Mamanti, told them to attack the next group that they saw traveling the road, so Sherman was spared near-certain death. The Kiowa did as their medicine man had instructed as a wagon train pulled into view. That night, a survivor of the subsequent wagon train massacre staggered into Fort Richardson, where Sherman was listening to complaints about the Kiowa from the Texas citizenry.

Nine days later, Sherman was at Fort Sill, Indian Territory, when the Kiowa raiders rode into their "sanctuary" to ask for the government annuities that were paid to the people on the reservation. Satanta even had the temerity to brag about the Salt Creek Massacre. Sherman ordered the Kiowa leaders arrested and sent back to Texas to stand trial for murder. Satank was later shot while trying to escape, but both Satanta and Big Tree were eventually sent to prison.

To carry out the new and more aggressive policy ordered by Sherman, the U.S. Army had in place an energetic young officer who would figure prominently in the Indian Wars in the West in the coming decades. An 1862 graduate of the U.S. Military Academy at West Point, Colonel Ranald Slidell Mackenzie had commanded troops in five battles in the Shenandoah campaign during the Civil War, and after the war he was tapped to command the new 41st Infantry Regiment. On February 25, 1871, he was assigned to lead the 4th Cavalry at Fort Concho, Texas. The regiment moved its headquarters to Fort Richardson in March, putting it in the forefront of operations against the Kiowa and Comanche.

During the summer and autumn of 1871, Mackenzie undertook a series of 4th Cavalry patrols into the remote Texas Panhandle and the Llano

General Ranald Slidell MacKenzie (1840–1889), left, West Point Class of 1862, led the 4th Cavalry Regiment in the important campaigns on the southern Plains. (*National Archives*) Quanah Parker (1853–1911), right, was a principal leader of the Quahadi Comanche in the 1870s. He was the son of Comanche leader Nocona, and Cynthia Ann Parker, who had been captured by the Comanche as a child in 1836. (*Author*)

Estacado in an effort to drive renegade Indians back onto their reservations. In addition to eight companies of cavalry, Mackenzie had a detachment of scouts drawn from the Tonkawa tribe, traditional enemies of the Comanche.

Early on October 10, Mackenzie's troops were ambushed by the Comanche at the mouth of Blanco Canyon in the Llano Estacado. Among them was the twenty-six-year-old Quanah Parker, the young raiding party leader whose mother, Cynthia Ann Parker, had been captured by the Comanche as a child in 1836, and whose father, Nocona, had been killed in 1850 at Pease River.

Lieutenant Robert Carter and a small detachment rode in pursuit, but about one hundred Comanche warriors surrounded the soldiers. Carter rallied the men, who successfully defended themselves from the much larger force. For his presence of mind and his bravery, Carter would be awarded the Congressional Medal of Honor, although not until 1900. The citation recalls that Carter "Held the left of the line with a few men during the charge of a large body of Indians, after the right of the line had retreated, and by delivering a rapid fire succeeded in checking the enemy until other troops came to the rescue."

Mackenzie pursued Parker and his warriors up Blanco Canyon for several days until a winter storm forced the 4th Cavalry to withdraw.

The following year, Mackenzie was again in the field with five companies of his 4th Cavalry, a company of 24th Infantry Regiment, and a contingent of Tonkawa scouts. On September 29, 1872, they detected and attacked a Comanche encampment on the North Fork of the Red River. In a firefight that lasted several hours, Mackenzie lost four troopers killed in action. Estimates of the Comanche dead vary widely, but average forty-five. The 4th Cavalry took 124 prisoners, mainly women and children, and destroyed the captured Comanche property. A large horse herd was also snatched, but the Comanche managed to take the horses back in a raid two nights later.*

The following spring, Mackenzie and his battle-hardened 4th Cavalry were sent south to deal with the cross-border raids by the Kickapoo and the Lipan Apache. While Mackenzie was under strict orders to not violate the Indian Territory's Red River boundary, he was given a green light to cross the Rio Grande, just as United States forces in Vietnam a century later were allowed to operate inside Cambodia and Laos as long as there was plausible deniability at the upper tiers of the chain of command.

At dawn on May 18, 1873, even as the Modoc War was reaching its crescendo in California, the 4th Cavalry launched a devastating attack on a large Kickapoo encampment near the town of Remolino in Mexico. The troops killed nineteen Kickapoo and captured forty-two, while losing only one man. Though it was technically an international incident, Mexico did not object to having the raiders removed from its territory, and the mission had the desired result of effectively ending cross-border raids by the Kickapoo.

---

*The Red River fight resulted in nine Congressional Medals of Honor being awarded, including one to Sergeant William Wilson. The latter was Wilson's second Texas Theater Medal of Honor awarded in 1872. His previous action had been chasing cattle rustlers in the Colorado Valley. Another 1872 Medal of Honor had been awarded to Private Franklin McDonald on August 5 for "Gallantry in defeating Indians who attacked the mail" near Fort Griffin, Texas.Medals were also given to Private Edward Branagan, farrier David Larkin, Corporal Henry McMasters, Sergeant William McNamara, Corporal William O'Neill, blacksmith James Pratt, Private William Rankin, and Sergeant William Foster.

In the meantime, the advocates of the peace process were lobbying for the release of the imprisoned Satanta and Big Tree. The negotiations came around to a promise from the government that they would be released if Kiowa raiding was curtailed. Things were reasonably quiet in the autumn of 1872 and through the summer of 1873. The two leaders were released in October and the Kiowa raids soon resumed. The 4th Cavalry struck back with an ambush of a Kiowa and Comanche raiding party on the West Fork of the Nueces River on December 10.

As the raids continued into the spring of 1874, the Kiowa and Comanche were joined by Cheyenne. On June 27, a group of raiders including members of all three tribes struck Adobe Walls, the trading post settlement on the Canadian River in the Texas Panhandle where Kit Carson had fought the Kiowa ten years earlier.

In the second Battle of Adobe Walls, two dozen buffalo hunters and a few shopkeepers managed to successful hold off a force of several hundred warriors. Among the warriors was Quanah Parker, who killed one of the defenders during the fight, while two others were killed in the initial assault in the predawn darkness. Among the defenders was an extraordinarily skilled marksman named Bartholomew "Bat" Masterson, who would go on to have a colorful career in the West as a frontier lawman, gambler, and newspaper editor. Using their highly accurate hunting rifles, Masterson and the others managed to kill more than a dozen of the Indians, while wounding many more, including Quanah Parker. When the attackers broke off the fight two days later, the outpost was abandoned as being too difficult to defend in the face of what was rapidly turning into a major war.

The Red River War

In the wake of the second Battle of Adobe Walls, General Sherman lobbied Secretary of War William Belknap and Secretary of the Interior Columbus Delano for the authority to recognize the deteriorating situation in northern Texas as a state of war and to revoke the sanctuary status of Indian Territory for the tribes who were involved in the raids in Texas.

The conflict that would be known as the Red River War began at Adobe Walls, but the U.S. Army offensive technically got underway on July 20, 1874, when Sherman received word from Washington that he had the official authorization that he had requested. His strategy called for a five-pronged pincer that would converge on the Texas Panhandle like spokes of a wagon wheel, sweeping the opposing forces into the headwaters of the Red River at the hub.

Sherman delegated operational command to General John Pope of the Department of the Missouri and General Christopher Augur, late of the Department of the Platte, now in command in Texas and the parts of Indian Territory that were not in Pope's command. Ranald Mackenzie would drive north from Texas with a 470-man 4th Cavalry contingent, forming the prong at the five-o'clock position on the wheel. Major William Price would be coming in from New Mexico with four companies of the 8th Cavalry at the nine-o'clock position. They would press south through Indian Territory. Driving through Indian Territory from the two-o'clock position to the east would be Lieutenant Colonel John "Black Jack" Davidson's 10th Cavalry Buffalo Soldiers out of Fort Sill, and Lieutenant Colonel George Buell's 11th Infantry Regiment at the four-o'clock position.

The one-o'clock prong would be the eight-hundred-man spearhead of Pope's force, Colonel Nelson Appleton Miles of the 5th Infantry Regiment, who took four companies of his own regiment, plus eight of the 6th Cavalry, into the field. Miles, like Mackenzie, was one of the Army's rising stars, although, unlike Mackenzie, he was part of a new generation of senior officers who had risen through the ranks during the war, rather than beginning his career with a West Point commission. During the Civil War, Miles had led troops at Antietam, Chancellorsville, and Fredericksburg, ending the war as a brevet major general. Though he was an excellent officer in his own right, it did not hurt his career to be married to Mary Hoyt Sherman, the niece of both Ohio Senator John Sherman and Commanding General William Tecumseh Sherman.

Among the Indians, many saw the large forces gathering and rushed to sign up at the agencies to become part of the reservations. One Comanche band, led by Big Red Food, arrived after the sign-up deadline, so Black Jack Davidson turned them away.

Big Red Food took his people up to the Anadarko Agency on the Washita River, hoping to turn themselves there among the Wichita, Caddo, and other tribes. That might have worked, had not the agents at Anadarko caught the Comanche stealing food that had been doled out to other tribes. They sent to Fort Sill for help. Davidson arrived on the scene with three companies of 10th Cavalry on August 22 and demanded that Big Red Food surrender. He countered by trying to stampede the cavalry horses. Shots were fired and the confrontation became a melee. The fight continued into the next day, with troopers trading fire with Big Red Food's people amid the encampments of hundreds of uninvolved Indians of various tribes. Four civilians at the Anadarko Agency were killed, along with an estimated sixteen Indians.

The first major battle after the Red River campaign officially started had occurred outside the context of the intended offensive—and it had the unexpected result of inflaming the emotions of the Indians who were predisposed to be hostile. These warriors, who might not have done so if not for the Anadarko incident, rode out to join Satanta, Quanah Parker, and the various groups of raiders.

Meanwhile, Nelson Miles and his forces had reached the headwaters of the Red River more than one hundred miles west of the Anadarko Agency, fighting the blistering heat and lack of forage for their livestock, and lack of water for both man and beast. By August 30, they were near the mouth of Palo Duro Canyon, when they were attacked by an estimated six hundred Comanche and Kiowa. The battle surged back and forth as the long column of soldiers organized themselves. As soon as the troops were able to bring their howitzers and Gatling guns to bear on the attackers, the tide of battle shifted abruptly. The cavalry was then able to carry the fight to the nearby Indian encampments, and the enemy was routed. Had Miles not been at the absolute limit of his supplies, he might have been able to have undertaken a pursuit, and to have forced another decisive battle. As it was, the Indians lost seventeen warriors killed in action, and a substantial quantity of supplies, while no soldiers were lost.

Miles linked up with the two hundred-man 8th Cavalry column out of New Mexico on September 7 in the Llano Estacado, where he was awaiting supplies that were coming south from the big depot at Camp Supply on the North Fork of the Canadian River. While Miles remained in place, Price's 8th Cavalry pressed eastward.

As Miles was camped with the largest concentration of forces in the general offensive, a substantial combined Kiowa and Comanche force was about to launch a withering offensive of their own—nearly one hundred miles to the north and east.

The second week of September would be marked by some of the most intense fighting in multiple locations that would ever be seen in Texas or on the Southern Plains. On September 9, Miles's supply train was ambushed. Three dozen wagons, escorted by a 104-man detachment of infantry and cavalry under the command of Captain Wyllys Lyman was attacked between the South Fork of the Canadian and the headwaters of the Washita by what was estimated at nearly five hundred Comanche and Kiowa, including those bands of the latter tribe led by Satanta and Big Tree.

Lyman circled the wagons in classic fashion and established a defensive perimeter. The siege continued for several days in heat that reached the century mark. The surrounded men were able to tap the supplies in the wagon, but ran desperately short of water until a rainstorm moved in. The siege was not lifted until September 14, when a scout who had slipped out returned from Camp Supply with a relief column.

Meanwhile, the combined Kiowa and Comanche bands were simultaneously in action against two other U.S. Army units. On September 12, they attacked both Price's 8th Cavalry column and a seven-man detachment that Miles had sent out to check on the progress of his supply train. Price's troops were ambushed on the Dry Fork of the Washita by a superior force consisting of many of the same warriors who had been tormenting the Camp Supply wagon train for the preceding three days. Recognizing that he was outnumbered, Price ordered his men into a defensive position. They managed to hold of the Indians for several hours, killing two before they finally withdrew. Price suffered no men killed in action, but the Indians did kill several cavalry horses.

The attack on the reconnaissance party that Miles had sent out resulted in a heroic defensive action, which like that at Beecher's Island in 1868, became a staple of Western folklore. They had reached the Washita River when they were surrounded by an estimated 125 Indian warriors.

Sergeant Zachariah Woodall, who was in command, and three others were wounded almost immediately as the men took refuge in a shallow buffalo wallow. It looked as though they would be quickly overcome and killed. As the Indians circled the wallow for the kill, the men returned fire and prepared to defend themselves. They held out for a day and a half, and miraculously only one man, Private George Smith, was killed. On September 14, after the Indians had given up and moved on, Price's 8th

A nineteenth-century Kiowa ledger drawing that may depict the Buffalo Wallow fight. (*University of Texas*)

Cavalry arrived on the scene. The men of the Buffalo Wallow Fight would all be awarded the Congressional Medal of Honor.*

While Miles was awaiting his supplies, Ranald Mackenzie had established a field depot at Blanco Canyon under the guard of three infantry companies, and moved the 4th Cavalry north into the Llano Estacado on September 20. By now, the Kiowa and Comanche were on an offensive roll, and on September 26, they rolled into the 4th Cavalry. It was an abortive, nocturnal, horse-stealing raid that failed to net any horses and alerted Mackenzie to the Indian presence in the area.

Within thirty-six hours, Mackenzie had located what turned out to be the primary encampment of the Kiowa and Comanche, and their Cheyenne

---

*They included five 6th Cavalry troopers, Sergeant Woodall, Private Smith, Private John Harrington, Private Peter Roth, and Corporal Edward Sharpless, as well as two civilian scouts, Amos Chapman and William "Billy" Dixon, a veteran of the Battle of Adobe Walls earlier in the summer. In 1916, the general review of all Medals of Honor rescinded those of civilians such as Chapman and Dixon. Dixon, who was still alive, refused to surrender his, and in June 1989, the U.S. Army Board of Correction of Records restored the honors to the scouts of the Buffalo Wallow Fight. The Medal of Honor was also awarded to a number of the other men involved in the actions of the bloody second week of September. From the 5th Infantry Regiment, they included Sergeant William DeArmond, Sergeant Fred Hay, Corporal John James, Corporal John J. H. Kelly, Thomas Kelly, Sergeant John Knox, Sergeant William Koelpin, and Sergeant John Mitchell. Those from the 6th Cavalry included Sergeant George Kitchen, Corporal William Morris, Frederick S. Neilon (aka Frank Singleton), and Josiah Pennsyl.

allies. It stretched for three miles, deep inside the steep walls of Palo Duro Canyon, near the mouth of which the Indians had clashed with Miles a month earlier. On September 28, Mackenzie launched his attack, sending an assault force down the face of the cliffs. Most of the Indians managed to escape, but they left behind an irreplaceable stockpile of food and supplies, as well as more than 1,400 head of horses. Their loss of this materiel would change the course of the Red River War.*

For the Indians, the offensive fervor of September evaporated after the Battle of Palo Duro Canyon. The U.S. Army now pressed its advantage. Judging by the number of abandoned villages and supplies that the five prongs found as they scoured the Plains during October, the Indians were not only on the defensive, they were on the run. Many, including Satanta himself, surrendered. Others, notably Quanah Parker, remained in action.

During November, there was a series of skirmishes along McClellan Creek, one of the headwater streams of the Red River. On November 6, a twenty-eight-man 8th Cavalry patrol under Lieutenant Henry Farnsworth clashed with about one hundred Cheyenne led by Grey Beard. The opposing sides lost two and four men, respectively, before Farnsworth withdrew under cover of darkness.

Two days later, Lieutenant Frank Baldwin of Miles's command was returning to Camp Supply with empty wagons when he came upon Grey Beard's camp. He put his infantry in the wagons and used them as precursors to twentieth-century armored personnel carriers to attack the encampment. It worked. As the personnel carriers rolled into the camp, Baldwin's cavalry chased the escapees. He lost none of his soldiers, while killing twenty Cheyenne.†

Most important, Baldwin's men were able to capture Cheyenne supplies, and recover Adelaide and Julia German, aged five and seven, who

---

*For actions on the Red River during the last week of September, the Congressional Medal of Honor was awarded to Private Gregory Mahoney, Private William McCabe, and Corporal Edwin Phoenix of the 4th Cavalry's Company E, and to Private Adam Paine of the Indian Scouts.

†Two men of the 4th Cavalry's Company A were awarded the Congressional Medal of Honor for actions during the first week of November, Corporal John Comfort and farrier Ernest Veuve. One Medal of Honor was awarded to Sergeant Dennis Ryan of the 6th Cavalry for "Courage while in command of a detachment" on December 2, and three additional 4th Cavalry Medals of Honor went to Private Frederick Bergerndahl of the regimental band, Private John O'Sullivan on Company I, and Lieutenant Lewis Warrington for actions on December 8.

had been taken captive when their parents were murdered by the Cheyenne in Kansas two months before. Their two older sisters were repatriated the following year, having been raped and badly abused. The story of the German girls' ordeal was embraced by the newspapers and became a rallying cry for popular support for the Red River War.

The howling winds and heavy snow of winter suspended offensive operations. As the troops returned to the crackling fires of their forts, the Indians shivered and starved on the Llano Estacado. By March 1875, the numbers of Indians surrendering was increasing dramatically.

The capitulation process was not without incident. On April 6, more than 150 Cheyenne prisoners escaped from the Darlington Agency on the North Fork of the Canadian River, and were pursued and surrounded by elements of the 5th Infantry and 6th Cavalry. Among the Cheyenne were those who had been identified as having raped the German girls. Most were captured and eleven were killed.

Those not killed or captured fled upriver, where they joined another band. They were trailed by Lieutenant Austin Henely, who caught up with them on April 23 at Sappa Creek in Kansas. While another thirty-plus escaped again, the troopers surrounded nineteen warriors and eight women and children in a dry creek bed and gunned them all down. Henely was later disciplined and reprimanded for what came to be called the Sappa Creek Massacre.

Paradoxically, eight men of Company H, 6th Cavalry, were awarded the Congressional Medal of Honor for the battle at Sappa Creek. Six of them to men who, according to their citations, "waded in mud and water up the creek to a position directly behind an entrenched Cheyenne position, who were using natural bank pits to good advantage against the main column. This surprise attack from the enemy rear broke their resistance."*

In contrast to Sappa Creek, real heroism prevailed just two days later. Lieutenant John Bullis of the 24th Infantry Regiment and three part-Seminole, part-African-American scouts ambushed a group of thirty Comanche who were attempting to take a large herd of stolen horses across the Pecos River in Texas on April 25.

---

*These six were Private Peter Gardiner, Private Simpson Hornaday, Private James Lowthers, Sergeant Frederick Platten, Private Marcus Robbins, and Sergeant Richard Tea. The other two medals went to Private James Ayers and trumpeter Michael Dawson.

They attacked, despite the Comanche being present in larger numbers and armed with Winchester repeaters. It a bitter, see-saw battle, they captured and recaptured the horses, but finally were forced to withdraw. The scouts made it to safety, but then turned to go back and successfully rescue Bullis, for which Private Pompey Factor, trumpeter Isaac Payne, and Sergeant John Ward were awarded the Congressional Medal of Honor.

In March 1875 Ranald Mackenzie was given command at Fort Sill and control over the reservations upon which lived the Arapaho, Cheyenne, Comanche, and Kiowa. The Indian Wars were over for neither him nor Nelson Miles.

The Red River War ended on June 2, when Quanah Parker arrived at Fort Sill with 407 of his followers and 1,500 horses. Satanta was later returned to prison in Texas, where he committed suicide in 1878. Parker adapted to reservation life, took up ranching, and made a good deal of money, which he invested wisely. A wealthy man, he was influential in both tribal and non-tribal politics. He became a friend to many prominent Texans, as well as to President Theodore Roosevelt, and he lived until 1911.

THE BLACKFEET

In the far north of Montana Territory, off the general beaten track of the emigrant rails and settlements, lived the Blackfeet people. Algonquian-speaking, they were linguistically related to the Cheyenne and Arapaho rather than to the Sioux. They are called Blackfeet, not Blackfoot, but are known in their own language as Siksika (pronounced as sheek-sheek-awah). They are not to be confused with the unrelated Sihasapa, or Blackfoot Sioux. The Blackfeet people consist of three major branches, the Blood, the Piegan, and the Blackfeet proper.

In the wars that preceded the arrival of Europeans and Euro-Americans, the Blackfeet had risen to a position of military prominence in their corner of the Plains that was analogous to that enjoyed by the Sioux peoples farther south and east. The Blackfeet were also greatly feared by the Kootenai, Salish, and Nez Percé people who live across the Rocky Mountains, and who ventured east to hunt buffalo in Blackfeet territory. In a major ongoing war that coincided with the last quarter of the eighteenth century, the Blackfeet repeatedly defeated, and nearly annihilated, the Shoshone.

The first confrontation between the U.S. Army and the Blackfeet had occurred on July 26, 1806. During his epic expedition with William Clark, Meriwether Lewis had separated from the main body of the Corps of Discovery to conduct a survey of the upper reaches of Maria's River (today's Marias River) in northern Montana. Because it was calculated to be the major northern tributary of the Missouri, it would define the northern extent of the Missouri River drainage, and hence the northern boundary of the Louisiana Purchase. President Thomas Jefferson had hoped that this boundary could be determined to be north of 50 degrees, thus pushing north the border between the United States and the British territory that would become part of Canada. It was a purely economic issue. The more territory that could be made part of the United States by this geographic feature, the more of the potentially lucrative fur trade that could be diverted to Americans.

Having made his sextant calculations, Lewis was on his way south with George Drouillard and Privates Joseph and Reubin Fields. They had crossed the Two Medicine River when they came upon a large number of horses and eight riders who turned out to be Piegan. They camped together for the night, a pipe was passed, and Lewis presented a Jefferson peace medal and other token gifts. Lewis explained that he had made peace with other tribes, hoping to imply that he now hoped to make peace between the Blackfeet and the United States government.

It has been suggested that the Piegan became angry when they interpreted Lewis as having said that he had allied tribes such as the rival Shoshone against the Blackfeet, but nobody will ever know for certain. In any case, shortly before dawn, the Piegan attempted to steal the men's rifles. In the ensuing scuffle, the rifles were recovered but Reubin Fields killed one of the Piegan with a knife. Other Piegan, meanwhile, were attempting to steal the horses. One of them shot at Lewis, and he returned fire. Lewis hit the shooter, and the rest of the Piegan fled.

The Piegan had earlier alluded to a large encampment of their tribe nearby, so it was a foregone conclusion that a large number of warriors would be returning soon. The four members of the Corps mounted up and headed toward the Missouri River at top speed. Lewis estimated that they rode sixty-three miles before they rested, and another thirty-seven miles before they made camp. By now it was past midnight and they were traveling by the light of the moon. This was the only violent encounter between members of the Lewis and Clark Expedition and the indigenous people of the West.

Over the next six decades, the Blackfeet had contact with traders and trappers working the Missouri and its tributaries. Their first treaty with the United States government was signed by Lame Bull in 1855. However, it was not until after the Civil War that ranchers and settlers began making their way into central and northern Montana Territory in sufficient numbers for them to come into serious conflict with the Blackfeet.

As would be the case many other places in the West, the conflict initially took the form of raids by the Blackfeet on livestock herds. Late in 1869, an increasingly aggressive round of such raids, led by Mountain Chief—and coincidently in the Marias River area—involved several settlers being killed. The U.S. Army was ordered to respond.

Major Eugene Baker was dispatched from Fort Shaw, near Helena, with four companies of the 2nd Cavalry, along with a mounted contingent of 13th Infantry Regiment soldiers. By the time that the troopers arrived, Mountain Chief and his Piegan band had fled.

Rather than continue the pursuit, Baker ordered his men to attack the Piegan bands associated with Bear Chief, Bighorn, Black Eagle, and Heavy Runner on January 23, 1870. These people, who had not been involved in the raids, had been on good terms with both the settlers in the region and with the United States government. Therefore, they assumed that they were immune from attack, so they had not taken defensive precautions. The soldiers killed 173 Piegan and took another 140 into custody and destroyed the villages. Mountain Chief's band had gotten away.

The Marias Massacre was the last major incident between the U.S. Army and the Blackfeet, but it would create a climate of mistrust and antagonism that would last for generations.

THE NORTHERN PLAINS

After the abandonment of Fort Phil Kearny and the Bozeman Trail in 1868, the Lakota bands led by Red Cloud, Spotted Tail, and their allies ranged freely in the Powder River country of Wyoming and Montana Territories, and in adjacent parts of Dakota Territory, the latter including the Black Hills. A vast "Great Sioux Reservation" had been granted to the

Sioux and Northern Cheyenne tribes, mainly in Dakota Territory, but there was tacit recognition by the United States government of their right to roam and to hunt in the Powder River country and throughout southeastern Montana Territory. Since the United States had agreed to abandon the Bozeman Trail, the Indians assumed that they had also ceded the region through which it had run.

Red Cloud and Spotted Tail visited Washington, D.C., and received visits from government officials. The Indian Bureau established agencies in the name of both men in the northwestern corner of Nebraska. This was south of the reservation, but the locations were easily served by wagon trains on the Platte Road which were bringing supplies and annuities to the tribal members. Additional agencies were also established on the Missouri River in Dakota Territory, the Standing Rock, south of present-day Bismarck, and the Cheyenne River, near present-day Pierre, South Dakota.

The Indians whose bands had become signatories to the Treaty of Fort Laramie were able to hunt in the Powder River country, and also drop into the agencies for handouts of bacon, blankets, coffee, hard tack, and hunting rifles. The latter were, of course, also useful during raids on isolated settlements and emigrant trains. Those Indians who wished to continue raiding also found the agencies a useful place to park their women and children to be fed and clothed while they took to the field. This process worked well for several years, but there were those who expected it ultimately to collapse under its own weight.

Many of those who were displeased by the agency system on the Northern Plains were among the Indians themselves. These people found the process of accepting handouts personally degrading. One of the most prominent voices speaking out against reliance on the annuities was that of Sitting Bull (Tatanka Iyotake, or Sitting Buffalo Bull) of the Hunkpapa Lakota. He was more a shaman than a chief, but he was very influential among the community of bands who had not acquiesced to the treaties.

Though the Bozeman Road had been relinquished, an even more permanent road was being built across Montana Territory north of the Powder River country. The Union Pacific Railroad and Central Pacific Railroad had joined their rails at Promontory, Utah, in May 1869 to give the United States a transcontinental rail link. Now, a second transcontinental line across the northern tier of the United States, the Northern Pacific, was being constructed westward from Minneapolis and St. Paul, and eastward from the Pacific by way of the Columbia River Gorge. The link between the two outer segments would be through Montana Territory by way of the Yellowstone River valley. The Northern Pacific would not be complete until 1883, but by 1871, surveyors were already at work in Montana Territory, and they depended on the U.S. Army for protection.

Occasionally, the troops escorting the railroad surveyors came to blows with the Cheyenne and Lakota. On August 14, 1872, Major Eugene Baker of the 7th Cavalry, the perpetrator of the unwarranted Blackfeet massacre of two years earlier, tangled with an estimated four hundred Indians near Pryor's Fork of the Yellowstone. An early morning horse-stealing gambit by the Indians turned into a short firefight and a standoff that lasted most of the day before the Indians rode away. Baker lost one man, while killing two of the Indians.

Another incident a year later would involve the man whose name is synonymous with the Indian War history of Montana. Lieutenant Colonel George Armstrong Custer was riding with ten companies of his 7th Cavalry as part of a large force under Colonel David Stanley. Custer was with Captain Myles Moylan and a small advance party on August 4, 1873, when a small group of Lakota swept into their camp near the mouth of the Tongue River, planning to steal horses, decoy troops into an ambush, or both. Custer who gave chase and was abruptly surrounded by an estimated three hundred warriors. He scampered back to Moylan's encampment and they formed a defensive perimeter. After several hours and a failed attempt to start a grass fire to smoke out the troopers, the Indians broke off the attack. The regimental veterinarian and two other solders were killed.

A week later, the 450-man 7th Cavalry contingent was camped near the mouth of the Bighorn River when they were surprised by an early morning attack from approximately the same number of Lakota—although Custer later reckoned there were a thousand. The troops managed to beat off one concerted attack, but the shooting continued through the day. Most of the gunfire was ineffective. The Lakota lost four confirmed dead, three of them killed by sharpshooter Private John Tuttle before he became one of three soldiers killed in action. The Stanley expedition, of which the 7th Cavalry was a component, would remain in the field until September 23, but the Bighorn River battle was the last major combat they would experience.

The 7th Cavalry, with its support column and wagons, during the Black Hills Expedition of 1874. Lieutenant Colonel Custer heads the column, wearing light-colored buckskins and riding a dark horse. (*National Archives*)

Meanwhile, the situation at the Red Cloud and Spotted Tail agencies was deteriorating. As could be expected in places where large numbers of people crowd for handouts and little else, petty crime became rampant, and unruly gangs of thugs and bullies formed. This was an ideal recruiting ground for idealist warlords looking for young men to fight and die for a cause.

Among the easiest causes to grasp would be that of the Black Hills, the picturesque mountain country in southwestern Dakota Territory—now the state of South Dakota. Comprising roughly six thousand square miles were the same sort of defensible redoubt for the Lakota that the Llano Estacado had been for the Comanche, or the Lava Beds for the Modoc. As with any such hinterland, the Black Hills were rich in sacredness for the Lakota. For non-Indians, the Black Hills of the early 1870s represented riches of a more tangible kind. There were rumors swirling about that gold had been discovered within these hills. Though the Treaty of Fort Laramie had been vague about the boundaries of the immense reservation promised to the Sioux, the Black Hills were definitely within the boundary. This meant that any attempt to exploit the mineral riches within this venerable land was guaranteed to create ill will.

Meanwhile, General Phil Sheridan, commanding the Division of the Missouri was eyeing the military consequences of the Black Hills as a redoubt. He was envisioning a U.S. Army post situated within it as a presence for his troops behind enemy lines in case of war. In 1873, he started lobbying his superiors, including President Grant, and finally he got the green light to send a tentative reconnaissance mission into the Black Hills. To lead what would be designated as the Black Hills Expedition, Sheridan picked his old protegé George Custer.

The 7th Cavalry left Fort Abraham Lincoln, near Bismarck in Dakota Territory, on July 2, 1874, and were in the field just short of eight weeks. As surveyors mapped the heretofore uncharted region, Custer located a good site for a fort and his men spent time seeing for themselves whether the rumors of "gold in them thar hills" were true. They were.

Custer's after-action report read like a travelogue. He wrote glowingly of the timber resources and lovely scenery as though he was promoting the Black Hills for settlement—and he was not shy about mentioning the gold. Of course, his was not the first news to reach the outside world. The scout Charley Reynolds had carried dispatches to Fort Laramie that reached the East Coast even before Custer got back to Fort Abraham Lincoln. This news, received against the backdrop of the Depression caused by the Panic of 1873, had the barely unintended effect of creating the Black Hills Gold Rush. Over the coming years, thousands of miners poured into the Black Hills, and the notorious mining towns of Deadwood, Central City, and Lead were established. By 1880, the gold and silver mines in the region had an annual yield of about $7 million (about $120 million in current dollars).

With the Northern Pacific Railroad having gone bankrupt in the Panic of 1873, the U.S. Army would spend the 1875 campaigning season riding not against the Indians harassing surveyors, but against the trespassers who poured into the Black Hills. The government did the best it could, offering to buy the Black Hills for the equivalent of $100 million in today's dollars. The Lakota leadership, as might be expected, turned down the offer. However, among the Lakota, there was a growing rift between the militants and the moderates. Those such as Sitting Bull who had no inclination whatsoever to do business with the United States government were insulted. In the coming year, Sitting Bull's role among the Lakota would grow to almost mythical proportions.

6

The 1876 Campaign and the Great Sioux War

By 1876, the United States had put the divisiveness of the Civil War behind it and the robust young nation was looking forward confidently to the beginning of its second century. American technology rivaled that of any nation on earth. Its railway and telegraph mileage was the envy of any country in Europe. Alexander Graham Bell would patent the telephone in March, and by the end of the year, Thomas Alva Edison had patented the mimeograph.

The Centennial Exposition, the nation's first world's fair, would take place in Philadelphia through the summer. People would marvel at exhibits ranging from Remington typewriters to Hire's root beer to Heinz ketchup. The United States was celebrating the hundredth anniversary of the Declaration of Independence, but more important, the United States was celebrating itself as a leader among the civilized nations of the world.

The Indian Wars in the West were nearly as distant to most Americans in 1876 as they are to most Americans today. They were already a thing of nostalgia, mere grist for tabloids and dime novels. Yet far distant from the bustle of carriages, street cars, plate glass windows, and daily newspapers on the streets of the great cities of the East, there was a world where people hunted the buffalo, lived in buffalo hide tipis, ate buffalo meat cooked over an open fire, and got their news from the wind and clouds. Both civilizations were within the borders of the United States, and they had been in conflict since before 1776, but this was the year that they would face their ultimate collision in what would later be referred to as the Great Sioux War.

In a round of White House meetings in November 1875, President Grant made a decision that would define the military operations in the coming year. He met with Secretary of War William Belknap, Secretary of the Interior Zachariah Chandler, and Chandler's subordinate, Commissioner of Indian Affairs Edward Smith. From the West, Grant brought in General Phil Sheridan, commander of the Division of the Missouri, and his subordinate, General George Crook, the hero of the Apache Wars, who now commanded the Department of the Platte with headquarters in Omaha. The decision was to get tough. After spending much of his two terms in office favoring diplomacy, Grant would take the same approach against the recalcitrant tribes of the Powder River country that he had used against Robert E. Lee's Army of Northern Virginia.

Instead of forcing the prospectors out of the Black Hills, the U.S. Army would go after the "roamers" among the Indians who had stayed away from the reservations. Beyond the Great Sioux Reservation granted by the Treaty of Fort Laramie there was still the Powder River country, a vast wilderness that the U.S. government had tacitly surrendered to the tribes.

That was to stop. It was time to compel the Lakota and Cheyenne to comply with the treaty and move onto the reservations. Kit Carson had forced the Navajo to comply. The Paiute and Modoc had been compelled to relocate. It seemed that Crook had forced the Apache into submission. After many hard years of campaigning, the Comanche and Kiowa had been forced to comply. Now it was time for the Lakota and Cheyenne to make way for the inevitable march of American civilization.

Grant issued an order that all of the Lakota and Cheyenne bands should be out of the Powder River country and on the reservation by the end of January 1876. If not, the U.S. Army was to take whatever measures it deemed necessary to force them.

Strategy and Scandal

The strategic plan worked out by Sheridan and Crook called for a multi-pronged campaign directed against the Powder River country and all of southeastern Montana Territory. One prong would drive north out of Fort Fetterman on the Platte River, about seventy miles upstream from Fort Laramie. An eastern prong would move west from Fort Abraham Lincoln on the Missouri River. By now, the Northern Pacific Railroad had reached this point, so supplies could come either by rail or by steamboat on the Missouri. The western prong would move eastward along the Yellowstone

River from Fort Ellis, near present-day Bozeman, Montana. The Yellowstone River, which runs west to east across the northern edge of the Powder River country, was navigable by steamboats and could be used as a logistical highway for the latter two prongs of the assault.

General Crook, commanding the Department of the Platte, would lead the southern prong personally, but with operational command in the hands of his subordinate, Colonel Joseph Reynolds of the 3rd Cavalry.

General John Gibbon of the 7th Infantry Regiment, a veteran commander of forces at Antietam and the Wilderness during the Civil War, would lead the western column out of Fort Ellis. It was widely anticipated that General Alfred Terry, the long-time commander of the Department of Dakota, would place the eastern column out of Fort Abraham Lincoln under the command of Lieutenant Colonel George Armstrong Custer. Indeed, Custer had been intimately involved in the planning for the offensive, that is, until he was abruptly summoned to Washington, D.C., to testify before Congress.

During the winter, a long-brewing scandal reached its crescendo in Washington. An investigative reporter for the *New York Herald* named Ralph Meeker had written a series of articles suggesting that Secretary of War Belknap was involved in graft and corruption in the management of the trading posts at the Indian agencies in the West. Since 1870, Belknap's office had directly overseen the appointment and management of the post traders at U.S. Army forts in the West. Because the forts were usually located near—or co-located with—Indian agencies, such traders usually handled the lucrative trade with the Indians as well. The competition for the valuable trading licenses was intense. In 1874, Belknap had revoked the licenses at the posts on the upper Missouri River, putting them out for bid. At this point, the president's brother, Orvil Grant, appeared on the scene, using his influence to secure licenses for those who paid him a bribe.

In February 1876, even as the Army's campaign was being readied to take to the field, the Committee on Military Expenditures of the United States House of Representatives decided to hold hearings on the Belknap Scandal. The matter soon grew so serious that Belknap resigned. Grant replaced him with Alonso Taft on March 8.

George Custer was called to testify because he was a regimental commander at Fort Abraham Lincoln, one of the posts involved in the alleged graft. Custer testified on March 29 and several times in April, stating that he had heard rumors of the bribes, but other witnesses had even more damning testimony. Among them was Orvil Grant himself, who admitted his misdeeds.

The Belknap Scandal hearings were an integral part of a Washington power struggle between President Grant and his rivals, who were using Belknap to discredit the president. As events unfolded through the spring, with charges and counter charges being hurled back and forth, the media began to paint the colorful Custer as a star witness against Belknap and Orvil Grant. In fact, he had little firsthand knowledge of the corruption.

The Belknap faction, meanwhile, tried to implicate Custer himself in an effort to discredit him. Among those who believed that Custer was guilty both of graft, and of perjury in slandering poor Orvil Grant, was President Grant himself. Grant was so infuriated with Custer that he ordered Taft to order Sherman to order Sheridan to order Terry to relieve Custer of any command responsibilities in the upcoming campaign. In an effort to set things straight, Custer called on Grant at the White House on May 1, but spent the whole day waiting, while Grant refused to see him.

Meanwhile, Sheridan had ordered General Terry to personally assume command of the eastern prong of the assault in the Powder River country. Custer set out for Fort Abraham Lincoln, learning on May 4, as he changed trains in Chicago, that he had been ordered not to participate in the upcoming campaign that he had helped to plan. With Sheridan's endorsement, Terry wired Grant that he felt that Custer's 7th Cavalry was necessary for the operation, and that he wanted Custer to lead it. Finally, on May 8, Grant relented. Custer could lead the 7th Cavalry—but only as part of Terry's overall command.

Had it not been for the Belknap Scandal, Grant might have run for—and won—a third term as president. Had it not been for the scandal, Custer might have commanded the third prong of the 1876 campaign, and how might that have changed the course of history?

THE OPENING GAMBIT

It had been hoped, indeed planned, that the 1876 operations would open as a winter campaign, and be under way in February, but an especially severe winter hampered both logistics and the U.S. Army's ability to get troops into the field. General Crook and Colonel Reynolds jumped off first, heading out of Fort Fetterman, and traveling up the old Bozeman Trail on the first of March. The command consisted of nearly a thousand men, including five companies each of the 2nd and 3rd Cavalry, and two companies of the 4th Infantry Regiment, who were included mainly to guard the supply trains.

Crook and Reynolds suffered through a severe blizzard during the second week of March as they searched the valleys for sign of their elusive quarry. On March 16, they were working their way along the Tongue River, when they caught sight of a pair of Indians. Crook ordered Reynolds to take six companies and pursue them, while Crook waited with the slower elements of the command.

The following day, Reynolds crossed into the valley of the Powder River, and came upon an encampment containing an estimated seven hundred Cheyenne and Oglala Lakota. The troops attacked, but they were hit by gunfire from the high ground surrounding the camp. Reynolds ordered a tactical withdrawal, which was executed amid confusion and disorganization, and with the loss of four men killed in action.

The following morning, the Indians attacked Reynolds's camp, taking back the horses. Once the column had struggled back to Fort Fetterman through the deep snowdrifts, Crook ordered Reynolds to be court-martialed for bungling the attack and essentially losing the Battle of the Powder River.

There were moments of heroism in the Powder River Fight. Hospital steward William Bryan was awarded the Congressional Medal of Honor for having "Accompanied a detachment of cavalry in a charge on a village of hostile Indians and fought through the engagements, having his horse killed under him. He continued to fight on foot, and under severe fire and without assistance conveyed two wounded comrades to places of safety, saving them from capture." Other Medals of Honor went to two men of Company M, 3rd Cavalry, blacksmith Albert Glavinski and Private Jeremiah Murphy. The latter, "the only member of his picket not disabled, attempted to save a wounded comrade."

Despite Reynolds's mismanagement, it was clear to everyone, including Sheridan, long an advocate of winter campaigning, that the weather had played a critical role in the failure of the opening gambit in the campaign.

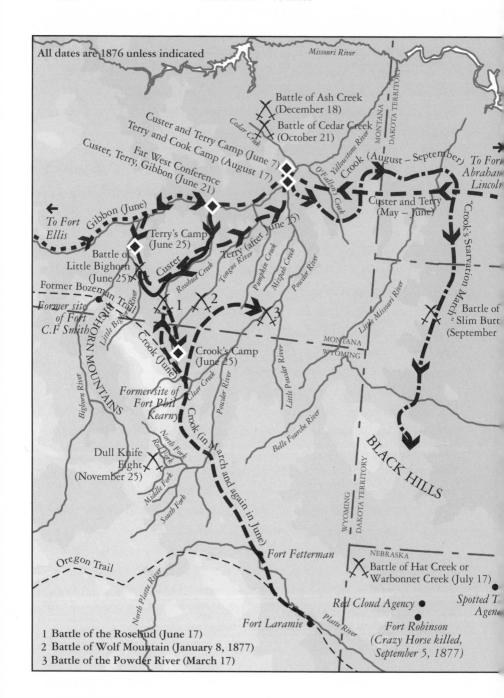

All dates are 1876 unless indicated

Missouri River

Battle of Ash Creek
(December 18)

Battle of Cedar Creek
(October 21)

Cedar Creek

MONTANA
DAKOTA TERRITORY

Custer and Terry Camp (June 7)
Terry and Cook Camp (August 17)
Far West Conference
Custer, Terry, Gibbon (June 21)

Yellowstone River
O'Fallon's Creek

Crook (August – September)

To Fort
Abraham
Lincoln

Gibbon (June)

To Fort
Ellis

Terry's Camp
(June 25)

Battle of
Little Bighorn
(June 25)

Custer

Rosebud Creek

Terry (after June 25)

Tongue River

Pumpkin Creek

Mizpah Creek

Powder River

Custer and Terry
(May – June)

"Crook's Starvation March"

Former Bozeman Trail

Former site
of Fort
C.F. Smith

BIGHORN MOUNTAINS

Little Bighorn River

Crook (June)

1   2   3

Crook's Camp
(June 25)

Little Missouri River

Little Powder River

MONTANA
WYOMING

Battle of
Slim Butte
(September

Bighorn River

Former site of
Fort Phil
Kearny

Clear Creek

Powder River

Belle Fourche River

BLACK HILLS

Dull Knife
Fight
(November 25)

North Fork

Red Fork

Middle Fork

South Fork

Crook (in March and again in June)

WYOMING
DAKOTA TERRITORY

Oregon Trail

North Platte River

Fort Fetterman

NEBRASKA

Battle of Hat Creek or
Warbonnet Creek (July 17)

Red Cloud Agency

Spotted T
Agen

Fort Laramie

Platte River

Fort Robinson
(Crazy Horse killed,
September 5, 1877)

1 Battle of the Rosebud (June 17)
2 Battle of Wolf Mountain (January 8, 1877)
3 Battle of the Powder River (March 17)

Often overlooked as a sideshow to the Powder River campaign was another skirmish involving the Lakota, some of whom would possibly later be involved in the summer's big battles. It is worth a mention for its having involved actions warranting the Congressional Medal of Honor.

A group of Lakota were observed in the vicinity of Fort Hartsuff in Nebraska, and the fact was reported to Lieutenant Charles Heyl of the 23rd Infantry Regiment at the post on April 28, 1876. He took a small detachment, including civilian volunteers, to investigate.

The Lakota were found near Gracie Creek, and Heyl decided to attack them at dusk. He took three men, and together they rode in, with their guns blazing at close range. One trooper and one of the Lakota were killed. Heyl and the surviving troopers were awarded the Medal of Honor.*

ORDER OF BATTLE

Colonel Gibbon had been ready to depart Fort Ellis at about the same time that Reynolds was being beaten on the Powder River and as Custer was arriving in Washington to testify. When news of the Powder River debacle reached him by telegraph, Gibbon stood down and did not move out until the end of March. Even then, his men found the snow still deep and the weather cold.

His 450-man command, about a third the size of Crook's, consisted of four companies of the 2nd Cavalry, six from his own 7th Infantry Regiment, and about two dozen Crow scouts. Among the scouts was Michael "Mitch" Boyer, the legendary part-Sioux tracker, who is often recalled in the same sentence as names such as the great mountain man and explorer Jim Bridger. Gibbon's role in the operation would be to patrol the Yellowstone River, waiting to cut off any Indians who escaped north from Crook's probe, or westward in the face of the column out of Dakota Territory.

General Terry was delayed for another six weeks in getting under way, both by weather-related supply issues and by his desire to await resolution of the Custer matter. The latter was sorted out by May 8, and the Terry-Custer command departed Fort Abraham Lincoln on May 17. By this time, the weather that had made things so difficult for Crook and Gibbon was

---

*They were Sergeant Leonard Patrick, and Corporal Jeptha Lytton. For Patrick, it was his second. He had earned his previous one at on the Little Blue River in May 1870.

no longer a major impediment, although there would still be occasional snow flurries and heavy rainstorms.

Custer's 7th Cavalry Regiment constituted the preponderance of the combat strength of the eastern prong of the 1876 campaign. In addition to this regiment's dozen companies and regimental band, there were a company from Captain Stephen Baker's 6th Infantry Regiment (which formed Terry's headquarters detachment), two from Captain Louis Sanger's 17th Infantry Regiment, and one company of the 20th Infantry Regiment, which was detailed to man a battery of Gatling guns under Lieutenant William Low. Custer also employed thirty-nine Indian scouts under the command of Lieutenant Charles Varnum. This detachment included Charles "Lonesome Charley" Reynolds, who had long been one of Custer's favorites. All told, the eastern column was comprised of fifty-two officers and 879 enlisted men, with thirty-two officers and 718 men being from the 7th Cavalry.

Among the other notables riding with Custer would be his brother and right-hand man, Captain Thomas Ward Custer, commander of the 7th Cavalry's Company C, who had the distinction of having earned two Congressional Medals of Honor during the Civil War. Commanding Company L was Lieutenant James Calhoun, who was married to the Custers' sister Margaret.

Also present for what many predicted would be yet another moment of glory for George Custer was another brother, Boston Custer, and nephew, Harry Armstrong "Autie" Reed. Even Custer's loquacious and high-spirited wife, Elizabeth Bacon "Libbie" Custer, accompanied the column for the first day out of Fort Abraham Lincoln, before turning back with the paymaster and a small contingent of escorting troops.

Though he was clearly expecting to achieve a career-polishing victory in Montana, Custer was uncharacteristically businesslike. He had even trimmed his normally long hair to a conservative collar length. However, just as there was nothing conservative about the carnival atmosphere to the regiment's departure from Fort Lincoln, there would be nothing conservative about the way that Custer planned to see the campaign portrayed in the eyes of the world when he rode back in triumph. To record the colorful details, Mark Kellogg of the *Bismarck Tribune* would be present as an embedded reporter, and he would also be serving as a stringer for the *New York Herald*, a newspaper that had an established fascination with the exploits of George Armstrong Custer. There were even whispers about presidential possibilities. It was an election year, and neither party had yet picked its candidate.

Logistics for the eastern column were handled both by an enormous wagon train guarded by the infantry and by steamboats, which would carry supplies up the Yellowstone River. The supply steamer *Far West* would also later serve as a floating command post on the Yellowstone. Fort Ellis would serve as Gibbon's forward operating base and forward supply depot. Terry would initially situate his on the Yellowstone River near the mouth of Glendive Creek, just west of the border of Montana Territory, but he would soon move it upstream to near the mouth of the Powder River. Crook's forward operating base would be on Goose Creek in the headwaters of the Tongue River.

Crook would leave Fort Fetterman on May 29 with about 1,300 combat troops. The cavalry, consisting of five companies of the 2nd Cavalry and ten of the 3rd Cavalry, were led by veteran commander Lieutenant Colonel William Royall. Leading two companies of the 4th Infantry Regiment and three of the 9th Infantry Regiment was Major Alexander Chambers.

In keeping with his doctrine of using a large number of Indian scouts, Crook would employ more than 250 Crow and Shoshone in this role. Reporters accompanying the troops included Reuben Davenport of the *New York Herald* and John Finerty of the *Chicago Times* and Joseph Wasson of the *San Francisco Alta Californian*.

Intelligence Estimates

Calculations of the number of Lakota and Cheyenne warriors present in the entire Powder River country varied between five hundred and eight hundred, although this was to prove to be an underestimation by several orders of magnitude. By June, when all three columns had, at last, reached the theater of operations, additional numbers of warriors had departed winter quarters and had converged on the Powder River country. In all, there have been as many as 15,000, and probably not many fewer than 10,000. Among them, were at least 1,500 warriors, and possibly as many as 4,000. The intelligence estimates had been done in March, when the campaign was expected to start. They had probably been correct at theat time, but two months later, they had grown stale.

What the U.S. Army planners did not know, and probably could not have predicted, was that a number of factors had converged that would bring together the biggest concentration of Indian warriors ever to be seen in the West since the Civil War. In addition to the Northern Cheyenne, there would be some Santee Sioux, including many who had fought in the Minnesota uprising of the 1860s. The majority, however, would be Teton Sioux, or Lakota. They would include Hunkpapa bands led by men such as Gall, and of course, Sitting Bull, as well as Minneconjou led by Hump and Lame Deer. Also present would be the Oglala led by Crazy Horse.

Rather than camping in separate bands across the vast landscape, as was logically expected, the majority of the Indians would be camped together, especially between June 17 and June 25. This would create an unprecedented critical mass of truly historic consequence. Ironically, the Army's biggest fear as May gave way to June in the centennial year was that the Indians would slip away without standing to do battle.

THE BATTLE OF THE ROSEBUD

On June 6, Crook passed the scene of the Fetterman Fight and moved north toward Goose Creek, where he would set up his forward operating base. On June 16, he crossed into the headwaters of Rosebud Creek.

Crook's scouts were giving him bits of information that a large Indian village was near, but the exact location was still unknown. However, the Lakota had also been monitoring the progress of the troops, which were moving in a ponderous slow-moving column—terribly uncharacteristic of the Crook doctrine.

On the morning of June 17, as the troops rested after an hour's march, the sound of gunfire was heard. The Crow scouts had made contact with a large war party, led by Crazy Horse himself, which soon was upon the troops. Crook organized counterattacks, but the Cheyenne and Lakota skillfully routed each of the counterattacking columns. It is recalled as having been the most skillfully conducted cavalry attack to be thrust upon a U.S. Army force since the Civil War. After the false start of the Reynolds fiasco, it was also the first major battle of the campaign, and of the Great Sioux War.

As the battle formed, Crook developed the misconception that the encampment from which the Indians had come was just a few miles upstream from where they were fighting. With this in mind, Crook ordered Captain Anson Mills of the 3rd Cavalry to disengage from the battle at hand and take several companies downstream to attack this camp. Seeing these troopers ride away from the battle simply energized the attackers and they renewed their efforts to overwhelm Crook. This, in turn, caused Crook to send word recalling Mills to the main battlefield.

Things were not going well for Crook, now locked in the largest battle of his career in the West, and indeed the biggest battle that most present would ever see outside the Civil War. William Royall's contingent was badly beaten and nearly surrounded as the roughly 750 warriors persisted with one relentless assault after another.

Though Crook had more men on the field, the terrain favored the attackers, and Crook's decision to separate Mills from the main force was ill advised. After Mills had returned to the scene, Crazy Horse finally chose to break off the battle and headed downstream. Crook ordered a pursuit, but the narrowing width of the valley looked too much like an ambush waiting to happen, and he called it quits.

Crook was still in possession of the battlefield and called it a victory, but, in fact, he had suffered the worst defeat of his otherwise brilliant career as an Indian fighter. At best, it was a costly draw. Estimates of U.S. Army casualties in the battles of the Indian Wars are usually precise, but for the Battle of the Rosebud, they vary widely from nine to twenty-eight men killed in action, and from twenty-one to fifty-six wounded. Crazy Horse would later be quoted as having said that his side lost thirty-six killed in action and sixty-three wounded.*

For the Army, the worst thing about the Battle of the Rosebud was that it effectively put the largest contingent in the 1876 offensive campaign out of action for more than a month. Rather than form up and continue his drive north, Crook gathered up his battered command and limped back to his forward operating base to wait for reinforcements. Within a few days, most of Crook's Indian scouts had left him. The fact

---

*Sergeant Joseph Robinson of Company D, 3rd Cavalry, earned a Congressional Medal of Honor at the Rosebud that day for bringing horses up to his skirmish line "with judgment and great coolness . . . at a critical moment." Other Medals of Honor went to 3rd Cavalrymen Sergeant Michael McGann, Sergeant John Shingle (aka John Henry), and trumpeter Elmer Snow, who was wounded in both arms.

that Crook's command was no longer in play would remain unknown to Terry and Gibbon until July.

Just as the Rosebud fight tarnished Crook's career, the reputation of Crazy Horse as a military leader was greatly enhanced. Already somewhat of a legend, he became a larger-than-life figure not only among the Oglala, but among all Lakota—and among the soldiers as well. There was even a rumor that this light-haired, light-skinned warrior had earlier attended the U.S. Military Academy at West Point under another name. This was not true, but his tactical skill and his leadership qualities are even now the subject of discussion for cadets in training at West Point.

RECONNAISSANCE AND PLANNING

Throughout May, as the eastern and southern columns were converging from farther distances, Colonel Gibbon's Fort Ellis command was moving down the Yellowstone, and finding plenty of evidence of the presence of the Lakota and Cheyenne. In fact, the opposing side was clearly aware of them. On May 3, some of the Crow scouts had their horses stolen by unseen raiders during the night, and on May 23, it was discovered that two soldiers and a teamster had been ambushed and killed. His scouts also reported seeing smoke from the fires of a large camp in the distance in the vicinity of the Rosebud, but Gibbon inexplicably failed to mention this in a dispatch that he sent to Terry by courier.

On June 9, a week before Crook's battle on the Rosebud, Gibbon had rendezvoused with Terry on the Yellowstone, near the mouth of the Rosebud. Here, they sat down to confer aboard the Far West.

The battle map for the fateful month of June consisted of the Yellowstone River flowing west to east across the top. Flowing south to north into the Yellowstone from below were four rivers and four major river valleys. From west to east, these were the Bighorn, the Rosebud, the Tongue, and the Powder. Each of the four had smaller tributaries feeding into it. The principal tributary of the Bighorn was the Little Bighorn River. It was considered unlikely that the enemy were camped farther to the west, because beyond the Bighorn was Crow territory. The Lakota were traditional enemies of the Crow, and would not enter their realm unless they were planning—or expecting—a fight.

Based on their pooled intelligence, Terry and Gibbon decided, correctly, that the large encampments of Lakota and Cheyenne—if there were more than one—were somewhere between the Bighorn and the Powder. Based on the intelligence that Gibbon had obtained, they assumed that one of the largest encampments—if not the single encampment—was on the Rosebud. On June 9, this was still a correct assumption, but the huge encampment would move to the Little Bighorn after Crook's battle on June 17.

Terry, as senior officer, devised the battle plan. His strategy was to first send part of Custer's 7th Cavalry to ascend the Powder River, then cross over and descend the Tongue River. If they did not sight the encampment(s) this would narrow the potential battlefield and tighten the noose. Next, Terry would have Gibbon's force move up the Rosebud, and Custer move upstream along the Tongue River.

A River Too Far

On June 10, Major Marcus Reno of Custer's 7th Cavalry undertook to search the Powder River, and the Far West chugged downstream to start moving Terry's supply base nearer the action. A Civil War veteran, Reno had served mainly in administrative jobs since 1865, and this was his first experience in Indian Wars operations. Instead of limiting his reconnaissance mission to the Powder and Tongue as Terry explicitly ordered, Reno decided to cross westward through the valley of the Tongue and descend the Rosebud to the Yellowstone. This would cover more territory, but it would also risk the possibility of the U.S. Army forces being detected by the enemy.

By June 17, the day of Crook's huge battle on Rosebud Creek, Gibbon was still moving upstream along the Yellowstone. Reno, meanwhile, was about sixty miles downstream from Crook on Rosebud Creek, moving away from Crook and the Indians toward the Yellowstone. None of the other commanders knew where Crook was, nor what was happening to him.

Reno reached the Yellowstone by June 19, and had seen made contact with Gibbon. He then started downstream on the Yellowstone—opposite Gibbon's direction—toward a rendezvous with Terry and Custer at the mouth of the Tongue River. Terry was furious with Reno for traveling a river too far on his scouting mission, but Reno had managed to return with valuable information. Reno reported finding a great deal of evidence of Indian camps (although some of them dated back into the winter), and fresh signs of a large party of Indians moving through the area into the valley of the Rosebud. Most important, as Reno pointed out, was that if they did not know where the Indians were, they now had a better idea of where they were not.

MARCHING INTO BATTLE

With the intelligence gleaned by Major Reno in his unauthorized reconnaissance, Terry was able to revise his plan for a more concise field of action. Both the Powder and Tongue Rivers were ruled out, leaving the Rosebud and the Bighorn. On June 20, Terry ordered Custer—with Reno's troops reattached—to move upstream along the Rosebud, and Gibbon to move upstream along the Bighorn. Custer would then cross over the ridge to the valley of the Little Bighorn—quaintly referred to by Terry as the "Little Horn"—and march downstream to meet Gibbon.

On the morning of June 21, Custer and Terry met with Gibbon for one final conference aboard the Far West, which shuttled back and forth on the Yellowstone between the Rosebud and the Bighorn. At this meeting, they came up with the plan for the climactic assault on the Indian encampment—wherever it was. Between them, Custer and Gibbon would have about a thousand troops, while the number of warriors in the Indian encampment was still estimated at about eight hundred, and probably fewer. From examining the campsites that Reno had discovered, his scouts had calculated the number of tipis, and extrapolated the number of warriors from this data.

The basic plan was straightforward: the two commands would converge on the Indian encampment and attack. Custer's 7th Cavalry, being the more mobile of the two, would act as a hammer, driving the enemy against Gibbon's anvil. Because Custer's command would be covering the most ground, the best scouts, including Mitch Boyer and Charley Reynolds, would ride with him.

No minutes from the meeting are known to exist, but it is probable that both Gibbon and Custer—certainly Custer—voiced the opinion that his force alone could defeat eight hundred warriors. Of course, no one present at the meeting knew that General George Crook's large command had been severely mauled by these same warriors just four days earlier, and that the Indians were in high spirits.

Also probably expressed at the meeting was the fear, not of overwhelming opposition, but that the large group of Indians traveling together might be splitting into smaller bands, and that most of them would simply slip away and not be caught in the huge dragnet that Terry, Gibbon, and Custer were casting.

Custer rode south at the head of his column at noon on June 22 with rations sufficient to support the 7th Cavalry in the field until July 6. This was considered more than enough time to accomplish the mission. Custer's command totaled thirty-one officers, 566 enlisted men, thirty-five Arikira, Crow, and Sioux scouts and inter-

Lieutenant Colonel George Armstrong Custer (1839–1876) of the 7th Cavalry Regiment. (*Library of Congress*)

preters, as well as about a dozen civilian scouts, mule packers, reporter Mark Kellogg, and Custer's two civilian relatives, Boston Custer and Autie Reed.

The troopers each carried a Springfield rifle with one hundred rounds of ammunition, and a Colt revolver with twenty-four rounds.

The Model 1873 Springfield rifle, which would remain standard with the U.S. Army for twenty years, had evolved out of a series of experiments done in the early years after the Civil War. Improvements began with modifying the Army's huge stock of war surplus Springfield rifled muskets to fire metal cartridges which were more durable and versatile than earlier paper cartridges. This and other innovations were incorporated into the Model 1873, which had a range of up to 1,100 yards. Meanwhile, the Colt Model 1873 pistol also evolved from a wartime predecessor, the Colt Model 1860. Like the Springfield Model 1873, this .45 caliber six-shooter would remain as standard equipment with the U.S. Army until the 1890s.

The regimental pack train carried additional ammunition totaling about fifty rounds for each man. Custer himself carried a pair of snub-nosed English revolvers, adequate primarily for close-range action. Terry had offered Custer the use of a detail of Gatling guns, but he declined. Reno had taken them on his previous scouting mission, but Custer felt that they were too cumbersome, and would slow him down. None of the officers carried their sabers because these also were considered too awkward.

As recorded for posterity in the *Annual Report of the Secretary of War*, Terry's direct orders to Custer were precise:

> The Brigadier General commanding [Terry] directs that, as soon as your regiment can be made ready for the march, you will proceed up the Rosebud in pursuit of the Indians whose trail was discovered by Major Reno a few days since. It is, of course, impossible to give you any definite instructions in regard to this movement, and were it not impossible to do so the Department Commander [Terry] places too much confidence in your zeal, energy, and ability to wish to impose on you precise orders which might hamper your action when nearly in contact with the enemy. He will, however, indicate to you his own views of what your action should be, and he desires that you should conform to them unless you shall see sufficient reasons for departing from them. He thinks that you should proceed up the Rosebud until you ascertain definitely the direction in which the trail above spoken of leads. Should it be found (as it appears almost certain that it will be found) to turn toward the Little Horn, he thinks that you should still proceed southward, perhaps as far as the headwaters of the Tongue, and then turn toward the Little Horn, feeling constantly, however, for your left, so as to preclude the possibility of the escape of the Indians to the south or southeast by passing your left flank. The column of Colonel Gibbon is now in motion for the mouth of the Bighorn. As soon as it reaches that point it will cross the Yellowstone and move up at least as far as the forks of the Big and Little Horns. Of course, its future movements must be controlled by circumstances as they arise, but it is hoped that the Indians, if upon the Little Horn, may be so nearly enclosed by the two columns that their escape will be impossible.
>
> The Department Commander desires that on your way up the Rosebud you should thoroughly examine the upper part of Tullock's Creek [a stream that entered the Bighorn River near its mouth, about twenty miles downstream from the mouth of the Little Bighorn], and that you should endeavor to send a scout through to Colonel Gibbon's column, with information of the results of your examination. The lower part of this creek will be examined by a

detachment from Colonel Gibbon's command. The supply steamer will be pushed up the Bighorn as far as the forks of the river if found to be navigable for that distance, and the Department Commander, who will accompany the column of Colonel Gibbon, desires you to report to him there not later than the expiration of the time for which your troops are rationed, unless in the meantime you receive further orders.

As explicit as Terry's orders were, the general clearly respected Custer sufficiently so as to give him some latitude if, in Custer's professional judgment, any alternative action was required. In permitting Custer to do as he wished when the battle was joined, Terry told him that he "places too much confidence in your zeal, energy, and ability to wish to impose on you precise orders which might hamper your action when nearly in contact with the enemy."

Gibbon, meanwhile, was taken aboard the *Far West* to catch up his troops, who were then marching westward along the Yellowstone, headed for the mouth of the Bighorn. From there, they would turn south on that river, arriving at its confluence with the Little Bighorn in time to take up position as Terry's anvil on June 26. Terry and his command staff would accompany Gibbon.

On June 23, Custer was seeing for himself, signs of a large group of Indians having recently moved through the valley of Rosebud Creek. Among the hoofprints and burned out cooking fires, Custer's Arikara scouts found evidence that the Lakota and Cheyenne had performed the sun dance, an annual ritual of renewal for warriors involving painful self-flagellation from which warriors were said to emerge fearless and ready for battle. This was a bad sign.

The Night Before

Custer and the 7th Cavalry camped for the night of June 24 at the point where Davis Creek flows eastward into Rosebud Creek. They had followed the Indian trail they had picked up the previous day to this point. From there, it led up Davis Creek and across the ridge separating the valley of the Rosebud from the valley of the Little Bighorn River.

The column had come seventy-three miles in two and a half days—or two days if one takes into account the long rest stop that Custer ordered on June 24. They were on schedule now to easily cross the ridge and trav-el downstream to meet Gibbon at the mouth of the Little Bighorn on June 26. If Custer was feeling a sense of urgency about finding the Indian encampment as soon as possible, it was not exhibited in his leisurely pace on June 24.

Custer had sent his Crow scouts to follow this Indian trail beyond the ridge and to determine which way it led from there. At about nine o'clock that night, the scouts returned. They explained that the trail was very fresh, meaning that the encampment had to be on the Little Bighorn. Furthermore, they assured Custer that there were no signs of it having split, meaning that no smaller bands had yet peeled off. The large group was still intact, and they were all camped together across the ridge. The location of the camp now appeared to be farther downstream, and closer to the Yellowstone, than had been surmised in the conference aboard the Far West.

Custer was energized and moved to action. On the previous days, reveille had been at dawn and the command was on the trail at 5:00 a.m. Now, Custer called his officers together at 9:30 p.m. and gave orders for an all-night march. The men were roused after having been in camp for less than three hours.

Custer's new plan was for the troops to move into the Little Bighorn valley, rest through June 25, and launch a three-column surprise attack at dawn on June 26. This would replicate his successful tactics at the Washita eight years earlier. June 26 was also the day on which Gibbon was expect-ed to arrive. Of course, now that it seemed the Indian camp was closer to the Yellowstone than expected, Custer extrapolated that Gibbon would arrive sooner than they had planned.

The scouts told Custer about an outcropping of high ground, known as the Crow's Nest, from which the Little Bighorn valley could be surveyed, and Custer sent Lieutenant Varnum, the chief of scouts. Arriving at the Crow's Nest around 2:30 a.m., he studied the distant campfires of the large encampment, sent a courier back to Custer, and napped until sunup.

As the 7th Cavalry saddled up in the darkness and undertook their exhausting night march, covering nearly twenty miles of ground they could barely see, the Indians slept. One of the largest encampments seen on the Northern Plains in recent memory, the village on the Little Bighorn consisted of between 990 and 1,200 lodges, containing an estimated seven thousand people. The nucleus of the camp was Sitting Bull's group of about four hundred lodges that had been on the Rosebud on June 17, and from which Crazy Horse's warriors had ridden to attack Crook. After that fight, they had pulled up stakes and moved north, where they linked up with the party that Reno and Custer had been following. On June 24, they had set up camp at their present location along a several mile stretch of the western shore of the meandering Little Bighorn River, a stream that they referred to as the Greasy Grass.

Tataanka Iyotanka, Sitting Bull, (1831–1890) was a leading Hunkpapa Lakota shaman who was the foremost Lakota spiritual leader for a generation. (*Author*)

The exact population of the Greasy Grass encampment is not known, and, indeed, it was probably not known on June 25, 1876. Interviews and extensive research done in the years following that date have given us a pretty good idea of the numbers, and certainly the demographics. It is estimated that 85 percent of the total lodges were Lakota Sioux of various subtribes, 12 percent were Northern Cheyenne, and less than 3 percent were Santee Sioux. A few Arapaho were also present.

To break down the Lakota demographics further, 24 percent of the lodges belonged to Sitting Bull's Hunkpapa Lakota, and another 24 percent to the Oglala Lakota led by Crazy Horse and American Horse. The Minneconjou accounted for 15 percent, 11 percent were Itazipacola (Sans Arcs or No Bows), and the remainder were comprised of Brulé (Burnt Thighs), Oohenonpa (Two-Kettle), and Sihasapa (Blackfoot Sioux). The latter three groups were camped together near the center of the larger encampment.

The Oglala and Northern Cheyenne were camped at the northern, or downstream, end of the Greasy Grass encampment, while the Hunkpapa anchored the upstream end. This was the direction from which the 7th Cavalry would approach.

The soldiers reached a point adjacent to the Crow's Nest, after marching for less than three hours, where they would eat breakfast and rest for several hours. Custer himself went up to the Crow's Nest around 9:00 a.m. on June 25 and peered toward the Indian encampment about fifteen miles to the north. A blanket of smoke and haze hung over the camp, so he was unable to glean anything more useful than to know that here was the object of the mission. He was not able to ascertain the size of the camp, nor the fact that there were approximately 2,500 warriors, rather than the eight hundred that prior intelligence estimates had reckoned.

As Custer had told his officers twelve hours earlier at the Davis Creek camp, his plan was to rest through the day and strike at dawn on June 26. However, this plan would suddenly be scrapped. As Custer was at the Crow's Nest, his scouts reported that they had seen and been seen by a Lakota hunting party—and that this party had probably seen the approaching soldiers.

In order for his plan to work, Custer depended on the element of surprise. As soon as these Lakota reported back to the larger village, surprise would be out the window. Foremost in Custer's mind was the fear that the camp would break up and bands would move away in separate directions. Experience told him that this would be the most typical reaction to their knowing that a large force of soldiers was nearby.

Custer surmised that to wait until June 26 would lose him not only the initiative, but the target itself. Custer ordered his column to move out. If not a dawn attack tomorrow, then there would be an afternoon attack today. If the Indians were warned, they would not have much warning. Custer would catch them before they had packed up to move.

PREPARING TO ATTACK

At 11:07 a.m. local time on June 25, 1876, Lieutenant Colonel George Armstrong Custer led the 7th Cavalry across the ridge that separated the drainage of Rosebud Creek from that of the Little Bighorn River. The official timekeeper, Lieutenant George Wallace, had his watch set to Central time, so he recorded the event as occurring at 12:07 p.m.

At this point, Custer divided his command into three attack columns and a support column. The three attack columns would advance abreast into the valley, gradually extending their separation until they were no longer within sight of one another.

Custer himself would lead the right column, consisting of 213 officers and men of two battalions comprising companies C, E, F, I, and L. The two battalions were companies E and F under the command of Captain Myles Keogh and the other three companies, under Captain George Yates, who also commanded Company F. Captain Tom Custer, the commander of Company C and de facto executive officer, would be with George Custer in this contingent. So too was young Autie Reed. Boston Custer initially remained with the supply column, but hastened to join his brothers after the shooting started.

The center column would be under the command of Major Reno—an Indian Wars novice—and would consist of 140 officers and men of companies A, G, and M, plus thirty-five scouts. The left column, led by Captain Frederick Benteen—who had been with Custer on the Washita—would be comprised of 115 officers and men of companies D, H, and K. Captain Thomas McDougall would lead Company B as the escort for the pack train carrying the supplies and the regiment's reserve ammunition.

Reno's mission in the center was to ride to the Little Bighorn River and follow it straight into the southern end of the Indian encampment. Custer would lead his column along the ridgeline to the east of the river. When they were abreast of the center of the camp, they would ride down, cross the river and attack. Presumably this would occur at about the same time that Reno was attacking from the south. Benteen's left column was to cross the river and ride northward along the west side, opposite Custer, and to stop any Indians who might be attempting to escape from the other two attacks. Then, he was to cross back and support Custer.

This was a logical division of labor for attacking a camp of four hundred lodges, but clearly not so when there were between 990 and 1,200 lodges. Apparently, Custer still did not know this, although his scouts would later insist that they had given him such estimates before the assault.

Benteen moved steadily away from the others, and the pack train lagged far behind all three. Reno and Custer were still fairly close together at 1:00 p.m. local time when they stopped to investigate a lone tipi containing the body of a warrior killed in action in the June 17 action against Crook. By this time, they had covered more than half the distance from the ridge to the base of the Indian encampment.

They could see a few Lakota, and clouds of dust in the distance, which the scouts interpreted as the camp beginning to move out to escape the troops. Because they were now in the valley, they did not have the overview that they would have had from higher ground.

Reno and Custer then separated, with Custer going right to climb the ridge along the east side of the valley. Reno crossed the Little Bighorn River from east to west, and continued toward the camp. While the hills and ridges in the area were open grassland, the valleys and riverbanks were heavily wooded, so it was impossible for Reno to see into the village until he was almost upon it. By 1:50 p.m. local time, Reno was passing through the outskirts of the long, narrow encampment, and his men were seeing a few tipis and horse herds. His scouts were now reporting that they had ridden ahead to within sight of the village, and that the Lakota were not moving out. They were preparing a counterattack.

RENO'S ATTACK AND RETREAT

At 2:10 p.m. local time on June 25, 1876, Major Marcus Reno signaled his three companies to attack the Hunkpapa Lakota camp at the foot of the huge village. He had ordered them to charge down the western shore of the Little Bighorn at full gallop in order to deliver a stunning blow against the foe. Instead, it was Reno's men who were shocked and awed, both by the size of the village, and by the aggressiveness of its defenders, who were led by the respected Hunkpapa war leader Gall, who was also the adopted younger brother of Sitting Bull.

Both Sitting Bull and Gall were present in the Hunkpapa Lakota encampment that day, but it was Gall who led the prompt and effective counterattack against Reno. Sitting Bull said he witnessed the action, but he is not believed to have taken a major part in the fighting. Reno ordered his men to halt and the two sides were quickly enveloped in a large gun battle. The Battle of the Little Bighorn was under way.

Suddenly a group of Lakota attacked his left flank, and Reno ordered his men to move back upstream, where they could take cover in some trees near the river. Here, they formed a skirmish line at about 2:20 p.m. local time. More and more Lakota piled into the fight from the camp, blasting away at the troopers with the Winchester repeating rifles that had been previously doled out by the Indian agents. In addition to the Lakota on the

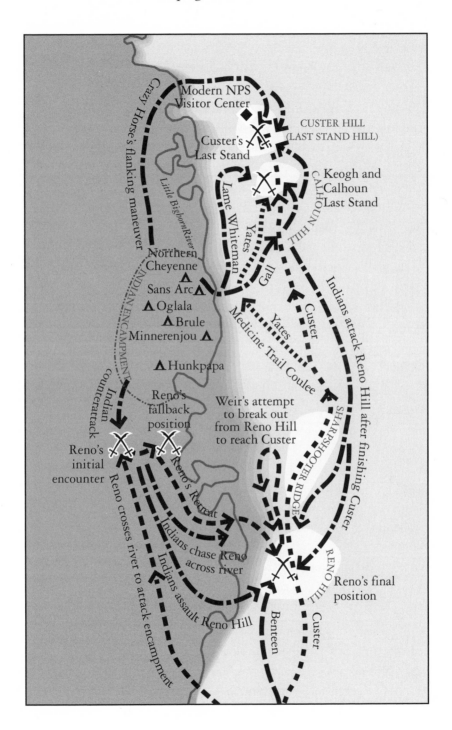

Modern NPS
Visitor Center

CUSTER HILL
(LAST STAND HILL)

Custer's
Last Stand

Keogh and
Calhoun
Last Stand

Crazy Horse's flanking maneuver

Little Bighorn River

CALHOUN HILL

Lame Whiteman

Yates

Gall

Northern
Cheyenne

Sans Arc

Oglala

Brule

Minnerenjou

Hunkpapa

INDIAN ENCAMPMENT

Medicine Trail Coulee

Yates

Custer

Indians attack Reno Hill after finishing Custer

Reno's
fallback
position

Weir's attempt
to break out
from Reno Hill
to reach Custer

Indian counterattack

Reno's
initial
encounter

SHARPSHOOTER RIDGE

Reno's Retreat

Reno crosses river to attack encampment

Indians chase Reno
across river

Indians assault Reno Hill

RENO HILL

Benteen

Custer

Reno's final
position

west shore, a few had crossed to the east side and were sniping at Reno's men from behind.

It was clear that Reno's hastily organized defensive position in the trees could not hold for long, so at 2:55 p.m. local time, he ordered the men to cross to the east side of the Little Bighorn and head for higher ground on the ridge. Most of the men in Companies A and M heard the order, but most in Company G did not. To these men, and to the Indians, it looked like a frantic retreat when Reno led the withdrawal across the river amid a hail of bullets the likes of which few men had ever seen.

With no organized covering fire, Reno's tactical withdrawal became a chaotic retreat. The Lakota recognized this, and chased the fleeing troops, shooting them off their horses as they struggled across the river and attempted to climb the steep bluffs on the opposite shore.

By 3:10 p.m. local time, Reno and his battered detachment had reached a defensive position on the ridge above the Little Bighorn valley that would henceforth be known as Reno Hill. Here, the remnants of his command frantically dug in to fend off what many feared would be their annihilation. Their rifle pits are still visible today.

As Reno took stock, he realized that only seven of his eleven officers had survived. Only eighty-four of his 129 enlisted men had made it to Reno Hill, and the wounded numbered thirteen. The men could recall seeing a few troopers go down, but many were trapped in the woods below and killed before they could reach, much less cross, the river. In the hour since his abortive attack had made contact with the enemy, Reno had suffered a 44 percent casualty rate. It was one of the worst such rates for an hour-long battle in U.S. Army history, but it would soon be topped.

CUSTER'S ATTACK AND RETREAT

After taking his leave of Reno at what the timekeeper noted as 2:37 p.m. Chicago time (1:37 p.m. local time), Custer had led his column into the hills, passing the location of Reno Hill before Reno had begun his charge into the village. By 2:00 p.m. local time, Custer had covered about a mile and a half and was in a position to observe the entire sobering panorama of the vast encampment. It was now obvious that the 7th Cavalry faced a far more formidable foe than Custer had imagined. At 2:05 p.m. local time, Custer sent Sergeant Daniel Kanipe back to find McDougall and to convey

Custer's order to bring the pack train with the extra ammunition straight across the ridge to Custer's position.

Ten minutes later, and a mile farther north, Custer rode to the higher ground of what is now known as Weir Point, looked down and watched as Reno reached the village with his attack. At 2:20 p.m. local time, as Reno went into his defensive posture in the trees, Custer rejoined the column and ordered his trumpeter, John Martin, to go find Benteen. Because the Italian-speaking Martin (born Giovanni Martini)

View westward toward the Little Bighorn River from Reno Hill. (*Author Photo*)

might not be understood, Custer's adjutant, Lieutenant William Cooke scribbled a note that read "Benteen. Come on. Big Village. Be quick, Bring packs. P.S. Bring packs." The packs contained the extra ammunition.

Cooke's postscript clearly underscored the extreme urgency felt by Custer's command, which by this point numbered just 210. This included his thirteen officers, Mitch Boyer, the three civilians and 193 enlisted men, reduced from its original strength because of the two men sent back with messages, and several whose horses had gone lame and who couldn't keep up.

With Reno already engaged, Custer was anxious to get into the fight, to take the pressure off Reno and to execute his own part of the battle plan. At about 2:30 p.m. local time, without waiting for the ammunition that he had requested, Custer ordered Yates and his battalion to take the first available direct path off the bluffs that led down to the Little Bighorn. Known as Medicine Tail Coulee, this broad, dry wash is located approximately halfway between the point of Reno's attack and the northernmost part of the encampment.

Before he crossed out of sight, Martin watched Yates run into a determined counterattack. Several soldiers fell as the abortive attack was quickly turned. The Lakota and Cheyenne swept across the Little Bighorn at

Medicine Tail Ford, chasing the troopers back up Medicine Tail Coulee. As Yates regained the high ground, Custer was looking for a defensive position and scanned the horizon hopefully for Benteen's 115-man force—and for the pack train.

BENTEEN AT RENO HILL

By 3:10 p.m. local time, the last of Major Reno's command was atop the bluff known as Reno Hill and digging desperately to build a defensive position. Had the Lakota that had so badly mauled the command in the valley chosen to charge up the hill, they could probably have finished Reno's group off to the last man. Instead, Gall rallied his warriors to ride north to face the threat posed by Custer.

Meanwhile, Benteen had scouted north a short way along the west side of the Little Bighorn River and then recrossed the valley to the east side, following the route that Custer had taken. He moved his column at a leisurely pace that was in marked contrast to the frantic urgency with which the other two columns were moving. It was as though he was on an entirely different battlefield far, far away.

At 2:13 p.m. local time, as Reno was up to his bridle in Hunkpapa warriors, Benteen reached the lone tipi that the others had passed an hour and a quarter earlier. By this time, he could see the pack train slowly approaching from the south.

At 2:38 p.m., Sergeant Kanipe passed Benteen, and four minutes later, he reached the pack train. Eleven minutes later, at 2:53 p.m. local time, Martini handed Cooke's memo to Benteen. At this point, Benteen's column was still five miles from Reno Hill, which was about two miles from Medicine Tail Coulee. Benteen ordered his column into a trot, and by 3:10 p.m. local time, he was close enough to see the last of Reno's troops reach the top of Reno Hill.

At 3:20 p.m., Benteen's intact column reached Reno Hill, finding Reno's decimated contingent desperately digging in. Major Reno ordered Captain Benteen to halt and assist him, and Benteen complied, rather than following Custer's orders and pressing forward. By now, only a few Lakota were still present, and the troopers were able to drive them off.

As things quieted down on Reno Hill, the troopers could hear the sound of intense gunfire farther to the north, but higher peaks in the ridgeline prevented them from seeing what was going on. At 3:55 p.m. local time,

Captain Thomas Weir took Company D north toward the sound of the shooting, but his unit ran into a large contingent of mounted Lakota a little more than a mile north of Reno Hill. He halted on the bluff now known as Weir Point, the highest point in the area. From here, Company D could see a huge battle ensuing about two miles farther north. This was Custer.

At 4:10 p.m. local time, Benteen followed Company D with his three companies, but they, like Weir's command, were halted at Weir Point by the Lakota. They arrived at about 4:30 p.m., and would remain for only a short time before all of the troops at Weir Point decided to backtrack to Reno Hill.

Meanwhile, at about 4:15 p.m., McDougall's pack train finally reached Reno Hill. By the time that Reno was able to pull his group together to follow the others, Reno met Benteen and Weir retreating from Weir Point to Reno Hill.

By about 5:30 p.m., the combined force of survivors from the three columns were all back at Reno Hill and digging in for the night when the Lakota and Cheyenne attacked again, killing five more troopers and bringing the number of wounded to nineteen. Even when this attack was over, Lakota warriors were taking up positions on higher ground from which they would pour relentless rifle fire into the defenses on Reno Hill until after dark.

Many of the men had seen, and all had heard, the enormous distant battle that had engulfed Custer's column, but as June 25 ended, no one in the 7th Cavalry was sure exactly what had happened.

Custer's Last Stand

As Reno was fighting his way across the Little Bighorn River, Custer had led the remainder of his force farther along what is now called Battle Ridge, parallel to the river and the large Indian encampment.

He had sent Captain Yates down Medicine Tail Coulee, either as an offensive probe into the Indian village or as an effort to prevent the Indians from crossing the river through Medicine Tail Ford until Benteen arrived to reinforce Custer's five companies.

On Battle Ridge, Captain Keogh, forming Custer's rear guard, had taken up a position north of Medicine Tail Coulee. Various theories suggest that Custer was with either Yates or Keogh, or that he was farther north. He was probably with Keogh on the ridge.

Yates was turned back at Medicine Tail Ford, probably at about 2:45 p.m. He retreated up Medicine Tail Coulee to the point about halfway up the ridge where a second gully, known as Deep Coulee, branched to the left. He led his men this way because it led north toward where Custer and Keogh were.

Meanwhile, having defeated Reno, Gall led his Hunkpapa warriors north through the village, across the Little Bighorn at Medicine Tail Ford and up Medicine Tail Coulee. Here, they clashed with Keogh's men. Keogh, a former Irish soldier of fortune and one-time papal guard, probably fought back fiercely.

When Yates arrived near where Keogh was fighting, the five companies probably joined forces and moved uphill and farther north to a location now known as Calhoun Hill after Lieutenant Calhoun, the Custer brother-in-law who commanded Company L in Keogh's battalion.

According to firsthand accounts later related by the attackers, the defenders of Calhoun Hill were fighting back with their Colts rather than their rifles. While the Springfields were useful at long range, the close-in fighting demanded the rapid repeating fire of revolvers rather than long-range accuracy. For their part, the Indians preceded their cavalry attacks with showers of arrows launched at great distance, which dropped into the defensive positions from above. This technique, used by the Indians at the Little Bighorn, and at other battles in the West, is reminiscent of the arrow storms that the English longbowmen used so effectively at Poitiers in 1356 and at Agincourt in 1415. Troops on the defensive, especially unarmored cavalry were especially vulnerable to the wrath of an arrow storm.

Tom Custer's Company C spearheaded a cavalry charge apparently designed to break out northward from Calhoun Hill, but he was turned back by a Cheyenne force led by Lame White Man. Nevertheless, both battalions continued to move north along Battle Ridge, spurred on by George Custer, either in a search for a better defensive location, or in his zeal to still find a way to attack the village. Indeed, Company C made another charge down the slope toward the village from the hill now known as Custer Hill that marked the northernmost progress of 7th Cavalry troops on June 25.

The climax of the Battle of the Little Bighorn came in a dramatic cavalry charge executed by the brilliant Oglala mastermind, Crazy Horse. While Gall and Lame White Man slammed the two battalions with a

Custer's last stand has inspired many renderings, including this fancifully inaccurate Kurz & Allen lithograph from 1889. Custer's last stand actually occurred at the *top* of the hill. (*Library of Congress*)

frontal assault up the ridge from the valley, Crazy Horse forded the Little Bighorn River north of the village and the battle, thus outflanking Custer Hill and Keogh's position farther south on Battle Ridge. Leading what may have been nearly a thousand warriors, Crazy Horse delivered a powerful and spectacular final blow against which the troopers had no realistic defense.

While both Crazy Horse and Gall were very much part of the action on Battle Ridge and Custer Hill, Sitting Bull would later explain that he had been in the village below, and had not seen Custer at the Little Bighorn.

When the battle actually ended is not known for certain. It still raged when Weir and Benteen were observing the faraway battlefield from Weir Point between about 4:10 and 4:30 p.m. local time. By the time that they returned to Reno Hill, the distant gunfire had subsided.

George Armstrong Custer made his last stand on Custer Hill, beneath the regimental headquarters flag and surrounded mainly by the men of Companies E and F. About forty men shot their horses and used them as breastworks as Crazy Horse attacked, first from behind, then from all directions at once. George Yates was at Custer's side, as was his brother Tom, although most of his Company C would die lower on the slope where they had made their last charge toward the Little Bighorn River. Both Boston Custer and Autie Reed were here as well, as was Mark Kellogg, whose story of the great battle would never be written.

All 210 men of Custer's command to whom John Martin bid farewell at 2:20 p.m. local time were killed in action. Only Martin lived to tell the tale. He remained in the U.S. Army until 1904. Martin retired from the Army with the rank of sergeant, and worked for many years as a subway ticket-taker in New York City. He died at his home in Brooklyn on Christmas Eve in 1922.

Of the 210 dead, most were killed either on Custer Hill or in the place on Battle Ridge a hundred yards or so to the south where Captain Keogh made his last stand with the last remnants of his battalion. The remainder were killed in the broad arc from the base of Medicine Tail Coulee through Battle Ridge to the slopes beneath Custer Hill.

The order in which they died is not known, although those on Custer Hill likely were the last. Custer had one bullet wound near his heart, and a second in his left temple. His body, unlike many of the others, was stripped but not mutilated.

There is an oft-repeated story that Hunkpapa warrior Rain in the Face had once been insulted by Tom Custer, and that he told Custer he would one day cut out his heart and eat it. This may or may not have happened, but it is a fact that both at the Battle of the Little Bighorn. Tom Custer died and was badly disfigured. Rain in the Face lived until 1905.

The Morning After

Reno and Benteen continued to take fire all through the night, and at daybreak on June 26, the Lakota and Cheyenne attacked yet again. It was rare, although not unheard of, that battles in the Indian Wars continued into a second day with scarcely diminished fury, but there was no sign that the Indians were going to abandon the field on June 26.

In a memo that he was preparing for General Terry, Reno made note of having led a charge toward the river at 2:00 p.m. (1:00 p.m. local time) that day, but that he had been forced back to the hills by the enemy. Among those on Reno Hill as the sun came up on June 26, seven more would be killed and an additional forty-one would be wounded. Men died of gunshot wounds while the relentless summer sun beat down on other men wasting away from thirst.

It is indicative of the desperate lack of water on the hot afternoon of June 25 on Reno Hill that most of the men who were awarded the

Itonagaju, Rain in the Face, (1835–1905), left, was a legendary Hunkpapa Lakota warrior present at the Battle of the Little Bighorn. He had a personal vendetta against Captain Tom Custer. (*Author*) Pizi, Gall, (1840–1894), right, of the Hunkpapa Lakota was a brilliant tactical commander who led forces against the 7th Cavalry at the Little Bighorn. (*National Archives*)

Congressional Medal of Honor at the Battle of the Little Bighorn received it for carrying water from the river under what many of their citations referred to as "a most galling fire."* Other Congressional Medal of Honor citations for the water carriers contain more information that helps convey the violence of the action that took place that day. That for Private Peter Thompson of Company C states that "After having voluntarily brought water to the wounded, in which effort he was shot through the head, he made two successful trips for the same purpose, notwithstanding remonstrances of his sergeant."†

---

*Among them were Private Neil Bancroft of Company A, Private Abram Brant of Company D, Private Frederick Deetline of Company D, Sergeant George Geiger of Company H, Private Theodore Goldin of Company G, Private David Harris of Company A, Private William Harris of Company D, Sergeant Rufus Hutchison of Company B, blacksmith Henry Mechlin of Company H, Private James Pym of Company B, Sergeant Roy Stanislaus of Company A, Private George Scott of Company D, Private Thomas Stivers of Company D, Private Frank Tolan of Company D, Sergeant Charles Welch of Company D, Private Charles Windolph of Company H, and Private Thomas Callen of Company B.

†Though his citation specifically notes that he was "shot through the head," this is certainly hyperbole. Thompson probably received a particularly bloody head wound. Injuries to the scalp and forehead tend to bleed profusely, giving the impression of a more serious wound.

Otto Voit, a saddler for Company H, "Volunteered with George Geiger, Charles Windolph, and Henry Mechlin to hold an exposed position standing erect on the brow of the hill facing the Little Bighorn River. They fired constantly in this manner for more than 20 minutes diverting fire and attention from another group filling canteens of water that were desperately needed." All four received the Medal of Honor.

Sergeant Benjamin Criswell of Company B earned his Medal of Honor when he "Rescued the body of Lieutenant Hodgson from within the enemy's lines; brought up ammunition and encouraged the men in the most exposed positions under heavy fire." Corporal Charles Cunningham of Company B, earned his Medal of Honor when he "Declined to leave the line when wounded in the neck during heavy fire." His citation noted that he "fought bravely all next day."

Sergeant Richard Hanley of Company C, "Recaptured, singlehanded, and without orders, within the enemy's lines and under a galling fire lasting some 20 minutes, a stampeded pack mule loaded with ammunition." Private Henry Holden of Company D "Brought up ammunition under a galling fire from the enemy," and Sergeant Thomas Murray "Brought up the pack train, and on the second day the rations, under a heavy fire from the enemy."

It was not until late in the day that the troops on Reno Hill saw any indication that the Cheyenne and Lakota were going to fold their tipis and pack up their camp. At sundown on June 26, they finally began streaming out of the valley of the Greasy Grass, heading back to the valley of the Rosebud.

On the morning of June 27, not a single Cheyenne or Lakota was anywhere to be seen on what had been the great battlefield. Reno and Benteen spent the day tending to their casualties and did not ride north to investigate the Custer battlefield.

As they relocated their camp near the river, they discovered that some of the missing—and presumed dead—from Reno's command had remained hidden for two days in the trees where Reno had formed his brief skirmish line on June 25.

TERRY REACHES THE LITTLE BIGHORN

General Terry had gotten under way from his Yellowstone bivouac on the fateful morning of June 25, moving upstream on the Bighorn River, bound for the mouth of the Little Bighorn. The going was slow, as Terry was leading an ungainly amalgam of cavalry and infantry, and because he wanted to carefully investigate Tullock's Fork of the Bighorn. Late in the day, some of Terry's Crow scouts reported seeing a great deal of smoke in the direction of the Little Bighorn.

On June 26, James Bradley of the 7th Infantry Regiment, who was spearheading Terry's advance with eleven mounted infantrymen and eighteen Crow Scouts, met three Crow riding downstream on

General Alfred H. Terry (1827–1890), while commander of the 10th Corps during the Civil War. (*National Archives*)

the Bighorn River. They were Goes Ahead, Hairy Moccasin, and White Man Runs Him, all of them scouts who had been with the 7th Cavalry. They told the incredible tale of what had occurred the day before. The troopers thought the narrative was a wild exaggeration, but Bradley rode back downstream and reported to Terry just as Gibbon arrived on the scene. Though they were unsure exactly what had happened, Terry and Gibbon could be sure that a battle of some kind had taken place up the Little Bighorn.

They waited for the 7th Infantry Regiment to catch up to the 2nd Cavalry detachment under Major James "Grasshopper Jim" Brisbin, and by early afternoon, the column had turned eastward, heading upstream on the Little Bighorn toward where the ominous cloud of dark smoke still hung.

The story of Custer's annihilation was too far fetched for Terry to believe, but he had not seen nor heard from Custer so he sent two scouts to ride quickly and deliver a message to the 7th Cavalry commander. The couriers returned late in the afternoon of June 26 to tell Terry that the valley up ahead was swarming with a large number of Lakota and Cheyenne. Indeed, the besieged Reno and Benteen were still fighting the Battle of the Little Bighorn.

At sundown, Lieutenant Bradley rode south to investigate for himself and saw the huge encampment being dismantled and moved out. Indeed, just as Bradley was watching them, the Lakota and Cheyenne scouts were monitoring his progress. That night, Terry's command camped under the watchful eye of the Lakota scouts, just eight miles from where Custer and his 210-man command lay dead.

The lead elements of Terry's column arrived on the scene early on the morning of June 27. They first came upon the detritus of the huge encampment, completely abandoned. They found a few dead Lakota, laid out ceremonially, and then they began to find discarded fragments of 7th Cavalry uniforms and gear.

The men of Terry's column were the first U.S. Army troops to ride up to Custer Hill since the battle nearly forty-eight hours before. Neither Reno nor Benteen had sent anyone to investigate what had happened to their commander. It was Terry's men who found Custer's body and who did a preliminary count of the dead bodies strewn across the hill. They counted 197 of the 210 within an hour or so. The others were all located later.

It was Terry himself who delivered the news to Reno and Benteen. A tally was taken: the battle had cost the lives of 263 soldiers and civilians, and there were fifty-nine wounded. Even Benteen's column, which had entirely missed the two major engagements of the battle, had suffered a dozen dead and nineteen wounded in the fighting overnight and on the second day. Those killed in action, most of whom had lain in the open under the scorching sun for more than two days, were hastily buried, generally where they had fallen.

The casualty count on the opposing side is unknown, and estimates vary widely from a couple of dozen dead to about the same numbers as were suffered by the 7th Cavalry. Because the dead belonged to many tribes and bands, and because these bands separated soon after the battle, it is probable that a total count was never made.

Terry had earlier ordered Captain Marsh of the *Far West* to bring his vessel up the Bighorn River—which had never before been navigated by a steamboat—as far as the mouth of the Little Bighorn. This was done, and the wounded were put aboard. Wriggling his way back down the narrow Bighorn, Marsh reached the Yellowstone on July 3. From there, he made the 710-mile run to Fort Abraham Lincoln in fifty-four hours. As the wounded men were transferred to the base hospital, the first news of the defeat of Custer's 7th Cavalry was telegraphed to the nation. It was major headline news, and it would remain so for weeks.

There would be a flurry of speculation and finger pointing that would go on for years. Who was responsible? The question was asked because it was assumed that someone had to be held accountable. Benteen was blamed for not being present on the battlefield sooner. Reno was blamed for retreating and not coming to Custer's aid. He was brought up on charges for this in 1879, but not convicted.

Finally, Custer is blamed for many things—for dividing his command, for misinterpreting or disobeying Terry's orders, for attacking too late in the day, with an exhausted command, without the element of surprise, and without adequate intelligence. All of

Looking toward the Little Bighorn from Custer Hill. Monuments include those for 7th Cavalry members, including George Custer (center), Tom Custer, and George Yates. (*Author Photo*)

these accusations are valid, and their aggregate effect proved fatal.

However, it can also be said that Custer lost because he faced an unusually large force of especially skilled and determined warriors. Custer and most of the 7th Cavalry probably fought bravely and fought well, but Gall, Crazy Horse, the Lakota, and the Cheyenne also fought bravely—and they fought better.

THE CAMPAIGN CONTINUES

The immense attention lavished upon the Battle of the Little Bighorn in the weeks that followed turned the impetuous Custer into a martyr and did a great deal to move the issue of United States government relations with the Indians of the West to the forefront of public consciousness.

There was a growing popular sentiment that the Great Sioux War must be won. The calls for decisive military action were voiced loudly, and they were heard in Congress, which appropriated funds for more troops to be sent to the West. General Sherman also ordered troop realignments, with units already in the West to be relocated to the theater of operations in Montana Territory. As soon as word of the Custer disaster reached his ears, the division commander, General Sheridan, had urged his field commanders to take swift action, but neither Crook nor Terry felt he was in a position to undertake an immediate pursuit until reinforcements arrived. It would be nearly six weeks before the troops in the field could go back into action.

Under Terry's command, the decimated 7th Cavalry had been the key mobile strike force, but it had lost more than half its men wounded or killed in action, and the rest were numb with post-traumatic shock. The same shock waves rippled through that portion of Gibbon's command who had seen the battlefield and who had helped bury the scalped, and otherwise mutilated, bodies.

Crook's command, who did not know of the Battle of the Little Bighorn until July 10, were also shaken by the news, having fought the nucleus of the same foe on June 17.*

Sheridan sent orders transferring the 5th Cavalry, then based in Kansas, but operating out of Fort Laramie, to Crook's command. Its new commander was Colonel Wesley Merritt, who had just taken over from the veteran Lieutenant Colonel Eugene Carr. Merritt took a detour en route to joining Crook to fight the first Indian battle in the West since the Little Bighorn on July 17.

Merritt received word that an estimated eight hundred Cheyenne warriors had left Red Cloud's Agency to join the hostile "army" in the Powder River country that had been responsible for the Little Bighorn fiasco. In fact, it was a band of fewer than one hundred being led by Lone Wolf, which may or may not have been the vanguard of a larger group. With Buffalo Bill Cody scouting for his column, Merritt laid a trap on Hat Creek in northwestern Nebraska, using a wagon train as bait. Merritt had three companies ready to pounce and infantrymen aboard the wagons. However, instead of taking the bait, seven of Lone Wolf's warriors went for two mounted riders. Merritt did not want to disclose the location of three companies to chase seven individuals, so Cody suggested that he and a couple of scouts go after the seven warriors.

---

*In the meantime, three men from Company E of the 7th Infantry had earned the Congressional Medal of Honor on July 9 for carrying the dispatch to Crook. They were Private James Bell, Private William Evans, and Private Benjamin Stewart.

Cody reached the Cheyenne first and almost immediately found himself in a duel with Yellow Hand, who was riding in the lead of his party. It was another of those moments in the folklore of the West that seems so unreal as to have been created by Hollywood. Cody, who was an excellent marksman, shot Yellow Hand's horse out from under him, but at that moment, Cody's own horse stumbled and fell.

Suddenly the two armed warriors stood facing one another, man to man. Armed with a Winchester repeating rifle and clad in buckskins, Cody faced Yellow Hand, who was armed with a Colt revolver, and—if the stories are true—wearing an enormous headdress of the type that was so dearly loved by the costume managers of classic westerns. Cody got off two shots, killing Yellow Hand with the second. He then took out his knife and lifted Yellow Hand's scalp, declaring it the "First scalp for Custer."

The remaining Cheyenne scattered and the 5th Cavalry gave chase for a little while, but there were no further casualties on either side. Eventually, Little Wolf's band returned quietly to the reservation. The battle at Hat Creek, now known as Warbonnet Creek, was not yet over, however. In the coming weeks and years, it would be embellished as a legend and replayed thousands of times. Cody's "heroism" would soon be the subject of many dime novels—and even a stage production.

On August 3, Merritt and the 5th Cavalry finally reached Crook's forward operating base on Goose Creek. When Crook went into the field again on August 5, he now commanded a force of two thousand troops. He organized twenty-five companies of the 2nd, 3rd, and 5th Cavalry into a brigade, with Colonel Merritt in command, and ten companies from the 4th, 9th, and 14th Infantry Regiments into a second brigade with Major Alexander Chambers in command. More than two hundred scouts, led by Shoshone Chief Washakie, rounded out the force that the U.S. Army wished had been at the Little Bighorn six weeks before.

Back in Montana Territory, General Terry mustered his own forces. By August 2, less than a month after news of the Little Bighorn reached the outside world, he had received two regiments of the reinforcements that he had requested. Colonel Nelson Miles, the ambitious young commander of the 5th Infantry Regiment, arrived with six companies, and Lieutenant Colonel Elwell Otis led six companies of the 22nd Infantry Regiment off the steamboat at the mouth of Rosebud Creek.

Terry formed an infantry brigade, giving Colonel Gibbon command of elements of the 5th, 6th, 7th, and 22nd Infantry Regiments. Terry also formed his cavalry into a brigade, under Grasshopper Jim Brisbin of the 2nd Cavalry. The brigade contained four companies of the 2nd Cavalry, as well as what remained of the 7th Cavalry. Reno now commanded the 7th Cavalry, which was had been reconstructed into eight rather than twelve companies. On August 8, Terry went into the field with his huge task force.

Crook moved into the headwaters of the Tongue River, then crossed into the valley of the Rosebud, where he picked up one of the many Indian trails that criss-crossed the Powder River country that summer. Terry meanwhile, ascended the Rosebud, retracing the steps taken by Custer as he began his last march on June 21. On the August 10, the columns led by Terry and Crook ran into a formidable armed force—each other!

The evidence contained in the Indian trail indicated that the large band was still holding together, but the evidence was more than a month old, and there was no way of knowing the current status.

In fact, it was at about the same time that Crook and Terry formed their joint task force on the Rosebud that the combined group of Cheyenne and Lakota fragmented. A few of the bands had peeled off in the weeks after June 26, but on August 9, as they broke camp near the mouth of the Powder River, the large remaining groups all went their separate ways. The Cheyenne went south, ascending the Powder River. Crazy Horse and the Oglala returned toward the Black Hills, while Sitting Bull's Hunkpapa moved northeast into Dakota Territory, and Long Dog's Hunkpapa crossed the Yellowstone River at Glendive Creek and rode due north.

Crook and Terry set out to follow the month-old Lakota and Cheyenne trail as it lead eastward toward the mouth of the Powder River. A week of bad weather made for slow going as the troops crossed the muddy gullies and wind-swept hills of southeastern Montana Territory. The formidable U.S. Army joint task force, nearly four thousand strong, reached the mouth of the Powder River on August 17, having found none of the warriors that they sought. The men were wet, cold, and tired, and their morale was sinking. Somewhere out on those Plains were thousands of Lakota and Cheyenne, but the troops that sought them had not seen a single one for weeks.

Just as the Indians had gone their separate ways, so too would the soldiers. Crook decided to take his command south and east toward the Black Hills, and Terry divided his command. It was late in the season, and the water was getting too low in the Yellowstone to run heavily laden supply ships into the Powder River country.

On August 26, General Sheridan had ordered Terry to establish posts at the mouths of the Tongue River and Glendive Creek and to station Miles's 5th Infantry Regiment and Otis's 22nd Infantry here through the winter. All of the available supply capability would have to be devoted to stockpiles to support this enterprise, so on September 5, Terry sent Gibbon and Brisbin back to Fort Ellis.

This essentially terminated the major three-pronged offensive that had begun in June, although it was not the end of major combat on the Plains during the centennial year.

THE ROAD TO SLIM BUTTES

For nearly two months following the Battle of the Little Bighorn, the enormous concentration of Indian warriors that had won that battle remained largely intact. It had taken most that time for the U.S. Army to field a force capable of confronting them, but the two armies were in the field simultaneously for nearly two weeks without meeting one another.

Despite a serious shortage of rations, Crook pressed on toward the Black Hills. His "starvation march" was a prescription for poor morale and diminished fighting strength—if not for disaster.

On September 8, as his men were subsisting on the meat of their own horses, Crook decided to send a supply train into the Black Hills mining town of Deadwood to purchase food for his beleaguered column. To escort the pack mules, he sent 150 men under the command of Captain Anson Mills of the 3rd Cavalry. This small detachment would succeed in doing what the huge task force had failed to do for a month. It made contact with the Lakota.

In the early morning of September 9, near the place known as Slim Buttes, Mills's troopers came upon thirty-seven tipis belonging to the band of Oglala led by Little Bighorn veteran American Horse. The troopers attacked, and the Oglala fought back fiercely. By the middle of the day, the almost accidental Battle of Slim Buttes had become the biggest engagement to occur on the Northern Plains since the Little Bighorn.

Crook arrived with his main force, as did a sizable number of Oglala from Crazy Horse's much larger camp, which was nearby but previously undetected by the soldiers.

The fight continued through the night and into the following day, albeit with diminishing intensity. Finally, Crook disengaged his hungry fighters in order to resume the principal task at hand, which was to find food.

Crook's command suffered only three men killed in action at Slim Buttes, but fifteen were wounded. The troops seized the camp's winter supply of dried buffalo meat, captured twenty-three Oglala, and killed an estimated fourteen. American Horse died later from wounds suffered in the battle.

Two men of the 3rd Cavalry's Company M, Sergeant John Kirkwood and Private Robert Smith, were awarded the Congressional Medal of Honor when they "Bravely endeavored to dislodge some Sioux Indians secreted in a ravine" at Slim Buttes.

On September 13, Crook's starvation march finally ended as his large column made contact with a supply train. Ironically, the U.S. Army had finally found its target, but only after the available troops were too exhausted to ride in pursuit of the Lakota. Crazy Horse, meanwhile, led his followers back into the Powder River country for the winter.

BEAR COAT, SITTING BULL, AND THE WINTER OF 1876

When the great offensive formations of the 1876 campaign were dismantled in September, Colonel Miles was left to hold down the fort—literally—in his newly established post on the Yellowstone River. Terry went back to the Department of Dakota headquarters at St. Paul, having created a new subsidiary District of the Yellowstone and naming Miles to command it.

As Miles went into his winter quarters, the coming months were expected to be filled with tedious garrison duty. In mid-October, however, Sitting Bull returned. He and Gall had come back from Dakota Territory with a contingent of as many as six hundred Hunkpapa, Minneconjou, and Sans Arc Lakota warriors.

Between October 11 and 15, Sitting Bull's warriors raided 22nd Infantry Regiment supply trains on the north side of the Yellowstone. On the latter date, Elwell Otis parleyed with a group of Lakota and they agreed to leave the supply trains alone.

Alerted to Sitting Bull's presence, Nelson Miles decided to go on the offensive. Taking the 449 officers and men of his 5th Infantry Regiment, Miles set out to track the Lakota. It took just two days, and on October 20, the 5th Cavalry located the Lakota on Cedar Creek about twenty miles north of the Yellowstone. Sitting Bull said that he wanted to talk to the 5th Infantry commander, whom the Lakota had dubbed "Bear Coat" because of his heavy winter overcoat.

The two leaders parleyed and argued for the better part of two days, with Miles demanding that Sitting Bull take his band back to the reservation, and the Lakota insisting that he and his people were not and would never be "Reservation Indians."

General Nelson Appleton Miles (1839–1925) was an important commander in Indian Wars operations both on the Plains and in the desert Southwest. He became the U.S. Army's commanding general in 1895. (*National Archives*)

On October 21, the talks broke down and Miles unleashed his army. Supported by artillery, Miles forced the Lakota—which may have outnumbered the 5th Infantry Regiment two to one—onto the defensive. Miles chased Sitting Bull downstream on Bad Route Creek to the Yellowstone, which the Lakota crossed on October 24. As Miles now suspended the chase, the Lakota had been forced to abandon a great deal of their gear, not to mention horses and large stockpiles of food.

On October 27, Miles was approached by a number of Minneconjou and Sans Arc, who asked to turn themselves in. Having no agency facilities to care for them in Montana Territory, Miles directed them to go to the Cheyenne River Agency on the Missouri in Dakota Territory. Some did, but others went south to join Crazy Horse's Oglala.

With Nelson Miles in the field, U.S. Army operations along the Yellowstone were more productive in the late autumn than they had been with a much larger force during the late summer. The same was true on the southern side of the theater in Crook's sector. Just as Miles had energized the Yellowstone salient, Colonel Ranald Mackenzie would invigorate operations in the upper Powder River country.

After a brief tour of duty in Washington, D.C., during which he commanded troops assembled to keep the peace if disruptions occurred during the presidential election in early November, Mackenzie came west. It is curious to link domestic unrest in an eastern city to the Indian Wars in the West, but 1876 was a contentious year in both places. Samuel Tilden had won the popular vote in the election, but he lost to Rutherford B. Hayes by one vote in the Electoral College. The squabbling and controversy would not finally be put to rest until Hayes was inaugurated in March 1877. Violence that had seemed probable was averted and MackKenzie was sent to take part in Crook's winter offensive against the Lakota.

Riding out of Fort Fetterman on November 14, Crook commanded a 2,200-man force, the size of that which he had fielded three months earlier. It consisted of fifteen companies drawn from the 4th, 9th, 14th, and 25th Infantry Regiments and 4th Artillery Regiment under Lieutenant Colonel Richard Dodge. Mackenzie would lead eleven companies of the 2nd, 3rd, 4th, and 5th Cavalry.

The plan was to find Crazy Horse, who was wintering the Powder River country near where he had beaten Crook in June, but the scouts brought word of a large encampment of Cheyenne. These were the people from the big encampment on the Little Bighorn who had traveled with the Lakota until mid-August before turning south.

Crook turned Mackenzie's cavalry loose to form and execute an attack. At dawn on November 25, 1,100 cavalrymen fell upon the large bands of Little Wolf and Dull Knife camped on the Red Fork of the Powder River. The four hundred warriors who were present fought ferociously, but so did the troopers, for whom the Custer fiasco still resonated. Mackenzie's command lost six men killed in action and twenty-six wounded. The Cheyenne battle deaths numbered perhaps as many as forty.

Sergeant Thomas Forsyth of the 4th Cavalry's Company M earned the Congressional Medal of Honor in the battle. As his citation states, "Though dangerously wounded, he maintained his ground with a small party against a largely superior force after his commanding officer had been shot down during a sudden attack and rescued that officer and a comrade from the enemy."

As Mackenzie's men secured the Cheyenne village, they found a large number of items, including a flag bearing 7th Cavalry insignia. These had obviously been looted from the Little Bighorn battlefield exactly five months earlier. Though many of the Cheyenne escaped, the troops burned the village and its contents, severely affecting the ability of the survivors to get through the winter. The Indians would travel overland through the snow and cold, finally linking up with Crazy Horse on the Tongue River in mid-December.

Crook remained in the field himself until mid-December, before coming in from the cold without finding Crazy Horse. Bear Coat Miles, in contrast, remained active through the harsh winter months. The weather created a climate in which many of the Lakota and the Cheyenne began thinking that reservation life might not be so bad after all. Having lost most of his people's property to Mackenzie, Dull Knife made surrender overtures to Miles, as did several Lakota chiefs. Crazy Horse did not, but he was apparently in the minority.

Miles would come very close to achieving a major negotiated resolution to the Powder River situation as the centennial year neared its end. It was almost within his grasp when it was snatched away by his own Crow scouts.

On December 16, as a delegation of chiefs was en route to meet with Miles at his base on the Tongue River, they were attacked by the Crow, who killed five of them. The people who might have been ready for peace turned again to the road to war, a detour that merely postponed the inevitable

Meanwhile, Miles was continuing to keep up the pressure on Sitting Bull's Hunkpapa. Even as the Crow were assaulting the delegation coming to parley with Miles, three companies of the 5th Infantry Regiment under Lieutenant Frank Baldwin were operating to the north, between the Yellowstone and the Missouri. On December 18, they attacked a village of 122 tipis located on Ash Creek. There was minimal fighting because most of the warriors associated with the encampment were on a hunting trip. Only one Lakota was killed, but the troops burned the tipis and the supplies at the site.

Operating from a forward location in the center of the theater, Nelson Miles was able to keep up the relentless pressure on the Cheyenne and the Lakota throughout the winter. In this campaign, Miles demonstrated that infantry could be very effective in operations against the Indians on the Plains. It had become axiomatic since the Civil War that cavalry was better suited for such a task, but Miles disproved the belief that winter. He probably made the best use of infantry in successful campaigning of any U.S. Army commander in the Indian Wars.

One of the most aggressive commanders that the Army had seen in the West in some time, Miles was also exhibiting the sort of drive and determination that would eventually take him to the top job, commanding general of the U.S. Army.

A large number of Congressional Medals of Honor would be awarded to the men of the 5th Infantry Regiment who had participated in Miles's campaign that winter. The citations read "Gallantry," and the place and date read "At Cedar Creek, etc., Montana Territory, 21 October 1876 to 8 January 1877." As was true of any roster of enlisted men compiled during the Indian Wars of the 1870s, a substantial number of these men had been born in Ireland.*

The early January actions were included in these citations because the last battle that can be properly counted among the closing battles of the centennial year actually took place one week into 1877.

Fresh from sorties against Sitting Bull, Miles departed his headquarters shortly after Christmas 1876 and marched upriver on the Tongue, hoping to make contact with some of Crazy Horse's Oglala. He led five companies of the 5th Infantry Regiment, plus two of the 22nd Infantry and an artillery detachment. On January 7, an attempt by the Cheyenne to

---

*The men thus awarded included musician John Baker of Company D, Private Richard Burke of Company G, Sergeant Denis Byrne of Company G, Private Joseph Cable of Company I, Private James Calvert of Company C, Sergeant Aquilla Coonrod of Company C, Private John Donelly of Company G, Private Christopher Freemeyer of Company D, Corporal John Haddoo of Company B, Sergeant Henry Hogan of Company G, Corporal David Holland of Company A, Private Fred Hunt of Company A, Corporal Edward Johnston of Company C, Private Philip Kennedy of Company C, Sergeant Wenelin Kreher of Company C, Private Michael McCormick of Company G, Private Owen McGar of Company C, Private John McHugh of Company A, Sergeant Michael McLoughlin of Company A, Sergeant Robert McPhelan of Company E, Corporal George Miller of Company H, Private Charles Montrose of Company I, Sergeant David Roche of Company A, Private David Rodenburg of Company A, Private Edward Rooney of Company D, Private David Ryan of Company G, Private Charles Sheppard of Company A, Sergeant William Wallace of Company C, Private Patton Whitehead of Company C, Corporal Charles Wilson of Company H, and Private Bernard McCann of Company F, 22nd Infantry.

ambush the column near Deer Creek backfired, and Miles captured a party of Cheyenne, including women and children. Attempts to recapture the prisoners that afternoon failed, and Miles prepared his troops to fight a defensive battle the following day near Wolf Mountain.

During a blizzard that lashed the Plains on January 8, Miles successfully used his artillery to fend off repeated attacks by Crazy Horse. The brilliant tactician who had successfully delivered the coup de grace against Custer in June had met his match in Bear Coat Miles.

With only three soldiers and five warriors killed in action at Wolf Mountain, it could be written off as a minor battle, but in fact it was probably the engagement that finally convinced both Crazy Horse and Sitting Bull—who was not there but who had been running from Bear Coat Miles all winter—that the soldiers would not be defeated.*

The Indian Wars during the centennial year had been characterized by disappointment for the U.S. Army. The great military campaign south of the Yellowstone had failed, but even this was overshadowed by the bad luck of the senior field commanders. Custer had lost in spectacular fashion, while Terry and Gibbon failed even to find a decisive engagement to fight. George Crook, regarded as the best general in the field, had been beaten to a stalemate on the Rosebud, and was perceived as having nearly lost his command to starvation. In the coming year, however, the U.S. Army would see the rise of one of its shining stars in the person of Nelson Miles.

---

*Three 5th Infantry Regiment officers earned the Congressional Medal of Honor specifically for their actions at Wolf Mountain: Captain Edmond Butler, Captain James Casey, and Lieutenant Robert McDonald, who, as his citation notes, "Led his command in a successful charge against superior numbers of hostile Indians, strongly posted."

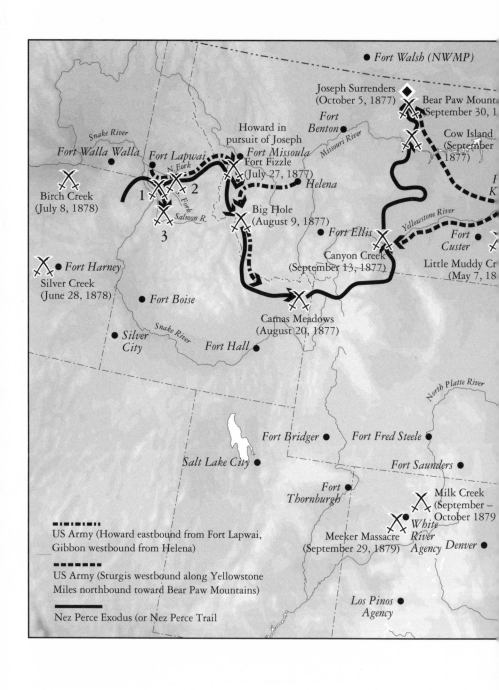

Fort Walsh (NWMP)

Joseph Surrenders
(October 5, 1877)
Bear Paw Mount
September 30, 1

Fort
Benton

Cow Island
(September
1877)

Fort Walla Walla
Snake River
Fort Lapwai
N. Fork
Fort Missoula
Fort Fizzle
(July 27, 1877)
Missouri River
Helena

Birch Creek
(July 8, 1878)
1   2
S. Fork
Salmon R.
3

Big Hole
(August 9, 1877)

Yellowstone River

Fort Ellis
Canyon Creek
(September 13, 1877)
Fort
Custer

Fort Harney
Silver Creek
(June 28, 1878)
Little Muddy Cr
(May 7, 18

Fort Boise
Camas Meadows
(August 20, 1877)

Snake River
Fort Hall
Silver
City

North Platte River

Fort Bridger
Fort Fred Steele

Salt Lake City
Fort Saunders

Fort
Thornburgh
Milk Creek
(September –
October 1879
White
River
Agency
Denver

Meeker Massacre
(September 29, 1879)

▬▪▬▪▬▪▬▪
US Army (Howard eastbound from Fort Lapwai,
Gibbon westbound from Helena)

▬▬▬▬▬
US Army (Sturgis westbound along Yellowstone
Miles northbound toward Bear Paw Mountains)

Nez Perce Exodus (or Nez Perce Trail

Los Pinos
Agency

7

A Culture Eclipsed

The centennial year of the United States had begun with the Indian Wars in the West far from the attention of most Americans. Against this backdrop, the Little Bighorn had been a profound shock because it was such an enormous loss, but mainly because it was so unexpected. Of course, the fact that Custer was such a media star made it a major story for journalists.

For the Lakota and Cheyenne who had rejected the treaties and reservations, the Little Bighorn was a moment to celebrate because it seemed to represent such a total victory over the U.S. Army, and over Custer. who was its symbol. The fact of Custer's stardom was as well known to them as it was the readers of the *New York Herald* on the streets of Manhattan. The celebration would not, and indeed could not, last. By year's end, the Indians' would lose the war was as inevitable as the completeness of their victories in the June battles.

The centennial year of the United States ended with the nation more united than at any time since the Creek War in its determination to end the resistance by the militants among the continent's indigenous people.

The U.S. Army and the Indian Bureau no longer squabbled over whether it should be done, but how it would be done. The year ended with the most militant of the Plains tribes shivering amid the snowdrifts wondering when and where Bear Coat Miles would strike next. Many were willing, and even anxious, to sign on at an agency. Even Crazy Horse was having second thoughts, and Sitting Bull would soon go into exile to escape Miles.

THE SLOW DEATH OF THE GREAT SIOUX WAR

The Lakota and Northern Cheyenne had ridden out from the Greasy Grass in June 1876 as a formidable and victorious fighting machine of epic dimensions. Despite having eluded the enormous dragnet cast by Crook and Terry in the closing weeks of the 1876 campaign, their power had eventually waned, crushed under its own weight. The logistical problems associated with keeping such a group, including its women and children, in the field through the Plains winter were insurmountable.

Less than a year later, they had been reduced to a handful of fugitive bands. In 1877, the U.S. Army returned to the Little Bighorn, constructing a fort at the center of what had so recently been the heartland of Lakota power. Located at the mouth of the Little Bighorn, it was called Fort Custer. Meanwhile, the outpost at the mouth of the Tongue River became Fort Keogh.

The constant pressure of Nelson Miles's winter operations, supported by a base in the center of the theater, was the primary reason that the tide had turned against the Lakota and Northern Cheyenne. Ranald Mackenzie's blow against the Cheyenne in November 1876 was another important factor, and the two men would be rewarded as the U.S. Army reorganized itself for the next phase of the Sioux War.

Miles and Mackenzie were now the in-theater field commanders. Terry commanded the Department of Dakota from his headquarters in St. Paul, and Crook the Department of the Platte from Omaha, but Miles and Mackenzie now commanded the troops in the field. Sheridan expanded the boundaries of Miles's District of the Yellowstone to include the entirety of the Powder River country. Rules of engagement were rewritten permitting operations across departmental boundaries during ongoing pursuit operations.

There would be few such operations in 1877. In the spring of 1876, the top concern had been Lakota and Cheyenne streaming off the reservation, but a year later, the tables had turned. As soon as the snows melted in the spring of 1877, the exodus was onto the reservations. Spotted Tail, whom the United States government tacitly recognized as the "super-chief" of all the Sioux, agreed to lead a peace mission to coax the bands in, and it seemed to work. Even though the concept of a Sioux super-chief was an absurd notion to the people themselves, Spotted Tail was widely respected.

There were exceptions to the stream of Indians coming back onto the reservations. In May 1877, Sitting Bull fled north to the land of the "White Mother" or "White Grandmother," as the Lakota described Queen Victoria's Dominion of Canada. Here, the U.S. Army could not touch him, and here he would remain there until 1881.

At the same time that Sitting Bull went north, Crazy Horse's Oglala and the Minneconjou band led by Lame Deer went west, returning to the Powder River country as so many had the year before. On May 1, Bear Coat Miles went in search of Lame Deer. He started up the Tongue River and crossed over to the Rosebud, just as Custer had headed up the Rosebud in the same direction a bit more than ten months earlier.

Miles had with him 471 men, a contingent of the 2nd Cavalry, as well as six mounted companies drawn from the 5th and 22nd Infantry Regiments. As guides, he took with him three men with whom he had recently been at war, the Cheyenne warriors Brave Wolf and White Bull, and Hump, a fellow Minneconjou of Lame Deer's.

On May 7, at a side stream of the Rosebud called Little Muddy Creek, Miles executed a dawn surprise attack, the same sort of attack that Custer had planned for June 26, 1876, but never made. Lame Deer and his nephew Iron Star ran, but found themselves cornered. Hump convinced them to come and parley with Bear Coat, and they did. Miles told them to put down their rifles, and they nervously complied, although they left them cocked and pointed forward. As they began to converse with Miles, a scout made a false move and up came the rifles. Lame Deer fired at Miles, he dodged, and the bullet killed another trooper. A ferocious gun battle ensued and Lame Deer fell.

When the smoke settled over the Battle of Little Muddy Creek, four troopers had been killed in action and nine were wounded. An estimated fourteen Minneconjou were dead, and twenty wounded. Lame Deer had died with seventeen bullet wounds. Miles took forty prisoners, but Lame Deer's son, Fast Bull, got away. His band would remain at large through the summer, but they were a minor annoyance compared to the situation during the previous summer.*

*Men of the 2nd Cavalry who were awarded the Congressional Medal of Honor for actions at Little Muddy Creek included Corporal Harry Garland, farrier William Jones, Private William Leonard, Private Samuel Phillips, and Sergeant Henry Wilkins. Garland, Jones, and Wilkins would have later actions included in their Medal of Honor citations.

Two days before the shootout on Little Muddy Creek, the most momentous event of the season occurred at the Red Cloud Agency. None other than Crazy Horse rode in to surrender himself and his Oglala band. Crook had made several attempts at making contact with him to negotiate his coming in. He had sent Spotted Tail to the Powder River country in the late winter, but Crazy Horse avoided him.

In late April, Red Cloud had gone out to meet with Crazy Horse and had conveyed the notion that Crook would consider designating an agency for Crazy Horse, not in Dakota Territory with the others, but in the Powder River country. The Oglala were hungry and running short of ammunition with which to hunt and to continue the armed struggle against the U.S. Army. Crazy Horse finally acquiesced.

He remained at a camp near the agency through the summer, making everyone—from the soldiers at nearby Fort Robinson to the agents to the other chiefs—nervous. He remained detached and unapproachable, scowling and pacing. He was waiting for the promised agency, but the others thought that he was planning trouble. He was invited to go to Washington to meet President Hayes, but he refused.

When the U.S. Army started to recruit Lakota for its corps of scouts, this infuriated Crazy Horse. He thought that they would be used against Sitting Bull. Crazy Horse became so agitated that it was feared he would incite a revolt among the Oglala, and that they would return to their previous state of war with the Army.

On September 2, General Crook ordered that Crazy Horse be confined at Fort Robinson. Crazy Horse escaped to the Red Cloud Agency to hide, but he was found and he agreed to go to the fort. Some soldiers and agency police went to arrest him on September 5. Among the agency police, he recognized Little Big Man, a fellow Oglala who had once fought as a warrior alongside Crazy Horse. To Crazy Horse, this was a tremendous insult.

At Fort Robinson, as Crazy Horse was about to be locked up, there was a scuffle and Crazy Horse suffered a stab wound. Whose blade was responsible has been debated ever since. Some say that it was a bayonet wielded by Private William Gentles on the order of Captain James Kennington. Others say it was Little Big Man, possibly in response to Crazy Horse pulling his own knife in an attempt to flee. In any case, Crazy Horse died of his wounds later that night at the age of thirty-five.

In October, many of the Oglala who were part of Crazy Horse's band left the reservation to join Sitting Bull in Canada, but the reservation remained fairly quiet. There were ongoing negotiations over the final location of the various agencies. The government wanted them near the navigable Missouri River for ease of movement of supplies, but the Lakota wanted them farther west in their familiar territory.

Red Cloud and Spotted Tail traveled to Washington to meet Hayes. Even Crook supported the chiefs. Finally, in 1878, the agencies were moved to the Dakota Territory (now South Dakota) locations where they remain today. The Spotted Tail Agency became the Rosebud Agency—although it is nearly three hundred miles southeast of Rosebud Creek—and the Red Cloud Agency became the Pine Ridge Agency.

The Northern Cheyenne, meanwhile, were sent south to the Cheyenne and Arapaho Agency in Indian Territory, rather that to Pine Ridge as they wished. In Indian Territory, they felt unhappy and out of place, and longing for the Northern Plains, they asked to be collocated with the Lakota.

On September 7, 1878, Dull Knife and Little Wolf made a truly desperate break to get back to Montana Territory. With just ninety-two warriors, they attempted to move a party of 268 women and children through country where the U.S. Army clearly had the upper hand. Captain Joseph Rendlebrock went out from Fort Reno to intercept them, accompanied by two companies of the 4th Cavalry and an Arapaho scout known as Ghost Man.

Rendlebrock sent Ghost Man to urge the Cheyenne to turn around. Little Wolf refused, a squabble ensued, Ghost Man pulled his gun, and a firefight broke out. When the dust settled, Ghost Man and two soldiers were dead, and the Cheyenne had gotten away with a few wounded.

To resume the pursuit of the Cheyenne, the Army assembled a larger force that included five companies of the 4th Cavalry Regiment, as well as three companies of the 19th Infantry Regiment under Lieutenant Colonel William Lewis. Little Wolf saw the troops coming and laid an ambush for them at Punished Woman's Fork of the Smoky Hill River on September 27. Lewis led his men into the ambush, but one eager warrior fired prematurely and the soldiers escaped with one man killed in action, and six wounded. Among the latter was Lieutenant Colonel Lewis, who bled to death later that night.

By October 23, Dull Knife and Little Wolf had made it all the way to the vicinity of Fort Robinson in northern Nebraska, where Dull Knife's party was taken into custody. Little Wolf and his people got away, and they would elude capture through the winter.

Dull Knife's band was placed in barracks at Fort Robinson surrounded by six companies of the 3rd Cavalry. Post commander Captain Henry Wessels attempted unsuccessfully to convince them to return to Indian Territory. In January, in a desperate effort to make them change their minds, he locked them up and cut off their food and firewood.

On January 9, 1878, they made a desperate attempt to break out. They ran into a hail of gunfire, in which sixty-four men, women, and children were killed. The rest managed to get away, but seventy-eight were rounded up over the next two weeks. As many as ten were never found and are presumed to have died from exposure in the bitter winter cold. The U.S. Army sent twenty people back to Indian Territory, but allowed fifty-eight to settle at Pine Ridge.

Little Wolf's band, meanwhile, managed to get as far as Montana Territory, where they were captured on March 27, 1879. They were allowed to remain at Fort Keogh at the mouth of the Tongue River, and in 1880, thanks to Bear Coat Miles's intercession, Dull Knife and his band were allowed to join them in Montana Territory at the Lame Deer Agency on the Rosebud, which became the administrative center of the Northern Cheyenne Reservation.

SITTING BULL IN EXILE

With Crazy Horse dead, and the Lakota and Northern Cheyenne contained at the agencies, the Great Sioux War was slowly grinding to a conclusion. The only missing piece in the puzzle was the elusive Sitting Bull. A major voice for rebellion in 1876, and an observer at the Battle of the Little Bighorn, the Hunkpapa shaman had become a larger-than-life figure since he had escaped to Canada in May 1877.

In Canada, Sitting Bull came under the jurisdiction of the North West Mounted Police, best known by their nickname, the Mounties. Established in May 1873 by Sir John Macdonald, the first prime minister of Canada, the Mounties were intended to institute law and order and assert Canadian sovereignty in the North West Territories, which encompassed today's provinces of Alberta and Saskatchewan.

The organizational structure of the Mounties was based on that of a nineteenth-century British cavalry regiment. Macdonald directed that the Mounties wear red uniforms to emphasize the British nature of the force, and to differentiate it from the U.S. Army's blue uniforms. Known since 1920 as the Royal Canadian Mounted Police, the Mounties today function as a national police force in Canada, with law enforcement powers roughly analogous to the American FBI.

On May 7, 1877, Sitting Bull and his Lakota refugees would be met by the North West Mounted Police detachment commanded by Major James Walsh, based at Fort Walsh in the southeast corner of what is now Saskatchewan. Walsh explained to the Lakota that they could stay in Canada as long as they obeyed the "White Mother's" rules. They agreed, and Sitting Bull showed Walsh a King George III peace medal that his grandfather had gotten at the time of the War of 1812.

The Canadian government was reluctant to have a Lakota leader of such notoriety as Sitting Bull within its borders, and they pressured the United States to send a team to negotiate his return. On October 17, 1877, General Terry went up to Fort Walsh to meet with Sitting Bull, Walsh, and North West Mounted Police Commissioner Lieutenant Colonel James Macleod. Sitting Bull flatly refused to go back with Terry.

Bear Coat Miles, meanwhile, suggested that he would not be opposed to just going up to Canada and grabbing the fugitive Lakota. There was a precedent of sorts in Ranald Mackenzie's 1873 cross-border incursion to strike the Kickapoo near Remolino, Mexico. However, neither Terry nor General Sherman had any desire to have Miles involved in an international incident involving the Mounties in Canada.

By the summer of 1879, it seemed as though Miles stood a chance of actually catching Sitting Bull on American turf, as the Lakota started to slip across the "medicine line" into Montana Territory to hunt buffalo. Miles stationed seven companies of the 2nd Cavalry, plus another seven of mounted 5th Infantry, in an effort to be ready for such an eventuality. In July, the U.S. Army was in a running gun battle with a Lakota hunting party, and Walsh and Miles exchanged some heated words.

Small unit actions involving the U.S. Army and the Lakota in Montana Territory well south of the border would continue through the end of the decade and beyond. A few are worth a brief mention, if only to show that the wars on the remote corners of the Northern Plains lingered long after Crazy Horse and Sitting Bull were no longer an active part of the picture.

Sergeant T. B. Glover of the 2nd Cavalry received the Congressional Medal of Honor for his actions in two such skirmishes in the Yellowstone River country, one on April 10, 1879 on Mizpah Creek, a tributary of the Powder River and another on Pumpkin Creek, a tributary of the Tongue River, on February 10, 1880. In the latter incident, Glover and a small patrol chased a band of Lakota horse thieves for sixty-five miles, finally cornering them. In the ensuing firefight, Glover killed one, wounded two, and captured three, while losing one of his troopers killed in action.

Meanwhile, on April 17, 1879, Lieutenant Samuel Loder and a detachment of the 7th Infantry Regiment were in a particularly bloody shootout with the Lakota in the headwaters of the Musselshell River in Montana Territory in which two soldiers and eight Lakota were killed in action. Three months later, on July 17, a detachment led by Lieutenant Philo Clark of the 2nd Cavalry was involved in a skirmish with some Hunkpapa from Sitting Bull's band along the Canadian border that cost the lives of three on each side.

On April 1, 1880, two 2nd Cavalry officers earned the Congressional Medal of Honor in an encounter with the Lakota on O'Fallon's Creek in the Powder River country. Lieutenant Lloyd Brett and Captain Eli Huggins surprised the Lakota and captured their horses. The latter were essential to the mobility required both for raiding and for hunting the dwindling number of buffalo on the Northern Plains.

Ultimately, it was the buffalo, Sitting Bull's own namesake, that forced his return. By the end of the 1870s, commercial hunting on the Plains in the United States had dramatically reduced the numbers of the big beasts available to be hunted by the indigenous people for whom they were long a dietary staple. Gradually the Lakota in Canada began looking upon the free food and supplies available at the agencies as an honorable alternative to going hungry. In 1879 and 1880, many Lakota returned south to Dakota Territory. Finally, in 1881, it was Sitting Bull's turn. On July 19, 1881, the fifty-year-old elder statesman of the Lakota rode into Fort Buford in Dakota Territory with forty-five men, sixty-seven women, and seventy-three children. Bear Coat Miles was not present.

After serving two years as a prisoner of war, Sitting Bull settled on the Standing Rock Agency, where he became a prominent member of the community, and a successful rancher. He had several wives and many children, whom he sent to reservation schools, despite his insistence on their not losing their Lakota culture. In 1885, he even dabbled in show business, touring with Buffalo Bill's Wild West Show.

The Nez Percé

The first contact that the U.S. Army had with the Nez Percé people living in the Clearwater River country of the Idaho panhandle came in September 1805, when Captain Meriwether Lewis, Captain William Clark, and the Corps of Discovery stumbled out of the Bitterroot Mountains after a horrible trek of near starvation.

The Nez Percé welcomed the strangers with open arms. The hospitality of the Nez Percé saved lives, and perhaps assured the success of the Lewis and Clark expedition. Of all the hospitable tribes that Lewis and Clark encountered during their two-way trek across the continent, there is perhaps none that truly fits the bill for being a participant in a real model for the first Thanksgiving than the Nez Percé. Like the Shoshone, they shared food when food was scarce, and they shared precious horses.

Horses probably reached the Nez Percé early in eighteenth century, and they had about the same effect as in the case of buffalo hunting Plains peoples. Horses gave them a mobility that had never before been possible. It is interesting that in the valleys above the Columbia River, the methods of using the horse were the same as in the Plains, and that along with this went a similarity in dress, furnishings, and the use of the tipi.

Over the years, the Nez Percé also became recognized as being among the best horsemen of all the indigenous people of North America. The popular and distinctive Appaloosa breed originated with the Nez Percé. The term Appaloosa is derived from the word "Palouse," the name of the region of the Palouse River drainage in northeast Oregon and southeast Washington that was part of the traditional homeland of the Nez Percé, as well as of the related Palouse people.

The name Nez Percé was given to the people because, when they were first encountered by the French, some members of the tribe were seen wearing pendants attached to their pierced noses. They traditionally hunted wild game, especially buffalo, but fished for salmon as well. The Penutian-speaking Nez Percé are linguistically related to other nearby tribes, including the Palouse, Umatilla, Wall Walla, and Yakima, who speak a dialect referred to by linguists as Shahaptin or Sahaptini.

The Nez Percé had generally good relations with Europeans and Euro-Americans beginning with the French and continuing with Americans such as Lewis and Clark. In 1831 they even sent emissaries to St. Louis requesting Christian missionaries. There was probably no tribe in the entire West that was less likely an antagonist in warfare than the Nez Percé. They had remained neutral in all the region's wars, including the Rogue River Wars of the 1850s. When war clouds next rolled across the valleys and forests of the Northwest, the Nez Percé would write one of the greatest epics in the history of the Indian Wars, and would see the rise to national prominence of one of the greatest Indian leaders of all time.

The tribe was actually two tribes, an Upper and Lower Nez Percé, with each occupying its own distinct lands but sharing certain common hunting grounds. This distinction, however, was lost on the United States government, which in 1863 entered into a treaty with the Upper Nez Percé, who signed away the lands granted to both Nez Percé groups in a previous treaty in 1855.

It took over ten years before immigrant population growth in Lower Nez Percé territory reached a level where it encroached on the people who still were not abiding by the treaty that had been signed for them. In 1873, President Grant signed an executive order creating a Lower Nez Percé reservation in the Wallowa Valley, but this order was rescinded in 1875 out of pressure from Oregonians and would-be settlers.

The Lakota and Northern Cheyenne resistance that had been unfolding through 1876 had been seen by many within the Nez Percé community as heroic, and as a model for how to deal with the mistreatment that the tribe seemed to be experiencing from the United States government.

A moderating force against the rising tide of militancy was an articulate and diplomatic thirty-six-year-old leader named Heinmot Tooyalakekt. Born in present-day eastern Oregon, he had been educated at mission schools and had taken the name Joseph. He was the son of Tuyakaskas, an equally respected leader, also known as Joseph, who died in 1871.

The younger Joseph, known to the people of the region as Chief Joseph, sought to arrange a negotiated settlement that would please everyone and avoid the type of bloodshed that had occurred in the Powder River coun-

General Oliver Otis Howard (1830–1909), West Point Class of 1854, left, commanded the Department of the Columbia during the operations against the Nez Percé. (*National Archives*) Heinmot Tooyalakekt, Chief Joseph, (1841–1904), right, was the astute Nez Percé leader who led his people from Oregon, through Idaho and Montana, successfully evading the U.S. Army for four months in 1877. (*Author*)

try since the summer of 1876. His opposite number was Brigadier General Oliver Otis Howard, who had taken over the Department of the Columbia in 1874. Previously a peacemaker to the Apache in Arizona Territory, Howard had been an advocate for African Americans as head of the Freedman's Bureau after the Civil War and was the founder of Howard University. Since taking over in the Columbia, Howard had immersed himself in the Nez Percé issue, convinced that a Wallowa reservation was a good idea.

It is hard to imagine two men ostensibly on opposite sides of the issue who were more predisposed to peace than Joseph and Howard. However, at a council held at the Lapwai Agency in November 1876, Howard was dismayed and angered at Joseph's unwillingness to compromise. He was also worried by the growing militancy of all the tribes on the Columbia in the wake of the huge defeat that the U.S. Army had suffered on the Little Bighorn.

In May 1877 at the U.S. Army's Fort Lapwai, Howard met again with Joseph, as well as other Nez Percé leaders, such as White Bird, Looking Glass, and Toohulhulsote (Toohoolhoolzote). Howard saw no reason why they needed to be on their ancestral land in the Wallowa, and the southern wing of the Nez Percé was ordered to move from the Wallowa onto the Lapwai Reservation.

In June, some young men from White Bird's band killed some settlers at Camas Prairie. On June 15, Howard, who was still at Fort Lapwai, ordered Captain David Perry to take elements of two companies of the 1st Cavalry and ride immediately to Camas Prairie. In the meantime, another fifteen settlers had been killed at Grangeville. None of the killings had the sanction of any Nez Percé leaders, but Howard had no way of knowing this.

Perry's orders were to cut the Nez Percé off from escaping across the Bitterroot Range. However, this didn't take into account the fact that the Nez Percé were about to undertake their annual trip across the mountains to hunt buffalo on the Plains—as the Nez Percé had done for many generations before Lewis and Clark had come.

White Bird Canyon and Its Aftermath

On the morning of June 17, Perry's command was on White Bird Creek, heading through the canyon of the same name toward the Salmon River. Meanwhile, Joseph and a large party were camped at the confluence of White Bird Creek and the Salmon, preparing for the annual trek across the Bitterroots. As the advance party of Perry's column, accompanied by some Idaho volunteers, approached Joseph's camp, Joseph sent some men out with a white flag, hoping to arrange a parley. The volunteers opened fire at the truce party and the fight was on.

From positions high on the steep slopes of White Bird Canyon, the Nez Percé quickly shot the volunteers and the advance guard. Perry and his men scrambled for defensive cover and proceeded to fight their way back out of the canyon, stunned by the marksmanship and efficiency of the Nez Percé, and the skill of their battlefield leaders.

The 1st Cavalry and the volunteers suffered thirty-four men killed in action, a figure that represented more than a third of the force with which Perry had left Fort Lapwai. The Nez Percé had three men wounded. Coming a week before the first anniversary of the Battle of the Little Bighorn, the Battle of White Bird Canyon came as a shock from an unexpected theater of operations. It was the worst defeat suffered by the U.S. Army in the Department of the Columbia since the 1850s.*

On June 22, as Howard worked to scrape together all the forces at his disposal, he sent Captain Stephen Whipple with two cavalry companies, backed by a Gatling gun battery, to capture the village of Looking Glass on Clear Creek. He ignored the fact that Looking Glass had vehemently declared his neutrality.

Whipple might have parleyed with Looking Glass and been mollified by his neutral stance, but again the Idaho volunteers riding with the soldiers opened fire without talking. In the gunfight, one Nez Percé man was shot and a woman and child drowned trying to escape across the stream. Looking Glass managed to evacuate the rest of his people before the troops streamed in to burn the village.

Howard's troops in the field had now managed to turn two of the most levelheaded Indian leaders in his department—and their followers—into enraged enemies. Howard's overeager troops had turned a contentious disagreement into a major war in a theater that had been generally quiet for two decades. Howard wired the headquarters of the Division of the Pacific at the Presidio of San Francisco, requesting that General Irvin McDowell send him reinforcements.

In the wake of the Clear Creek battle, Whipple's command continued their pursuit. In contrast to the open Plains of the Powder River country, where their brother soldiers had campaigned the previous year, the 1st Cavalry found themselves operating in very difficult terrain. The Idaho panhandle is characterized by sharp ridges and steep canyons that twist and turn into a veritable vertical maze with few flat, level areas.

Within this labyrinth, some of the civilian scouts operating with Whipple went missing. Unknown to Whipple, they had detected a Nez Percé presence near a trading post on Cottonwood Creek and were trying to find him.

On July 3, Whipple was told by a stage driver of a band of Nez Percé, probably the same one seen by the scouts. Sending eleven men under Lieutenant Sevier Rains to find the missing scouts, Whipple went to

*Two men of the 1st Cavalry were awarded the Congressional Medal of Honor for actions at White Bird Canyon that day. According to his citation, Sergeant Michael McCarthy "Was detailed with 6 men to hold a commanding position, and held it with great gallantry until the troops fell back. He then fought his way through the Indians, rejoined a portion of his command, and continued the fight in retreat. He had two horses shot from under him, and was captured, but escaped and reported for duty after three days' hiding and wandering in the mountains." Lieutenant William Parnell's citation noted that "With a few men, in the face of a heavy fire from pursuing Indians and at imminent peril, returned and rescued a soldier whose horse had been killed and who had been left behind in the retreat."

search for the Nez Percé. The Nez Percé ambushed Rains, killing him along with his entire detachment. Whipple happened on this battle, confronting a band of about 150 Nez Percé. Outnumbered two to one, Whipple retreated.

On July 4, Captain Perry, late of the White Bird Canyon fight, joined Whipple's command, and they rode to the trading post on Cottonwood Creek. Here, surrounded by Nez Percé, they went into defensive positions. The next day, a group of seventeen Idaho volunteers led by D. B. Randall rode to the aid of the more than one hundred soldiers surrounded on Cottonwood Creek. The volunteers fought their way to within sight of the trading post, when they too were surrounded. Whipple broke out with forty-two men and came to the aid of the seventeen. As a result of the day's fighting, Randall, two other volunteers, and at least one Nez Percé were killed. The Nez Percé were clearly demonstrating their fighting effectiveness and tenacity.

THE BATTLE ON THE CLEARWATER

By the beginning of the second week in July, Looking Glass had joined Joseph's band and they had decided to leave the Clearwater River country of Idaho and cross over the Bitterroots in to western Montana Territory, using the long-used Nez Percé trail across Lolo Pass that Lewis and Clark had used in 1805 and 1806. The Nez Percé party that Joseph now led numbered eight hundred, with just three hundred being men capable of bearing arms. The rest were women and children.

Also by this time, General Howard had taken to the field with his own large task force, which incorporated Whipple's and Perry's commands. Numbering five hundred troops, Howard's column contained elements of four companies of the 1st Cavalry, six companies of the 21st Infantry Regiment, and five companies of artillerymen from the 4th Artillery that he would use mainly as infantry. Captain James Jackson's Company B of the 1st Cavalry was also en route from Fort Klamath to join the force.

Howard's plan was to go after Joseph's band, round them up, and take them to the reservation. Outnumbered, and with women and children slowing him down, Joseph seemed to be easy pickings.

On July 11, Howard discovered the Nez Percé encampment in the valley of the Clearwater as he was working his way across a ridge. He attacked with artillery, but at too long a range for accuracy. The troops worked their way into the valley through difficult terrain only to find the Nez Percé shooting at them from three sides. The Nez Percé kept the soldiers pinned down through the night and into the following day. Howard found himself in a difficult position from which he hoped to extricate himself by a breakout maneuver.

The siege was finally broken by the fortuitous arrival of Captain Jackson from Fort Klamath, who entered the scene, coincidentally, from the Nez Percé rear. They scrambled to avoid being surrounded and escaped across the Clearwater. As Joseph slipped away, Howard licked his wounds. He had lost seventeen of his men killed in action, with twenty-seven wounded. Joseph meanwhile, lost at least four, although Howard claimed twenty-three killed in action and forty-six wounded.

Lieutenant Charles Humphrey of the 4th Artillery earned his Congressional Medal of Honor on July 11 when he "Voluntarily and successfully conducted, in the face of a withering fire, a party which recovered possession of an abandoned howitzer and two Gatling guns lying between the lines a few yards from the Indians."

Howard waited until the next day to undertake a pursuit, permitting the fast-moving Joseph a considerable head start. This would haunt Howard later. He sent Major Edwin Mason of the 21st Infantry Regiment with elements of five cavalry companies to chase the Nez Percé, while he pulled his cumbersome column through the mountains. Mason was ambushed on July 17 at Weippe Prairie—ironically the same place that the Nez Percé had welcomed Lewis and Clark with open arms seventy-two years before. After a brief gun battle, the Nez Percé slipped away. Forced by the terrain to dismount his cavalry, Mason could not keep pace and lost them.

Things were not going nearly as well for Howard as he had predicted.

THE BATTLE OF FORT FIZZLE

Within a week of the Clearwater Fight, Joseph and the Nez Percé were across the Bitterroots and out of the Department of the Columbia. Nevertheless, General Sherman demanded that Howard continue the pursuit across the mountains into Colonel John Gibbon's District of Montana. Based at Fort Shaw, across the continental divide near Helena, the veteran of the previous year's campaign began mobilizing the forces at his disposal to intercept the Nez Percé who had just slipped into his area of responsibility. Joseph would now have two U.S. Army contingents to dog his trail.

As Gibbon formed up to march west into the Bitterroot country, the opening move for the Montana troops fell to a small detachment of the 7th Infantry Regiment from Fort Missoula. Augmented by Montana Territorial volunteers, they went to fortify the base of the trail across Lolo Pass, in order to intercept the Nez Percé. The fortification was built, and the defenders waited anxiously to snare Joseph in their trap.

The Nez Percé scouts, meanwhile, had spied the defensive structure built by the Missoula men, and Joseph simply led his people around it. The Nez Percé had already moved southward, up the Bitterroot River valley away from Missoula, before the troops knew what had happened. Local residents mocked the would-be defenders, nicknaming their useless defensive structure "Fort Fizzle." The name is still remembered to this day, being the official name of a state park on the site.

Joseph had demonstrated a knack for elusiveness that would become legendary in the coming weeks.

THE BIG HOLE AND BEYOND

On August 6, the Nez Percé crossed the continental divide by way of the 7,264-foot pass now named for Chief Joseph. This was the same route that William Clark had used on his return trip in 1806, while Meriwether Lewis traveled north into Blackfeet country. By the first week of August, the Nez Percé had been on the move for three weeks, and asked their leaders to stop and rest. Believing that they had eluded the US Army for the moment, Joseph agreed. The camp was made on the south side of the Big Hole River, in the Big Hole Basin near the site of present-day Wisdom, Montana.

The Nez Percé were unaware of the U.S. Army's use of telegraph communications, and of Howard's having alerted Gibbon to locate and attack them. Gibbon reached Missoula after Fort Fizzle had fizzled, and was now making his way south along the Bitterroot with 161 troops and forty-five civilian volunteers. They included elements of two companies of the 2nd Cavalry, and five of the 7th Infantry Regiment. Gibbon has been criticized for moving to pursue such a highly mobile Nez Percé throng with infantry, but he was working with what he had, and he was hoping for a single decisive battle to end the campaign. Howard's own advance party, meanwhile, was crossing Lolo Pass and was about two days behind Gibbon.

Gibbon observed the Nez Percé encampment on the Big Hole River on August 8, and prepared to launch a surprise attack at dawn on August 9 from the high ground on the north side of the river.

Looking Glass (c. 1830–1877) in an undated photograph. (*National Archives*)

There were numerous Nez Percé casualties in the initial assault, but White Bird, Looking Glass, and Joseph rallied their people to counterattack. The marksmanship of the Nez Percé snipers was so effective that the troops were forced back across the river. Gibbon's force took up defensive positions, where they would remain until the following morning. The crew of a twelve-pounder mountain howitzer, manhandling their gun through a jackpine forest, arrived after the battle had begun and managed only two rounds before they were outflanked. The Nez Percé then captured and dismantled the howitzer.*

The Nez Percé withdrew on the morning of August 10, having badly mauled the troops, who were unable to pursue them. Troops under Howard's command arrived shortly after the Nez Percé had escaped.

Gibbon had lost twenty-nine of his men killed, and forty were wounded—including the colonel himself. His battered force would be unable to

---

*Private Lorenzo Brown of the 7th Infantry Regiment was awarded the Congressional Medal of Honor for actions in the Big Hole battle when, "After having been severely wounded in right shoulder, [he] continued to do duty in a most courageous manner." Other Medal of Honor recipients in regiment for actions in the clash included Sergeant William Edwards, musician John McLennon, and Sergeant Patrick Rogan, who "Verified and reported the company while subjected to a galling fire from the enemy." Sergeant Milden Wilson earned his Medal of Honor for "Gallantry in forming company from line of skirmishers and deploying again under a galling fire, and in carrying dispatches at the imminent risk of his life." Sergeant Wilfred Clark's Medal of Honor citation noted his "especial skill as sharpshooter."

undertake the pursuit. While Gibbon licked his wounds, this job would go to Howard. A year earlier, Gibbon had missed the Battle of the Little Bighorn by a couple of days, but he had now suffered his own major defeat. Like the Little Bighorn, the Battle of the Big Hole is still one of those moments in the Indian Wars in the West that are noted with pride by American Indians.

The Nez Percé suffered between fifty and ninety battle deaths, of which only about thirty were warriors. Joseph's initial plan had been simply to get away from the Clearwater country, and hope that Howard would give up the chase. Now he was thinking long term, of trying to make a break for the Canadian border, across which he might be able to join forces with Sitting Bull.

Though the Battle of the Big Hole was a Nez Percé victory, it was a turning point in the campaign because it demonstrated to Joseph that there would be no rest for his people until and unless they were able to escape into Canada.

After pulling up stakes at the Big Hole, the Nez Percé raided several ranches to steal horses, and ambushed a wagon train, killing several people in the process. Joseph and the Nez Percé crossed briefly into the Snake River drainage in Idaho, camping at Camas Meadows on August 18. The following day, Howard's cavalry vanguard reached the Camas campsite, now just a day in Joseph's wake.

On the morning of August 20, two hundred Nez Percé warriors boldly rode back to Camas Meadows to steal the cavalry horses, managing to steal 150 mules and scatter the horses. Major George Sanford led a retaliatory force to recapture the stolen livestock, but he was turned back after only partial success, the loss of two men killed in action, and nearly a dozen wounded.*

From here, Joseph led the still undefeated Nez Percé through Yellowstone National Park, which had five years earlier been designated as

---

*Captain James Jackson of the 1st Cavalry earned the Congressional Medal of Honor at Camas Meadows when he "Dismounted from his horse in the face of a heavy fire from pursuing Indians, and with the assistance of one or two of the men of his command secured to a place of safety the body of his trumpeter, who had been shot." Three men of the 2nd Cavalry were awarded the Medal of Honor with citations mentioning the battle of Camas Meadows, as well as their actions on May 7 at Little Muddy Creek. They were Corporal Harry Garland, farrier William Jones, and Sergeant Henry Wilkins.

America's first national park. Coincidently, one of the park's most recent visitors was General William Tecumseh Sherman, who had just departed and who was now in Helena. When Howard had the audacity to suggest that he now break off the pursuit of the Nez Percé, Sherman became furious, instructing him to resume the chase and follow Joseph "to the death."

In early September, Joseph exited Yellowstone park on the east, thereupon following the Clark Fork of the Yellowstone River north and east. By now it had been several weeks since the Nez Percé had had any contact with their pursuers. Joseph no doubt knew that this happy condition would not last. He had now moved into Nelson Miles's District of the Yellowstone, and the domain of the 7th Cavalry, George Armstrong Custer's old outfit.

Colonel Samuel Sturgis, now commanding the 7th Cavalry, moved forth with six companies of the regiment, augmented by elements of three companies of the 1st Cavalry. Sturgis's plan was to intercept the Nez Percé as they made a southerly turn before reaching the Yellowstone River. This was a mere deception, but Sturgis bought it and lost the Nez Percé. He soon found himself facing Major Sanford and Howard's vanguard.

Having deceived Sturgiss, Joseph raided some settlements along the Yellowstone River near the site of present-day Laurel, Montana, and proceeded to cross the river. Having made a U-turn, Sturgis also forded the river, hoping to cut Joseph off as the Nez Percé moved up Canyon Creek, out of the river valley and onto the plateau beyond. Again, as at the Big Hole and at Camas Meadow, the skill and discipline of the Nez Percé warriors proved too much for the U.S. Army. Their marksmanship and horsemanship proved superior to the 7th Cavalry, as they outmaneuvered Sturgis repeatedly.

The Battle of Canyon Creek on September 13, 1877, was not nearly the kind of defeat that the 7th Cavalry had suffered just eighty miles to the east on June 25 the previous year, but it was hardly the sort of showing that Sturgis might have liked. He lost just three troopers killed in action and eleven wounded, but he had failed to stop a slightly smaller force that was encumbered with large numbers of women and children.

Unmolested by the U.S. Army for the moment, Joseph managed to lead his people north from the Yellowstone River to the Missouri River in ten days. Here, they skirmished with a small contingent of troops at Cow

Island on September 23, killing three. The next day, on Cow Creek, north of the Missouri, they accosted a wagon train, offering to trade for supplies. Negotiations continued into September 25, when Major Guido Ilges of the 7th Infantry Regiment arrived on the scene with two dozen militiamen. They attacked the Nez Percé and were driven back after an extended gun battle. The Nez Percé burned the wagon train and escaped again.

In the meantime, General Howard, thoroughly outdistanced by the Nez Percé, had wired Nelson Miles after the Canyon Creek fight, asking him to try to head off Joseph's march to the north. Miles had been preoccupied with Sitting Bull, but as the pursuit of the Nez Percé seemed to be evolving into the key campaign of the season, so Bear Coat was only too happy to get involved.

Miles assembled a task force that included three companies of the 2nd Cavalry under Captain George Tyler, three companies of the 7th Cavalry under Captain Owen Hale, and four mounted companies from the 5th Infantry Regiment under Captain Simon Snyder. Miles took his command across the Missouri near the mouth of the Musselshell River as the distant Cow Creek Fight was playing out, and hastened westward toward Joseph's path.

The End of the Line for the Nez Percé

Knowing that Howard was far behind, and unaware of Miles, Joseph agreed to allow his people to take a break from their relentless and exhausting march. On September 29, they camped just north of the Bear's Paw (now called Bear Paw) Mountains on Snake Creek, a tributary of the Milk River. They were just south of today's town of Chinook, Montana, and about forty miles from the Canadian border. Matching the pace they had traveled after the Canyon Creek fight, the Nez Percé were only about three days from the goal they had been moving toward for two and a half months. Without the women and children, it was only a day's ride for the warriors.

Winter had arrived on the Northern Plains. Temperatures dipped below freezing, and the Nez Percé awoke on September 30 to Snake Creek being iced over. They also awoke to an attack by the 7th Cavalry. Skilled as any military force against which the U.S. Army had fought, the Nez Percé quickly rallied and beat off the charge. Aiming for officers, the Nez

Percé marksmen managed to kill or incapacitate six in the initial volley, greatly crippling Miles's command structure. Not only did Miles's initial attack fail, so too did a secondary assault by the 5th Infantry and later attempts by the 2nd Cavalry to stampede the Nez Percé horses. Miles had lost a staggering twenty-four men killed in action, and forty-six wounded.

Had it not been for the weather and their general exhaustion, the Nez Percé might have picked up and moved out as they had at the Big Hole. Had Miles been Gibbon, he might have let them. But this was not to be. Miles still had the troops—and the artillery—to surround the Nez Percé encampment and put it under siege.

On October 1, Miles came forward under a truce flag, and Joseph agreed to a parley. The talks were inconclusive and the standoff dragged on for four days, with snipers on both sides continuing to take shots at the other.

Howard's column finally arrived on October 4, taking up positions in the cordon around the Nez Percé. Though he was now the senior officer on the scene, Howard graciously permitted Miles to remain in command of the siege—and to take responsibility for the outcome, whatever it was.

Within the Nez Percé camp, there was less unity, less cordiality and a great deal of disagreement over what to do. Of the principal leaders, Toohulhulsote had been killed in the initial attack, Looking Glass and White Bird favored an attempt to break out, and Joseph favored negotiations. On October 5, the three surviving chiefs decided to separate and follow different paths. Suddenly, a sniper's bullet killed Looking Glass.

Joseph decided that surrender was the only course of action, so he signaled his willingness to parley with Howard and Miles. His final speech, delivered on October 5, is ranked with one of the greatest ever spoken by any military leader in defeat:

> I am tired of fighting. Our chiefs are killed. Looking Glass is dead. Toohulhulsote is dead. The old men are all dead. It is the young men who say yes or no. He who led the young men is dead. It is cold and we have no blankets. The little children are freezing to death. My people, some of them, have run away to the hills and have no blankets, no food. No one knows where they are—perhaps freezing to death. I want to have time to look for my children and see how many of them I can find. Maybe I shall find them among the dead. Hear me, my chiefs. I am tired. My heart is sick and sad. From where the sun now stands I will fight no more forever.

That night, White Bird slipped away with a handful of followers. They caught up with a number of people who had escaped on September 30 and slipped across the border. In turn, they linked up with Sitting Bull and his Lakota band, and shivered together through the winter under the watchful eyes of the Mounties. Had it not been for Bear Coat Miles, all of the Nez Percé would have made it.*

The following July, White Bird and his warriors would return through Montana Territory to the Lapwai Reservation. Near Missoula, they raided some outlying settlements, and were pursued by Lieutenant Thomas Wallace out of Fort Missoula with a small mounted detachment of the 3rd Infantry Regiment. He caught up with the Nez Percé party on the Middle Fork of the Clearwater River on June 21, 1878, where he managed to kill six and capture a number of their horses.

Joseph had made a masterly retreat of over a thousand miles. It was one of the great epic tales of human history, coming to a tragic conclusion so close to the final goal.

After surrendering, Joseph and his followers were not permitted to go to the reservation they had first refused. Joseph was initially confined as a prisoner of war at Fort Leavenworth, Kansas, and later sent to Indian Territory with his followers. He pleaded with the Indian Bureau for his

---

*Congressional Medals of Honor were awarded to nine men for actions at the Bear Paw Mountain clash. They included 5th Infantry Adjutant, Lieutenant George Baird, as well as Lieutenant Mason Carter of the 5th Infantry and Lieutenant Edward McClernand. Lieutenant Oscar Long of the 5th Infantry earned his when, as his citation states, "Having been directed to order a troop of cavalry to advance, and finding both its officers killed, he voluntarily assumed command, and under a heavy fire from the Indians advanced the troop to its proper position." Major Henry Tilton, the surgeon in Miles's command earned his Medal of Honor when he "Fearlessly risked his life and displayed great gallantry in rescuing and protecting the wounded men." Sergeant Henry Hogan of Company G, 5th Infantry, had been awarded the Congressional Medal of Honor for his actions centering on the Battle of Cedar Creek six months earlier. He was awarded his second Medal of Honor at Bear Paw Mountain for carrying a severely wounded Lieutenant Henry Romeyn off the field of battle under heavy fire. Lieutenant Romeyn also earned the Congressional Medal of Honor for leading his command into "close range of the enemy, there maintained his position, and vigorously prosecuted the fight until he was severely wounded." Two 7th Cavalry veterans of the Battle of the Little Bighorn, Captains Edward Godfrey and Myles Moylan, who were wounded at Bear Paw Mountain were both awarded the Congressional Medal of Honor for their leadership in the final battle of the Nez Percé War. They were Captain Edward Godfrey and Captain Myles Moylan.

people to be sent back to the Pacific Northwest, but the political powers in the region strongly opposed such a move.

It would be more than two decades before Joseph was permitted to return to the Pacific Northwest, and then not to the Wallowa, but to the Colville Reservation in Washington, where he died on September 21, 1904.

The Great Basin Wars

By the time that Chief Joseph said that he would fight no more forever, the same could be said by most of the tribes that had been at war with the U.S. Army through the nineteenth century. The exceptions were in the most remote parts of the West, namely the Southwest and the Great Basin. In the late 1860s, General George Crook had waged an effective campaign against the Paiute in the deserts of eastern Oregon that had left the region generally quiet for a decade.

Technically the people of the northern Great Basin, the Bannock, Paiute, Shoshone, and Ute, were required to remain on reservations, but Indian Bureau estimates done in 1878 indicated that only about 14 percent of a population of eight thousand actually did. The rest roamed far and wide over an area the size of the state of Oregon that encompassed parts of Idaho, Nevada, Oregon, and Utah. Because the area was sparsely populated, they had little contact with settlers, so little was done by the U.S. Army in the way of offensive action.

Within a few months of Joseph's surrender, however, tempers were beginning to flare and the region was moving toward conflict. At the Fort Hall Agency, near present-day Pocatello, Idaho, the January 1878 murder of a Bannock man led to serious discord among the Indians living at the agency. A number of factions of the various tribes began planning for hostilities, which finally boiled over in the spring.

On May 30, a Bannock shot and wounded two settlers at Camas Prairie in Idaho Territory, near the scene of Nez Percé battle a year earlier. This touched off a wave of violence by a group of about fifty Bannock and Paiute, who killed ten people across the southern part of the territory.

On June 8, near Silver City, some volunteers under J. B. Harper tangled with the raiders, wounding their leader, Buffalo Horn, who later died. Harper lost two men killed in action. Over the next three weeks, the band gradually mushroomed in size to an estimated 450 warriors. Under a new leader, Egan of the Paiute, the raiders had crossed into Oregon. Here, they were joined by a party of Klamath warriors.

General Oliver Howard, commanding the Department of the Columbia, now faced the second war in as many years in a department that had been quiet for a decade. Captain Reuben Bernard had taken to the field from Fort Boise on May 31 with a detachment of the 1st Cavalry, and Howard sought to augment this small force. He ordered Colonel Frank Wheaton at Fort Lapwai to send elements of the 1st Cavalry, the 4th Artillery, and the 21st Infantry Regiment into action.

Howard came east to Fort Boise to observe operations himself, and to attempt a peaceful settlement of the growing conflict. He even enlisted the venerable Chief Winnemucca of the Paiute and his daughter Sarah in an unsuccessful effort at negotiations.

During the last week of June, Captain Bernard trailed, located, and attacked Egan's force on Silver Creek in southeastern Oregon with three companies of 1st Cavalry on the morning of June 28. Bernard surprised them, forcing them to abandon their camp for defensive positions in the hills. He was unable to dislodge them, and the battle turned into a stalemate in which the two sides traded shots through most of the day. At the end of the day, both sides withdrew, with Bernard having lost three men killed in action, and Egan at least five. Egan himself had been wounded, and a mercurial shaman known as Oytes took over his leadership role.

Oytes and Egan led their force north across the Oregon desert toward the Columbia River Gorge, hoping to join forces with factions among the Umatilla people who were also looking for a fight. Though Bernard was making better time than the infantry that Howard had sent to back him up, it was slow going for all because the barren landscape offered little in the way of forage for the horses, or water for both man and beast.

On July 2, on the North Fork of the John Day River, Oytes ambushed the scouts riding ahead of Bernard's task force, killing two and wounding three. Bernard arrived and drove off the attackers, but did not give chase because of wanting to keep his column together. Five days later, at Pilot Rock, Bernard linked up with the other troops from Howard's command. The Bannock-Paiute confederacy, meanwhile, had taken up defensive positions on nearby Birch Creek.

Though several senior officers, including Howard himself, were present, Howard had a great deal of admiration for Captain Bernard's leadership and tactical abilities, and chose him to lead the attack on the Bannock-Paiute positions. On July 8, Bernard launched his assault, using seven companies of the 1st Cavalry to attack the enemy who were dug in to the slopes of Pilot Butte. Though it was tough terrain, the troopers managed to overwhelm the Indian positions, forcing them to retreat to the top of the hill. From here, the Indians fled down the other side. Bernard was unable to give chase because his horses were exhausted.

Despite the difficult fighting, casualties on both sides had been light, with only one trooper killed in action. After the battle, Lieutenant Colonel James Forsyth assumed command of the combined companies of the 1st Cavalry Regiment.

Oytes continued north, where he made contact with the Umatilla at their agency. He also ran into Captain Evan Miles (a veteran of the Nez Percé campaign), with seven companies of the 21st Infantry Regiment, one of the 1st Cavalry, and two of the 4th Artillery.

Instead of joining Oytes against Miles, the Umatilla deliberately remained on the sidelines when the two sides met in battle. On July 13, Miles surrounded the Umatilla Agency, and the warriors came out to meet him. When the Umatilla stood aside, Oytes's warriors made a few half-hearted attacks, then turned tail and ran. Two days later, the Umatilla caught up with Oytes. They coaxed the wounded Egan away from the rest of the party, killed him, and later presented his scalp to Miles.

By now, with not only a large U.S. Army task force on his tail, but with the Umatilla actively hostile toward him, Oytes was clearly on the defensive. On July 20, Forsyth's 1st Cavalry again caught up with Oytes, this time back on the North Fork of the John Day River. Though the battle was essentially a draw, it hastened the final breakup of the combined Indian force. The Paiute and Bannock escaped, but as separate bands in different directions, not the single large raiding party that it had been a month before.

General Howard ordered a massive sweep of the Oregon desert to pick up Paiute stragglers as one group of Bannock rode east. Their plan was to head for Canada, following roughly the same route as the Nez Percé had a year earlier. They crossed through Yellowstone National Park and turned north into Montana Territory on the Clark Fork of the Yellowstone. Here, they found themselves in Nelson Miles's District of the Yellowstone.

On August 30, the Bannock tangled with troops of the 2nd Cavalry under Lieutenant William Clark, and on September 4, Miles hit their camp with the 5th Infantry Regiment in a surprise attack. Miles suffered one man killed in action, but managed to kill or capture forty-two of the Bannock, along with a large part of their horse herd, and to force them to abandon their plan to go north into Canada.

The Bannock wintered in remote central Idaho Territory with the related Shoshone band that were known as the "Sheepeaters." During the spring of 1879, as reports came in of Indian attacks on far-flung settlements, General Howard ordered search and destroy operations to probe the rugged mountain country of the region. Reuben Bernard led his 1st Cavalry force in the operation, Lieutenant Henry Catley took a mounted detachment from the 2nd Infantry Regiment, and Lieutenant Edward Farrow went out with a contingent of Umatilla scouts.

The operation played out over the summer as a cat-and-mouse game in the extremely rugged Salmon River country, with the soldiers finding evidence of Indian trails, but no Indians. On July 29, Catley's fifty-man force was ambushed by an estimated fifteen Indians near Big Creek. The following morning, they were ambushed again at Vinegar Hill. This time, Catley ordered the men to abandon their pack train and flee. For this retreat, which was the only contact that the U.S. Army had with the enemy in the theater all summer, Catley was reprimanded.

It was Farrow and his scouts who finally caught up with the Indians, but not until September 21. On that date, they captured two women and two children, stragglers from the Sheepeater band. Knowing that they were hot on the trail, they moved quickly, nearly catching up with the fast-moving Indians several times over the ensuing week. On September 28, a huge storm blew into the mountains, bringing rain mixed with snow, sleet, and freezing temperatures. On October 1, the Sheepeaters came into Farrow's camp to give themselves up.

The campaign of 1879 in Idaho had been a mere footnote to the larger war against the Bannock and Paiute the previous year, but to the south, the Ute War of 1879 had evolved into a major conflict.

The Ute War

The Ute had not figured prominently in the military operations in the West since the Civil War years. The Treaty of 1868, which Kit Carson had helped negotiate, had granted them substantial portions of western Colorado and eastern Utah in perpetuity in exchange for their claims on land in New Mexico. This had been agreeable to all sides, but a decade later, prospectors had begun to swarm into Ute land in increasing numbers. In 1873, Ouray, one of the most respected of the Ute leaders, had agreed to cede a large swath of land in southwestern Colorado in order to keep the peace, but within a few years, there were demands for further concessions.

When Colorado achieved statehood in 1876, there were further demands that the Ute be removed from the new state entirely. This did not sit well with Ouray, nor with any of the Ute. Trouble was brewing.

The main troublemaker for the Ute was the eccentric Nathan Meeker, who in 1878 assumed the post of agent at the White River Agency in northwestern Colorado. The largest of the Ute agencies, White River accounted for 48 percent of the total Ute population of about 4,200. With the zeal of a man with a mission, Meeker demanded that the Ute begin farming immediately. When the Ute resisted his demand, Meeker called for the U.S. Army to intervene to help him bend the Ute to his will.

Though Colorado was in General John Pope's Department of the Missouri, the nearest Army post was Fort Steele in Wyoming Territory, part of General Crook's Department of the Platte, so Major Thomas Thornburgh was dispatched from Fort Steele to aid Meeker. Thornburgh brought a 153-man contingent containing elements of the 3rd and 5th Cavalry and a 4th Infantry Regiment company to accompany him part of the way.

The Ute sent word that they wanted to parley at the agency. Thornburgh said he agreed, but continued his advance, planning to get his cavalry force within a short distance of the agency before he rode in for the discussions. This sent mixed messages to the Ute leader named Jack, who interpreted the continued advance as Thornburgh's having decided to fight rather talk. On September 29, at Milk River, about a day's ride from the agency, Jack confronted Thornburgh. Again, the major sent mixed messages, deploying his men in an attack formation while sending Lieutenant Samuel Cherry to open discussions.

A single shot was fired, by whom it was uncertain, and the fight was on. The Battle of Milk Creek would rage far and wide for nearly a week, but Thornburgh would not experience it. He took a bullet in the head from a Ute sniper in the early stages of the fighting on September 29. Before the day was out, eleven soldiers had been killed in action and most of the Army horses had been shot.

Thornburgh's column was not alone in being attacked that day. Nathan Meeker would also meet his end. As the Battle of Milk Creek began, a group of Ute rode into the White River Agency, where they killed the much-despised Meeker and eight or nine others, meanwhile torching the agency buildings. Mrs. Meeker, along with a woman named Flora Price and three children, were taken hostage.

Captain Scott Payne assumed command of Thornburgh's column, circled the supply wagons, and prepared a defensive position at which the Ute would continue to hammer for days. Captain Francis Dodge arrived three days later with thirty-five men of the 9th Cavalry, but they too found themselves besieged within Payne's circle of wagons. Captain Dodge would receive the Congressional Medal of Honor for having led his command an all-night ride to the scene of the battle, joining the action, and fighting the attackers for another three days.

Finally, on October 5, Colonel Wesley Merritt reached the scene with five companies of the 4th Infantry and four of the 5th Cavalry, a force sufficient to break the impasse. In one of the longest sieges of the Indian Wars, the U.S. Army had suffered thirteen men killed in action and forty-seven wounded, including Payne and the regimental surgeon. The number of Ute killed in action was estimated at about thirty-seven.*

There were virtually no horses left alive among the besieged units, and the sea of festering animal carcasses lying in the sun for nearly a week made the scene look—and smell—especially horrible.

Merritt would not reach the White River Agency to discover the bodies of Meeker and the others until October 11. When news of what came to be known as the "Meeker Massacre" reached the outside world, it incensed the nation as nothing since the Little Bighorn. Those in the War Department favored a swift and punishing response, but the Interior Department cautioned that an all-out war was undesirable, especially when the lives of the hostages taken at the White River Agency hung in the balance.

Barring word to the contrary, the U.S. Army prepared for a powerful offensive on the scale of the 1876 campaign against the Lakota and Northern Cheyenne. Merritt had commanded seven hundred troops on the day that he rode into the White River Agency, but General Pope had ordered elements of the 3rd Cavalry, as well as detachments of the 4th, 7th, 9th, and 14th Infantry Regiments to be placed at his disposal. Colonel Edward Hatch had come up from the District of New Mexico with units of the 9th Cavalry. Hatch's command was ready to go at Fort Lewis on the San Juan River, along with the 15th, 19th, and 22nd Infantry Regiments.

General Ranald Mackenzie, whose 4th Cavalry had been the primary defensive force in north Texas for a decade, was ordered to lead six companies into the Colorado Theater of operations. Infantry reassigned to him as he made his way to Fort Garland raised his effective total to 1,500 troops.

Despite this huge task force converging on western Colorado, the Interior Department was able to win its case for an attempt at a negotiated settlement of the Ute War. Former Ute Agent Charles Adams was sent into the region to begin a dialogue with the tribal leadership through Ouray, who had not been a party to the White River Agency incident.

On October 21, a council was held at Grand Mesa, in which Ouray's people threatened to intervene against the perpetrators of the agency murders. Adams was able to obtain the release of the captives taken at the agency, along with a promise that the individuals responsible for killing Meeker and the others would be turned over for trial.

---

*Sergeant Edward Grimes of the 5th Cavalry was awarded the Medal of Honor for having "voluntarily brought up a supply under heavy fire at almost point blank range" during the siege. Lieutenant William Hall of the 5th Cavalry earned his Medal of Honor when his small reconnaissance party was attacked by thirty-five Indians, and he "several times exposed himself to draw the fire of the enemy, giving his small party opportunity to reply with much effect." Sergeant Henry Johnson earned his Medal of Honor when he "Voluntarily left fortified shelter and under heavy fire at close range made the rounds of the pits to instruct the guards, fought his way to the creek and back to bring water to the wounded." Wilhelm Philipsen, a 5th Cavalry blacksmith, earned the Medal of Honor for attacking and capturing an enemy strongpoint, and Corporal Hampton Roach of the 5th Cavalry acquired his Medal of Honor when he "Erected breastworks under fire; also kept the command supplied with water three consecutive nights while exposed to fire from ambushed Indians at close range." Other Medals of Honor with less detailed citations also went to Sergeant John Lawton, Sergeant John Merrill, Corporal George Moquin, Corporal Edward Murphy, Sergeant John Poppe, and Sergeant Jacob Widmer, all of the 5th Cavalry, for actions during the six-day siege.

The establishment of a commission headed by Adams and Ouray, along with Colonel Hatch, was appointed to sort things out, and the threat of further major combat in the Ute War was diffused. To ensure that the situation remained that way, much of the large task force that had been assembled in October would remain on alert in Colorado through the winter.

Though it had garnered intense media attention, the Meeker affair was essentially a side issue that was largely unrelated to the overriding matter that had been the focus of Ute relations prior to 1879. This was Colorado's demand for cessation of the Ute lands in the western part of the state. The Meeker matter had brought the political conflict to a head by making it a military issue, but now that the war was settled, the cessation matter was back on the table.

In 1880, the Indian Bureau and the tribal leaders met in Washington to resolve the issue of further Ute relocation. Ouray, who was suffering from kidney disease and near death, attended. He agreed that the majority of the Ute, including those currently assigned to the White River Agency, would allow themselves to be relocated to new reservations in Utah in exchange for cash payments. Ouray died on August 24, having proven himself a statesman capable of understanding the cultural divide, and of making tough choices.

The ultimate disposition of the Ute War was emblematic of the way that diplomacy was being brought into play to resolve issues relating to relations between the tribes and the rising tide of demand for settlement. By 1880, such was the case throughout the West. It was often a difficult middle ground that pleased no one and greatly angered the warhawks on the extremes, but it averted further major combat.

8

THE SOUTHWEST, THE LAST
THEATER

The wars on the Plains that garnered the headlines during the 1870s
were characterized by large unit actions and dramatic battles. It is
still hard to think of these campaigns without fixating on the Little
Bighorn and warfare on that scale.

The wars in the Southwest, certainly those after the 1864 campaign
against the Navajo, were the direct opposite: small unit actions in difficult
terrain. The primary foe was the Apache, who operated in small, guerrilla
bands using their uncanny understanding of the Southwest environment.
For the U.S. Army, campaigns in this theater were tailor-made for the kind
of tactics that General George Crook had used so successfully during the
early 1870s.

When the conflict resumed at the end of the decade, the U.S. Army
would again turn to Crook, its master of unconventional warfare, to resolve
the conflict in the Southwest. After his poor showing at the Battle of the
Rosebud, the immediate harbinger of the Little Bighorn, Crook's reputation as a field commander had dimmed, but only somewhat. It was, after
all, a conventional battle against the formidable Crazy Horse, and Crook's
forte was unconventional warfare. His new opponents would share that
specialty.

When war clouds again gathered over the mesas of the Southwest, a
new generation of leaders would emerge to inspire the Apache, and the
imaginations of the American media. Cochise, the principal war chief of
the Chiricahua Apache in the 1860s, had died in his mid-sixties in June
1874, and for a time, the peace to which he had finally agreed, had prevailed in the Southwest though the 1870s. In the 1880s, that would
change brought about by a new generation that included a Mimbres

Apache known as Victorio, and a Chiricahua Apache named Goyathlay, but best known to the world and to posterity, by his Spanish-language name, Geronimo.

Born in 1829, Geronimo had grown up in the Sierra Madre of northern Mexico, a region that he always saw as his home. In 1858, Geronimo watched Mexican troops murder his mother, his wife, and his children, and this event would mold his opinion of the outsiders who settled in Apache lands. In the 1860s, he rode with Cochise, and after Cochise passed from the scene, Geronimo would be most renown of the leaders who filled the void.

The match between Crook and Geronimo would pit against one another the leader from each side who was perhaps the most suited to the tactics and battles that would play out in the last major campaigns of the Indian Wars in the West.

THE SOUTHERN FRONT

Two separate military actions of 1873 had brought quiet—albeit temporarily—to the Southwest Theater. If Crook's campaign of 1872-1873 had succeeded in curbing Apache raiders in Arizona Territory, Ranald Mackenzie's incursion into Mexico at Remolino in May 1873 had demonstrated that Mexico was not a durable sanctuary for raiders crossing into Texas. Though Mackenzie's target were the Kickapoo, the Lipan and Mescalero Apache operating south of the Rio Grande also got the message. Once loud and clear, Crook's and Mackenzie's messages would fade by the end of the decade.

As was demonstrated in Vietnam in the 1960s and 1970s, and in Southwest Asia at the beginning of the twenty-first century, every effective insurgency benefits from a sanctuary in which conventional opposition forces cannot operate for political reasons. Politics constrain conventional armies, while unconventional forces respect no borders.

In the 1870s, there were effectively two sanctuaries on the United States-Mexico border that were exploited by the Apache for cross-border raids. One such sanctuary was the Mexican state of Coahuila, which was used by the Lipan and Mescalero for raids into Texas. The other was the Territories of Arizona and New Mexico, which served as sanctuaries for the Chiricahua Apache to make raids into the Mexican states of Chihuahua and Sonora.

As Mackenzie's crack 4th Cavalry was relocated to the north of Texas during the Red River War, the principal commander on the Southern Front opposite Coahuila was Lieutenant Colonel William Rufus "Pecos Bill" Shafter, heading the 24th Infantry Regiment. He had earlier made a name for himself in the Llano Estacado campaign, where he commanded a combined brigade that included elements of the 24th and 25th Infantry Regiment, as well as the 10th Cavalry Buffalo Soldiers and a company of Seminole scouts. Having conducted relentless sweeps of the Llano Estacado, he was only too willing to cross the Rio Grande if the tactical situation called for it. In this, he had the acquiescence of the Department of Texas commander, General Edward Otho Cresap Ord, a veteran Civil War commander who had previously headed both the Department of California and the Department of the Platte.

The first test of the Ord-Shafter policy came in July 1876, a month after the Little Bighorn when most journalists' attention was focused on the Northern Plains. After a raid by Lipan Apache into Texas, Shafter ordered an incursion into Mexico by three companies of the 10th Cavalry under Lieutenant George Evans and elements of the two infantry regiments at his disposal, headed by Lieutenant John Bullis. On July 30, they launched a dawn attack on a Lipan Apache encampment near Zaragosa. Three troopers were killed in action, as were fourteen Apache.

Mexico complained formally, but local Mexican authorities were apparently not bothered to have the U.S. Army chasing Apache that strayed south of the border. Of course, at this time, Mexico was embroiled in one of its many revolutions, and President Porfirio Díaz was fighting an insurgency of his own, and one that was of more immediate concern.

Díaz defeated the revolutionaries at about the same time that Rutherford Hayes was sworn in as the new President of the United States in March 1877, after his own war of uncertainty in the Electoral College. Díaz, desiring United States recognition for his regime, seemed to leave the window open for a possible tacit agreement on "hot pursuit" operations in Mexico. However, when the Hayes administration acted unilaterally on June 1, giving such authority to Ord and Shafter, Díaz sent his army into northern Mexico to block the U.S. Army. Despite the presence of the Mexican forces, detachments from Shafter's command made another raid against the Apache in the Zaragosa area on September 26, and into the Sierra del Carmen at the end on November.

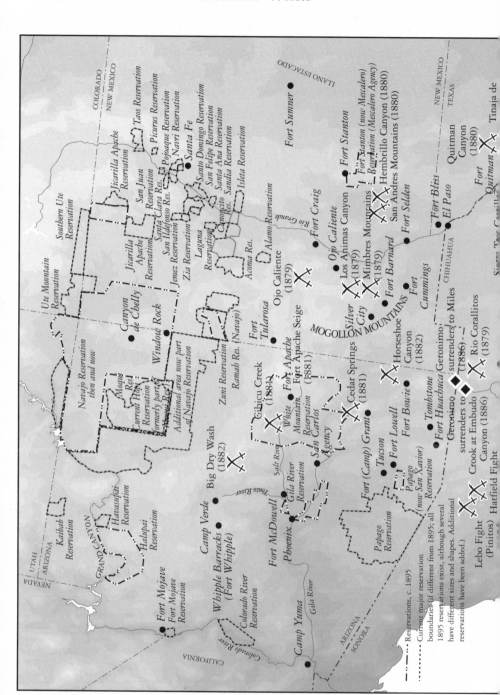

In December 1877, Sherman sent Mackenzie and the 4th Cavalry back to the Southern Front to reinforce Shafter, and in June 1878, the two officers led a thousand-man sweep into northern Mexico backed by artillery.

On two occasions, at Remolino and at Moncloca Viejo, the Mexican army prepared to block the progress of Mackenzie's cavalry, and on two occasions, the Mexicans backed down. The two national armies maneuvered threateningly, but never came to blows. In the process however, they probably served as a deterrent to the Apache. The controversial order permitting the cross-border raids was a point of contention between the two governments until Hayes finally rescinded it in February 1880.

Farther west, the American hostilities against the Chiricahua Apache had been resolved by the Chiricahua agreeing to settle on reservations and not raid American settlements. However, as was the case throughout the lightly populated sections of the West, the people who were technically living on reservations routinely left the reservations to hunt.

In the case of the Apache reservations in the Southwest, the same people who had formally agreed not to raid settlements in Arizona saw no reason not to leave their agencies to cross the border for a an occasional raid into Chihuahua. Indeed, the Chiricahua used their Ojo Caliente Agency in southwestern New Mexico as a virtual base camp for raids into Mexico.

After he largely brought the Apache situation under control in his 1872-1873 operations, General Crook had remained to enforce the tenuous peace in Arizona Territory until he was transferred to command the Department of the Platte in 1875. Though Crook was succeeded as departmental commander by Colonel August Kautz of the 8th Infantry Regiment, the real power in Arizona would, for a time, be a civilian, John Clum, a former Rutgers divinity student who served as the Indian Agent for the San Carlos Agency from 1874 to 1877.

As noted earlier, the U.S. Army had always divided the Southwest Theater between two military departments. While Kautz commanded the Arizona department, his counterpart in the District of New Mexico was Colonel Edward Hatch, who had recently played an important role in the Ute War in Colorado, which was outside his own command area.

In 1876, two years after the death of Cochise, the Indian Bureau had decided to move the Chiricahua people from the Ojo Caliente Agency north to the San Carlos Agency. This so angered the Chiricahua that it had the unintended effect of reviving raids by militant Chiricahua within Arizona. This, in turn, saw the emergence of Victorio and Geronimo as the new generation of leaders, and the beginning of a new Apache War.

The transfer of the Chiricahua to San Carlos also provided young John Clum with his own moment of stardom in the Indian Wars. On April 20, 1877, Clum and a detachment of his agency police force rode into Ojo Caliente to take the last of the Chiricahua into custody. Major James Wade was inbound from New Mexico with a backup force of eight companies of 9th Cavalry, but before he had arrived, Clum had the matter in hand. When Geronimo balked at leaving, Clum and his agency promptly arrested him and sixteen other Chiricahua leaders and put them in irons. Though in future years Geronimo would give himself up on several occasions, Clum was the first and only man to ever successfully capture Geronimo. Clum would resign later in 1876 to go on to other pursuits, including a stint as mayor of Tombstone, Arizona.

Conditions at the San Carlos Agency would gradually deteriorate, and within five years both departmental commanders would change, setting the stage for the next chapter in the history of the theater. In Arizona, Kautz would be succeeded by Colonel Orlando Willcox of the 12th Infantry Regiment in 1878, while in the District of New Mexico, Colonel Hatch would later be replaced by Ranald Mackenzie.

With Geronimo subdued, the focus of major combat actions in the Southwest Theater of operations would shift east to New Mexico, but only for a few years.

THE VICTORIO WAR

For the Apache, the situation at the crowded San Carlos Agency was unpleasant to say the least, and in September 1877, Victorio led about three hundred Mimbres and Chiricahua Apache off the reservation. Most were captured, but Victorio remained at large, leading a sizable raiding party across the Southwest—in both the Arizona and New Mexico military departments—for the next three years.

As had been the case with Cochise in the previous decade, the U.S. Army undertook to pursue Victorio whenever they could find his trail. On May 29, 1879, a detachment of men from two companies of the 9th Cavalry led by Captain Charles Beyer and Lieutenant Henry Wright cornered Victorio on the continental divide in the Mimbres Mountains of New Mexico. An attempt to parley devolved into a shootout, in which Wright was saved from being captured by Sergeant Thomas Boyne, who earned the Congressional Medal of Honor for his action. The brief fight left one soldier dead, and two men on each side wounded. Victorio and his band managed to escape, but he was forced to abandon a large volume of food and other supplies.

In September, Victorio's band went on the offensive, with a series of major raids across southwestern New Mexico that are often referred to as the Victorio War. On September 4, they attacked the U.S. Army post at Ojo Caliente, killing five soldiers and three civilians while making off with a substantial number of livestock.

After the Ojo Caliente raid, Lieutenant Colonel Nathan Dudley took four companies of the 9th Cavalry and a number of Navajo scouts in search of Victorio. On September 18, they tracked the Apache into the upper reaches of nearby Las Animas Canyon, where they came under fire from Victorio's well-entrenched marksmen. During the vicious shootout that followed, five soldiers were killed in action, and three others earned the Congressional Medal of Honor.*

Victorio led his men away from Las Animas Canyon to continue their raiding. On September 28, after they had struck a mail carrying detachment, Major Albert Morrow led a mixed detachment of 6th and 9th Cavalry to follow their trail, catching up with them the following day at Cuchillo Negro Creek. The ensuing firefight kept the troops penned down overnight, and Victorio escaped having killed two troopers while losing three of his men.

---

*The Medal of Honor citation for Lieutenant Matthias Day reported that he had "Advanced alone into the enemy's lines and carried off a wounded soldier of his command under a hot fire and after he had been ordered to retreat." Sergeant John Denny "Removed a wounded comrade, under a heavy fire, to a place of safety," while Lieutenant Robert Temple Emmet was in Company G, which was sent to relieve a detachment of soldiers under attack. During a flank attack on the Apaches made to divert them, Emmet and five of his men became surrounded. "Finding that the Indians were making for a position from which they could direct their fire on the retreating troop," reads Emmet's Medal of Honor citation, "the Lieutenant held his point with his party until the soldiers reached the safety of a canyon. Lieutenant Emmet then continued to hold his position while his party recovered their horses. The enemy force consisted of approximately 200."

Morrow would continue to pursue Victorio for the next month, crossing south into Mexico, and finally catching him on the Rio Corralitos on
October 27. By this time, the troopers were exhausted and short of ammunition, but they had come all this way to fight, and fight they did. Rather
than let the Apache get away, Morrow ordered a night attack, which cost
him one man killed in action. Once again, Victorio got away, but he rode
south into Mexico, rather than north into the United States. For the next
couple of months, he would be pursued by Mexican General Geronimo
Trevino.

The fighting resumed early in 1880, as Victorio returned from Mexico,
once again to find Morrow and the 9th Cavalry on his trail as soon as his
raiders were seen north of the border. Leading six companies in hot pursuit,
the major caught up with his Apache nemesis at Percha Creek, New Mexico
on January 12. As had been the case in their previous encounters, the two
sides traded fire for several hours before Victorio was able to flee. Again,
Morrow lost a man killed in action, with Apache casualties being unknown.

As the chase continued, Morrow and the 9th Cavalry followed Victorio
into the mountains of southern New Mexico. In a series of four engagements between January 17 and February 9, Morrow's command lost four
men killed in action, but kept the pressure on the Apache, and kept
Victorio on the run.

By April, the conflict had escalated on both sides. Victorio and his band
had managed to join forces with the Mescalero Apache in the San Andres
Mountains east of the Rio Grande. The Mescalero were assigned to the
Tularosa Agency in central New Mexico, but as with most Apache, the
warriors spent little time on the reservation.

Meanwhile, Colonel Hatch had decided to concentrate a large force on
the San Andres in an effort to both disarm the people living at Tularosa,
and round up the Apache not at the agency. In addition to the 6th Cavalry
contingents under Merritt and Captain Curwen McLellan, Colonel
Benjamin Grierson would come in from Texas with five companies of 10th
Cavalry, and Captain Henry Carroll would ride out of Fort Stanton with
four companies of 9th Cavalry. The plan was to converge on Victorio's
camp in Hembrillo Canyon on April 7.

Carroll's command was the first to arrive, but they had run out of water
when the water hole they planned to use en route turned out to be alka-

line. Knowing that the Apache were camped near a spring, they hoped that the converging columns would be able to make quick work of battle so that they could get a drink. As it turned out, Hatch and McLellan had been delayed for a day and did not arrive as planned. Carroll found his troops in a firefight and nearly out of drinking water. The Apache kept the troops penned down through the night, but just as Victorio moved in on the morning of April 8 to finish them off, McLellan reached the canyon with the 6th Cavalry. Victorio and the Apache broke off the attack and melted away before the soldiers could form up to give chase.

Victorio left three of his men killed in action, having wounded Captain Carroll and seven others. All the troopers drank from the spring, but the Apache had managed to slip through their fingers and back into the Mogollon Mountains to the west.

Four days after the Battle of Hembrillo Canyon, Colonel Hatch and his command rode into the Tularosa Agency to carry out the plan to disarm the Mescalero. They were met by Grierson's 10th Cavalry column, who had tangled with the Apache on April 9 on their way in from Texas.

The process of disarming the people at the agency turned into a brawl on April 16, shots were fired and fourteen Apache were killed. Twice that number escaped to join Victorio, but they were intercepted by Major Morrow's cavalry the next day in Dog Canyon, near White Sands, where three Apache were killed.

On May 7, a raiding party that Victorio set out to attack the San Carlos Agency, was spotted and reported to Captain Adam Cramer of the 5th Cavalry at the agency. He rode out with about twenty troopers and a like number of scouts to cut off the Apache. They crossed paths near Ash Creek of southeastern Arizona Territory, but the Apache escaped back into the mountains after a short running gun battle in which Cramer lost two men killed in action.

Late in May 1880, Colonel Hatch sent his chief scout, Henry Parker, into the Mogollons with sixty scouts to hunt for Victorio. In a turn of events that seemed almost scripted, he found the elusive Apache leader's encampment on the Palomas River in two days—and in a box canyon.

Parker deployed his men around the camp in position for a dawn surprise attack, which he launched methodically on May 24. Pouring withering fire into the camp, they had Victorio trapped. Parker sent for backup, but withdrew when Hatch did not respond. Had Parker more men and more ammunition, the Victorio War would have ended there that day on the Palomas.

Parker suffered no losses, but thirty of Victorio's band were killed, and the chief himself was among the wounded. As the Apache headed south toward Mexico, hoping to regroup and recoup, the tenacious Major Morrow caught one group at Cooke's Canyon, north of the border, with four companies of the 9th Cavalry. Most escaped, but Morrow's men managed to kill ten, possibly including Victorio's son, Washington. The battered band also was compelled to abandon a large number of horses as they fled.

In Mexico, Victorio found his people pursued and harassed by Colonel Adolfo Valle's Mexican cavalry, so he headed east and north, hoping to pass into Texas unnoticed. However, since February 1880, the Mexican and United States governments had agreed to cooperate against Victorio, so Valle telegraphed Colonel Grierson of the 10th Cavalry, who posted companies at various Rio Grande crossing points.

Grierson himself staked out the Tinaja de Las Palmas, an isolated water hole in south Texas that he knew Victorio would need. He was not disappointed. On July 30, Grierson's Company G managed to keep Victorio and an estimated 150 warriors at bay for two hours until additional 10th Cavalry Buffalo Soldiers rode up, whereupon the Apache fled south without having watered their horses. Grierson lost one man killed in action, and Victorio left seven dead. A week later, Victorio again crossed the border, but again Grierson was waiting for him at a necessary water hole. During his escape, Victorio was tempted to attack a wagon train, which was actually a decoy for another of Grierson's traps, and at least one Apache was killed.

In September 1880, under the new spirit of cooperation between Mexico and the United States, plans were laid for a three-prong sweep through northern Mexico. Colonel George Buell would lead a force out of New Mexico, while Colonel Eugene Carr would ride south from Arizona with the entire 6th Cavalry. The third fork was Colonel Joaquin Terrazas with the equivalent of three regiments of Mexican cavalry. It was to be the largest multinational force to be fielded during the Indian Wars in the West.

Unfortunately, this great coalition operation was doomed to failure. As the U.S. Army should have learned in its massive offensive operation in Montana Territory in 1876, large formations deployed against a highly mobile irregular force are unwieldy and ineffective. However, as often happens in such operations, it was ill fated not for technical reasons, but political factors. It seems that the politically ambitious Terrazas wanted Victorio for himself.

Eventually, the Mexican colonel had his wish. On October 16, 1880, the Mexican army cornered the Apache in the Sierra Tres Castillos of Chihuahua and attacked. The Apache suffered sixty warriors killed, along with eighteen women and children. Victorio himself took a fatal bullet from the rifle of a Tarahumara scout.

On October 28, a group of Apache fleeing the Sierra Tres Castillos fight crossed the Rio Grande near Ojo Caliente, where they attacked a small 10th Cavalry detachment. Five of the troopers died before the Apache escaped back across the border.

The Apache raiders resumed their cross-border forays early in 1881, killing two people in an attack on a stagecoach in Quitman Canyon, Texas. Pursued by Texas Rangers under Captain George Baylor, they escaped, but not before the Rangers killed four warriors and four women and children who were riding with them on January 29.

OLD NANA'S REIGN OF TERROR

The remains of Victorio's band coalesced under Nana, a sort of Apache elder statesman who had ridden with Victorio over the preceding years of raiding across the Southwest. Roughly eighty years old at the time, Nana was an unlikely candidate to be the scourge of the U.S. Army in 1881, but he was fit physically and able to both lead and keep up with the few dozen younger warriors who rode with him that year.

The series of Apache raids for which Nana is best remembered in the annals of the Indian Wars began on July 17, 1881, with an attack on a U.S. Army pack train in Alamo Canyon, New Mexico, near Fort Stanton. Lieutenant John Guilfoyle began a gunfight-filled pursuit that would be tailor-made for an action-adventure movie. Many of the encounters rank among the truly epic small unit actions of the Indian Wars, and five Congressional Medals of Honor would be awarded for actions that summer on Nana's trail.

After hitting the wagon train, Nana killed a group of Mexicans at an isolated location near White Sands, but Guilfoyle overtook the Apache in the San Andres Mountains on July 25, killing two of them in a shootout.

The chase then led westward across the Rio Grande and into the San Mateo Mountains. Nana killed at least seven people in two raids, which only served to get the local settlers angry enough to organize a posse. On August 1, however, Nana ambushed this posse in Red Canyon, killing one man, wounding seven, and stampeding almost all of their horses.

Two days after the Red Canyon fight, Guilfoyle found Nana's band in the San Mateo Mountains, managing to wound at least one Apache, but Nana escaped and the chase resumed. The exhausted Guilfoyle gave up the chase, which was taken over by Captain Charles Parker and Company K of the 9th Cavalry. When Parker's command cornered Nana's in Carrizo Canyon on August 12, the encounter quickly turned bloody. Five soldiers and at least one Apache were killed in action.*

After leaving Carrizo Canyon with one hostage—whom they subsequently murdered—Nana's raiders attacked a ranch near Alamosa Creek, where they killed a woman and her two children and stole some cattle.

Four days after Carrizo Canyon, Lieutenant George Burnett of the 9th Cavalry's Company I overtook the Apache herding their booty along Cuchillo Negro Creek. Nana quickly led his band into defensive positions in the cliffs and began peppering the soldiers with rifle fire. When four troopers became surrounded and were about to be overwhelmed, Lieutenant Burnett personally led Private Augustus Walley and Sergeant Moses Williams in a rescue effort. For this, all three would be awarded the Congressional Medal of Honor. The lieutenant's citation notes that he "Saved the life of a dismounted soldier, who was in imminent danger of being cut off, by alone galloping quickly to his assistance under heavy fire and escorting him to a place of safety, his horse being twice shot in this action." The citation for Sergeant Williams recalls that he "Rallied a detachment, skillfully conducted a running fight of three or four hours, and by his coolness, bravery, and unflinching devotion to duty in standing

---

*Sergeant Thomas Shaw was awarded the Congressional Medal of Honor when, as his citation noted, he "Forced the enemy back after stubbornly holding his ground in an extremely exposed position and prevented the enemy's superior numbers from surrounding his command." Sergeant George Jordan of the same company also earned the Medal of Honor at Carrizo Canyon, when he "stubbornly held his ground in an extremely exposed position and gallantly forced back a much superior number of the enemy, preventing them from surrounding the command." His medal was awarded both for this action and for a previous engagement on May 14, 1880. While commanding a detachment of 25 men at Fort Tularosa, New Mexico, "he repulsed a force of more than 100 Indians."

by his commanding officer in an exposed position under a heavy fire from a large party of Indians saved the lives of at least three of his comrades."

Nana and the Apache disappeared into the desert under cover of darkness, but both the 9th Cavalry and civilian volunteers were now swarming after him. Lieutenant George Smith and forty-six men from Companies B and H of the 9th Cavalry followed Nana southward into the Mimbres Mountains, accompanied by forty scouts and volunteers.

On August 19, the Apache ambushed Smith's column in Gavilan Canyon. Smith and three volunteers were killed almost immediately. The volunteers quickly retreated, but Sergeant Brent Woods assumed command as two more soldiers went down. Despite the initial disarray, Woods rallied the troops to return fire. For this, he would be awarded the Medal of Honor.

Nana again slipped away unscathed again, and rode across the border into Mexico, his late-in-life adventure essentially over. He would later surrender to the U.S. Army and serve prison time in Florida. When he was released, he was sent to Fort Sill, where he died in 1896, estimated to be nearly one hundred years old.

NAKAIDOKLINI'S CHILDREN

Within a week of Nana's having left the stage of the Southwest Theater of operations, a new cast of characters came upon the scene to take his place.

In almost Shakespearian progression, the first among these was young shaman named Nakaidoklini (also known as Nochaydelklinne), who had actually served as a scout with Crook a decade earlier and who had visited Washington, D.C. He had now become an herbalist and mystic, whose visions were considered important by many Apache. One such discernment saw a future in which the Apache were all-powerful and the Euro-Americans had disappeared. By the summer of 1881, Nakaidoklini had a growing number of enthusiastic devotees, especially among the Apache living on the squalid refugee camp that was the San Carlos Agency in southeastern Arizona Territory.

Through the winter of 1879-1880, when the agency was managed by the U.S. Army, circumstances had improved under the administration of 6th Cavalry Captain Adna Chaffee. However, when the Indian Bureau had resumed management in 1880, it was back to business as usual.

Conditions at San Carlos were poor, with people from numerous Apache bands living on top of one another. Corruption on the part of the agents and their commercial suppliers was rampant, and the agency was a breeding ground for anarchy. Nakaidoklini would be the prophet of the coming insurrection, and soon he would be its martyr.

In late August 1881, even as Nana was disappearing across the horizon, The Indian Bureau agent at San Carlos, J. C. Tiffany, convinced departmental commander Colonel Orlando Willcox that Nakaidoklini was a clear and present danger. Willcox, in turn, issued orders to veteran Indian fighter Colonel Eugene Carr, now the commander of the 6th Cavalry, to arrest Nakaidoklini. Although he rode out from Fort Apache to do as instructed, Carr questioned the orders. Doing a bit of soothsaying himself, he predicted that interfering with a medicine man could invite more trouble among his followers than it prevented.

Carr reached Nakaidoklini's camp on Cibicue Creek on August 30, with elements of two companies of cavalry and a two-dozen-man detachment of White Mountain Apache scouts under Lieutenant Thomas Cruse. The scouts spoke with Nakaidoklini, explaining that he had to come with the soldiers. If he did not, they told him, he would be killed. Nakaidoklini predicted that he would never be killed and went with the soldiers.

As the troops made camp, Nakaidoklini's disciples attacked in force. The Apache scouts promptly revolted and joined in, shooting wildly at the soldiers. Having been ordered to shoot Nakaidoklini if anything happened, Sergeant John MacDonald did so, although it took several shots to bring him down. Various accounts of the incident have Nakaidoklini's wife and members of his family also being killed.

The soldiers took cover and the two sides traded shots until dusk, at which time, Carr organized a withdrawal under cover of darkness. He had lost four men killed in action, and another man would later die of his wounds.*

News of the death of Nakaidoklini spread quickly, liberally enhanced by exaggeration. This was the catalyst that led to a general uprising. It probably would have happened soon anyway, but the assassination of the

---

*Three of the 6th Cavalry troopers would be awarded the Congressional Medal of Honor for their bravery at Cibicue Creek that day—Sergeant Alonzo Bowman, Lieutenant William Carter, and Private Richard Heartery.

shaman was the direct cause. Over the next three days, five civilians and three soldiers were killed by the Apache in remote locations in east-central Arizona near Fort Apache. They even laid siege to Fort Apache itself, during which Private First Class Will Barnes of the Army Signal Corps earned the Medal of Honor for bravery in the defense of the post.

Meanwhile, other rumors had spread all the way to Washington, D.C., that Carr's entire command had been wiped to the last man. Before the initial reports could be corrected, the national papers ran with the story, which naturally recalled news of the obliteration of Custer's command five years before.

The outcry for revenge was referred to the desk of William Tecumseh Sherman, who telegraphed Colonel Willcox back in Arizona with great urgency. Even though Carr's death toll was eventually confirmed to have been merely five, the reports of the "massacre"—and the fact of the Fort Apache siege—had done their deed. This, in turn, had escalated the Apache revolt by inciting public opinion among Arizona settlers against the Apache.

Apaches who had been anxious to desert the agency used this sudden turn of events to do so. Among the Apache to leave the San Carlos Agency were leaders such as Naiche (also known as Nachez, the youngest son and successor of Cochise) and Geronimo. While Naiche was technically the chief of the Chiricahua Apache, Geronimo had the charisma and the skill that made him their leader.

Other less prominent leaders who took to the hills with small bands of disaffected warriors was Natiotish of the White Mountain Apache, who would figure prominently in the Apache battles the following year.

Geronimo and the Chiricahua at War

Geronimo and Naiche left San Carlos together, leading a group of about six dozen Chiricahua. On August 2, 1881, they paused near Cedar Springs to attack and loot a wagon train. In an almost cinematic moment, the cavalry arrived, specifically elements of three companies from the 1st and 6th Cavalry, led by departmental commander Willcox himself.

The Chiricahua withdrew quickly into defensive positions in nearby hills. Willcox eagerly followed, leading his cavalry into what turned out to be a snare, hastily and skillfully laid by Geronimo. The Chiricahua escaped at nightfall with no losses. Three soldiers and seven people at the wagon train had been killed.

Smarting from his poor showing at Cedar Springs, Willcox blamed Carr for having mishandled of the Nakaidoklini arrest, despite Carr's having correctly predicted that interference with a holy man was a prescription for disaster. Called up on charges, Carr was largely cleared of wrongdoing, but the court of public opinion in Arizona would not be nearly so kind to Willcox. Their cries were heard at the War Department in Washington. Within a year, Willcox would be gone—replaced by the territory's favorite Indian fighting general, George Crook.

Having wintered in Mexico in his old home country in the Sierra Madre, Geronimo led his growing Chiricahua band back across the border in April 1882. In Mexico, Geronimo had linked up with Nana's band, and, crossing back into Arizona, they were joined by Loco's band. The latter had wintered at the agencies, and were now ready to bolt.

The return of Geronimo to the hostile list sent reverberations throughout the Southwest Theater of operations. District of New Mexico commander Colonel Ranald Mackenzie's troops were the first to see action in the new year. Specifically, it was Lieutenant Colonel George "Sandy" Forsyth and a detachment of the 4th Cavalry—Mackenzie's old outfit—that crossed paths with the Apache at Horseshoe Canyon in Arizona. The unit had been trailing the Apache into the Pelloncillo Mountains, when their advance scouts were ambushed by Loco's band on April 23.

After the firefight had been raging for a while, Forsyth himself arrived on the scene with four companies and began the difficult task of assaulting the Chiricahua, who held the higher ground. By day's end, Loco set a grass fire to cover his exit and escaped. Sandy Forsyth had lost four scouts and two troopers killed in action, and he counted two Apache dead. Two men of the 4th Cavalry, wagoner John Schnitzer and Lieutenant Wilbur Wilder, earned the Congressional Medal of Honor at Horseshoe Canyon for rescuing a wounded comrade under heavy enemy fire.

Loco slipped twenty miles into Mexico and set up camp in the Sierra Enmedio, thinking his band immune from the long arm of the U.S. Army. In fact, both Forsyth and a 6th Cavalry detachment led by Captain William Rafferty and Captain Tullian Tupper had picked up their trail and followed them. On April 28, just five days after Horseshoe Canyon, the

Geronimo, left, and Naiche giving themselves up for a second time. (*National Archives*)

6th Cavalry sprung an attack on Loco. The fierce shootout ended only when the troops ran short of ammunition and withdrew.

Forsyth linked up with the exhausted 6th Cavalrymen, who convinced him to rest overnight before resuming the combined offensive. By April 29, the Chiricahua had pulled up stakes and gone, but Loco had been wounded, and the battle had cost him fourteen warriors, along with seven women, killed. The 6th Cavalry had only one man killed in action.

Back in Arizona, trouble was brewing among that contingent of the White Mountain Apache, who had followed Natiotish into the rugged Tonto Basin Country. They used the area, scene of the Tonto Basin War a decade earlier, as a base for raiding forays into surrounding communities. In July, after the White Mountain band killed a civilian police chief and three others at the San Carlos Agency, the U.S. Army entered the Tonto Basin to pursue Natiotish.

The coming battle was going to be a classic instance of the outcome hinging on the quality of intelligence. Natiotish could see Captain Adna Chaffee's single company of 6th Cavalry troopers coming as he climbed the Mogollon Rim, moving toward General Springs, an important water hole on the trail that led northwesterly across the Tonto Basin. He knew that his intelligence was good, because his people knew the lay of the land so intuitively. His mistake was overconfidence. He thought, incorrectly, that he had the whole picture.

Natiotish's observers had missed seeing Major Andrew Evans, as he joined Chaffee at the end of the day on July 16 with five companies of the 3rd and 6th Cavalry. As Natiotish prepared an ambush for the following day on East Clear Creek, his intelligence was nearly a day old. Meanwhile, Chaffee's own scouts, led by the veteran Al Seiber, had spotted Natiotish, and had figured out that the White Mountain leader was under the impression that he would be springing a surprise attack.

Chaffee proposed, and Evans concurred, that he lead a flanking movement to outflank each of the Apache positions overlooking the trail with two companies. When the Apache attempted to spring the trap, the troopers would be behind them.

On July 17, as Evans moved into the canyon with two companies, Natiotish struck from both sides, believing that he was attacking the entire U.S. Army force. Suddenly, each of his flanks was, itself, under attack. The usual endgame for an Apache ambush had been for to simply pull back and fade away. This time, Natiotish found his exit route blocked. Chaffee had forced him to fight to the finish.

This fight—known as the Battle of Big Dry Wash although it occurred on East Clear Creek—was a major victory for the U.S. Army, and a major defeat for the Apache. The estimates of Apache dead range from sixteen to twenty-seven, with Natiotish himself among them. Virtually all of the rest were captured.*

This battle was marked the last major combat between the Apache and the U.S. Army within Arizona, but raiders would continue to strike in the territory for nearly a decade. After 1882, however, the main focus of the action, as well as the events leading to the ultimate end of the Apache Wars, would take place not in Arizona, but across the border in Mexico.

---

*Two 6th Cavalry lieutenants, Thomas Cruse and Frank West, and Lieutenant George Morgan of the 3rd Cavalry were awarded the Congressional Medal of Honor for their actions in the battle. Cruse, a veteran of the Cibicue Creek fight in 1881, earned his medal when he "Gallantly charged hostile Indians, and with his carbine compelled a party of them to keep under cover of their breastworks, thus being enabled to recover a severely wounded soldier." Morgan was cited when he "Gallantly held his ground at a critical moment and fired upon the advancing enemy until he was disabled by a shot."

CROOK VERSUS GERONIMO

In July 1882, the climactic steps were taken that would bring the last major campaign of the Indian Wars to its final conclusion. The same week as Captain Chaffee's victory in the Tonto Basin, the War Department officially replaced Colonel Orlando Willcox with General George Crook as commander of the Department of Arizona. His tenure in the Department of the Platte had been less than a total success, but in the Southwest, Crook's reputation was legendary. Now he was back, essentially to finish the job that he had started a decade before—to end the Apache Wars and bring peace to the Southwest.

A week later, the long-sought diplomatic agreement allowing the U.S. Army to operate in Mexico was signed by the administrations of presidents Chester Arthur and Porfirio Díaz. The two nations had theoretically been cooperating since February 1880, but now, the U.S. Army could operate in Sonora as easily as in Arizona.

Having received his orders in July, Crook arrived at Whipple Barracks on September 4 to take command. In the meantime, the Indian Bureau had seen fit to assign a new agent to San Carlos, Philip P. Wilcox, who was no relation to Colonel Willcox, whose name had a different spelling. Crook made it a point to make contact with Wilcox and to see that military officers were assigned to the agency and that military discipline would replace the poor management practices so ingrained in the direction of the agency. The general correctly believed that a necessary prerequisite to his accomplishing his mission was to get things under control at the refugee camp that was the breeding ground for the discontent that allowed insurrection to get out of hand.

Within his own military command, Crook would return to practices that had served him so well previously. These included the liberal use of Apache scouts to work with detachments fighting the insurgent Apache. Crook sought Apache scouts from the same subtribes and even the same bands as the Apache who he expected to be trailing. One of the most important would be a former White Mountain Apache raider named Tzoe, whom the soldiers nicknamed Peaches.

Across the border in the states of Chihuahua and Sonora, the Chiricahua in bands led by Geronimo and Chato, spent the winter raiding Mexican towns and settlements as they had during previous winters. In early 1883, both leaders began to look north, where their plunder was more likely to yield the arms and ammunition that they needed to sustain their operations. The Southwest had been generally quiet through the winter, but that would abruptly change.

During the last week of March, Chato made a particularly bloody foray into southeastern Arizona Territory and southwestern New Mexico that left eleven people dead, and culminated in an incident on March 28 that provided a graphic symbol for the resumption of hostilities. Judge Hamilton McComas, his wife, and six-year-old son were picnicking south of Silver City, New Mexico when the Apache raiders happened by. The judge was shot repeatedly, his wife was bludgeoned to death, and the boy was never to be seen alive again.

The publicity surrounding the McComas affair led to a public outcry that could only be answered by George Crook. The general carefully laid his plans, coordinating operations with Ranald Mackenzie in New Mexico, and making contact with the authorities in Mexico. He wanted to be sure that there would be no surprises, such as had greeted Colonel Carr when Joaquin Terrazas decided that he wanted Victorio all to himself.

Crook himself led the expedition, which crossed into Sonora on May 1, headed for the Sierra Madre where Geronimo had his redoubt. The centerpiece of Crook's command were six companies of the 3rd Cavalry under Captain Emmet Crawford. Also included were elements of the 6th Cavalry and nearly two hundred Apache, Mojave, and Yuma scouts, including Peaches. The latter had only recently switched sides and would prove valuable in the hunt for the raiders.

The Sierra Madre, Geronimo's home turf, had never before been probed by a U.S. Army task force. In fact, even the Mexican army regarded it as so dangerous as to be off limits. However, the splendid job that Geronimo and the Apache had done in turning the Sierra Madre into a sanctuary actually worked to their disadvantage. On May 15, they were not expecting it when the 3rd Cavalry attacked Chato's encampment, killing nine combatants and capturing women and children.

Just as Geronimo was regarded by Arizona settlers as a larger than life antagonist, so was Crook considered by the Apache to be a warrior of considerable power. His sudden presence in the heart of the sacred Sierra Madre—with a large body of soldiers and with Apache scouts—was seen as an event of tremendous significance. With this, the Apache agreed to

General George Crook back in the American Southwest for another round of fighting with Geronimo and the Chiricahua. Crook is accompanied by two Apache scouts, Dutch, left, and Alchise, far right. (*National Archives*)

parley rather than fight. Crook met with all of the Apache leaders, from Chato to Geronimo, and even with old Nana, who had essentially retired to the Sierra Madre. He negotiated from a position of strength by demonstrating his own power. The Apache could run, but they could not hide.

Amazingly, Crook managed to get all of the Apache leaders to agree to turn themselves in—although not all at once. Geronimo explained that it would take time to pull everyone together. His supplies running short, Crook decided that it would be better to go back with some of the Apache rather than allow his command to become stranded in Sonora. He returned to Arizona with more than three hundred Apache and a promise that the Apache leaders would soon follow.

Initially, Crook was celebrated for his nearly bloodless "victory" in Mexico, but as the months passed and Geronimo remained at large, skeptics began questioning his judgment. However, much to the amazement of all, the Apache leaders did as promised. After the first of 1884, they gradually came north to the once dreaded San Carlos Agency. Naiche and Chato had arrived by February, and when Geronimo himself reached Arizona a month later, Crook's mission seemed complete. It was not. Now that he had captured the Chiricahua, the question arose of what to do with them. At the San Carlos Agency, Philip Wilcox feared the Chiricahua, so he begged Washington to let the Army house them at Fort Apache. Crook accepted responsibility for the Chiricahua.

With Geronimo back under watchful eyes, Apache relations moved into a new phase that was more administrative than military. As had been the case throughout the West for the previous quarter century, there was an ongoing jurisdictional turf war between the Army and the Indian Bureau. The latter wanted a free hand at the agencies, but the ability to call upon the former when force was needed—and to have the Army take sole responsibility for people such as the Chiricahua that agents thought were too hot to handle. Crook felt that the Army should have the authority to go with the responsibility, and that it should be the lead agency in Indian matters in the Southwest. If he was going to have to pick up the pieces if agency policy created problems, he wanted a hand in setting that policy.

As with many such organizational matters in a bureaucracy, the topic remained in limbo until it became a crisis. In May 1885, two years after Crook's triumph in the Sierra Madre, and nearly four years after their last major insurrection, the Apache rebelled.

Though Crook's treatment of the Chiricahua was seen by all as more humane that the treatment of other people by the Indian Bureau, there were still complaints. This time the catalyst for rebellion was a good deal more mundane than the death of a shaman that started things in 1881. In 1885, the motivation was Crook's crackdown on the abuse of Chiricahua women by Chiricahua men, and the drunkenness that came with the practice of home-brewing tizwin, a traditional Chiricahua beer made from the mescal plant.

On May 17, Geronimo, Nana, Naiche, and other leaders took nearly 150 followers and headed for Sonora. On the way, they passed through New Mexico, where they killed several miners. Crook responded by sending two fast-moving cavalry task forces to pursue the Chiricahua into Mexico. One was under Captain Wirt Davis, the other under Captain Emmet Crawford, a veteran commander of the Sierra Madre campaign, who knew the enemy and the terrain as well as anyone in the U.S. Army. Guiding them was none other than Chato, the former Apache leader, now turned Apache scout.

This time the going was not so easy. Geronimo and his followers proved to be more elusive than ever. Two years before, Crook had penetrated the Sierra Madre and had gotten Geronimo to the bargaining table in a couple of weeks. This time, Davis and Crawford pursued the Chiricahua through the summer and into the fall. During June, each side managed to attack a small detachment camp of the other, but the results were minimal. Finally, on August 7, Davis's 4th Cavalry found and attacked Geronimo's own camp near Casas Grandes in Chihuahua. Though two of his wives were captured, Geronimo himself got way, as did the venerable Nana.

By November, Davis, Crawford, and Crook had little to show for their efforts when the brazen Chiricahua resumed their cross-border raids. One young leader, Josanie took about two dozen warriors on a month long spree across Arizona and New Mexico that left nearly forty people dead and created a public outcry of epic proportions. The fact that all of the forces available to Crook at the time had failed to curb the violence or even to intercept the relatively small raiding party led to intense criticism of the once-beloved Indian fighter.

General Phil Sheridan, who has succeeded William Tecumseh Sherman as commanding general of the U.S. Army in November 1883, came west to Arizona to have a word with Crook, and to micromanage the campaign. The two met at Crook's field headquarters at Fort Bowie near Tucson.

Sheridan explained to Crook that it was now clear to both the Secretary of War William Endicott and him that the problem of the Chiricahua in the Southwest could be resolved only by taking them out of the Southwest. Crook's humane treatment of the Chiricahua may have been seen as benevolent and desirable until they revolted, but it now appeared to those at the head of the chain of command that he had allowed himself to be duped. Rounding up the Chiricahua and shipping them to be interned in the East was seen to be the only solution.

When Crook explained that some of his best scouts were Chiricahua, Sheridan explained that he and the Secretary of War were also displeased with Crook's reliance on the use of indigenous scouts. When Crook had been successful, such tactics had been seen as innovative. Now that things were not going well, those in Washington had decided that the scouts were untrustworthy. More reliance on regular troops, Sheridan had decided, was the way to go.

One thing both of the officers agreed upon was that capturing Geronimo was the key to the goal of a peaceful Southwest. With him remaining as a beacon to the Chiricahua raiders, there could be no peace.

Finally, in January 1886, after eight months of relentless campaigning, Emmet Crawford had success within his grasp. Using mainly Apache scouts rather than regulars—contrary to Sheridan's new strategy—Crawford had located Geronimo on the Rio Aros, deep inside Mexico. Geronimo sent word to Crawford's camp. He was ready to talk.

On the appointed day, January 11, as Crawford waited to parley, an unexpected third party intervened. The Mexicans had triumphed over Victorio, and they intended to have the elusive Geronimo as well. As Crawford watched from the sidelines, a band of Mexican irregulars, consisting mainly of Tarahumara Indians, attacked. As the captain tried to intervene to arrange a cease-fire, he took a bullet in the head, reportedly fired by Mauricio Corredor, thought to have been the same Tarahumara who killed Victorio. As the gun battle evolved, it seemed that the Mexican irregulars were just as willing to trade shots with the U.S. Army's Apache as with Geronimo's Apache. One of Crawford's scouts shot and killed Corredor.

After the battle, Geronimo and the Mexicans scattered in separate directions, and the U.S. Army contingent, now led by Lieutenant Marion Maus, headed north thinking that the expedition had been a failure.*

Two days later, as the column was nearing the border, some Apache women approached Maus to explain that Geronimo was still ready to talk, but he would deal only with Crook. Maus suddenly had some good news to report when he reached Fort Bowie.

Arrangements were made, and on March 25, 1886, Crook and Geronimo met once again, this time at Embudo Canyon, a dozen miles inside Mexico. Crook accepted Geronimo's surrender, as well as those of Nana, Naiche, and others. As in 1883, Crook went north without Geronimo, who promised that he would be along soon. Lieutenant Maus would escort the Chiricahua back to the United States. Once again, it seemed to be over, but once again it was not.

Two days after the conference and the surrender, the Chiricahua got hold of some mescal, had a few drinks, and had a few second thoughts. Lieutenant Maus returned to Fort Bowie with old Nana and about sixty other people, mainly women and children. Geronimo, Naiche, twenty war-

*For his actions on January 11, for assuming command and leading the force out of Mexico, Maus would be awarded the Congressional Medal of Honor.

riors, and thirteen women were once again in the wind. Unfortunately, Crook had already wired Sheridan to report Geronimo's capture.

On April 1, 1886, Crook wired Sheridan again, asking to be relieved of his command.

As George Crook headed north, returning to his former post in the Department of the Platte, Geronimo was on his way back to the Sierra Madre.

MILES VERSUS GERONIMO

With Crook having failed to deliver, Phil Sheridan turned to the commander who ran Sitting Bull ragged and accepted the surrender of Chief Joseph—Brigadier General Nelson Appleton Miles. Only a year earlier, Miles had taken over command of the Department of the Missouri after a stint in command of the Department of the Columbia. Sherman saw the energetic Miles as his ace in the hole. Among the U.S. Army's senior leadership, he had an extraordinary record and a reputation for getting the job done.

Sheridan placed a quarter of the total active-duty troop strength of the U.S. Army at Miles's disposal. On paper, Miles was ready to handle any contingency. All he had to do was make contact with the enemy. He did not have to wait long. Before the end of April 1886, Geronimo and Naiche were back across the border on another raiding spree. After some settlers were killed, Captain Thomas Lebo led Company K of the 10th Cavalry in pursuit, chasing the Chiricahua for 200 miles into the Sierra Pinito of Sonora. On May 3, Geronimo decided to stand and fight. Two of the African-American Buffalo Soldiers fell, one dead and one wounded.*

Miles had brought a new face to the campaign, but he was chagrined by the inability of the troops to intercept the cross-border raid that marred his first month in office. Meanwhile, his offensive tactics were essentially the same as Crook's. If Geronimo was to be recaptured, it would be through the deployment of mobile cavalry detachments on long patrols deep inside Mexico—using Apache scouts.

---

*Second Lieutenant Powhatan Clarke would earn the Congressional Medal of Honor that day for saving the wounded man. His citation notes that he "Rushed forward to the rescue of a soldier who was severely wounded and lay, disabled, exposed to the enemy's fire, and carried him to a place of safety."

As a field commander for the Mexican operations, Miles picked a veteran 4th Cavalry officer, Captain Henry Lawton. He headed south from Fort Huachuca, Arizona, on May 5, just two days after Lebo's battle in the Pinitos, with a detachment that included fifty-five men from the 4th Cavalry and the 8th Infantry Regiment, as well as twenty Apache scouts. They took a hundred-head pack train in order to support operations for four months.

It would an epic expedition into a harsh and unforgiving environment in the hottest time of the year. The cavalry became infantry for lack of water and forage for the horses. Only the heartiest were able to tough it out through the whole summer. Most of the troops had to abandon the campaign and return to Arizona Territory to be replaced by fresh troops. Both Lawton and his contract surgeon, Dr. Leonard Wood, did remain in the field, and did survive the ordeal. For Wood, it would be the campaign that launched a stellar career.*

From a tactical point of view, the campaign in Sonora in the blistering summer of 1886 was a disappointment, though. Only brief and fleeting contact was made with the Apache. On May 15, Captain Charles Hatfield, commanding elements of Company D of the 4th Cavalry located and attacked an Apache encampment on Rio Bavispe in the Santa Cruz Mountains. The Apache got away, allowing the troops to capture some of their horses and equipment. As they were leaving however, the troops were ambushed by the same Apache. During the ensuing fight, two men were

---

*Wood was awarded the Medal of Honor for the campaign that summer, though not until 1898. His citation noted that Wood had "Voluntarily carried dispatches through a region infested with hostile Indians, making a journey of seventy miles in one night and walking thirty miles the next day. Also for several weeks, while in close pursuit of Geronimo's band and constantly expecting an encounter, commanded a detachment of Infantry, which was then without an officer, and to the command of which he was assigned upon his own request." A Harvard Medical School graduate, Wood would get military service into his blood that summer in the Sonoran desert and never lost it. Wood went on to serve as personal physician to Presidents Grover Cleveland and William McKinley, and got to know Theodore Roosevelt, who was then assistant secretary of the Navy. At the start of the Spanish-American War, Wood and Roosevelt organized the 1st Volunteer Cavalry Regiment, better known as the "Rough Riders." During the war, Wood served as commander the 2nd Cavalry Brigade in Cuba, and later as Military Governor of Cuba until 1902. Promoted to major general, Wood commanded American forces in the Philippines through 1906, and was named U.S. Army Chief of Staff—the equivalent of the nineteenth-century commanding general's post—in 1910 by President William Howard Taft.

Apaches during a stop as they were moved by rail to the east. Geronimo is third from the right in the front row. (*National Archives*)

killed, and Sergeant Samuel Craig was seriously wounded. Despite this, he fought bravely and was awarded the Congressional Medal of Honor for his "conspicuous gallantry."

On July 14, the scouts for the main column located an Apache camp, but by the time Lawton had men in position for an attack, the Apache had gotten away. The Lawton expedition of 1886 was essentially a tactical duplicate of the Crook expedition of 1883, except that it failed to yield results.

Whereas his offensive operations mirrored those of Crook, on the defensive side, Miles can be credited with being the first to provide the U.S. Army with a distant early warning system utilizing leading edge technology. Cross-border raids were problematic because they were difficult to intercept, and if they were observed, it would take a fast moving horseman riding at top speed to report the incursion to the nearest Army post. Communications were the Achilles heel of operations anywhere in the West, especially in the Southwest.

Miles solved this problem through a system of twenty-seven distant early warning posts located on mountaintops and equipped with heliographs. He situated these all across the Mexican border. If an Apache raiding party crossed the border in daylight, news of the incursion could be transmitted throughout the entire border region within minutes. A cavalry strike force could be alerted just as quickly. As would be the case with radar during the Battle of Britain in 1940, the opposing side never grasped the importance of the new technology. However, it was good only as a defensive measure, and it was essentially useless in the primary mission at hand—catching Geronimo.

Having been unsuccessful in snaring him with a stick, Miles finally decided to use a carrot. Lawton was still in Sonora, but he had come up empty-handed, so Miles let it be known that he wanted to parley with Geronimo.

In the meantime, Miles had decided to clear his plate of the Chiricahua, including old Nana, who had been brought in by Crook's command in March. They had bolted from the reservation before, and there was no reason to suppose they wouldn't again. Sheridan had long been pressuring his field commanders to get the Chiricahua under lock and key, so finally, Miles took action. On August 29, even as Miles's emissaries were presenting his olive branch to Geronimo, the general rounded up the Chiricahua in his care, loaded them aboard a train, and sent them to Fort Marion, Florida, for incarceration.

On August 24, Lieutenant Charles Gatewood, who had served under Crook and who had known Geronimo when he was at Fort Apache, had met with the Chiricahua leader at Rio Bavispe. He acknowledged that the Chiricahua were running scared, that they had the enmity of the Mexicans, as well as the Americans and that they could not go on for long this way. It was like the conversation between Miles and Joseph in the Bear Paw Mountains of Montana Territory nearly a decade before. Geronimo knew that his situation was nearing an end, but was reluctant to admit it.

Geronimo finally surrendered to Bear Coat Miles at Skeleton Canyon, south of Fort Bowie on September 4, 1886. Miles, like Crook, said that Geronimo would be held as a prisoner of war in Florida, which is where most of the Chiricahua had been sent in August.

There were demands from Arizona Territorial civil authorities that Geronimo be turned over to for trial—and almost certain hanging—but the United States government abided by the terms under which he had surrendered.

CLOSING THE CHAPTER

Though major combat in the Southwest seemed to have come to an end, no campaign involving action against a guerrilla force ever ends abruptly on a specific day with the signing of a specific surrender document. As we see through the records of those awarded the Congressional Medal of Honor, the U.S. Army's job in the Southwest Theater of operations did not end with Geronimo's capitulation.

On May 11, 1889, two men of the 24th Infantry Regiment who were escorting a paymaster earned the Medal for intervening in an attempted robbery. Although he had been shot in the abdomen, Sergeant Benjamin Brown did not leave the field until he was again wounded through both arms. After the fight, Corporal Isaiah Mays walked and crawled two miles to a ranch for help.

Nor did the skirmishing with the Apache end when Geronimo's Chiricahua band went east. Nearly four years after, on March 7, 1890, a running gun battle took place in which three men were awarded the Congressional Medal of Honor. Sergeant William McBryer of Company K, 10th Cavalry earned his for having "Distinguished himself for coolness, bravery and marksmanship while his troop was in pursuit of hostile Apache Indians." Sergeant James Daniels of Company L, 4th Cavalry was awarded the Medal for his "Untiring energy and cool gallantry under fire in an engagement with Apache Indians."

When he had left the Southwest, Brigadier General George Crook had gone back to command the Department of the Platte, where he continued to deal with minor skirmishing on the Plains. However, by now, the Indian Wars consisted mainly of fights involving small gangs of bandits with no formal support from tribal leaders. When a Ute hunting party got intro a shootout with a Colorado game warden over out of season hunting in 1887, Crook refused to intervene. He felt that it was a matter for local law enforcement.

In 1888, when the long-serving Alfred Terry retired, President Grover Cleveland gave Crook his second star and transferred the newly minted major general to Chicago to command the entire Division of the Missouri. The man who had achieved his greatest success as a military leader in the West with compact mobile units now commanded a 13,000-man force that was the largest in the U.S. Army.

Throughout his later years, even as he rose in rank within the U.S. Army, Crook was an outspoken advocate of Indian rights. He had tried to run his stewardship of the Chiricahua in Arizona with even-handed honesty, and he advocated no less in the government's policies nationally. Crook especially lobbied for the Chiricahua to be treated in accordance with the terms of their surrender.

Crook suffered a heart attack and died in Chicago on March 21, 1890, while still commanding the division. He was originally buried at Oakland, Maryland, but he and his wife were reinterred in Arlington National Cemetery in 1898.

Crook was succeeded as commander of the Division of the Missouri by Nelson Miles, a man whose career was now on the fast track. In 1894, after leading the U.S. Army in the controversial suppression of the Pullman Strike violence in Chicago, he was sent to take command of the Department of the East, with headquarters at Governors Island, New York. When General John Schofield retired in 1895, he became the commanding general of the U.S. Army, a post that he would hold until his retirement in 1903 at the rank of lieutenant general. During the Spanish-American War, he personally led U.S. Army operations in Puerto Rico. He published two volumes of memoirs and lived until 1906.

General Ranald Mackenzie, whose career as an able campaigner on the Plains and in the Southwest was overshadowed by those of Crook and Miles, would meet an unhappy end. He served as commander of the District of New Mexico from 1881 to 1883, when he was promoted to brigadier general and assigned to head the Department of Texas. He had planned to marry and retire on land that he owned near Boerne, Texas, but in December 1883, shortly after assuming the Texas command, he was diagnosed as suffering "paralysis of the insane." Taken under escort to New York, he was hospitalized and retired from the Army in March 1884. He died in 1889 and was buried in the military cemetery at West Point.

Geronimo and five hundred Chiricahua were initially interned at different locations in Florida, where disease decimated their numbers. In 1888, the Indian Rights Association, with George Crook's support, successfully campaigned for their being reunited at a location in Alabama. There was still a great deal of opposition in Arizona to their being returned to their original home, but Crook lobbied for their being sent to Fort Sill in Indian Territory, which had, at least a somewhat more familiar climate.

In 1894, with deaths among the women and children about double the normal rate, and because of unsanitary conditions, Geronimo and his band were finally moved to Fort Sill. Geronimo, though technically still a prisoner of war, was allowed a certain amount of freedom after his relocation to Fort Sill. In 1905, at the age of seventy-five, he was invited to ride in President Theodore Roosevelt's inaugural parade, and in 1908 he was invited to join Pawnee Bill's Wild West Show.

Geronimo died of pneumonia at Fort Sill on February 17, 1909, but the Chiricahua continued to be held as prisoners of war until 1914, when they were given permission to return to their old home in the Southwest.

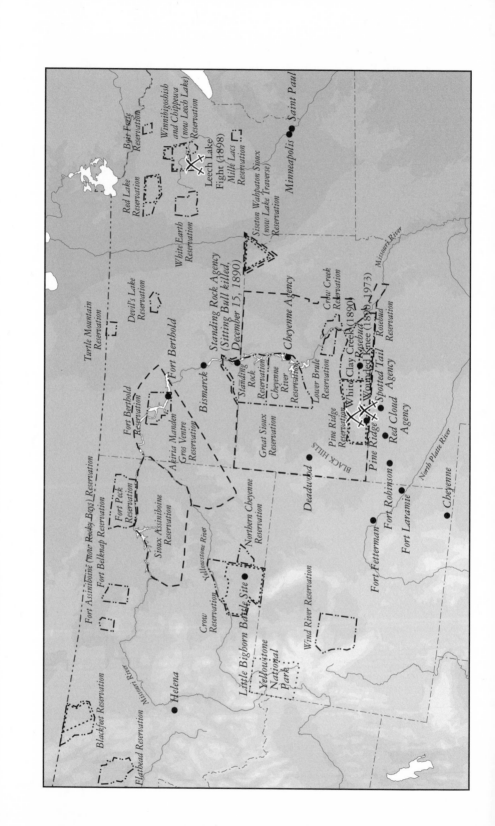

9

WOUNDED KNEE

In 1890, the same year that George Crook died, the United States Census Bureau officially declared the nation's western frontier closed. No longer could one identify a vertical line on a map as the limit of westward expansion. The U.S. Army's mandate in the West since the beginning of the Grant administration two decades earlier had been to move the Indians onto reservations, and force them back if they strayed. This job had been essentially complete by 1880, except in the Southwest, and with Geronimo's surrender in 1886, the Army's job seemed done. Upon his retirement as commanding general of the U.S. Army in 1883, William Tecumseh Sherman had declared, "Indians as substantially eliminated from the problem of the Army."

With the frontier closed, the West was fast integrating itself into the fabric of the nation. Among the geographic divisions in the West, only Arizona, New Mexico, and Indian Territory were no longer states, and the "unused" Indian land in the latter had been opened to outside settlement in 1889.

Even the notion of the existence of Indian Territory itself was beginning to be considered archaic. It had been many decades since anyone had considered the once popular idea that large swaths of the West should be set aside as "Permanent Indian Country." Indeed, this concept was officially abandoned in 1868 in favor of the reservation system. In 1890, the western part of what is now the state of Oklahoma was organized as Oklahoma Territory. As Oklahoma Territory and neighboring Indian Territory were surrounded by states, both territories began lobbying for statehood. In 1905, the two parallel efforts merged, and the United States Congress was petitioned to admit the two as a single state. In 1907, they were merged and admitted to the Union as the state of Oklahoma. Arizona and New Mexico would round out the forty-eight contiguous states in 1912.

Outside Indian Territory, the indigenous people of the West had been assigned to reservations across the western half of the country. Those in Montana, Wyoming, and the Dakotas alone had an aggregate area larger than New England, and the Navajo Reservation in Arizona was the largest of all.

In 1890, the six reservations in South Dakota constituted the largest concentration of Indian land outside Indian Territory. These were organized in three groups of contiguous pairs. The smallest of the pairs contained the Lower Brulé and Crow Creek, straddling the Missouri River south of Pierre. The other two pairs were larger, each about the size of the state of Maryland. In the south, adjacent to the Nebraska line, were the Pine Ridge and Rosebud Reservations, which were the former Spotted Tail and Red Cloud Agencies. In the north were the Cheyenne River and the Standing Rock (which extended into North Dakota). The latter was also home to Sitting Bull, seen by most as the most influential of Lakota leaders.

Like Sitting Bull, all the great Indian leaders who had figured prominently in the Indian Wars of the West during the nineteenth century were either dead, in custody, or living quietly on the reservations by 1890.

As the end of the frontier was declared in 1890, it seemed that the epoch of the Indian Wars in the West had also come to a close. That was not to be. Trouble would flare up again, and there would two more battles, though some would call them massacres. They would be separated by eighty-three years and an infinitely complex transition in American culture and society, but they would occur in the same place.

DANCES WITH GHOSTS

The closing of the frontier in the American West was accompanied by the end of a chapter in the history of the indigenous people that had lasted for centuries. Nowhere were the ramifications of this closing chapter more pronounced than on the Plains. In other regions, such as the Southwest, where agriculture had been adopted by most tribes prior to the arrival of Europeans and Euro-Americans, the change was less dramatic. On the Plains, where all aspects of life and culture had centered on a nomadic people following the great herds of buffalo, the change was profound.

The buffalo, which had once numbered 75 million or more, had been pushed to the point of extinction. There were too few to hunt, and certainly there were too few around on which to maintain a way of life. The once-nomadic people, for whom the Plains were once an infinite ocean of grass with no obstacle other than rival tribes, were now confined to prescribed reservations, their very livelihood dependent on the whims of the bureaucrats of the Indian Bureau.

The well-meaning Indian agents had taken it upon themselves to open schools to educate the children, while teaching the adults the trades of "civilized" society, from farming to carpentry to blacksmithing. Because religious groups had been given a role in managing the reservations, religious education was also a part of the transformation of Indian life and culture. In 1887, the Dawes Act had paved the way for private ownership of reservation land. The idea was that Indians could become property owners. Unfortunately, this also permitted non-Indian ownership of parcels of reservation land.

As beneficent as their intentions may have been, the agents were essentially replacing indigenous culture with an alien culture. Especially on the Plains, the agents were endeavoring to turn a nomadic people—whose concept of land ownership was that all land was owned equally by everybody and nobody—into landed farmers.

The by-product of the reservation system was the dismantling of Indian culture. A full discussion of this process and its implications to indigenous life and culture is beyond the scope of this work and could easily fill several volumes. I mention the matter simply as a backdrop for understanding the movement that precipitated the climactic battle of the nineteenth-century Indian Wars in the West.

With the collapse of an ancient, well-ordered system of cultural and religious beliefs, a void is created. Into this void can step a revelator who can claim divine guidance by which he can lead a people back to a happier time, before the traditional way was threatened by alien doctrines imposed by outsiders. Such voids and such people have occurred throughout history, and often they lead to religious warfare. The rise of Islamic fundamentalism in the twenty-first century can be seen as such a circumstance. In the context of nineteenth-century cultural conflicts, Tenskwatawa, the Shawnee Prophet who had a large following in the early nineteenth century, was such a shaman.

In the 1880s, similar prophets, from Nakaidoklini of the Apache to Sword Bearer of the Crow, came and went, usually exiting violently after stirring their devotees to religious hysteria. They arrived on their respective scenes after all seemed lost, presenting themselves as the last hope to lead people back to the purity of the old ways. The most important and influential of such prophets at the end of the century was Wovoka (also known as Jack Wilson) a thirty-four-year-old Paiute shaman. Though he was based in Nevada, his message would have its most profound resonance on the Lakota reservations of South Dakota.

Wovoka created a messianic dogma that borrowed elements from both native creeds and Christianity. He taught that the next life would be a happy and peaceful one, in which a person would live forever, following the bygone way of life without any material wants, in the company of previously departed friends and relatives.

The Ghost Dance was the essential ritual of Wovoka's teaching. By singing and dancing, a Ghost Dance adherent could put himself or herself into a trance so as to glimpse the wonderful world beyond. To his credit, Wovoka cautioned that a condition of reaching this special place was to live peacefully and nonviolently.

Even Sitting Bull became curious about the Ghost Dance, and he sent Short Bull from the Rosebud Reservation and Kicking Bear from the Cheyenne River Reservation to visit Wovoka and learn what they could. They came back to South Dakota as converts.

As often happens with religions, Wovoka's Ghost Dance was hijacked by an element of Lakota extremists who decided that a short cut to paradise would be to eliminate all of the Euro-Americans. By eliminating them from the traditional Lakota lands, a paradise on earth might be created on the Northern Plains. This is not unlike the preaching of twenty-first century Islamic fundamentalists, who want to eliminate Christians and Jews from the Middle East.

Short Bull and Kicking Bear became the leading proponents among the Lakota of the extreme version of the Ghost Dance religion. By November 1890, the Ghost Dance movement had swept the Northern Plains like a prairie fire. The Ghost Dance was being danced throughout South Dakota, and on reservations throughout the West. Reportedly, the Ghost Dance religion had so engrossed the reservation population that work and other activities came to a virtual standstill.

Ghost Dancers photographed in 1890. (*National Archives*)

Short Bull and Kicking Bear had added to Wovoka's doctrine, teaching that special Ghost Dance shirts could be worn, which rendered the wearer impervious to bullets. This, along with the fanaticism being seen at some of the dances, greatly alarmed both the Indian Bureau and the U.S. Army.

Important leaders, such as Big Foot of the Minneconjou and Sitting Bull of the Hunkpapa, were overtaken by events. Though he was more of an observer of the Ghost Dance movement than a leader, Sitting Bull's influential position in the Lakota community demanded that he accept it. Big Foot, meanwhile, had embraced it.

Nelson Miles had assumed command of the Division of the Missouri when George Crook died in that office in March 1890. An activist commander, Miles was only too willing to get involved. It was only a matter of determining the appropriate action. He considered sending Buffalo Bill Cody, with whose Wild West Show Sitting Bull had toured, to speak with the chief. However, Standing Rock Agent James McLaughlin urged that Sitting Bull simply be arrested, and his hard-line view prevailed. Cody arrived at Standing Rock but left without seeing his old colleague. Events were starting to spin out of control.

Miles ordered Lieutenant Colonel William Drum at Fort Yates to use 8th Cavalry personnel to take Sitting Bull into custody. However, McLaughlin convinced Drum that it would be better if Indian Police rather than U.S. Army troops made the arrest, and on the morning of December 15, they knocked at Sitting Bull's door.

According to McLaughlin's report to Commissioner of Indian Affairs Thomas Morgan, Sitting Bull

> at first seemed inclined to offer no resistance and they allowed him to dress, during which time he changed his mind and they took him forcibly from the house. By this time the police were surrounded by Sitting Bull's followers, members of the Ghost Dance, and the first shot was fired by Catch the Bear, one of the hostiles and the Lieutenant of Police, Henry Tatankapah [Bull Head], who was in command of the detachment of 42 men, was struck; the fighting then became general, in act it was a hand to hand fight. Sitting Bull was killed, shot through the body and head in the early part of the fight by Bull Head and Marcelus Chankpidutah [Red Tomahawk] who each shot at him.

Ironically, the Ghost Dance religion probably prevented an armed insurrection on a scale that the Northern Plains had not seen since 1876. The death—and presumed murder—of Sitting Bull was provocation on a monumental scale. However, most Ghost Dance disciples believed that armed insurrection was unnecessary because the dance would soon drive away the Army and the agents, while restoring the happier times and the great buffalo herds.

They could rise up and kill all of the soldiers and settlers, but why bother? According to the Ghost Dance religion, they would all soon be gone anyway.

WOUNDED KNEE I

While McLaughlin botched the arrest of Sitting Bull, Lieutenant Colonel Edwin Sumner had been tasked with arresting Big Foot. Sumner hesitated, permitting Big Foot and his Minneconjou followers ample time to slip off the Cheyenne River Reservation. They went south, accompanied by some of Sitting Bull's Hunkpapa band, heading toward the Pine Ridge Reservation, where the Oglala chiefs had invited them to a council.

With Sitting Bull dead and Big Foot on the move, Nelson Miles donned his bear coat, left his headquarters in Chicago, and headed west to personally take command of operations in South Dakota. He put elements of three regiments into the field in an effort to catch Big Foot. These included the 6th Cavalry under Colonel Eugene Carr, the 7th Cavalry

Brigadier General Nelson A. Miles and William F. "Buffalo Bill" Cody view the Lakota encampment near the Pine Ridge Agency on January 16, 1891. (*National Archives*)

under Colonel James Forsyth, and the 9th Infantry Regiment under Major Guy Henry.

On December 28, 1890, a four-company detachment of the 7th Cavalry led by Major Samuel Whitside succeeded in intercepting their quarry on Porcupine Creek near Pine Ridge. The two sides parleyed, and Big Foot explained that they were going to the Pine Ridge Agency. The chief, who was suffering from pneumonia, agreed to their being escorted to the agency.

That night, Whitside's men and the Lakota camped at Wounded Knee Creek, where they would soon be joined by Colonel Forsyth and the balance of the 7th Cavalry, along with a battery of the 1st Artillery Regiment. The troops were posted around the perimeter of the Lakota encampment. The number of Lakota present was estimated at 120 men and 230 women and children.

On the morning of December 29, Forsyth ordered the Minneconjou and Hunkpapa to be disarmed, and their weapons were stacked. Forsyth then ordered a search for concealed weapons, and two rifles were found. One man, Black Coyote, balked at giving up his gun, there was a scuffle, and a shot was fired. As had been the case so many times during similar situations earlier in the Indian Wars, a ferocious firefight broke out instantly. Soldiers began firing into the crowd as the Lakota grabbed their weapons. The 1st Artillery cut loose with a withering barrage from their 1.65-inch Hotchkiss light mountain guns, which had been positioned on a hill overlooking the Wounded Knee campsite.

The Lakota death toll in the shootout at Wounded Knee on December 29 stood at 153, including an estimated sixty-two women and children, although some who escaped may have died from their wounds without having been counted. Big Foot was found among the dead. Meanwhile, the 7th Cavalry suffered its greatest number of casualties of any engagement since the Civil War with the exception of the Battle of the Little Bighorn. The regiment lost twenty-five men killed in action, and thirty-five wounded.*

Generally considered to have been the last battle of the Indian Wars, Wounded Knee was not even the last battle of the week. The following day, a large number of Lakota burned a building near the Drexel Mission and attacked a wagon train on White Clay Creek, killing one soldier.

Forsyth rode from Wounded Knee with most of his command. Instead of giving chase, the 7th Cavalry was pinned down under heavy rifle fire for most of the day until they were relieved by four companies of the 9th Cavalry. Forsyth lost two men killed in action and seven wounded in the last battle of 1890.†

---

*A number of 7th Cavalry personnel would be awarded the Congressional Medal of Honor for actions in the Wounded Knee battle. Both Sergeant William Austin and Sergeant Albert McMillan of Company E were cited for assisting men on the skirmish line, directing their fire, and "using every effort to dislodge the enemy" who were concealed in a ravine. Wounded during the same action, Lieutenant John Gresham was cited for having "Voluntarily led a party into a ravine to dislodge Sioux Indians concealed therein." Sergeant James Ward of Company B received his Medal of Honor for continuing to fight "after being severely wounded." Among the artillerymen, musician John Clancy, Private Joshia Hartzog, and Corporal Paul Weinert of the 1st Artillery and Lieutenant Harry Hawthorne of the 2nd Artillery were awarded the Congressional Medal of Honor for actions at Wounded Knee. Weinert's citation stated that "Taking the place of his commanding officer who had fallen severely wounded, he gallantly served his piece, after each [firing] advancing it to a better position." Other Medal of Honor awardees among the 7th Cavalry at Wounded Knee included Private Mosheim Feaster, Lieutenant Ernest Garlington, Private Mathew Hamilton, Private Marvin Hillock, Private George Hobday, Sergeant Bernhard Jetter, Sergeant George Loyd, Private Adam Neder, Farrier Richard Nolan, Sergeant Theodore Ragner, Private Thomas Sullivan, Sergeant Frederick Toy, and Sergeant Jacob Trautman

†After the action, Corporal William Wilson of the 9th Cavalry was awarded the Congressional Medal of Honor. Captain Charles Varnum of Company B, 7th Cavalry, earned the Medal of Honor at White Clay Creek. "While executing an order to withdraw, seeing that a continuance of the movement would expose another troop of his regiment to being cut off and surrounded, he disregarded orders to retire, placed himself in front of his men, led a charge upon the advancing Indians, regained a commanding position that had just

Soldiers detailed to begin the process of removing the Indian bodies from where they fell. (*National Archives*)

On New Year's Day 1891, Captain John Kerr led elements of two companies of the 6th Cavalry in action against hostile Lakota on the north bank of the White River, near the mouth of Little Grass Creek.*

Back at Wounded Knee Creek, wagons came out from the Pine Ridge Agency on New Year's Day to collect the nearly two hundred dead in the subzero cold.

Controversy continued to swirl around the Wounded Knee incident for more than a century. It has been called a massacre, although the Lakota compelled the Army to pay a heavy price. In the very least, Forsyth badly

---

been vacated, and thus insured a safe withdrawal of both detachments without further loss." Meanwhile, Private Hermann Ziegner of Company E, 7th Cavalry, was awarded a Medal of Honor for actions at both Wounded Knee and White Clay Creek.

*Awarded the Medal of Honor, he was cited for having "defeated a force of 300 Brulé Sioux warriors, and turned the Sioux tribe, which was endeavoring to enter the Bad Lands, back into the Pine Ridge Agency." In the same action Lieutenant Benjamin Cheever was awarded the Congressional Medal of Honor for heading "the advance across White River partly frozen, in a spirited movement to the effective assistance of Troop K, 6th US Cavalry." German-born Sergeant Fred Myers, meanwhile, earned his Congressional Medal of Honor at White River, when "With 5 men [he] repelled a superior force of the enemy and held his position against their repeated efforts to recapture it." Corporal Cornelius Smith earned his Medal of Honor as part of Myers's team. Other 6th Cavalry soldiers awarded the Medal of Honor for this action included Lieutenant Robert Howze and Sergeant Joseph Knight.

mishandled the situation. Miles attempted to censure him for incompetence, but Commanding General Schofield overruled Miles.

In January 1891, Miles went into the field himself, leading 5,500 men. Through the prudent use of a show of force, he was able to gently urge the remaining Lakota bands back to the reservations without further loss of life. On January 15, Kicking Bear handed his Winchester to Miles.

Within a month, the Ghost Dance was beginning to fade from its earlier popularity. Soon it was all but forgotten. The last Indian War campaign was finally over.

THE LAST BATTLE

The U.S. Army's Center of Military History reckons Wounded Knee to have been the last nineteenth-century Indian engagement to fall in the category of warfare. Later incidents were considered to be more in the realm of civil disturbance.* As the frontier faded from reality to quaint folklore and the U.S. Army stood down in the West, the Army would fight one last battle that was certainly on the scale of incidents that had earlier been worthy of being included as a battle in the annals of the Indian Wars. It encompassed the last Medal of Honor action of the Indian Wars.

In October 1898, two months after the major combat phase of the Spanish-American War came to a close, the U.S. Army fought the last battle of the Indian Wars in a most unlikely place—Minnesota.

Just as Minnesota was considered to have been long past its Indian War era when the 1862 uprising occurred, it was certainly thought to be beyond the point of such hostilities thirty-six years later. The background story was a familiar one involving disagreements between the tribes and the federal government over land issues. The catalyst was also familiar, a largely avoidable incident that was allowed to escalate.

In September 1898, a Chippewa man named Bug-onay-gee-shig (nicknamed Old Bug) was arrested at Onigum, Minnesota, on charges of failing to appear to testify at a trial in Duluth. A group of fellow Chippewa intervened and managed to wrestle Old Bug away from the deputies that arrested him, and to take him to Bear Island in Leech Lake.

---

*Private Allen Walker of Company C, 3rd Cavalry, earned the Congressional Medal of Honor in Texas on December 30, 1891, a year and a day after Wounded Knee. His citation stated that, "While carrying dispatches, he attacked a party of three armed men and secured papers valuable to the United States."

Officers of the 6th Cavalry who fought at Wounded Knee, including John J.
Pershing, standing at right center. (*National Archives*)

The U.S. Army sent a twenty-man 3rd Infantry Regiment detachment
from Fort Snelling to intervene and to compel Old Bug to surrender. He
refused, so the Army reinforced its contingent for a further show of force.
On October 5, eighty soldiers—mostly young and inexperienced
recruits—under the command of Major Melville Wilkinson boarded a
barge, which was pushed by a steamboat to Bear Island. The island was
abandoned, so they proceeded to Sugar Point, where Old Bug's cabin was
located. As the troops went ashore, they found themselves under the
watchful eye of roughly twenty Chippewa armed with Winchester rifles.

Fearing someone would get hurt, Wilkinson ordered the troops to stack
their arms. His best intentions were for naught. As had happened so often,
a single shot was fired that led to bloodshed. According to the Army, one
soldier did not lock the safety on his gun, and it fell and went off.
According to the Chippewa, a soldier opened fire on some women in a
canoe. As the battle erupted, Major Wilkinson took three rounds and fell
dead. The steamboat that had brought the barge pulled out, abandoning
the troops on the shore.

On October 6, the steamboat returned, but was driven off in a hail of
gunfire after taking just one wounded soldier aboard. The Minnesota
National Guard arrived later in the day with 214 men and a Gatling gun,
but they were not deployed until October 7. By this time, the Chippewa

had withdrawn, allowing the besieged troops to board the barge. The battle resulted in seven soldiers killed in action, and another sixteen wounded. There were no casualties among the Chippewa. On October 10, the tribal members involved in the battle surrendered, but no charges would be filed.

Private Oscar Burkard of the U.S. Army Hospital Corps was awarded the Congressional Medal of Honor "For distinguished bravery in action against hostile Indians." In an indication of the long duration of the Indian Wars, Burkard had been born in Aachen, Germany on December 21, 1877, a year and a half after the Battle of the Little Bighorn.

WOUNDED KNEE II

The Indian Wars in the West conveniently ended with the end of the nineteenth century, but there is one twentieth-century armed conflict which brought quasi-military forces of the United States into armed conflict with American Indians. Ironically, the battlefield in this 1973 incident was Wounded Knee, South Dakota.

This action that seemed to be plucked from the distant past occurred in the era of live television transmission, naturally making it a major media event. It had been only a few weeks since the final Apollo lunar landing, the apex of twentieth-century technological achievement, when suddenly there was an occurrence that seemed to belong to a previous century. Americans in the East were marveling at the invention of the telephone in 1876, when suddenly they heard news of the Little Bighorn. Nearly a century later, Americans of the modern media age suddenly found themselves watching an Indian War—televised from Wounded Knee, of all places.

In 1973, the 1890 Wounded Knee incident was not an obscure action from the dim past, but a high-profile milestone in American history thanks to Dee Brown's best-seller *Bury My Heart at Wounded Knee* and the film *Little Big Man*, featuring Dustin Hoffman, both released in 1970.

Though the U.S. Army had long been withdrawn from combat actions within the United States, the weapons and tactics that would be wielded by the Federal Bureau of Investigation and other agencies in 1973 were sufficiently similar to those that would have been used by the Army that this incident deserves inclusion in this history of Indian Wars.

The complex political and cultural history of the relations between the United States government and the indigenous people of this land during the twentieth century are beyond the scope of this work. So too are the intricate nuances of tribal governments and of intra-tribal politics. However, we will touch briefly on these because they form an essential part of the background.

The 1960s in the United States are well remembered as a period of social discord and widespread protest movements, involving both civil rights and opposition to the Vietnam War. At the same time, a similar—albeit much smaller—protest movement emerged that involved grievances by American Indians living on reservations.

The latter spawned the creation of an organization known as the American Indian Movement, which was started in 1968 by Clyde Bellecourt and Dennis Banks, both members of the Chippewa (Anishinabe) tribe, and a host of others. Coincidently, Banks was from the Leech Lake area of Minnesota, the scene of the last battle of the Indian Wars that was fought by the U.S. Army. Among its more extreme protest activities, the American Indian Movement was involved in the 1969-1971 occupation of the former federal penitentiary on Alcatraz Island in San Francisco Bay, and in a highly publicized 1972 sit-in at the Bureau of Indian Affairs headquarters in Washington, D.C.

By 1973 Banks was active on the Pine Ridge Reservation in South Dakota, along with an Oglala Lakota activist named Russell Means. Banks and Means had come into a confrontation with Tribal Chairman Dick Wilson, who had obtained an order from the tribal court barring American Indian Movement people from speaking at public meetings. The issue was further complicated by charges made by other tribal members that accused Wilson of corruption and mismanagement of tribal funds. The Bureau of Indian Affairs was criticized for not getting involved in the matter. Of course, if they had been more involved, this would not have gone without criticism.

The event that caused the situation to turn violent was the January 21, 1973, stabbing of a young Lakota named Wesley Bad Heart Bull. When manslaughter charges were brought in what seemed to be a murder case, there was a wave of protests organized by the American Indian Movement, culminating in a riot in Custer, South Dakota, in which a number of police officers were injured and more than two dozen Indians were arrested.

On February 27, an estimated two hundred Indians led by the American Indian Movement took over the small town of Wounded Knee, South Dakota, which is located near the final resting place of Lakota killed in the 1890 incident. As the Indian activists fortified Wounded Knee, both the media and the federal government responded.

Though the U.S. Army was not involved, a mixed force of U.S. Marshals, along with agents of the Bureau of Indian Affairs and the FBI were sent to the Pine Ridge Reservation. They were supported by armored personnel carriers and helicopters, reminding broadcast news viewers of the military operations during the recently concluded Vietnam War.

The force, with a numeric strength about the same as that of those occupying Wounded Knee, established a perimeter around the town and demanded that the activists surrender. It was a scene reminiscent of the Indian Wars of the nineteenth century. A substantial, well-armed United States government force was surrounding a group of Indians that included women and children. Also as in the nineteenth century, the Indians had a much better sense of the terrain. This permitted those occupying Wounded Knee to slip in and out of the besieged town with relative ease, and for supplies to be brought in.

Just as in many of the nineteenth-century sieges, the principal fighting involved marksmen on both sides sniping at one another. Two individuals within Wounded Knee were killed by snipers, a Cherokee named Frank Clearwater and a Lakota named Buddy LaMonte.

The siege finally reached a negotiated conclusion after seventy-one days, but many of the political issues that had led to occupation would remain unresolved. Indeed, the crisis on the Pine Ridge reservation in the mid-1970s has been characterized as a virtual civil war. Over the ensuing two years, a succession of beatings, shootings, and murders resulted in more than one hundred deaths among tribal members. In 1975, two FBI agents were killed in a shootout on the reservation, and American Indian Movement activist Leonard Peltier was arrested and convicted.

Dennis Banks was acquitted of charges related to the Wounded Knee incident, but convicted of assault stemming from the confrontation at Custer. He became a fugitive, and remained at large until 1985, when he surrendered to South Dakota authorities to serve an eighteen-month sentence. Russell Means served one year of a four-year prison term on South Dakota riot charges, and was released in 1980.

Like Sitting Bull more than a century before them, both Banks and Means went on to careers in show business. Both had roles in the Hollywood feature *The Last of the Mohicans*. Banks also appeared in *Thunderheart*, while Means appeared in *Natural Born Killers*, and was featured as the voice of Powhatan in the animated film *Pocahontas*.

Today, a stone monument stands at the site of the mass grave that is the final resting place of many of the victims of the 1890 massacre. A bill introduced in the United States Congress in 1995 would have set the area aside as the Wounded Knee National Tribal Park, but it was never enacted.

South Dakota Department of Tourism

Epilogue

The Indian Wars were the longest campaign ever waged by any of the United States armed forces, and the wars that were fought in the West consumed most of the active duty resources of the U.S. Army for most of the nineteenth century.

The Indian Wars in the West were fought on a vast landscape the size of continental Europe that was, for much of the nineteenth century, mainly an open trackless wilderness devoid of the sorts of infrastructure that the majority of Americans east of the Mississippi took for granted.

The tactics employed by the opposing sides were dramatically different, though on both sides they evolved over time. Initially, the U.S. Army's tactics were geared toward the protection of a few trails and roads. After the Civil War, as the goal became putting the Indians on reservations and forcing them back if they strayed, the strategy changed to one of putting large task forces into the field for seasonal sweeps. This might have worked in a conventional war against a predictable enemy, but in the Indian Wars, it had mixed results because the enemy combatants were generally flexible and highly mobile.

The basic Indian tactics centered on small groups of mounted warriors operating as raiding parties. This approach to warfare had been developed during the seventeenth and eighteenth centuries after the descendants of Spanish horses became available to the Indians. Long used for inter-tribal warfare, these tactics were naturally employed against emigrant wagon trains, settlements, and against the U.S. Army in the nineteenth century. So skilled were the warriors that analysts often ranked them among the best cavalry in the world. Indeed, the U.S. Army found them a formidable opponent. They could strike quickly, strike hard, and just as quickly break off the fight and disappear to fight another day.

To counter such tactics, U.S. Army commanders such as George Crook eventually developed the doctrine of small, highly mobile special operations detachments of their own. Using such tactics, Crook succeeded in winning two particularly obstinate campaigns. The U.S. Army came to understand what their opponents had figured out a century before, that the man on horseback is the ultimate warrior in the rugged, trackless terrain that constituted most of the American West. It can be said that such a doctrine is still applicable for this type of terrain. In 2001, U.S. Army Special Forces operated on horseback in similar topography in Afghanistan.

Had the Indians in the West been able to form and maintain the sort of unified intertribal command that Tecumseh had envisioned earlier in the century, and had this command indulged in long-range strategic planning, the history of the Indian Wars would have been much different. As we said in the Introduction, the Indian nations were never monolithic. Confederations, such as that involving the Comanche and Kiowa, did exist, but they were rare and often seasonal. The massive combined Lakota and Northern Cheyenne force that won the Battle of the Little Bighorn in 1876 was a formidable force that can be considered to have been one of the most powerful ever to operate in the West, but when this large group disbanded later in the year, it was never reconstituted.

The Indians also had a very different chain of command structure than the U.S. Army. Indian leaders held no rank. They led solely by their ability to inspire their followers, and to win their battles. A leader today was a leader tomorrow only if he was successful today. Some leaders came and went, others remained important for many years. This system could be criticized for its lack of continuity, although its strength lay in the fact that the battle leaders most suited for command were the ones who continued in leadership positions.

In large operations, the U.S. Army may have been clumsy tactically, but it always had the edge logistically. The large Lakota and Northern Cheyenne force that rode together and fought together during 1876 was powerful, but it depended on its ability to carry all of its own supplies, and it had to support the women and children that were part of the constituent bands.

As mobile as the Indian warriors were, they suffered time and again from their inability to collect and move their supplies as quickly as their horsemen. As Kit Carson demonstrated in the Navajo campaigns, destruction of supplies and infrastructure was as effective in conquering an enemy as defeating his troops in battle.

The Indian Wars in the West produced many great—and many more highly competent—leaders. Among the greatest military leaders were Crazy Horse and Geronimo, who are remembered for very different styles of warfare. If only for his masterful cavalry leadership at the Rosebud and the Little Bighorn in 1876, Crazy Horse deserves a place in the roster of great commanders in American history. He dealt the U.S. Army two of its largest defeats in conventional warfare in the West. Geronimo, in contrast, was a master of unconventional warfare whose victories were numerous, and who was defeated only when he decided to give up. Even then, he proved that he could change his mind.

There were other great Indian combat leaders. Among the Apache, Cochise, Nana, and Victorio were masters of small unit actions. Among the Lakota, Gall's cavalry leadership at the Little Bighorn deserves a place shoulder to shoulder with that of Crazy Horse. Among the Nez Percé, Chief Joseph was a great orator, and a political leader who inspired his people, but he also led them in a truly epic 1,700-mile evasion. The skill and discipline of the Nez Percé warriors themselves deserves them an honored place in military history.

The U.S. Army, too, had great leaders in the West. Kit Carson's name must come to mind among those who led troops before and during the Civil War. After the war, both Ranald Mackenzie and Nelson Miles earned a place in history. After an inauspicious start in the Red River War, Miles emerged from obscurity after the Little Bighorn and had the career that Custer might have had, if not for his fateful day in 1876. Miles was in the right places at the right times to figure prominently in the final chapter of the Nez Percé War, as well as the end of both the Great Sioux War and the Apache Wars.

Two of the most well known leaders, Custer and Sitting Bull, were not among the greatest from a tactical point of view, but are recalled for their larger than life images, and for the way these images inspired events. Custer had proven himself in the Civil War, but the boldness that had been the key to his glory then led to his downfall on the Plains. Thanks both to that boldness and his Civil War success, though, Custer had the sizzle that made him a media star in life, and the circumstances of his death assured that he would always be remembered. Sitting Bull's reputation among his own people was that of a political, and even spiritual, leader. He inspired more than he led. He was embraced by the mass media in the 1880s for much the same reason as Custer—he had great charisma, and he made himself available to the national spotlight.

Perhaps the greatest of the U.S. Army's senior tactical leaders in the Indian Wars in the West was George Crook. His career began on the Oregon-California border before the Civil War and continued through two of Geronimo's four surrenders three decades later. He is justifiably criticized for his mishandling of the Battle of the Rosebud, but he fared better against Crazy Horse than Custer would a week later.

More than anything, Crook can be credited with developing innovative unconventional tactics and successfully practicing them in the field. In so doing, he won the Paiute War and achieved a victory over the Apache that brought peace to the Southwest for a decade.

In remembering the generals, we are reminded that their triumphs are achieved on the shoulders of thousands of enlisted men, many of them foreign born, who endured hardships and boredom, as well as vicious battles. We should also recall great officers of lesser rank, but not of lesser courage or lesser skill. Among these were men such as Captain Reuben Bernard of the 1st Cavalry, Captain James Whitlock of the 5th California Infantry, Captain Louis Carpenter of the 10th Cavalry, Lieutenant Walter Scribner Schuyler of the 5th Cavalry, and Colonel Eugene Carr, who commanded units of several regiments in numerous campaigns across the West for many years.

The names of a few leaders are still well known, but as with most conflicts, these wars were fought mainly by many men whose names are long forgotten, or remembered by only a few. The Indian Wars in the West consumed the lives and careers of several generations of warriors from many walks of life. The Indian warriors came from many tribes, and they fought on both sides. The non-Indians included both soldiers and civilians.

During those generations, the nature of the Indian Wars changed as the nature of the West itself changed. In the 1840s, the West was a vast place that few non-Indians had crossed. Within a generation, it was a place that was routinely crossed by non-Indians, and during the succeeding generations, non-Indians came to stay, and they came in greater and greater numbers. It was this, rather than evolving weapons and tactics, that ultimately decided the outcome of the Indian Wars.

The tactics of the Indians changed little, while the U.S. Army gradually adopted a tactical doctrine that was more and more like that of the Indians. As exemplified by the operations on the Plains during Red Cloud's War, or in the Southwest during the long-running Apache Wars, the Indians succeeded by launching fast, hard-hitting surprise attacks against lightly guarded targets. This was the same tactical doctrine that had existed in intertribe warfare for years, so there was little reason to modify it when the opponents were non-Indians—especially when it worked so well.

The Indian warriors generally avoided heavily defended forts, and dealt best with large U.S. Army formations by leading them into traps. Such tactics continued to work favorably in the early years of the Indian Wars, when the vastness of the West offered sanctuary, and the Army was restricted to its well-defended forts. Later, as the population balance in the West tipped against the Indians, sanctuaries became fewer.

Another key advantage that served the Indians in every part of the West well throughout most of the nineteenth century was their knowledge of the terrain and of the geography of the open West. This advantage cannot be overemphasized. For the most of the Indian Wars, the troops were operating in areas where they had never been before, and they were operating against a foe whose people had been living and hunting there for generations. U.S. Army leaders, such as Crook, who made a point of learning and understanding the lay of the land, always fared better than officers who did not.

The Indians operated as they always had because their tactical doctrine worked. The U.S. Army entered the conflict under a tactical doctrine that had proven itself in Europe during the Napoleonic Wars. In Europe, large formations of infantry and cavalry, supported by artillery, fought one another on battlefields where victory was as much attributable to manpower and firepower as it was to tactical skill. In the West, large formations thus equipped could overwhelm the lightly armed Indians in a pitched battle, so the Indians simply avoided pitched battles against large formations.

Most battles throughout the Indian Wars in the West were fought between small numbers of men—usually on horseback—just as they had been for the preceding centuries. Because these engagements relied on tactical skill, victory went to the most skillful, and where the skills were evenly matched, to the most lucky.

In field operations, the U.S. Army succeeded best when it abandoned the large operations supported by complex logistics for small mobile special operations units who carried their supplies on a few pack mules. This was clearly demonstrated by leaders such as Schyler and by Crook during his operations against the Paiute and Apache. Crook's worst moments in the field came when he was trying manage a large and unwieldy force.

The U.S. Army's key advantages in terms of concentrated manpower and firepower began to change the balance when there was a shift from tactical to strategic warfare. When the U.S. Army used economic warfare against the Indians' ability to wage war, the balance shifted. For example, it was the Army's destruction of crops and stored supplies, rather than years of skirmishing, that convinced the Navajo that continued warfare was counterproductive.

With the Plains tribes, it was economic warfare of another kind. The gradual, then dramatic, decline in the number of buffalo in the 1870s and 1880s destroyed the economic basis of a culture and compelled the Plains people to make the decision to submit to the largesse of the Indian Bureau and to cease living off the land.

Another example of economic warfare was the practice of attacking Indian villages. In places outside the Plains, where villages were fixed in long-standing locations, they were particularly vulnerable. On the Plains, the people were nomadic for much of the year, so their villages were mobile, except during the winter. Whenever the cavalry was able to launch a mounted attack against encamped Indians, the troopers always had the advantage of speed and mobility. The Indian warriors, because they were dismounted, and defending their women and children, were usually at a tactical disadvantage. This supposition of Indian disadvantage, of course, led to Custer's cocksure overconfidence at the Little Bighorn, despite his being outnumbered.

In terms of weaponry, the key technological improvement that came during the Indian Wars was in the area of repeating arms. The U.S. Army first went west with single-shot muzzle-loading muskets. Because they took a long time to reload, they were dangerously impractical. The Indians could shoot and reload a bow much faster than a trooper could fire and reload a musket—and large volleys of arrows were as deadly and as fearsome in 1876 as they were in 1840.

After the Civil War, breach-loading, single-shot Springfield rifles became standard with the U.S. Army, and were useful because of their long-range accuracy. The introduction of seven-shot Spencer and Sharps repeaters gave the troops excellent firepower in close-in fighting where being able to fire quickly was more important than long-range accuracy, but these guns were not widely distributed. A great deal has been said about the irony of the Winchester Model 1876 repeater, one of the signature weapons in the West, being more readily accessible to the Indians through the Indian Bureau than it was to the U.S. Army through the normal supply channels. Another repeating weapon that became a legend in the West, the Colt .45-caliber six-shooter, was made available to the U.S. Army in sufficient quantities to make it very useful.

Artillery was brutally effective when it was actually deployed, but this was rarely. Until the introduction of the Hotchkiss gun into the West in the later 1870s, artillery usually stayed at the fort. Like wheeled supply wagons, cannons could not easily move over much of the terrain where the Army was compelled to operate, and it could rarely keep pace with a cavalry force. For example, Custer was offered the use of Gatling guns on his final campaign, but he declined for reasons of mobility.

Had Custer had Gatling guns at the Little Bighorn, things would have been different. How different is just one of many intriguing speculations that still fascinate us when we look back upon the Indian Wars. In that half century of conflicts, there were numerous turning points in which battles might have turned differently. What would not have changed, however, is the tenacity and the bravery exhibited by the warriors on both sides. This bravery was played out at numerous battlefields that are well remembered—and a myriad of others that are long forgotten.

It is this bravery and these battlefields—so distant in both time and place—that make the Indian Wars such an endlessly compelling subject. It is this, rather than their outcome, that has assured the Indian Wars an enduring place in American culture and tradition.

With hindsight it is easy to say that the eventual outcome of the Indian Wars in the West was inevitable, and perhaps it was. To those on both sides who fought bravely through most of the nineteenth century, though, it was not.

APPENDIX

I. THE EVOLUTION OF INDIAN TERRITORY SHOWING MAJOR TRIBAL AREAS

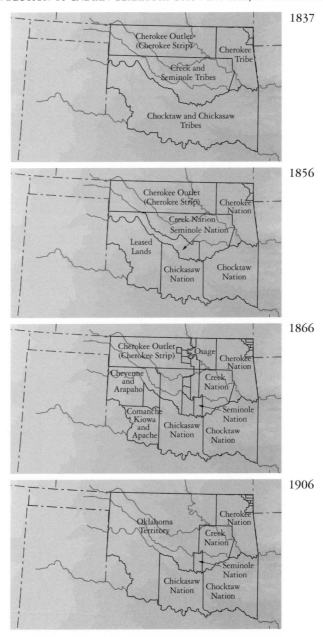

II. Bureau Heads During the Western Indian War Period

From 1789 to 1832, Secretaries of War were responsible for American Indian Affairs. In 1832, the post of Commissioner of Indian Affairs was created within the War Department, and in 1834, the Office of Indian Affairs was established. The Indian Bureau was transferred to the newly created Department of Interior on March 3, 1849.

Heads of the Indian Affairs Office (Department of War)
1824-1830 Thomas L. McKenny
1830-1831 Samuel S. Hamilton
1831-1832 Elbert Herring

Commissioners of Indian Affairs
1832-1836 Elbert Herring
1836-1838 Carey A. Harris
1838-1845 T. Hartley Crawford
1845-1849 William Medill
1849-1850 Orlando Brown
1850-1853 Luke Lea
1853-1857 George W. Manypenny
1857-1858 James W. Denver
1858-1858 Charles E. Mix
1858-1859 James W. Denver
1859-1861 Alfred Greenwood
1861-1865 William P. Dole
1865-1866 Dennis N. Cooley
1866-1867 Lewis V. Bogey
1867-1869 Nathaniel G. Taylor
1869-1871 Ely S. Parker
1871-1871 H. R. Clum (acting)
1871-1872 Francis A. Walker
1872-1873 H. R. Clum (acting)
1873-1875 Edward P. Smith
1875-1877 John Q. Smith
1877-1880 Ezra A. Hayt
1880-1880 E. M. Marble (acting)
1880-1881 Rowland E. Trowbridge
1881-1884 Hiram Price
1885-1887 John D. C. Atkins
1887-1889 John H. Oberly
1889-1893 Thomas J. Morgan
1893-1897 Daniel M. Browning
1897-1905 William A. Jones

III. Commanding Generals of the U.S. Army During the Western Indian War Period

1821-1828 Jacob Jennings Brown
1828-1841 Alexander Macomb (1782-1841)
1841-1861 Winfield Scott (1786-1866)
1861-1862 George Brinton McClellan (1826-1885)
1862-1864 Henry Wagner Halleck (1815-1872)
1864-1869 Ulysses Simpson Grant (1822-1885)
1869-1883 William Tecumseh Sherman (1820-1891)
1883-1888 Philip Henry Sheridan (1831-1888)
1888-1895 John McAllister Schofield (1831-1906)
1895-1903 Nelson Appleton Miles (1839-1925)

IV. Post-Civil War U.S. Army Organization

1868:
Headquarters, U.S. Army
Department of the Cumberland (Louisville, KY)
Department of the East (Philadelphia, PA)
Department of Georgia, Florida & Alabama (Atlanta, GA)
Department of the Gulf (New Orleans, LA)
Department of the Lakes (Detroit, MI)
Department of Mississippi and Arkansas (Vicksburg, MS)
Department of the Potomac (Richmond, VA)
Department of the South (Charleston, SC)
Department of Washington (Washington, DC)
Division of the Missouri (St. Louis, MO)
Department of the Missouri (St. Louis, MO)
Department of Dakota (St. Paul, MN)
Department of the Platte (Omaha, NE)
Division of the Pacific (San Francisco, CA)
Department of California (San Francisco, CA)
Department of the Columbia (Fort Vancouver, WA)

1875:
Headquarters, U.S. Army
Division of the Atlantic (Governor's Island, NY, NY)
Division of the South (Louisville, KY)
Division of the Missouri (Chicago, IL)
Department of the Missouri (Fort Leavenworth, KS)
Department of Dakota (St. Paul, MN)
Department of the Platte (Omaha, NE)
Department of the Gulf (New Orleans, LA)
Department of Texas (San Antonio, TX)

Division of the Pacific (San Francisco, CA)
    Department of California (San Francisco, CA)
    Department of the Columbia (Fort Vancouver, WA)
    Department of Arizona (Whipple Barracks, AZ)

1884
HEADQUARTERS, U.S. ARMY
Division of the Atlantic
    Department of the East (Governor's Island, NY, NY)
Division of the Missouri (Chicago, IL)
    Department of the Missouri (Fort Leavenworth, KS)
    Department of Dakota (Fort Snelling, MN)
    Department of the Platte (Omaha, NE)
    Department of Texas (San Antonio, TX)
Division of the Pacific (San Francisco, CA)
    Department of California (San Francisco, CA)
    Department of the Columbia (Fort Vancouver, WA)
    Department of Arizona (Whipple Barracks, AZ)

1891
HEADQUARTERS, U.S. ARMY
    Department of the East (Governor's Island, NY, NY)
    Department of the Missouri (Fort Leavenworth, KS)
    Department of Dakota (St. Paul, MN)
    Department of the Platte (Omaha, NE)
    Department of Texas (San Antonio, TX)
    Department of California (San Francisco, CA)
    Department of the Columbia (Fort Vancouver, WA)
    Department of Arizona (Los Angeles, CA)

Sources for Further Reading

Of the myriad of works concerning the Indian Wars, there are several that deserve mention above all others. First and foremost there is Robert Utley's remarkable two-volume study of the U.S. Army in the West. His *Frontiersmen in Blue* covers the 1848 to 1865 period, while *Frontier Regulars* continues from 1866 to 1891. Utley also wrote the official National Park handbook for the Little Bighorn Battlefield.

A more recent book which is a magnificent reference work cataloguing hundreds of individual battles in minute detail is Gregory Michno's *Encyclopedia of Indian Wars*. Robert Utley has said that Michno's work belongs "on the shelf of every student of the Indian wars of the American West," a recommendation with which I heartily concur.

For the definitive account of the Battle of the Little Bighorn and the campaign of which it was part, John S. Gray's *Centennial Campaign: The Sioux War of 1876* is the single most detailed and valuable work.

Custer's own book, *My Life on the Plains*, provides an interesting insight, and Dee Brown's classic *Bury My Heart at Wounded Knee* tells the social and cultural history of the American West from the Indian point of view. It would take more than just one large and sturdy bookcase to hold all of the books on Custer, but Evan Connell's *Son of Morning Star* is an enjoyable read and Stephen Ambrose's *Crazy Horse and Custer* is a good paired biography of the two leaders. Another joint biography of note is Peter Aleshire's *The Fox and the Whirlwind*, which pairs George Crook and Geronimo.

INDEX

About the Author

Bill Yenne is the San Francisco-based author of more than four dozen works of historical nonfiction. A native of Western Montana and a graduate of the University of Montana, he has written extensively about both the American West and its native peoples, including *On the Trail of Lewis & Clark, Yesterday and Today*; *The Opening of the American West*; and *The Encyclopedia of North American Indian Tribes*. He has visited the scenes of the actions of the Indian Wars from Killdeer Mountain to the Mogollon Mountains, and from the Big Hole River to the Rogue River, and has walked the Little Bighorn Battlefield several times. He served as a consultant for the History Channel Command Decision program on the Battle of the Little Bighorn.

Yenne has also contributed to encyclopedias of both world wars, and has written *Black 41: The West Point Class of 1941 and the American Triumph in World War II*, *Operation Cobra and the Great Offensive: Sixty Days that Changed the Course of World War II*, and *Aces: True Stories of Victory and Valor in the Skies of World War II*.